Železnice
Chemins de fer
Railway
Eisenbahn

LODZ

CZESTOCHOWA

Bytom
Sosnowiec

GLIWICE

KATOWICE

KRAKÓW

Tarnów

Przemysl

AVA

Frýdek
Mistek

Čadca

Nowy Sacz

Žilina

Tatr. Lomnica

Kežmarok

Bardejov

WALDOV

Trenčín

Ružomberok

Poprad

Starý
Smokovec

Prešov

Humenné

Brezno

Dobšiná

Klátorisko

Košice

Kremnica

Branská
Bystrica

Rožňava

Michalovce

ava

any

Zvolen

Jaškiná Domica

Užgorod

C.C.C.P.

Nitra

Banská Stiavnica

Rim.Sobota

LAVA

Levice

Lučenec

MISKOLC

N.Zámky

Komárno

Vác

Nyíregyháza

BUDAPEST

Jászberény

DEBRECEN

YARORSZÁG

© EDITIONS NAGEL

CZECHOSLOVAKIA

NAGEL'S
ENCYCLOPEDIA-GUIDE

Awards
Rome 1958, Paris 1961, Vienna 1968

CZECHOSLOVAKIA

480 pages
1 map and 1 plan in colour
17 pages of black-and-white plans

Fifth edition

NAGEL PUBLISHERS
GENEVA · PARIS · MUNICH

ISBN 2-8263-0387-2

CONTENTS

MAPS AND PLANS

Plan of Prague (in three colours) at the beginning of the book.
Map of Czechoslovakia (in three colours) at the end of the book.

PUBLISHER'S NOTE
(1st edition)

In our constant endeavour to serve our readers by providing an increasingly complete collection of accurate guidebooks we are glad to be able to offer the public this guide to Czechoslovakia.

It is our aim to publish guidebooks for every country in the world. To this end we have for some time begun to include the countries of eastern Europe in our programme. The guidebooks "Yugoslavia", "Moscow and Leningrad" and "Hungary" are the result of our efforts to give the reader objective and exact information. Thus our guidebooks offer those who have no immediate intention of visiting these countries a concise documentary survey of permanent value.

We should like to express our thanks to the **Czechoslovak Travel Bureau Čedok** and also to **Dr J. Chyský** and his collaborators **Dr V. Adamec, F. Bunzl, Eng. B. Bušek, J. Čížek, F. Patočka, Dr M. Skalník** and **F. Škrobánek** for their contribution to the compilation of this work.

The maps and plans were produced by the Nagel Guides cartographical department.

PUBLISHER'S NOTE
(Second, Third and Fourth editions)

The first edition of this guide on Czechoslovakia appeared in 1959. Devoted to a country with so many links with the West and a culture so close to our own, the guide enjoyed a great success: many letters from our readers showed that it had filled a real gap in tourist publications and responded to a genuine need.

Several years have passed, and Czechoslovakia's attraction as a tourist country has become firmly established. Hotels have been improved, and foreign visitors are being given wider facilities. It became necessary to publish a new edition containing the latest information and giving additional facts and new plans.

This work has now been completed and we are happy to introduce to our readers a new edition, mostly re-set, of our Czechoslovakia Guide. The task of our editors has been lightened immeasurably by the kind collaboration of the Czech authorities: we should like to thank, first of all, the **directors of the Čedok Agency,** notably Messrs **Jindřich Cinkl, Karel Holan** and **Karel Chaloupka,** and their collaborators, Mrs Moscova, **Dr L. Zajíček,** and others. We should also like to thank the Ministry of Health, especially Mrs **Šubertova** and **Dr J. Hanycz,** the director of Karlovy Vary, and **Dr Sever,** the director of Františkovy Lázné.

PUBLISHER'S NOTE
(Fifth edition)

Czechoslovakia has made great headway, particularly in the field of tourism, and this has prompted us to produce a fifth edition, taking into account all the changes that have occurred since the last one.

We have endeavoured to give a faithful picture of a country in great favour with tourists. Indeed, there were over 1,300,000 visitors in 1967, and their number is rapidly rising. It was necessary to acknowledge this, and to resume our task with only one aim in mind: to produce an even better and more practical guide. As usual, we shall be grateful for any constructive comment which our readers who have visited Czechoslovakia and wish to give us the benefit of their experience, might care to make. We thank them in advance.

It should also be pointed out that the Nagel Encyclopedia-Guides contain no paid advertisements so that all recommendations are entirely objective.

General
Introduction

GEOGRAPHY

One can see from a glance at the map of Europe that Czechoslovakia lies in the middle of the continent. Its very position has often thrust it into the foreground of many historical events. Traces of human civilisation are to be found here, beginning with the cave-dwellers and the settlements of the mammoth hunters. To the south of the country lay the northern frontier of the Roman Empire. It was over the frontier mountains that the nomad Celtic, German and Slav tribes poured in, and this was the farthest point reached by the Mongol and Turkish invasions. In the 14th century here was the easternmost territory reached by Western civilisation and today, just as a thousand years ago, it is the meeting point of West and East. Here the conflict between Catholicism and Protestantism degenerated into a war which almost exterminated the Czech people and nearly destroyed their culture.

Population

Czechoslovakia is a state composed of two peoples: about 9.5 million Czechs and 4.4 million Slovaks, approximately 160,000 Germans, 400,000 Hungarians, 80,000 Poles and 75,000 Ukrainians also live in Czechoslovakia. Each of these nationalities has its own cultural institutions, schools and newspapers.

Czechoslovakia has an area of 49,300 sq. miles and a population of more than 14.5 million. It has common frontiers with the German Federal Republic, the East German Democratic Republic, Austria, Hungary, Poland and the U.S.S.R. The frontier is 2,260 miles long. The distance from the Czechoslovak frontier to the Black Sea and the North Sea is roughly 434 miles; from the Adriatic and Baltic 280 miles. The rivers Elbe, Danube and Oder connect the country with the sea.

Historically and geographically, and also administratively, Czechoslovakia consists of two parts: the west, which includes the provinces of Bohemia, Moravia and Silesia, and the east, Slovakia. For purposes of administration, Czechoslovakia is divided into 11 divisions. The capital Prague with about 1,000,000 inhabitants is situated in the centre of Bohemia. The second largest town is Brno in Moravia and the capital of Slovakia is Bratislava, with populations of 350,000 and 250,000 respectively. The country is divided as follows: the capital Prague, Central Bohemia (with Prague as its chief town), North Bohemia (Ústí), South Bohemia (České Budějovice), West Bohemia (Plzeň), East Bohemia (Hradec Králové), Southern Moravia (Brno),

Northern Moravia (Ostrava), West Slovakia (Bratislava), Central Slovakia (Banská Bystrica), and East Slovakia (Košice).

The most important rivers in Bohemia are the Vltava (Moldau) and the Elbe with numerous tributaries, in Moravia the Morava and the Dyje, in Silesia the Oder and in Slovakia the Váh, Hron, Hernád and Danube.

The mountain peaks which rise to over 5,000 feet form a natural frontier in the west. In the south-west the frontier is formed by the Bohemian Forest, in the north-west by the Ore Mountains, in the north-east by the chain of the Sudetes, the Iser, Giant and Eagle Mountains, ending in Moravia in the Králicky Sněžník massif and the Jeseník heights. The Beskids mountains are characteristic of Northern Moravia.

The frontier between Bohemia and Moravia is formed by the Bohemian-Moravian highland; between Moravia and Slovakia by the ridge of the Little Carpathians.

Slovakia is a paradise for all mountain-lovers, for the whole northern part is formed by three spurs of the Carpathians. The northernmost spur is the most beautiful, with the peaks of the High Tatra Mountains, Gerlach, the highest, rising to 8,788 feet. The peaks of the Lower Tatra, the Little and Great Fatra, are not so high and the mountains of the Slovak Ore Mounts are of moderate height. The not very high Drahanská Vysočina plateau occupies the middle of Moravia; on it is the Macocha with its stalactite caves. Similar phenomena are also to be found in Slovakia, mostly in the central Slovakian massif (Demänov caves) and in the South Slovakian mountains (Domica caves). The ice cave at Dobšiná in central Slovakia is also a singular formation.

Climate

The climate in Czechoslovakia is generally mild, the annual average temperature 8–10° C, and winds which blow preponderantly from the west and the north-west bring sufficient moisture with them and contribute to the fresh appearance of the Czechoslovak landscape. There are only very few regions where drought is regular in the course of the year; woods and meadows full of moisture make the landscape especially attractive. The largest wooded areas are mainly in the mountain regions where there are still remains of primeval forest. More than 30% of the total area of the country is timbered.

Numerous mineral springs also add to the wealth of the country; around them many health resorts have sprung up, some of them, such as Karlovy Vary (Karlsbad), Mariánské Lázně (Marienbad) and Piešťany, of world-wide reputation.

HISTORY

The earliest traces of human settlements which have been discovered in the territory of Czechoslovakia go back to the Stone Age. It was here that the *Celts*, who played such an important part in the history of Western Europe, came to settle in vast numbers, and their descendants, the Boii, gave their name to the country—**Bohemia**. This name is still used today in several Western European languages.

When in the first millennium B.C. the first **Slavs** appeared in the stretch of country between the Dnieper and the Elbe they also settled in the territory which is now Czechoslovakia. They were the ancestors of both the **Czechs** and the **Slovaks**.

The first state to be founded on Czechoslovak soil was the so-called **Samos Empire**, in the middle of the 7th century, but it did not last long. There are data from the 9th century about the existence of a **Pribina Principate** in Slovakia, but this soon became part of a new state formed in Moravia, which expanded its power in the direction of both Bohemia and Slovakia and was known as the **Great Moravian Empire**. At this time **Christianity**, introduced by the Greek missionaries Cyril and Methodius, spread over the land which is now Czechoslovakia, counteracting the efforts of the German Empire in the west to convert the Great Moravian Empire to Christianity from that side. So from the earliest times the country was already exposed to civilising influences from both west and east. Cyril and Methodius preached in the Slav tongue, introduced a new Slav alphabet and translated religious writings into the Slav language. In this way they laid the foundations for the development of Slav literature and culture. This Slav Christianity, however, aroused the displeasure of the ruler and his entourage and it was suppressed in favour of the Latin-Germanic Christianity. At the beginning of the 10th century the Great Moravian Empire disintegrated, partly through internal quarrels and partly as the result of attacks by Hungarian tribes which had appeared in the Danube valley. In consequence Slovakia, Moravia and Bohemia were separated and **Bohemia** became the political centre of a new state, already more subject to western than to eastern influence.

In the middle of the 10th century the Czech state was ruled by the House of **Přemysl** from which Prince Vaclav (Wenceslaus) descended; at that date the first coins were minted; **Prague** became the principal centre between the Orient and Central trading

Europe. Gradually the Czech territory was surrounded by the Germans, and the Czechs had to struggle constantly to defend themselves. In the 11th century, the Hungarians seized Slovakia, which they occupied for several centuries. When the first townships were founded, German infiltration of the Czech provinces began, and the Bohemian monarch gave preferential treatment to German immigrants. The great economic progress of the country in the 13th century also strengthened the power of the Czech princes who during that period acquired crowns, which they were to keep for a long time and, after extending their sovereignty as far as the Adriatic, even attempted to gain the throne of the German Empire (Přemysl Otokar II.). He only succeeded however in expanding the realm of the House of the Premyslids to include neighbouring Poland and a part of Hungary. At that time Bohemian money, the **groschen,** coined from the silver mined at Kutná Hora, became the safest European currency.

When the last member of the Přemyslid dynasty died in 1306 the House of **Luxembourg** came to the throne of the kingdom of Bohemia and brought with its accession, after a short interval, a new political ascendency. The Bohemian kings Charles IV and Wenceslas II, were also emperors of the Holy Roman Empire. The country came into very close contact with Latin and French culture, and Prague became one of the most important cities in Europe. In 1348 the first university north of the Alps was founded here, there was a marked advance in economic life, great buildings were erected and Gothic art reached its peak.

The religious and moral enthusiasm of the Czech people found expression in the **Hussite Reformation Movement,** influenced by the ideas of John Wycliff. The memory of Jan Hus is held in honour throughout the world. The resounding victories of the Hussite armies led by Jan Žižka of Trocnov (he introduced a novel battle technique by the use of armed wagons) compelled the Church to negotiate with the "heretics" on equal terms. The Czechs repelled all attack from outside and thus became masters in their own land. This period is the most glorious in Czech history. But later King George of Poděbrad, also named "Hussite King" (he died in 1471) again tried to bring some Czech Reformation ideas into foreign politics and proposed a permanent union of European states for the purpose of achieving a lasting peace. In the 16th century the Czechs elected a **Hapsburg** to their throne in the hope that by so doing they would make it easier to repel the growing menace of the Turks.

Trade flourished and its highest point was reached in the reign of Rudolf II, (died 1612) when Prague was for the second time one of the most important cities of Europe.

The Hapsburgs, who also ruled in the Alpine countries and in Hungary, endeavoured to form a centralised, absolutist, Catholic state. And so they came into conflict with the Czechs, the majority of whom were Protestants and wished to preserve their liberty and sovereignty. This was at the time when the whole of Europe was split into two camps preparing for war. (This European conflict, the Thirty Years' War, began in Bohemia with an anti-Hapsburg rising in 1618 (defenestration of Prague). The Czechs however were defeated in 1620 at the **Battle of the White Mountain** (Bilá Hora) and cruelly punished. 28 leaders of the rebellion, Czech nobles and citizens, were executed in the Old Town Square (Altstädter Ring) in Prague on the 21st June 1621.

The Czechs were deprived of their rights guaranteed by the constitution, the Czech language was suppressed, Czech property confiscated and given to foreigners as a reward for having fought against the Czechs. The people were faced with the alternative of either renouncing the Protestant faith or going into exile abroad. And so the cream of the country, under the leadership of **Jan Amos Komenský (Comenius)** left their homeland. The minor nobility, which played an important part in the life of the nation, disappeared almost entirely and the cities fell into decline. The new industrial production which developed later was almost exclusively in the hands of the foreign nobility and foreign officials. The Hapsburgs financed their policy with the export of Czech products, principally glassware, cloth and linen.

The Czech state was also formally deprived of its independence in the second half of the 18th century. The reforms of the age of enlightenment actually strengthened centralism and Germanisation, but on the other hand they gave religious freedom and abolished serfdom in 1781, thus helping the lower classes of the population who, despite harsh persecution, still remained Czech. These measures opened up possibilities of both social and cultural advancement. They resulted in a **Czech national renaissance**, at first confined to language and literature, but which later spread to economic and political life. The Slovaks, too, made their contribution to the revival of the nation. The greatest Czech historian **František Palacký**, born in Moravia (Hodslavice), was the first to formulate a programme based on the principles of humanity and democracy.

In the year of revolutions 1848 the Czechs tried to regain their political rights, but without success albeit in this very year the political foundations of the nation were widened. The peasants were completely emancipated and the working class made its appearance. The **Industrial Revolution** in the 19th century entirely altered the picture and the composition of society. Note also the importance of the gymnastic societies, the **Sokol,** in which the national ideal was revived.

In the 1914–18 war Czechs and Slovaks sided against Austria–Hungary and gained their independency; with the help of the victorious western powers, they established a new united state, the **Czechoslovak Republic,** which was proclaimed on the 18th October 1918. **T. G. Masaryk** was elected as its first president. The new Czechoslovak state fell a victim to its western neighbour when in 1938 Hitler's Germany attacked it. After the occupation of the frontier region in the autumn of 1938 the whole of Bohemia, Moravia and Silesia were occupied and incorporated into the so-called Protectorate of Bohemia and Moravia in March 1939. Slovakia was again separated and a "Slovak State" formed.

Then, with the outbreak of the Second World War, there began for the Czech people yet another period of tribulation.

Liberation came to them in 1945 and marked a sudden turn in the history of both nations of Czechoslovakia. The wounds caused by the Second World War and the occupation were soon healed and Czechoslovakia rebuilt her industry which, already remarkable at the end of the 19th century, again put her at the forefront of the most industrialised countries in the world.

In spring 1945, after the liberation of the eastern part of the Republic, a government programme issued at Košice laid down the fundamental principles of the country's future development: equal rights for the Czech and Slovak peoples, alliance and friendship with the Soviet Union, the institution of national committees as the elected organs of government, confiscation of the possessions of the occupiers and their accomplices, and punishment of collaborators. Furthermore, numerous measures were taken in social and cultural matters. In autumn of the same year, the government programme was completed by the decree nationalizing finance, mining and heavy industry. By this means, 60% of industrial production came into the hands of the State which also redistributed some 1,700,000 hectares of land to 170,000 small farmers. The first Two Year Plan, covering the years 1947 and 1948, and primarily concerned with the rebuilding of the national economy which had been heavily hit by the war, provided for the industrialization of Slovakia, social insurance for all workers, new laws on the organization of education, etc. One of the prime objectives of this plan was the attainment of the pre-war level of industrial production, and this was achieved in the first year of the plan.

A new Constitution, voted in 1960, made Czechoslovakia a "Socialist Republic" (ČSSR).

ECONOMY

In the economy, the **means of production** are either state-owned or run by cooperatives. This is the case in mining of natural concerns, banks and insurance, railways, road and air traffic, post and telegraph, radio and television, films and large scale agricultural production. We are, of course, dealing with a socialist regime.

The people earn their living in widely different occupations, roughly as follows: 39% in industry and the building trades, 33% in agriculture and forestry, 6.4% in the communications and postal services, 6.6% in commerce and the rest, about 15% in other fields.

During the years 1919 to 1939, the **natural resources** of the Czechoslovak Republic were not adequately exploited (with the exception of coal mining and the building materials industry) and for the most part the country purchased its raw materials abroad. While even in 1948 **iron ore extraction** amounted to only 1,428,000 tons, it rose to 3,120,000 tons in 1966. There has also been a rapid increase in the extraction of **non-ferrous metals**, and new deposits have recently been discovered in the surroundings of Zlaté Hory. The production of non-metallic raw materials is proceeding at an increasing rate in various parts of the country, e.g., pyrites in the Prachatice region, magnesia in the Košice district, etc. Large new limestone and building stone **quarries** have been opened in various parts of the country—often in places where the existence of these resources was completely unsuspected.

New **coal and lignite deposits** have been discovered, notably in the neighbourhood of Ostrava and at the foot of the Ore Mountains; this has led to the building of a vast network of factories and power stations whose annual capacity attains 14 thousand million kwh in the North Bohemian basin alone—i.e., some 3.5 times as much as before the war.

The increase of production of **electric power** naturally goes hand in hand with the building of new hydraulic power works on many waterways. During the first Czechoslovak Republic, hydraulic power was used on a very limited scale. New dams on the Czech rivers confine hundreds of millions of cubic metres of water whose power is at the service of the State. 13% of the total electric power produced in the country is accounted for by hydraulic power stations. A system of dams has been built on the rivers throughout the country, chiefly on the Váh in Slovakia and on the Vltava in Bohemia. These dams are of course of importance both for agriculture and traffic. The biggest constructions of this kind are the dams on the Orava in the north-west of Slovakia and in Bohemia at Lipno, Orlik and Slapy on the middle and upper Vltava.

Industrial production occupies a very important place in the Czechoslovak national economy. Even before the Second World War, Czechoslovakia was among the 10 most highly industrialised countries in the world. In the 25 years since the end of the last war, Czechoslovakia has not only come close to the most advanced countries in the world in per capita production, but in some cases has equalled and surpassed them. Thus, for instance, Czechoslovak production per capita of steel and cement now surpasses that of Great Britain and the United States, and its production of cement and electric power is maintained at roughly the level of that in the German Federal Republic.

Particularly encouraging results have been achieved in the industrialization of the eastern part of the country, Slovakia, formerly a backward country. Since 1945, production of power in Slovakia has almost increased tenfold compared with 1937; in the same period, chemical production has increased fortyfold, mechanical production nineteenfold, and so forth. In the field of the machine industry alone, 29 new works have been built in Slovakia since 1945. This spectacular increase in industrial production is reflected in the growing employment figures which have quadrupled compared with the pre-war period (population increase amounting to 10%).

The principal recent achievements include, first of all, the "Klement Gottwald New Ironworks"—nicknamed the **Czechoslovak Donbass**—near Ostrava, the **Žiar nad Hronom** aluminium works covering an area of 158 hectares, in Central Slovakia, and the East Slovak Ironworks at Košice which produce large quantities of pig iron, steel, coke, laminated products, and a whole series of products needed for the development of various branches of industries, especially the chemical industry.

However, the most important link in the Czechoslovak economy is the **machine industry**. Today one in every three industrial workers is employed in the machine industry whose exports cover 50% of Czechoslovak imports from abroad. Czechoslovakia produces complete capital goods such as cement works, lime-kilns, mills, screening and transporting machines for the building industry, heavy moulding machinery (presses, power hammers), shovel and wheel excavating machinery, bridge cranes and other special cranes, drilling equipment, ball-bearings, snow-ploughs, all kinds of motor vehicles, suction dredgers, electric railway engines, special types of railway carriages, all sorts of motor vehicles, and many other varied kinds of machinery.

The **chemical industry** has also experienced a spectacular growth in the Czechoslovak Socialist Republic. It is based on the crude petroleum brought from the Soviet Union by a 4,000-km long oil pipe. The raw material is subsequently processed at the great "Slovnaft" oil works near Bratislava. Also in Slovakia —at Humenné—is the largest Czechoslovak synthetic fibre factory, "Chemko", which produces a new, exceptionally light fibre called **chemlon**. Other important chemical works include the "Soviet-Czechoslovak Friendship Chemical Works" of Záluží near Most, which produce 80 kinds of motor fuel for vehicles and planes, synthetic ammonia, domestic gas (for Prague, Liberec, Karlovy Vary and even some towns in Moravia) and a whole series of similar products. It is one of the largest works of its kind in central Europe.

Of course, the Czechoslovak chemical industry is continually evolving and closely follows technical progress: to this end Czechoslovakia is continually building new chemical works whose production will not only supply the needs of the home market but also the growing orders from foreign customers. This is particularly true of synthetic rubber, a most important raw material whose consumption in Czechoslovakia attains 1.1 kg per head of population annually. Czechoslovakia is the fifth largest rubber-consuming country in the world.

Since the 16th century **Bohemian glass articles** have delighted the whole world. In some dozens of works all kinds of glassware is manufactured, primarily utilitarian glassware, cut glass, various glass ornaments and objets d'art, Bohemian crystal chandeliers and other typically Czech specialities. The centres of the national glass industry are at Jablonec on the Nissa, Nový Bor, Kamenický Šenov, Teplice and Karlovy Vary. The ceramics and porcelain industry (Karlovy Vary) as well as Czechoslovak pottery and paper (South Bohemia and Slovakia) also enjoy a splendid reputation in the main markets of the world. Also famous are the products of the shoe factories at Gottwaldov (the former Bata factories of before the war).

The Czechoslovak **food industry** is famous for Czech **beer,** a delicious drink usually sold in the bottles manufactured by the Czech and Slovak glassworks and very much sought after abroad. From as early as the 12th century beer has been brewed in Bohemia, and the most famous breweries are at Plzeň (Pilsen).From there the famous "Pilsner Urquell", a light beer of 12 degrees and the best quality, is exported to all parts of the world. There are also very good breweries at Prague and at České Budějovice whose breweries produce and export the excellent bottled "Budvar" to practically all countries in the world. Beer is, so to speak, the national Czechoslovak drink; there are many kinds of beer of varying quality, from the 7-degree light to the 20-degree dark beer. The Czechoslovak brewing industry is founded on the cultivation of excellent Bohemian hops and the famous Czech malt both of which are also exported as raw materials to all parts of the world.

The cultivation of high-quality hops would not be possible without a highly developed state of **agriculture.** The Czechoslovak government takes great care to see that the arable land worked by the State farms and people's agricultural cooperatives (United Agricultural Cooperatives) are tended in the best possible way. Only a minute percentage of the soil remains in the hands of private farmers working independently.

The most common crops in Czechoslovakia include first of all cereals, especially wheat (surface sown: about 722,000 hectares), barley (about 670,000 hectares; barley is needed in the preparation of the malt for breweries), and oats. About 630,000 hectares are devoted to potato growing and in this respect Czechoslovakia is one of the leading countries in the world. As we said above, Czechoslovakia is renowned for its hops; the largest hop-fields are in the outskirts of the towns of Rakovník and Žatec in West Bohemia, and near Roudnice on the Elbe, in Central Bohemia. Sugar beet production also occupies an important place, and after processing in the Czechoslovak sugar refineries, various types of sugar are exported to all parts of the globe.

Czechoslovakia's **timber and paper** industries (furniture manufacture, matches, etc.) can draw on the tremendous forest resources of the country; in fact, Czechoslovak forests cover some 4 million hectares. The most wooded regions are in Slovakia (about 34% of the total surface); the frontier mountains of Bohemia, Moravia and Silesia are also covered with dense forests, occupying some 60% of the total area of these provinces. The forest zone continues to an altitude of 4,000 to 5,000 feet. The most common varieties of trees are the spruce-fir, fir, pine, oak, beech and yoke-elm; the Czechoslovak State exploits the forests either through its own administrative organs or through the United Agricultural Cooperatives.

Although Czechoslovakia is a relatively northern country (Prague is situated on the 50th parallel) grapes are also grown here. We find extensive vineyards chiefly in South Moravia, e.g in the neighbourhood of Mikulov and in south-western and southern Slovakia (wine-growing district of Modra, Sv. Jur). The wine from these regions has a good reputation. But the same can be said of the wine from the vineyards in central Bohemia near the towns of Mělník, Roudnice and Žernoseky where viticulture has a tradition of many hundred years.

Czech **fish-breeding** has a glorious tradition which goes back several centuries and is due to the innumerable natural and artificial lakes in the country, some of which were laid out in the 14th century. The total area of Czechoslovak lakes amounts to some 46,500 hectares; most of them are concentrated in the surroundings of Třeboň in the south of Bohemia where splendid carps are hatched in both small and large lakes (for example, Rožmberk lake has a surface of 720 hectares, Staňkovský lake 350 hectares, Horusický 439 hectares, Bezdrev 522 hectares, etc). Net-fishing in these lakes, which is organized every autumn, is a very interesting event not only for the local population, but also for foreign tourists visiting the region. Besides carp, other kinds of freshwater fish are hatched in Czechoslovakia, especially trout. For fishing as a sport see the special section at the end of this book.

Table of Main Products

Coal (million tons)	26.9
Lignite (million tons)	74.1
Electricity (thousand million kwh)	36.4
Steel (million tons)	9.1
Cars (thousands)	92.7
Tractors and lorries (thousands)	47.1
Rayon and synthetic fibres (thousand tons)	69

Corn (million tons)...............................   2.10
Maize (million tons) 0.52
Beet (million tons) 7.4
Cattle (1,000 head)   4,518
Pigs (1,000 head)   5,500

CULTURAL LIFE

Science

The supreme scientific body in Czechoslovakia is the **Czechoslovak Academy of Sciences** founded in 1952. Before that, Czechoslovak scientists belonged to the Czech Royal Society of Science, created in 1771 and the National Museum which was established in 1818, and subsequently to the "Czech Academy of Sciences and Arts".

The world owes many eminent scientists and scholars to the Czech and Slovak peoples, e.g., the linguist **Josef Dobrovský**, the historian and historiographer **František Palacký**, the founder of Slavonic studies **Pavel Josef Šafařik**, the physiologist **Jan Evangelista Purkyne, Jan Svatopluk Pressel**, the inventor of the ship propeller, **Petr Diviš**, the inventor of the lightning-conductor, **František Křižik**, the eminent electronic scientist, the Orientalist **Bedřich Hrozný**, the decipherer of Hittite script, etc.

This brillant tradition is now carried on by the leading figures in the Czechoslovak Academy of Sciences, the first institution of its kind to adopt a single programme of scientific work and research, a programme which includes every sphere and level of scientific work and research, from basic and applied research to the work of development and construction. Moreover, scientific research forms part of the curriculum of institutions of higher education of which Czechoslovakia has some fifty, with 108 faculties and about 120,000 students. The oldest of the country's great educational institutions is undoubtedly the Charles University of Prague, founded in 1348, and the School of Advanced Technical Studies, also in Prague, whose origins go back to 1707. Most students at institutes of advanced education receive scholarships, and more than half are lodged in State colleges.

In the last few years Czechoslovak science has had a remarkable success in an original, new scientific field, polarography, which was founded by the Academician **Jaroslav Heyrovský**, the first Czechoslovak Nobel Prize winner (1959). At the Brussels World Fair in 1958 the products and items exhibited by the Czechoslovak Academy of Sciences carried off 3 top prizes, 4 diplomas of honour, 2 gold medals, 1 silver medal and 2 bronze medals.

Architecture, Sculpture and Painting

Every branch of art has been practised in the territory which is now Czechoslovakia. However, in Bohemia, Moravia and Slovakia, artistic activity did not begin to flourish until after the Czech princes had adopted Christianity.

In the countries under the Czech crown, the arts first developed within the framework of Roman civilization, and later in the cultural climate of influences from western and southern Europe. The first expressions of **romanesque art** made their appearance as early as the beginning of the 10th century in the form of feudal strongholds and simple, round ecclesiastical buildings (rotundas); in the following two centuries romanesque art attained a very high technical and aesthetic standard, as is shown by the basilicas built during that period, e.g., at **Prague** (basilica of Saint George) and at **Třebíč** in southern Moravia, and in the capitular church at **Spiš** in eastern Slovakia.

The beginnings of a new era, the **gothic era**, which reached its peak in the 14th century, go back to this period of flourishing romanesque culture. The economic and cultural conditions at the time of the reign of the last Premyslids and the first sovereigns of the Luxembourg dynasty (Jean of Luxembourg and his son Charles IV) created a climate which was particularly favourable to the rapid expansion of the arts in this part of Europe. Especially in the reign of King Charles IV the arts attained an exceptionally high level in Bohemia, surpassing that in other European countries at that time, except perhaps in France.

Prague became the veritable centre of the German part of the Empire and the residence of the Emperor who founded the first university of central Europe there in 1348. At that time, too, a large number of exceptionally lovely churches, monasteries and other buildings were built there, so that the city was nicknamed the "city of a hundred towers". From this period, too, dates the building of the Charles Bridge—the second stone bridge in central Europe—across the Vltava; it has been preserved almost completely intact to this day. In the country, too, magnificent buildings went up, e.g., the royal stronghold of **Karlštejn** near Prague; the first stone of Saint Vitus' Cathedral was laid at Prague castle, etc. The gothic era gave birth to such famous architects as Matthew of Arras, Peter Parler of Gmünd, Benedikt Rejt of Pístov and Matěj Rejsek of Prostějov whose works are still admired. In Slovakia, too, numerous valuable mementos of the art of the time have come down to us, at Bratislava, Košice, Levoča, Spišská, Nová Ves and Bardejov.

It was, however, in painting and sculpture that Czech gothic art achieved its highest peak. When an exhibition of gothic art was held in Paris in 1957, the art world was astonished by the unsuspected wealth and tremendous beauty of the collection from the National Gallery in Prague. In this connexion we should at least mention the magnificent works of Master Theodoricus, of the Masters of Třeboň and of Vyšší Brod, and of Master Pavel of Levoča. A brilliant illustration of this art can be found especially in the portraits of the "Madonnas of Bohemia" dating from this period.

The **Renaissance** reached the country from Italy in the 16th century. It did not however give rise to such creative expression as the Gothic period had done, although it left some rare monuments for posterity, such as the **Castle of Opočno, Pardubice, Litomysl** in eastern Bohemia, **Telc** in southern Moravia and the embellishment of several towns built upon Gothic foundations. But the very compromise between the old native Gothic tradition and a new art form introduced from abroad gave rise to a new style, the **Bohemian Renaissance**. Some towns in Bohemia built in this style and still preserved are examples of it (e.g. **Telč Slavonice, Pardubice, Litomyšl, Nové Město**). In Slovakia, too, the Renaissance left many monuments, e.g. in **Levoča, Ležmarok, Bardejov and Prešov**. These towns owe their charm and grace to the Renaissance buildings.

Baroque made great strides in the 17th and 18th centuries, reaching the provinces of Czechoslovakia, chiefly Bohemia, after the end of the Thirty Years' War. The baroque **Prague** of today dates from this time, as do hundreds of religious and secular buildings in the country and thousands of art treasures, painting and statuary. Naturally the originally foreign Baroque art was assimilated locally, resulting in a Bohemian Baroque.

Besides such foreign—mainly Italian—artists as Pieroni, Rossi, Canevale, Luragho, and Mathei, native artists or artists who had been living in the country for many years, such as the architects Santini and Diezenhofer, the painters Škreta, Brandl, and Reiner, the sculptors Brokoff, Braun, Platzer and others, also created some splendid works. At that time the fame of Czech artists spread far beyond the frontiers of their country; those who enjoyed the greatest success abroad included the portraitist Jan Kupecký who worked in Vienna and Nuremberg, and the engraver Václav Hollar.

In Slovakia we find fewer traces of baroque art. Nevertheless, there are some interesting **wooden churches** whose form recalls the great baroque buildings and which contain many pictorial and sculptured decorations on religious subjects, most of them the work of local craftsmen.

At the end of the 18th century Bohemia and also Slovakia came under the influence of the **Rococo** and **Classical** styles, which found local expression in Empire style. Not only were chateaux built in this style (one of the finest examples is **Kačina** near Čáslav in Central Bohemia), but also many other notable town buildings (town halls, museums, theatres). In this period extensive English parks were laid out in the grounds of the chateaux.

The arts which attained a high standard of perfection in Bohemia in the 19th century include, first of all, Czech **painting** with its classic exponents **Josef Navrátil and Josef Mánes** whose work was a happy synthesis of the old and new elements in Czech pictorial art and laid the foundation of the splendid tradition of national painting. Towards the middle of the 19th century, the Czech painters **Karel Purkyně**, **Soběslav Pinkas**, and **Viktor Barvitius** formed close links with French modern painting by their attachment to the realism of the Barbizon school. The famous landscape painter **Antonín Chittusi** was one of the great Czech masters of this period.

The second half of the 19th century saw the rise of a rather large group of outstanding painters, including **Mikoláš Aleš**, **Vojtěch Hynais**, **František Ženíšek**, **Václav Brožík** and **Josef Mařák**; at that time, too, a group of excellent sculptors was formed, headed by **Josef Myslbek**, a pupil of Auguste Rodin, and a group of architects under **Josef Zítek**, the designer of the National Theatre in Prague. At the beginning of the 20th century, the portrait painter **Jan Preisler** and the Impressionist landscape painter **Antonín Slavíček** achieved international renown. The chief exponent of the following generation of Czech painters was **Max Švabinský**, whose work—particularly in the field of graphic art—earned him the title of National Artist after the Second World War.

Modern Czech painters, among whom there are such outstandingly talented artists as **Bohumil Kubišta**, **Rudolf Kremlička**, **Antonín Procházka**, **Josef Čapek**, **Václav Špala**, **Josef Rabas**, **Vincenc Beneš**, **Vlastimil Rada**, **Josef Lada** and many others, have renewed the link with the traditions of the French school of painting. In the field of sculpture, the founder of modern **Czech** sculpture, **J. V. Myslbek** has been succeeded by sculptors such as **Jan Štursa, Otto Guttfreund, Josef Mařatka, Ladislav Šaloun, Vincenc Makovsky**, and others. In Czech architecture, **Jan Kotěra** achieved international standing and taught a whole generation of contemporary Czech architects, including **Josef Gočár** (who created a modern district in the capital of East Bohemia, Hradec Kralové), **Pavel Janák, Jarmil Krecar**, etc.

Today, artists are organized in the Union of Czechoslovak Artists, and their works—as well as those of their predecessors—are shown as widely as possible in numerous permanent and temporary exhibitions and art galleries; not only in Prague but in all the chief towns of departments and many other towns.

Protecting the Cultural Heritage

In no other country in the world are buildings of cultural importance protected as efficiently as in Czechoslovakia. In fact, in the Czechoslovak Socialist Republic, historic, artistic and cultural buildings are placed under the direct protection of the State, which delegates this task to central bodies such as the Ministry of Education and Culture, the Central National Commission for the Protection of Historic Monuments (a consultative body) and the State Institute for the Protection of Historic Monuments and Nature. In each department, in every ward, and in every locality which possesses a certain number of important monuments or sites, special commissions have been set up for the protection of these monuments, as well as State consultative bodies, i.e., national Committees of the department, ward and locality.

Each year, the Czechoslovak State devotes some hundred millions of crowns to the protection of historic buildings, for this is regarded as an integral part of the State's educational and cultural duties. The State undertakes the repairs and up-keep of these buildings, and this work is carried out skilfully by highly qualified experts. This ensures not only the protection of monuments such as strongholds and feudal residences (of which there are several hundred in Czechoslovakia), but also the preservation and renovation of such art treasures as paintings, sculptures, and items of historic value. More than forty Czecho-slovak towns are scheduled as historic sites and effectively pro-tected against the ravages of time.

Music

Czechoslovak music has an old and splendid tradition, and Czech musicians are well known throughout the world. The excellent reputation enjoyed by Czech music derives from the numerous works by Czech composers who became known in Europe at the beginning of the 18th century, a period when many musical performers, composers and theoreticians worked in various European countries, especially in Austria (Vienna), Germany, France, and Italy. It also owes much to the numerous foreign tours made by Czechoslovak orchestras and other musical groups in the last few years. There are, mainly, the **Czech Philharmonic Orchestra** and **Prague Symphony Orchestra**, and some chamber music groups such as the **Smetana, Janáček, Vlach** and **Novák Quartets** which have, with great success, conveyed the spirit of Bohemian music in various parts of the world.

The first musical works were produced in Bohemia in the 11th and 12th centuries, but it was the religious music of the Hussite period (15th century) which made its influence felt throughout the country and even beyond its frontiers. In the reign of Rudolph II (Habsburg), i.e., between 1676 and 1712, there was a large orchestra composed of the finest artists of the period at the royal Czech court. At that time, fine works were composed by the Czech Kryštof Harant of Polžice. It is well known that the Czechs—and particularly the citizens of Prague—are great music connoisseurs and music lovers who, as early as the end of the 18th century, knew how to appreciate the operas of one of the greatest musical geniuses, Mozart, whose "Don Giovanni" had its *première* (and a very successful one) in the capital of Bohemia on 29 October 1787. At this period, too, dozens of Czech musicians were living abroad where many of them, e.g., **Jan Huge Voříšerk, Vojtěch Jírovec, Leopold Antonín Koželuh, Jan Dismas Zelenka, Jiří Antonín, Jan Václav Stamic, Antonín Rejcha, Jan Ladislav Dusík, Josef Mysliveček** (known in Italy as "il divino Boemo") **Jan Mareš,** etc. enjoyed a brilliant success. In their own country, however, the works of Czech composers were not properly appreciated until quite recently, but now they form an integral part of the repertoire of a whole series of chamber music ensembles and of Czechoslovak orchestras; many have also been recorded on the Czechoslovak "Supraphon" records.

It was **Bedřich Smetana** (1824–1884), the world famous composer, who created modern Czech music and opera. His most frequently performed works include the series of tone poems

"My Country" and the operas "The Bartered Bride" and "Dalibor". Smetana's pupil, the composer **Antonín Dvořák** (1841–1904) achieved immortal fame with his nine symphonies and numerous compositions of chamber music and vocal works. Other composers who contributed to the international renown of Czech music include **Zdeněk Fibich, Josef Bohuslav Foerster, Vítězslav Novák, Josef Suk, Otakar Ostrčil, Leoš Janáček, Bohuslav Martinů, Ladislav Vycpálek, Alois Hába** and—among the younger generation—**Iša Krejčí, Jarmil Burghauser, Eugen Suchoň, Ján Cikker, Petr Eben** and many others. Their works are performed all the year round in concert halls and on the wireless and are even recorded.

To this galaxy of composers we must add the many performers who are no less famous. In the past, the entire musical world unfailingly admired the unsurpassed mastery of the Czech violinists **Josef Slavík, František Ondříček, Jan Kubelík** and **Jaroslav Kocián** who have found worthy successors in the contemporary violinists **Alexandr Plocek, Ladislav Jásek** and **Josef Suk**. The brilliant tradition established by the violincellist **Hanuš Wihan** is now being carried on by **Miloš Sádlo, Josef Chuchro** and **Saša Večtomov**. The famous Czech school of pianists is today represented by **František Maxián, František Rauch, Jan Panenka, Josef Páleníček, Ivan Moravec** and **Zuzana Růžičková**.

Contemporary Czech conductors also enjoy a high reputation throughout the world, notably **Karel Ančerl**, conductor of the Czech Philharmonic Orchestra, **Václav Smetáček** and **Václav Neumann**, conductors of the FOK Prague Symphony Orchestra who carry on the fine traditions of **Oskar Nedbal** and **Václav Talich**.

The Czech people have also produced many great singers, e.g., **Ema Destinová, Jarmila Novotná, Karel Burian** and **Josef Zitek**. Czech choral groups, such as the choirs of the Czech Philharmonic Orchestra and of the Czechoslovak Radio and the male-voice choir of Prague of Moravian Teachers have a good reputation on the international scene.

Music plays an important part in Czechoslovak life, and there are thousands of concerts and operas each year. The Czechoslovak Socialist Republic has 12 professional opera companies, numerous light-opera companies and dozens of permanent symphony orchestras. Musical education is provided by three Conservatoires, three Colleges of Music and several regional institutes. Four Czechoslovak Universities have instituted chairs of music and train the new generation of performers, composers and theoreticians.

The most important musical event in Czechoslovakia is undoubtedly the "Prague Spring Festival" which has been held regularly since 1946. At this great musical event, which has international renown, numerous opera companies, symphony orchestras, orchestras of chamber music and artists from all parts of the world perform the works of ancient and modern composers, both Czech and foreign. The "Prague Spring Festival" is always inaugurated on 12 May, that is on the anniversary of the death of the founder of modern Czech music, Bedřich Smetana, and it lasts for three weeks. This international music festival which attracts visitors from all parts of the globe, has become a sort of gesture of international good will on the part of the entire musical world, aimed at creating an atmosphere of international friendship and thus contributing to world peace. Besides the set date on which the festival always begins, it als characterized by its programme which is based on a set theme. Thus, for instance, the 1954 festival was held on the theme of "The Year of Czech Music", that of 1956 on Mozart, while at other times it was devoted to the music of the 20th century, etc. The festival always ends with a double performance of Beethoven's Ninth Symphony with its choral hymn on friendship between nations.

The Theatre

The theatre is as popular in Czechoslovakia as music. Formerly theatre life was concentrated only in the big cities, Prague, Brno and Bratislava. Today every provincial town has a permanent theatre capable of putting on operas as well; in the whole republic there are 60 to 70 permanent theatres and hundreds of amateur theatre groups. Three academies of dramatic art train future actors, producers, playwrights, scene painters, dancers, puppeteers and even music critics. The best known of all Czech theatres is the National Theatre in Prague which enjoys a universal reputation. The Spejbl and Hurvínek puppet theatres are also known all over the world.

Czechoslovak films have likewise won a world-wide reputation, particularly with cartoon puppet films, short documentary and scientific films. An international Film Festival is held every year at Karlovy Vary (Karlsbad).

Czechoslovakia has achieved a world-wide lead in combining various techniques of the film and theatre with the poly-screen, based on the principle of simultaneous projection on several screens. This new art form, which has been named "Magic Lantern", achieved world-wide popularity at the Brussels World Fair in 1958, and has been very successful in other European capitals since then.

Literature

A survey of Czech culture would not be complete without mention of some outstanding literary works and their authors, many of whom have made their mark abroad. The only names we need mention of old Czech literature are **Thomas Štítný** (1331–1401) who endeavoured in his writings in Czech to win over simple people to a Christian philosophy, and **Jan Hus** the reformer (born after 1364 and died 1415), whose literacy activity signifies a new era in Czech literature, because he pioneered a new approach to written Czech. Another famous figure is **Jan Amos Komensky (Comenius)** (1592–1670). This philosopher and teacher, who had to go into exile after the Battle of the White Mountain, died in Holland and is buried at Naarden near Amsterdam. His fame rests mainly on his works: "The Labyrinth of the World", "The Gate of Languages Opened" (Janua linguarum reserata), "Tuition for Kindergardens", "Gate of Things" (Janua rerum) and "Opera didactica omnia".

The best known names in modern Czech literature are: **Kafka, Karel Hynek Mácha, Božena Němcová,** the brothers **Karel** and **Josef Čapek, Jaroslav Hašek** and **Julius Fučik.**

Folk Traditions

Czechoslovakia is rich in **folklore**. In some regions folk songs, dances and national costumes still survive, as well as ancient customs with vestiges of superstitions from the distant past. The most noteworthy are the beautiful, richly coloured national costumes, almost each article of which is a work of art. This applies equally to men's and women's dress. The gaily embroidered kerchiefs and scarves and the various decorations of hammered copper, brass and silver are unique, as are the axe-shaped sticks carried by the men.

The finest costumes are to be found in Slovakia and the eastern districts of Moravia on the Slovakian border. Popular customs and folk songs have been preserved and the people dance and sing on every important occasion, such as when children are born, at marriages, christenings, deaths and funerals. Great **popular art festivals** are held annually in Czechoslovakia. The best-known and gayest festivals, which are known even beyond the frontier of Czechoslovakia, are held at the end of June at Strážnice in southern Moravia and usually at the beginning of July at Východná in central Slovakia.

Wooden cottages, houses with picturesquely decorated gables, little wooden churches, village cemeteries, chapels and belfries are other instances of popular art.

Furthermore pottery ware and things made of wood or straw are very well known, but pride of place must be given to the lovely embroidery work, unique in its fantastic patterning and execution. Today these can be found not only in museums, but they can be bought in shops which, run as cooperatives, specialise in popular art.

Today the government is making a great effort to preserve these precious traditions—the costumes, dances and songs—for future generations; to this end it supports the setting up of groups devoted to traditional crafts which aims to revive popular traditions in the realm of art, dancing and singing. This worthy movement, disorganized at its beginnings, was subsequently organized under the form of "Contests of Traditional Crafts". To qualify for the finals of this splendid competition the groups had first to win the communal, district and regional contests. At present there are some 20,000 "Traditional Crafts" groups and circles in Czechoslovakia, and they cooperate closely with some 450 consultative district committees specially set up for this purpose.

MEDICINAL SPRINGS AND TOURISM

In the territory of Czechoslovakia there are countless mineral springs, many of which are used for medicinal purposes. They have given rise to the development of famous Czechoslovak spas which are visited year after year by sick people from all over the world seeking relief from their suffering. Most of these spas are situated in romantically beautiful surroundings and are not only equipped with every comfort, as regards accommodation and care, but also provide the most up-to-date methods of treatment.

The best known abroad are the volcanic spas in western Bohemia. The most famous is **Karlovy Vary** (Karlsbad) with its hot springs (42–71° C) where mainly gastric disorders are cured. Among other well-known spas are **Marianské Lázně** (Marienbad), nestling in a beautiful wooded landscape, 2,080 ft. above sea level, where treatment is given for diseases of the heart, rheumatism, gastric disorders, etc; **Františkovy Lázně** (Franzensbad) with 24 springs, where gynaecological diseases are treated; **Teplice** with its radio-active springs with a temperature of 46° C used for a variety of cures, principally of rheumatic ailments. There is also **Jáchymov** in western Bohemia with the most radioactive springs in the world. **Poděbrady** Spa, in central Bohemia, lies about 50 km east of Prague in the Elbe plain and here excellent results have been obtained in the treatment of heart disorders. Nor must we omit in this short survey **Janské Lázně** in the Giant Mountains where hot carboniferous mineral springs (29.6° C) are effective for the treatment of poliomyelitis.

In northern Moravia on the foothills of the beautiful Jeseník Mounts lies **Jeseník** Spa, formerly known by the name of Gräfenberg, where nervous diseases are treated in the Preissnitz Sanatorium. **Luhačovice** in south-east Moravia should really be counted as one of the Carpathian health resorts which lie in ideally beautiful natural surroundings. Here disorders of the respiratory system are effectively treated. All the spas in Slovakia are in the Carpathians. The best-known are: **Piešťany** in the valley of the river Váh with springs of temperatures up to 67° C used for the treatment of rheumatism, **Sliač** (30° C) in central Slovakia (heart diseases) and near **Trenčianske Teplice** (14° C). There are moreover in Slovakia a number of smaller health resorts with special cures, such as **Číž** and **Darkov** (iodine springs), **Rájecké**

Teplice (33° C), **Bojnické Teplice** (38° C), **Štubnianke Teplice** (48° C), **Vyšnie Ružbachy** (24° C) and many others.

Because of the mountainous nature of much of the country there are many high altitude health resorts in Czechoslovakia, notably **Špindlerův Mlýn** in the Giant Mountains (Bohemia), **Karlova Studánka** (Moravia) and in the High Tatra (Slovakia) **Tatranská Lomnica, Smokovec** and **Šrbské Pleso**. These are the most important out of a total of about 500.

The natural beauty of Czechoslovakia makes the country a tourist's paradise.

Climbing tours are possible anywhere in Czechoslovakia. There are hotels, tourists' hostels and belvederes in the mountains; and 40,000 km of footpaths are provided with sign-posts for hikers, and many also for skiers. The loveliest country for tourism in Bohemia is in the frontier mountains, especially in the Giant Mountains, the Iser Mountains, the Eagle Mountains and in the Bohemian Forest.

In Moravia and Silesia the **Králický Sněžník**, the **Jeseník** and the **Beskids** are the mountains most attractive to tourists. The greater part of Slovakia is of course mountainous. The most beautiful region is that of the High Tatra, magnificent and wild, with steep crags and clear, transparent lakes high up in the mountains and splendidly preserved old forest-land. Here, covering an area roughly 25 km by 17 km, a **State Natural Reserve Park** has been created, the Tatra National Park (abbrev. TANAP) where unique mountain flora and fauna (e.g. bears, approx. 600 chamois, 900 marmots) and important scientific research. But the other mountainous district of Slovakia, like the Lower Tatra (highest peak Dumbier, 6,748 feet), the Great and Little Fatra (rising to 5,600 feet), the Slovakian Ore Mounts and others are very lovely and attractive to tourists.

The "Underworld" of Czechoslovakia also belongs to the sights of Europe. In the Moravian **cave district** (north of Brno) there is a labyrinth of caves, subterranean lakes and abysses (Macocha); in central Slovakia there are vast subterranean regions of Demänova caves near the town of Liptovský Mikuláš, the Dominica caves in southern Slovakia, which are partly in Hungary and a large number of caves and abysses in the south Slovak cave district (near Plešivec and Rožnava, not yet entirely explored). Also fascinating is the ice cave of Dobšina, situated on the edge of the romantic limestone region known as the Slovakian Paradise, characterised by primeval-like forests with many waterfalls and cataracts in gorges and ravines.

Every year thousands of tourists visit the villages and labyrinths of the cliffs, celebrated for their many echoes. There are on the one hand, the cliffs of Děčín in northern Bohemia (known as Bohemia-Saxon Switzerland) and the Tiské Stěny; and in western Bohemia the cliffs at Prachov in the so-called "Bohemian-Paradise" near Turnov and Jičín, the rock formations at Adršpach and the Teplite cliffs in eastern Bohemia as well as the Sulov rocks in western Slovakia (near the town of Žilina).

But not only mountains and crags, but also rivers and highways play a great part in the tourism of Czechoslovakia. Hundreds, nay thousands of "water tourists" travel on the many navigable rivers in canoes, skiffs and other pleasure boats and enjoy the beauty of the valleys and the surrounding sights. Tens of thousands of tourists yearly make trips on the thousands of miles of well-kept highways in the summer, on bicycles, motor cycles, automobiles and buses to enjoy the beauty of their country.

The many mountains and peaks are suitable country for climbers. Their favourite and most extensive region is of course the High Tatra, its precipices offering the best practice ground, but this sport is indulged in wherever possible. Today the Czechoslovak mountaineering regions are also visited by many foreign climbers.

Czechoslovakia is also a hunting paradise, as good natural conditions, preservation of game as well as a strict observation of the hunting season make it possible to keep up a comparatively large supply of game in a comparatively small area. The same is true of angling which can be practised in the rivers, streams and weirs. Hunting areas are plentiful, for they are to be found in the high mountains, in picturesque valleys, in dense forests and in game parks. Accommodation in huts, hotels and hunting lodges, intended for this special purpose, is also comfortable. Sportsmen can assure themselves of the high state of development of this sport by visits to hunting museums, hunting lodges and reservations where they will find unusual species of game. The fees for shooting permits vary with the kind of game in question on the one hand, on the other, with quality of the bag, determined by the international rules of the C.I.C. (Conseil International de la Chasse), laid down in 1937. More precise information on the subject can be obtained from the Czechoslovak Travel Bureau (Čedok) or its agents.

FOOD AND DRINK

Like every other country Czechoslovakia has its own specialities in the preparation of food and drink. To be sure, the so-called "Bohemian cuisine" is not nearly so varied as the cooking of other countries in western and eastern Europe. The Slovak cuisine on the other hand has some resemblance to the Czech while, owing to the free use of spices and paprika, it is like the Hungarian; this applies primarily to southern and eastern Slovakia where excellent local wines are also drunk.

Czech cuisine is very filling, tasty and somewhat heavy, for its dishes consist of more meat than vegetables, and dumplings —a real speciality of the "Bohemian kitchen"—are served with them. The most popular meat is pork, prepared in a number of different ways; roast pork, well-done with sour-kraut and dumplings, has more or less become a national dish. In Slovakia, however, this national dish takes the form of a goulash cooked the Hungarian way with paprika, but likewise with dumplings or also with potatoes. Of course other kinds of meat are eaten, e.g. beef, veal, mutton, game and poultry. The fowl preferred is a well-roasted goose, also eaten with sour-kraut and dumplings. For a Czech, the thought of a well-prepared meal evokes the image of a well-roasted piece of pork with a golden crust accompanied by a dish of **knedlíky** (dumplings made of wheat flour bread rolls) and a pot of delicious sour cabbage—or alternatively a succulent roast goose with the same. A fresh, sparkling Czech beer is served with the food.

Dumplings are not only served with meat, but they are also a delicious sweet in the form of fruit dumplings, filled with cherries, morellas or apricots and in autumn with plums. They may be served with grated curds or gingerbread or strewn with poppy seeds with melted butter poured over them. The most popular are made with a kind of damson and when these are in season eating contests are often held.

There are other favoured meat dishes with a kind of white sauce, e.g. fillet of beef with dumplings or gravy. Fish also are greatly enjoyed, particularly the Czech carp, bred on an enormous scale in the ponds of southern Bohemia. This tasty fish can be baked or cooked **au bleu**, in aspic or with a sauce the main ingredients of which are beer, almonds and raisins. The Czechs are very fond of all kinds of smoked meat and specially of hot dogs, sausages sold in pairs (horky parky) and these are not only to be bought in shops, but are sold, like roasted chestnuts, in the street, on railway platforms, at football matches and at all times by day and night. They are best with a glass of good Pilsener beer. A speciality among the varieties of smoked meat is Prague ham, justly famous far beyond the confines of Czechoslovakia for its delicate flavour.

The national soup is "bramboračka" (the Czech word for potato is brambor), a potato soup flavoured with mushrooms.

Sweets are the "pièce de résistance" of the Czech menu. Besides the usual dishes of this kind, pancakes, sweet omelettes, flat cakes, etc. there are all sorts of cakes and pastries. One can see them in the window of any confectioner's. Most of them are common to the Austrian kitchen, and include buns filled with jam, strudel, kugelhupf, open fruit tarts, puff pastry, etc. The Czech and Slovak pastry-cooks are masters of their art and are in demand all over the world. If a luxury hotel, the restaurant of an ocean liner or a health resort has a reputation for the excellence of its patisserie, you can bet your bottom dollar that there is a Czech pastry-cook working in the kitchen.

The bread in Czechoslovakia is different from the bread of other countries in that it is generally baked with rye flour. Rolls are made of white flour.

The most popular drink in Czechoslovakia is undoubtedly beer (pivo), as the best beer in the world is brewed here. It is drunk everywhere: in large restaurants, in small inns and taverns and at home. It helps the digestion of some of the heavy dishes in Czech cuisine. Both light and dark beers are brewed in Czechoslovakia and fall into different categories according to their alcoholic content. The weakest beer is generally 7%, the strongest kinds are up to 20% and are known as "ležák". Strong dark beer is called "kozel" or "Prelat".

Wine is more widely drunk in the eastern parts of the state. Grapes are grown and pressed at Pezinok and Sv. Jur in Slovakia, in the country round Mikulov in southern Moravia and at Mělník in Bohemia. A special alcohol drink is plum brandy (Slivovice). It is very potent (60–70% and anyone not accustomed to drinking schnapps should be wary of it. The best slivovic is distilled in south-east Moravia ("Slovácká Slivovice"). A kind of bourbon is distilled in the so-called Haná district of central Moravia; it is called "Hanácká Režná".

Description
and
Itineraries

1.   PRAGUE

History and Art

The city of Prague lies on both banks of the Vltava, enveloped in the magic of its glorious and tragic past. Since the early Middle Ages it has been known as one of the most beautiful cities in the world. It won the admiration of the Arab merchant Ibrahim Ibn Jakub in the 16th century. He paid this tribute to its importance: "Prague is the biggest trade centre in the Slav countries where Russians and other Slav merchants from Cracow exchange their beaver pelts and other precious furs for the goods offered by the Moslems, the Jews and the Turks." As early as the 12th century, the beauty of Prague was eulogized by Kosmas, the first Czech chronicler who particularly admired the castle and other stone buildings. Later, during the reign of Charles IV, Prague welcomed the nuncio Rudolph who was enchanted by its beauty and wrote as follows: "There are few countries in the world that can boast of a town whose beauty even remotely approaches that of Prague. I would even say that the Bohemian capital surpasses Nuremberg, Vienna and Wroclaw, even the old Cologne, and I really don't know if such cities as Rome, Venice, Florence and other towns in the world can rival the beauty of this gem set in the very heart of Europe."

In the 14th century Prague surpassed all other central European towns. The Vltava was already spanned by stone bridges which are still among the greatest treasures of architecture. The tall spires of churches and the towers of fortifications rose above the roofs of the houses, the whole town nestling among the greenery of vineyards. It is not therefore surprising that in the 15th century so well-travelled a man as Aeneas Silvius, later Pope Pius II., was enraptured by Prague and described it as the queen of cities, for Prague seemed to him in no way inferior to Florence. Likewise Czech kings and Queen Elizabeth Stuart, daughter of King James I. of England rated it a truly royal city. And at that time Prague was still untouched by Baroque which in the 18th century made it one of the wonders of the world. Similarly in later times Prague never failed to arouse the enthusiasm of its visitors who have often known every country in Europe and even the whole wide world. The German poet Goethe called Prague the most beautiful jewel in the stone crown of the globe. The French writer Fouqué wrote in 1823: "Kingly Prague! Indescribable, incomparable is the splendour of the churches, the beauty and sublimity of thy palaces. No words can convey the almost miraculous impression made on the observer by the splendour of Prague and the Hradšin." The German historian Ranke also came under the spell of its magic and wrote in 1827: "But Prague is glorious! When I drove down from the Hradšin and reached the spot from which one can see at once the 100 towers of the Old Town, the river and the Petřin, I realised that I had never yet seen such a city."

Others, too, admired the beauty of Prague. Thus, for instance, the famous German naturalist and explorer Alexander von Humboldt preferred Prague to Constantinople, Naples and Lisbon which were considered the loveliest European cities in his time.

We may further mention the French sculptor Auguste Rodin, who called Prague the Rome of the North, and the French historian Ernest Denis who wrote in his History of the Czech People: "The history of Prague during the time of its oppression is tragic and a heroic drama could well be written about every stone."

But wherein actually lies the beauty of the capital of Czechoslovakia? No doubt there are two contributing factors: natural and human. Prague lies open towards the south, and is protected to the north, so that its mild climate, as well as its beautiful and favourable location must have attracted settlers from very early times, especially as the rest of the country was entirely covered with forest. Its position on the river was also of great importance. A settlement at the spot where the river was crossed by a ford sprang up 3,500 years ago; it later became Prague, the capital of the Slav Czechs. 1,000 years ago a settlement of wooden buildings was erected there which thanks to its central position became the focal point of the whole country; especially as in the 12th century Prague was built of stone. The descendants of Přemysl, the ruling dynasty, united all the Czech races into a single nation. Thus Prague became important not only to the Bohemian provinces but in the last 1,000 years it has often aroused the attention of all Europe.

The face of the Prague of today has been mainly formed by two art periods: the Romanesque-Gothic, A.D. 900–1500, and the Renaissance-Baroque, A.D. 1500–1800. Thus we find in Prague traces of all architectural styles, from Romanesque to a marked modern style.

The most important **Romanesque** buildings are, first: the **Basilica of Saint George** in the Pražsky hrad, the **Rotunda of Saint Martin** on the Vyšehrad and the **Rotundas of the Holy Cross** in the Old Town and of **Saint Longinus** in the New Town.

There are a number of magnificent **Gothic** monuments in Prague—partly rebuilt Romanesque edifices and partly of the Gothic period—resulting from the expansion of the city. At the very beginning of this period the following parts of the city were founded: the **Old Town** 1232, the **Inner Town** (Malá Strana) 1257, the **Hradčany** 1320 and the **New Town** 1348. It was not however until the reign of Charles IV and of his son Václav IV that Gothic architecture in Prague reached its zenith, especially on the Hradčany. It was at that time that the name "hundred-towered Prague" was coined. The outstanding Gothic buildings in Prague are:

The **Bethlehem Chapel,** in which Magister Jan Hus preached in the 15th century, the churches of the **Virgin Mary in front of the Týn,** of the **Virgin Mary Snow,** of **Saint Stephen, Saint Martin in the Wall** and many others. The foundation stone of **Saint Vitus' Cathedral** in the Hradčany was also laid then.

The most important secular buildings are:

The **Old Town Town-Hall,** the **New Town Town-Hall,** the **Carolinum,** seat of the first Prague university, the **Charles Bridge** (the wonderful decoration of statues dates from the Baroque period), the **Powder Tower** and remains of the fortifications of the Old Town. Prominent are the monuments in the **old Ghetto,** notably the Old Jewish Cemetery, the Synagogue, the oldest in central Europe, and other buildings.

The **Renaissance** added comparatively little to the embellishment of Prague, except the external decoration of buildings and façades. But we must not overlook the **Royal Pleasure Palace** and the beautifully planned gardens, laid out at the time the palace was built, and the peculiar construction of the summer palace **Hvězda** (Star), erected on a ground plan in the form of a star.

The greatest number of architectural and other artistic monuments are of the **Baroque period** which, although it was closely connected with the most tragic epoch of Czech history, created in Prague a complex of magnificent palaces and churches. During the Baroque age (1630–1780) one might say that the city was entirely rebuilt on its originally Gothic ground plan. The Baroque artists, mostly Italian and later also native, completely mastered the panorama of Prague and its terrain, understanding so well how to enhance the magic of its churches and palaces by giving them a setting of extensively planned gardens. We have but to mention the gardens of the **Vrtba, Ledeburg, Fürstenberg** and **Valdštejn** (Wallenstein) palaces. It is due to the work of these artists that Prague is one of the most beautiful cities in the world. During this period the building of **Prague Castle** was also finished.

The oldest parts of the city are filled with reminders of this age which, together with the monuments of earlier periods, give to Prague its indescribable enchantment. This is true above all for Prague Castle, Hradčany and Malá Strana. This is dominated by the **Church of Saint Nicholas,** Baroque at its best; but its palaces and private houses are also unique examples of this style. We must not however forget the monumental **Černin** palace and the **Loretto** monastery with its church opposite the palace. Not far away is **Strahov,** once a Gothic Premonstratensian monastery and today the **National Museum of Literature,** forming with the **Church of the Virgin Mary** and the **Church of Saint Roch** a unique monument of Baroque architecture. The most remarkable buildings in the Baroque Old Town are in the **Křižovnická,** particularly the **Clementinum,** the second largest edifice after Prague castle, with four courtyards and four churches. The church of **Saint Francis** with its remarkable cupola adjoins this huge edifice. Nor must we omit the churches of **Saint James** and **Saint Nicholas** which both enhance the Old Town. In the New Town the most notable monuments are near the Karlovy náměsti: the church of **Saint Ignatius** with the former Jesuit College, **Faust's House,** the church of **Saint John on the Rock,** the church of the **Holy Trinity** and others.

In the 19th century Prague was enriched by some important buildings in Czech Renaissance style, far superior to the experimental architecture of the period. The most notable of these are the **National Theatre** on the bank of the river, the **National Museum** at the top end of the **Václavské námesti,** the **Smetana Museum** near the Charles Bridge, the **Artists' House,** seat of the Czech Philharmonic. In recent times Prague has acquired a number of statues, the finest are: the equestrian statue of Saint Václav (by Myslbek, the originator of modern Czech statuary), the Jan Hus group in the Staroměstské náměstí, the F. Palacký group memorial, the statue of Josef Jungmann, the equestrian statue of Jan Žižka on Mount Vítkov facing the "Liberation Memorial".

From 1918 onwards when Prague was again the metropolis of the Czechoslovak state and especially after its liberation from the Nazi yoke at the end of the Second World War, Prague has successfully vied with other capital cities in the construction of modern residential districts, new undertakings and parks, shops, public buildings, etc.

The centre of modern Prague is the square **Václavské namesti** into which the following streets debouch: ulice 28 rijna (28th October St), Na Mustku, Vodičkova, Jindřišska, Opeltalova, Stepanska and Vinohradská. Here are almost all the most important shops, hotels, restaurants and places of amusement. The main railway stations are also not far away.

The list of Prague's cultural institutions must be headed by its many **museums.** The largest and most important are: the National Museum, the City Museum, the Technical Museum, the Arts Museum, the Náprstek Ethnographical Museum, the Military Museum, the Jewish Museum and others. Art collections are housed in different buildings of the National Gallery, e.g. the collection of ancient art is in the Sternberg Palace on the Hradčany and contains outstanding works by Gothic painters and sculptors; the works of 19th century Czech painters are collected in what was once the riding-school of the Waldstein Palace. The most important library is the National and University Library (some 2 million volumes) housed in the Clementinum; the library in Strahov is also famous. It stands next door to the National Museum of Literature which provides a detailed survey of the development of Czech literature from its beginnings down to the present day.

The **musical life** of Prague is concentrated in three opera houses and concert halls, the most notable of which are the Smetana Hall and the hall in the Artists' House. Concerts and performances given in the gardens of some of the old palaces are very popular. Gramophone record concerts are given in the Music Theatre. Serious musical works are also played at concerts in the old churches. The existence of two operetta theatres should also be mentioned.

The "Prague Spring" International Music Festival is held every year in which prominent artists and music-lovers from all over the world participate.

The most important monuments in Prague, listed according to style

Romanesque (11th–13th century): Rotunda of the Holy Cross (Karoliny-Světlé, Old Town), Rotunda of Saint Martin (Vyšehrad), Rotunda of Saint Longinus ("Na rybníčku", New Town), Saint George's Basilica in the castle, subterranean rooms of the castle and Saint Vitus' Cathedral with remains of the Carolingian Rotunda (926–929), the Spytihněv Basilica (1060–1096), the princely palace of Soběslav I. (1135–1173) under the Vlasislav Hall, all in Prague Castle (Pražský hrad).

Gothic (13th–15th century): **Early Gothic**—the Convent of the Blessed Town. **High Gothic**—the Church of Our Lady of the Snow (New Town), the Emaus monastery (New Town), the churches of Karlov, Saint Henry and Saint Stephen (all New Town), the Charles Bridge, the Old Town Bridge Tower, the bay of the Carolinum and the Old Town Hall (O.T.) and the choir of Saint Vitus' Cathedral. **Late Gothic**: The Tyne church—Sv. Maria Týn (Old Town), the Powder Tower (Old Town), the New Town Hall, the window left of the entrance into the Old Town Hall, the Vladislav Hall in Prague Castle, the Oratory of Saint Vitus' Cathedral.

Renaissance (1530–1620): the Týn Court (Old Town), the "Minute House" next to the Old Town Hall, the houses opposite the Tyne Church, the Slavata or Thun Palace by the New Castle Stairs (Malá Strana), the Schwarzenberg Palace, the Hradčany Town Hall, the Ball house in the Royal Gardens (Hradčany), Belvedere, the Hvězda castle (Liboc), the Jagellon Palace in Prague Castle.

Baroque (1620–1780): **In the Old Town**: the Kinský Palace, the Clam-Gallas Palace, the Clementinum, the churches of the Knights of the Cross, of Saints Salvator, Clement, Nicholas and Gall.

In the New Town: the Villa America, the Sylva-Taroucca Palace, Faust's House, the churches of Saint John on the Rock and of Saint Catherine.

In the Malá Strana: the Valdštejn (Wallenstein), Kolovrat, Nostitz, Buquoy, Morzini, Thun, Fürstenberg and Ledebourg

Palaces, the Abbot's Palace and the churches of Saint Nicholas, Our Lady of Victory (Saint Maria Viktoria), Saint Thomas, Saint Joseph. The Smiřický house ("U Montágů").

Castle and Hradčany quarter: 1st, 2nd, 3rd and 4th courtyards, the Archiepiscopal Palace, the Tuscan Palace, the Sternberg and Černín Palaces. Churches: the Loretto Church and the Strahov Monastery Church.

Also Saint Margaret's Church and Convent, in Břevnov Troja Castle.

Empire (1780–1850): the Strahov Library, the Exhibition Palace "U Hybernů" (New Town), the "Platýz" Palace (Old Town), the Church of the Holy Cross (Na Příkopé) and the "Slovanský Dům (New Town), the ethnographical section of the National Museum in Petřín Park (Villa Kinský).

19th-century buildings: Romantic Gothic—the Summer Palace in the "Baumgarten", the new part of Saint Vitus' Cathedral.

Neo-Renaissance: the National Theatre, Saint Václav's Church in Smíchov, the Gröbr Villa in Prague 12, the National Museum, the government "presidium" building (Straka Academy in the Malá Strana), the Gottwald Museum (New Town), the Wiehl House (New Town), at the corner of the Václavské náměstí and the Vodičkova).

Modern buildings: see below, "Modern Prague".

Modern Prague

As the Renaissance and Baroque styles of architecture become outdated and attempts to revive the Classical style failed to establish it, Prague and the whole of Europe fell into a certain stagnation, a decline of architectural development. Jan Koteřa was the first modern Czech architect to find a solution in Prague. He aimed to free architecture from the bonds of historical styles and proved by his creations that even in the Bohemian provinces a new artistic era had dawned. As examples we may take his own villa in the Letohradská ulice in Prague 12 or the Urbánek house in the Jungmannová třída in the New Town. Kotěra taught his pupils a simple and functional style. There were admittedly architects who went different ways;

an obvious instance is the house, already mentioned, the "Black Mother of God" in the Celetná (No 569). This creation by Josef Gočár in spite of its cubist style in no way disturbs the general impression of a typical street in the Gothic Old Town and also aroused well-deserved interest among experts abroad.

The search for new ways led moreover to the exploitation of popular building designs. Evidence of this is to be seen in Prague in the former "Legiobank" building in the "Na Poříčí" (No 1046), designed by Josef Gočár and the buildings of the Riunione Adriatica de Sicurta at the corner of the Národní trída and the Jungmannová in the New Town (No 748), designed by Pavel Janák. After the First World War modern Czech architecture found its expression, on the one hand, in office blocks and public buildings, e.g. administrative buildings, schools, cinemas, etc. and, on the other hand, in the erection of whole districts of villas and private houses (e.g. Vořechovka in Prague 5, Hanspaulká in Prague 6, Spořilov in Prague 4 and Barrandov in Prague 5).

During this period, an up to the present day, the panorama of Prague has been enriched by a number of important buildings.

The National Memorial on Vítkov Hill (Žižkov), erected by the architect Jan Zázvorka. The monument is suitably completed by the equestrian statue of Jan Žižka of Trocnov (Bohumil Kavka).

The Trades Union Council building in Žižkov (Architects J. Havlík and K. Honzík).

The Transport Board building in Holešovice (architects Adolf Beneš and J. Kříž).

The former Industries Fair building, also in Holešovice (architects Oldřich Tyl and Josef Fuchs).

The new Crematorium in Strašnice (architect Al. Mezera).

The Law Faculty of Charles University in Pařížská ulice in the Old Town (architects Jan Kotěra and Lad. Machoň).

The **Philosophy Faculty of Charles University,** Náměstî Krasnoarmějčů (Red Army Square) in the Old Town (architect Jos. Sakař).

The **Municipal Library,** Dr Vacek náměsti in the Old Town (architect František Roit).

The **Technical Museum,** Letná district, Prague 7.

Barrandov, restaurant overlooking the river, the swimming stadium in Prague 16 and the nearby film studio.

There are also a number of modern **church buildings** (the **Heart of Jesus** church in Vinohrady, designed by Plečník, **St. Vaclav's** in Vršovice, designed by Gočár); some new **bridges** (the Jirásek Bridge, the **Jana Švermy Bridge** with new embankment and the **Letná tunnel),** as well as other buildings which reveal the strides made by modern architecture.

The modern residential districts in the outer suburbs of Prague are continually expanding.

A. THE CASTLE (HRADČANY)

Prague Castle (Pražský hrad) was built in the second half of the 9th century as a Slav fortress. Originally made of wood, it was rebuilt in stone, and enlarged, in the 12th century.

The castle, later damaged by fire, was reconstructed by Matthias of Arras, and became the imperial palace of the Emperor Charles IV and King Wenceslas IV. Vladislav Jagellon II built his seat on its ruins in the late Gothic period. The central part of Prague Castle with its very famous Vladislav Hall has been preserved from that time until the present. In the 17th and 18th centuries the Castle was reconstructed in Renaissance style under Hapsburg rule and, finally, in the reign of the Empress Maria Theresa, between the years 1753 and 1755, it was given its uniform appearance as a late Baroque palace. There were no alterations until 1918 when it became the residence of the President of the Czechoslovak Republic, and the reception rooms of the castle were only modernised in the years that followed.

The **main entrance** to the Castle is in the **Hradčanské náměstí,** separated from the first courtyard by a wrought iron railing supported by eight pillars.

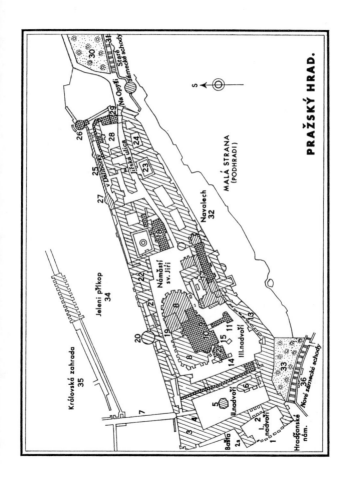

The statues of two giants on pillars by I. Platzer stand above the present entrance and the monogram MTI (Maria Theresia Imperatrix) can be seen on the railings, a proof that this gate was erected in the 18th century when the castle moat was filled in. Opposite the entrance gate in the middle of the new wing is the **Matthias Gate**, dating from 1614 (by Scamozzi), through which we come into the second courtyard. On the right of this gate a staircase leads to the President's reception rooms and on the left we enter the Hall of Pillars (by Plěnik) leading to the banqueting rooms.

By a lateral gateway (to the left) one enters the garden "Bašta". From here is an entrance to the well-known *Spanish Hall*, one of the largest in Europe (178 × 79 × 39½ feet) which was built in the 16th century to the plans of the architect Giovanni Giargiolli. The statues are by Adrien de Vries and Giovanni Guardi, the paintings by Vredeman de Vries and Christian Schröter. The present decoration of the Hall is pseudo-Rococo (1865-68).

The **second courtyard** was made when the second moat was filled in, in the 16th century. From this courtyard one can either pass into the third courtyard or to the second exit from the castle. Noteworthy are the **Baroque wells** (1886) with wrought iron railings and the **Chapel of the Holy Cross** (1753 and 1858) with internal decorations of a later period and a fine collection of religious objects. From the second courtyard one also enters the Picture Gallery where the Emperor Rudolf II (Hapsburg) assembled his famous art collections. Gates allow passage into the **third courtyard** opposite the portal of Saint Vitus' Cathedral.

Explanation of the Plan of Prague Castle

First Courtyard (Maria Theresa period, 1740-80): entrance gate with statues by Ignaz Platzer (1); this was formerly the site of the castle moat (from the Romanesque period) and a bridge led to the gate. The Matthias Gate (1614 Vincenzo Scamozzi) (2), the garden "Bašta" (2a).

Second Courtyard. There was a moat here in the Middle Ages. Buildings of the time of Ferdinand I and Rudolf II (1526-1612). It looks now as it did in Maria Theresa's time. Spanish Hall on the first floor (3), stables on ground level (both of the time of

Ferdinand I and Rudolf II). Picture gallery (former collections of Rudolf II), (4), stables on ground level. Well of the time of Leopold I. (Jer. Kohl, Francesco de Thore, 1686) (5). Chapel of the Holy Cross of Maria Theresa's time, restored in 1852 (6). Powder Bridge (7).

Third Courtyard. Saint Vitus' Cathedral (founded in 1344, the new part in 1873) (8). Remains of the Rotunda of Saint Vitus (926) (9) and the Spytihněv Basilica (1060) (10). Remains of a Romanesque chapel, late 12th century (11). Priory (residence of the bishop) built in 973, with remains of the chapel of Saint Mauritius (12). Building of the time of Ferdinand II (1637–57), rebuilt in Maria Theresa's reign, with remains of Romanesque fortifications under the pavement (13). Monolith (1929) (14), well with statue of Saint George (1372, repaired in the 16th century) (15). The old Royal Palace (Vladislav Hall, Bohemian Chancellor's Office, equestrian stairway, Hall of Justice, etc.). All Saints' Church (castle chapel of the time of Charles IV, repaired in 1572) (17). Saint George's Church (920) and Benedictine Monastery (973) (18). Vikar Lane (19). Mihulka Tower of the time of Přemysl Otokar II (1252–78) (20). Houses of the cathedral chapter, late 19th century (21, 22). Institute of the "Nobility (1755) (23). Lobkowitz House (1680–1891) (24). The "Golden Lane" with remains of ramparts of the time of Přemysl Otokar II (25). "Daliborka" Tower of the same period and the time of Vladislav II (1496) (26). White Tower of the time of Přemysl Otokar II (27). Old Burgrave's Palace (Giovanni Ventura, 1559) with the arms of different noble families (28). East Gate in the Black Tower (1135) (29). The so-called "Opyš" vineyard of Saint Václav (30). Old Castle Steps (31). The garden "on the ramparts" (32) and the "Paradise" garden (33). Jelenkí Příkop (Stag's Ditch) 34), Royal Gardens (35), New Castle Steps (36).

In the third courtyard is the old **Rectory**, originally the Romanesque **residence** of the 11th-century bishops. Next to it, on the east side, we see, protected by a roof, the remains of the Romanesque Chapel of Saint Maurice and the Spytihněv basilica, founded in about 1060 A.D. In the second half of the 17th century the seat of the Rector was rebuilt in Baroque style and is adorned by the statue of Saint Václav by Josef Bendl. Also worthy of note is the bronze equestrian statue of Saint George (1373) which was damaged in 1541 and recast its present form in 1928. In that year, the tenth anniversary of the foundation of the republic, a monolith of granite, 60 feet high, was erected in this courtyard.

Below the **pillared balcony** of Maria Theresa's time is the entrance to the chancellery of the Presidence of the Republic. In the southwest corner the **Romanesque "White Tower"**, once the state prison, is still preserved. Here one can also see above the entrance to the former court chapel the monogram "F III" (Ferdinand III). In the opposite corner a monumental staircase leads to the adjacent gardens.

From here one can make one's way, also beneath an architecturally beautiful balcony, into the most interesting medieval part of the castle, in which is the late **Gothic Vladislav Hall** with its unique vaulted ceiling and the monogram "W" (Vladislav II).

The equestrian stairs are a reminder that riding tournaments were once held in this hall. In the adjoining rooms (the old Diet Hall, Appeal Hall, Bohemian chancellery, the Imperial Council Chamber) the Bohemian kings were elected and all important state matters debated. Today the President of the Republic is elected in the Vladislav Hall. One of these rooms was the scene of the famous "Defenestration of Prague" (1618).

The old royal palace is connected with Saint Vitus' Cathedral by a Gothic passage under which one reaches the **Romanesque Basilica of Saint George** and the **convent.** Saint George's church is not only closely connected with the beginnings of Christianity in the lands of Bohemia, but is also the earliest Romanesque building which is still in use today.

According to the latest archaeological research, the Basilica of Saint George also contains the tombs of the princes of Bohemia. 12th-century frescoes have also been discovered there.

It was built of wood in about 920 A.D. and when Prague was promoted to an episcopal see in 973 the first Benedictine convent was founded there. In about 1000 A.D. the church was rebuilt in stone. Directly opposite the royal palace is the **Church of All Saints**, originally built in 1173 as part of the palace of Prince Sobeslav. In the reign of Charles IV it was reconstructed by the architect of Saint Vitus' Cathedral, the famous Peter Parler of Gmünd, destroyed by fire in the 16th century and rebuilt in its present form between 1570 and 1574. The altar-piece is the work of the painter Václav V. Rainer.

The adjacent classical pillared entrance leads into the so-called **Institute of Nobility**, the part of the palace constructed out of three private houses and the Rosenberg Renaissance Palace during alterations in the time of Maria Theresa (architect O. Avostatis).

Behind the convent and church of Saint George is the famous **Golden Lane** where a long time ago goldsmiths and later royal archers lived. It consists of 16 tiny houses built into the castle walls in 1541. One comes out from the Golden Lane into the **castle keep "Daliborka"** (1496). In the same year the first captive of the knight Dalibor of Kozojed was held prisoner here; the tower is named after him. This event is also the subject of Bedřich Smetana's well-known opera "Dalibor". The Dalibor Tower is one of the four towers of the old castle wall, the others being the Black Tower, the White Tower and the Mihulka Tower; the two latter towers overlook the Stag Ditch. One can leave the east side of the castle through the Black Tower, coming out into the old Castle Steps.

Also part of the castle is the former **Riding-school** which is reached from the second courtyard. This has been recently rebuilt as an Exhibition Hall.

Opposite the former Riding-school is the entrance to the **royal garden** with, in its eastern part, the **superb royal summer-residence (Belvedere)** built in Renaissance style between 1535–1560 after the designs of the architect Paolo della Stella and is now transformed into a magnificent exhibition hall and gallery. From the belvedere we have one of the most splendid views of Prague Castle. The royal Garden is not open to the public.

Saint Vitus' Cathedral, a characteristic and inseparable part of the outline of Prague Castle, is not only the most important church edifice in Czechoslovakia, but is also extremely rich in art treasures.

It stands where originally stood the rotunda with the tomb of Prince Václav I (Wenceslaus, 926–929 A.D.) and later a basilica dating from 1060–92. When the Prague episcopal see was raised to the see of an archbishopric, Charles IV founded a cathedral there, summoning the premier architect, Matthias of Arras, to Prague from Avignon.

A special chapel was erected, dedicated to Saint Václav (Wenceslaus). This was later enlarged by the famous Gothic architect, Peter Parler of Gmünd. He also started the building of the main tower. Building was interrupted for a time by the Hussite wars in the lands of Bohemia and it was not until 1509–11 that King Vladislav Jagellon continued the work. Another interruption was caused by a conflagration in 1541, and the attempts of the Emperor Leopold I in 1673 met with failure because of the outbreak of war against the Turks. Likewise the third attempt to complete the building of the cathedral in 1729 in the reign of Charles VI failed and it was only thanks to the efforts of the "Association for the Completion of the Building of Saint Vitus' Cathedral" in the second half of the 19th century that the cathedral was finished in 1929. Consequently every architectural style is represented, from the Romanesque to the modern.

Among the most precious monuments are the oldest works of statuary from the time of Charles IV and his successor Václav IV, of the period 1380–1420. Pride of place must be given to the statue of Saint Václav in the chapel dedicated to this saint; then to the 21 stone effigies of members of the Luxemburg family who contributed to the building of the cathedral, of the archbishop the master builders and the architect. This gallery of medieval sculpture which adorns the triforium was all executed in Peter Parler's stonemason's workshop; some of the statues he made himself, notably the tufa statue of Saint Václav.

Saint Vitus' Cathedral consists of two parts; the old and the new. The nave of the former is 118 feet high. As early as the time of Václav IV the Bohemian kings were crowned there before the high altar. In it are also 11 of the **19 chapels** of the cathedral, to wit: The Chapel of Saint Václav containing the tomb and relics of the saint, his shirt of mail and helmet. From it steps lead to the Regalia Chamber, where the Bohemia crown jewels are kept (the crown of Saint Václav from the time of Charles IV, sceptre and orb).

The Chapel of the Holy Cross with the picture of the head of Christ as imprinted on Veronica's handkerchief ("veraicon", a gift to Charles IV from the Pope).

The Valdstejn Chapel with the tombs of Matthew of Arras and Peter Parler. Behind them is the Vladislav oratatory (1493).

The Sternberg Chapel with the tombs of King Přemysl Otokar I and II, both by Peter Parler.

The Imperial Chapel with the tombs of Brětislav I and Spytihněv II, the founder of St. Vitus' Cathedral.

The Vlašim Chapel with the tombs of Očko of Vlašim, the first Czech cardinal; altarpiece by Peter Brandl.

The Chapel of St. John the Baptist (1352) with the tomb of Bořivoj II and Břetislav II, with the statue of a saint by the Czech sculptor Václav Levý and the statue of Cyril and Methodius by Joseph Václav Myslbek.

The Pernštein Chapel, with tombs of the archbishops, in front of which stands a larger than life-size of the kneeling Cardinal Schwarzenberg by J. V. Myslbek.

The Nostitz Chapel with a shrine containing relics (1266) on the altar which was preserved in Trier until the French Revolution.

The Chapel of St. Sigmund and St. Martin, both richly decorated.

In the oldest part of the cathedral is also the Royal Mausoleum by the Dutch sculptor Alex. Colin (1564–1598) and in the crypt below the mausoleum is the vault in which the Bohemian kings lie buried; in it the bones of Charles IV and his four wives, of Ladislav his successor, Jiří of Poděbrady, Rudolf II and other members of the royal house are piously preserved. The decoration of the vault dates from 1928. This however by no means exhausts the artistic treasures of this part of the cathedral.

There are also many remarkable things in the new part of the cathedral. The stained glass windows in the individual chapels should also be noted and the window in the front wall depicting the Creation by František Kysela. The west wall of the cathedral with two slender towers is adorned by 14 statues of saints and of Charles IV as well as by busts of the last architects of the cathedral, Josef Mocker and Kamil Hilbert (by the sculptor

Václav Sucharda, 1929). The sculptures on the doors recount the history of the cathedral from 925 to 1929, and show St. Wenceslaus and St. Adalbert. These are almost exclusively works by modern Czech artists (V. H. Brunner, Otokar Španiel and others). The stained glass window of the façade consists of 26,740 pieces of glass and covers 118 square yards. The work took two and a half years (Josef Vlasák).

On the south side of the cathedral stands a great tower, extended in height after the fire of 1541 and provided with a copper roof. This tower is enhanced by seven great bells, the largest of which, the "Sigmund" bell, dates from 1549. Next to the tower is the former main door, the so-called Golden Door, with mosaics of 1371, depicting the Resurrection of Christ, the Bohemian saints, Charles IV and his wife Elizabeth of Pomerania.

In the third courtyard beneath the paving-stones are excavations of the remains of the oldest part of the Castle preserved from the Romanesque period. They are principally the remains of the Rotunda of 926 and of another Rotunda of the second half of the 12th century (it is not known to which saint it was dedicated) with a Romanesque passage leading to St. Vitus' Cathedral. There is an entrance from the Chapel of the Holy Cross to the cathedral.

KEY TO THE PLAN OF ST. VITUS' CATHEDRAL

1 Chapel of St. Ludmilla
2 Chapel still undedicated
3 Thun family chapel
4 Chapel of the Holy Sepulchre
5 Interior of the main tower
6 7, 8 Undedicated chapels
9 Former Cathedral treasure chamber
10 New sacristy
11 Tomb of St. Adalbert
12 Wohlmuth's choir
13 Royal mausoleum
14 High altar
15 St. Václav's chapel
16 St. Andrew's (Martinic family) chapel

17 Chapel of the Holy Cross
18 Royal oratory
19 Chapel of St. Mary Magdalen
20 St. Jan Nepomuk (Vlašim) chapel
21 Tomb of St. Jan Nepomuk
22 Sternberg chapel
23 Chapel of the Virgin Mary
24 Chapel of St. John the Baptist
25 Chapel of the Archbishop
26 St. Anne's (Nostitz family) chapel
27 Old sacristy
28 St. Sigmund's chapel

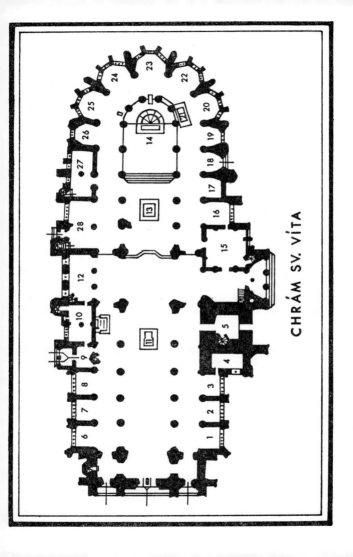

CHRÁM SV. VÍTA

B. WEST OF PRAGUE CASTLE

Leaving the first courtyard of the castle by the Rococo wrought irongate, whose pillars support enormous statues of gladiators, we come to the *Castle Square* (Hradčanské námĕsti) where elegant palaces and canons' houses follow on from the castle.

Quite close to the Castle is the **Archbishop's Palace** (No. 56). Its present form is the result of several reconstructions. The front wall dates from 1764–1765. The passage on the left of this building leads to the **Sternberg Palace** (No 57) in which today are housed the art collections of the **National Gallery.** The collection of Gothic works of art is one of the most valuable collections and its exhibition in Paris in 1957 literally created a sensation. The Sternberg Palace is a splendid Baroque building, erected between the years 1698–1730 by the architects Giovanni Santini and Giovanni Alliprandi to the plans of Domenico Martinelli.

The **Schwarzenberg Palace** (No 185) is a magnificent match for the Archbishop's Palace; it is actually a combination of two palaces, the oldest of which, the Lobkowitz Palace, was built in 1563. The large "S" above the entrance is the monogram of the archbishop Wilhelm Salm, its architect. Today the interesting historical War Museum is housed in the west wing. The beautiful graffito decoration (roughly 3,700 square feet) was restored in 1957.

On the west side of the Hradčanské námĕstí there is the fine **Tuscan Palace** (1691), built by the architect Pietro A. Fontana, decorated with figures of gods and goddesses from the workshop of Jan Brokoff, and at the corner of the old Hradčany Town Hall (No 173), built in 1598, stands the statue of Saint Michael by O. Most from about 1700. In the centre of the square we see the column commemorating the Prague with a group of statuary by F. M. Brokoff, from the beginning of the 18th century.

The Loretánská ulice leads into the Loretánské náměsti which goes back to the 17th century when the Capuchin convent and **church of Loretto** were built on the north and east side and **Černín Palace** on the west.

The Loretto Church is one of Prague's most valued monuments and is richly adorned with works of statuary and painting. Its façade was reconstructed by Kilian Ignatius Dienzenhofer between 1720 and 1722. The treasure chamber of the Loretto Church is in the west wing and contains vessels for divine worship from the 16th to the 18th century. The carillon, dating from 1694, still plays in the belfry. It is not long since that the ceiling was also restored.

The Černín Palace (No. 101—today the Ministry for Foreign Affairs) is the largest palace in Prague. It was begun by the Bohemian nobleman Jan Humprecht Černín in 1669. The work was later resumed by Czech and foreign architects in 1720. Among others, the famous Prague Baroque artists, the painter V. V. Reiner and the sculptor Ignaz Platzer, helped to decorate it. In 1851 the palace was acquired by the military administration and was turned into a barracks. It was not until 1918 that the palace was reconditioned and taken over by the Ministry for Foreign Affairs.

It is only a few yards from the Loretto Square to the Pohořelecké náměsti. Here at the corner of the west side stands the north façade of the former **Kučera Palace** (No 114), built by the architect J. Wirch between 1760–65, now repaired. We also see in the square a Baroque statue of Jan Nepomuk (Saint John Nepomucen) (1752). Close by, at the very beginning of the Pionýrská ulice in the school courtyard are the ruins of the house in which the famous

astronomer Tycho Brahe lived. From the Pohořelec
the staircase of No 147 leads to the courtyard of the
monastery of Strahov.

We have come to one of the outstanding historical monuments of Prague; it stands in an exceptionally beautiful
position commanding an unforgettable view of Prague and
Prague Castle. Strahov was founded 800 years ago, but its
present appearance dates from the Baroque period in the middle
of the 18th century. The fame of Strahov rests principally on its
library which contains valuable illuminated manuscripts of the
15th and 16th centuries, a 9th-century manuscript and others.
The monastery and church of the Virgin Mary were founded in
the 12th century, but a long period of building activity has left
its mark. The interior decoration is also valuable, chiefly because
of a number of old paintings, wood carvings and statues. The
church of St. Roc (1603–1612) at the west entrance forms part
of this picturesque whole. Today the **National Museum of
Literature** is housed in the former monastery and invaluable
collections of Czech literary works of all ages are stored there.

We pass the **church of Saint Roc** and return to the
Pohořelec through a very beautiful Baroque portal
(1742). From there we take No 22 tram to the terminus of the line on the "White Mountain" (**Bílá
Hora**). After visiting the little **Baroque church of Our
Lady,** built between 1706–40 in memory of the
victory on the White Mountain (which of course
meant the bitter defeat of the Czech nation) we
take a walk through the former deer **park "Hvězda"**
(Star) to the pleasure palace of the same name. This
today contains the Museum of Alois Jirásek, the
classic Czech author.

About 15 minutes walk brings us to the extensive block of
buildings consisting of the **Břevnov Monastery** and **church of
St. Margaret.** This monastery is one of the oldest in Bohemia
and probably dates back to the time of Prince Boleslav II (967–
999). St. Vojtěch, the second bishop of Prague, also had a hand
in the foundation of the monastery. After being reconstructed
several times it was given its present form between 1708 and
1721 by the famous Baroque architects Christof and Kilian

Ignaz Dienzenhofer. Today the monastery buildings are used for other purposes. Not far away is the "Museum of the Beginnings of the Labour Movement".

C. THE MALÁ STRANA

The Malá Strana (lit. Small Side), the most picturesque district of Prague, is more than 700 years old. With its labyrinth of crooked alleys, its Baroque palaces, old cloisters, its hidden gardens and tiled roofs it is a romantic island of peace where one is oblivious to the bustle of modern Prague.

Following the **Valdštejnská** from Klárov we are soon in the heart of the Malá Strana with its splendid palaces and picturesquely situated gardens; the Fürstenberg Palace (No. 153–158), built by an unknown architect (1743–1747), the Kolovrat Palace (No. 154, about 1780) and the Ledeburg Palace, architect Ign. Palliardi, the Palfy Palace (No. 184), the Auersperg Palace (No. 16), built in 1690. The Wallenstein Palace (No. 17), 1624–1630, with its memories of Albrecht von Wallenstein, is full of treasures. In the former riding school belonging to the palace are today collections of the National Gallery comprising the works of 19th-century Czech painters. In the summer, concerts and theatrical performances are given in the beautifully laid-out garden, and ballet and dance groups appear here.

From the Wallenstein Square (Váldštejnské náměstí) we enter the Sněmovní (Parliament Street) and unless we go slightly out of our way to visit the picturesque terrace restaurant "Zlatá studně" (No. 166) we then pass the Thun Palace (date about 1700—once the Diet), the Lažanský Palace (No. 175), the Černín Palace (No. 174) and the Bilandt-Rheidt Palace (No. 171, built in 1700 and today occupied by "Charitas"). Now we turn right, uphill, and come to another Thun Palace (No. 180) below the New Castle Stairways. This stairway dates from 1674. From here there is one of the finest views of Prague, especially with the Renaissance gables of the Hradetz Palace in the foreground.

Half way up the stairs we turn left, back into the Thunovská, from where we reach the Nerudova through a passage, coming out by the Theatiner Church (1691–1717). Leaving it on the right we can descend to the Malostranské náměsti, but we will remain for the moment in the **Nerudová** which is artistically the finest street in the Malá Strana. It was formerly part of the royal road, i.e. it was used by the coronation procession of the kings of Bohemia, as it connected the city with the castle. The street is named after the Czech writer, poet and journalist Jan Neruda who lived here at No. 233 at the sign of the "Two Suns". One of the most important buildings is the Morzini Palace (No. 256); its present form dates from 1713–1714. The doorway with its statues of Moors and allegorical representations of Day, Night and the four Continents is the work of F. M. Brockoff. The coat of arms, an eagle and the figures of Jupiter and Juno, on the Thun-Hohenstein Palace (No. 214) is by Matthias Braun. The interior decoration (paintings) of the hall date from 1870. Apart from magnificent palaces the Nerudová is enhanced by a number of old houses with interesting and picturesque escutcheons, e.g. No. 210—"The Three Litte Fiddles", No. 212— "The Golden Goblet", No. 220—"The Golden Horseshoe".

As far back as can be remembered the **Malostranské náměstí** has been the hub of the district. At the dawn of Czech history there was a marketplace here, in the centre of which stood the little church of St. Václav. In 1283 the church of St. Nicholas was built in Gothic style. It was given its Baroque form in the 18th century by native and foreign architects (D. Orsi, K. and K. J. Dienzenhofer, A. Lurago, J. Kramolin, J. Kracker, K. Škréta, F. X. Balko, I. Platzer, L. Kohl, R. Prachner). This group of houses with the church of St. Nicholas divides the square into two parts, the upper, west part being adorned with a Plague Memorial Column and a group of statuary representing the Holy Trinity. The church portal faces the square, as does the front of the Lichtenstein Palace (No 258). This palace was originally erected in 1591 and rebuilt in 1791.

In the lower, eastern part of the square stand a series of houses, each of which is rich in memories. In the house called "U Montagů" (Smiřický) the conference was held which set off the Czech rebellion against the Hapsburgs in 1618. The next house (No.7), which belonged to the Sternberg family stands on the spot where, in 1541, the conflagration broke out that destroyed about two thirds of the houses in the Malá Strana, part of the Hradčany and even part of Prague Castle and St. Vitus' Cathedral. Both houses were rebuilt in Baroque style in the late 17th century. The whole south side of the Malastranské náměsti consists of several large houses with arcades. All these houses are very old and were rebuilt in Baroque style in the 17th and 18th centuries. The most important building in the Malostranské náměstí is the former Small Side Town Hall, the corner house at No. 35 on the east side of the square. It was given its present appearance between 1618 and 1630. Next to the Town Hall is the 16th-century No 36, rebuilt in 1720. Next to it is the Kasserstein House (No 37); this dates from 1700 and its architect was G. B. Alliprandi. It is decorated by statues representing the four seasons.

We proceed along the **Mostecká** (Bridge Street) where we again find a number of houses with picturesque gables and escutcheons. Here there are houses which go back to the 14th–16th centuries and the Rococo Kaunitz Palace (No 277, 1773–75). Near the smaller bridge tower stands the interesting so-called Saxon House or Steinitz's and just opposite, at No 47, in the courtyard is a 15th-century tower of what was once the episcopal residence. One can also reach the Mostecká from the Malostanské náměsti by making a short detour through the Letenská and Josefská. On leaving the square we observe the statuary group of Saint Hubert with the stag at No 26, the "Golden Stag", in the Tomášská: also the church of Saint Thomas in the Letenská, a Gothic edifice, partly rebuilt in Baroque style, between 1725 and 1731, by Kilian Ignaz Dienzenhofer. The date of the Renaissance portal is 1617, the roof paintings are by V. V. Reiner. A home for old people is housed in the adjacent cloisters.

We now turn right into the **Josefská**. On the left hand side is the very beautiful Carmelite Monastery Church of Saint Joseph, late 17th century, embellished with valuable statuary and paintings. From the Josefská we return to the Mostecká and continuing in the same direction we come to the Maltese, also one of the finest squares in Prague. The Lázeňská, too, is interesting, for here at No 483, Adrian de Vries, the famous court architect of Rudolf II, had his workshop. In 1796 Ludwig van Beethoven lived at No 285 in the former inn, the "Golden Unicorn", and opposite at No 286, once the best hotel in Prague, the Czar Peter the Great stayed in 1698. A hundred years later the Russian general Suvorov and in 1835 the French poet Chateaubriand also stayed there.

In the **Maltese Square** the most important and striking building is the Church of **Our Lady "Under the Chain"** with mighty Gothic towers, a reminder that a powerful fortress stood here in the Middle Ages, dominating the entrance to the Charles Bridge from the Malá Strana end. The church was founded as early as 1158 and was later rebuilt several times. Old palaces and houses with arcades form the square; all of them have kept their old names (the sign of the "Golden Goose", the "Golden Bear", the "Ship", etc). On the south side stands the Nostitz Palace (1660 and 1770), in which the Dobrovský Library is housed.

Near the **Maltese Square** is another attractive and picturesque corner of the Malá Strana, the **Velkopřevorské Square** with the Palace of the Maltese Abbot (No 485), (1726–38), built by the architect Bartholomeus Scotti with sculptures from the workshop of Matthias Braun. Here also, at No 486, stand the Buquois Palace (1719) and the Hržan Palace (No 490. 1585, where the Czech composer J. B. Foerster was born in 1859). We cross an arm of the Vlatava by a little bridge, the so-called "Čertovka" (Čert=devil), on to the Kampa island, most of which has been made into a park. Beyond No 501, in front of which stands a memorial with the bust of Josef Dobrovský, we turn right and come back into the southern part of the Maltese Square to the Nostitz Palace. Proceeding along the Harantová we reach Karmelitaská Street.

From here we go towards the Malostanské námĕstí as far as the Church of "Our Lady of Vilbory", the earliest Baroque edifice in Prague, begun in 1611 and completed in 1654. The interior decoration is in Renaissance style and the church contains the world-famous Prague Infant Jesus (1628), a gift of Polyxena of Lobkowitz. Various foreign architects shared in the embellishment of the church, among them Peter Brandl and the sculptor Peter Prachner. In the same street on the opposite side we observe the Tyrš House (No 450), formerly the palace of Paul Michnas of Vacínov, built between 1640 and 1650 by Italian artists and a splendid example of Renaissance and Baroque. The palace was modernised in 1922 for the Czech Gymnastic Association Sokol and named after Dr Miroslav Tyrš, the founder of the Sokol, whose statue by Ladislav Šaloun stands in the entrance courtyard. It is occupied today by the Faculty of Physical Culture and the State Museum of Czech Physical Culture and Sport.

Following the Karmelitaská back in the direction of the square we visit the charming Vrtba Gardens with statues by Matthias Braun. The gardens belong to the palace of the same name (No 373). Further on we also observe the Schönborn Palace (No 365), the Lobkowicz Palace (No 347) and the Welsch Hospital block (No 335) in the building of which a number of well-known artists participated. At the end of our walk we go through the Tržištĕ (Market Street), the Betřislav or Vlašská as far as the Janský vršek ulice. Every house we pass is historically valuable, not only for its age and form, but also by reason of its exterior and interior decoration. From here we return to the Nerudova where we can find our bearings again. If we turn off to the right half way up the hill, a winding lane below the striking Schwarzenberg Palace brings us to the Hradčanské náměsti which we have already visited on our previous walk. If we continue along the Nerudova we come back into Pohořelec Square which we already know, passing some lovely, very old houses on the way. From both streets we enjoy an exceptionally beautiful view of Prague.

D. THE CHARLES BRIDGE

From its earliest days the "Stone Bridge" was the pride of Prague and the whole of Bohemia. It was built at the command of the Emperor Charles IV, by the famous Peter Parler of Gmünd, the architect of Saint Vitus' Cathedral and other notable Gothic buildings erected from 1357 onwards. This work is evidence both of his technical mastery and his artistic merit. At the far end of the bridge, by the old town, he constructed a splendid large *tower* for the purposes of defence and adornment. Together with the gate of the fortress of Prague. The medieval bridge was a main highway and thus of strategic importance. It was therefore necessary to protect it against attack. When it was completed the Charles Bridge was soon heard of abroad, not merely because of its fortification, but chiefly because it was one of the greatest undertakings of its kind, for the only existent bridge longer than the Charles Bridge was the bridge spanning the Danube at Regensburg, and it was only surpassed in architectural beauty by the bridge over the Elbe at Dresden. The length of the Charles Bridge from tower to tower is 660 yards.

But its reputation in Europe was established mainly by the statues which decorate it.

THE STATUES ON THE CHARLES BRIDGE

1 Saint Ivo (original by Matthias Braun 1711, copy by Fr. Hergessel 1908)

2 Saint Barbara, Saint Margaret and Saint Elizabeth (Ferd. Maxm. Brokoff 1707)

3 Pietá (Eman. Max 1859)

4 Saint Joseph (Jos. Max 1854)

5 Saint Francis Xavier (original F. M. Brokoff 1711, copy Vinzenz Vosmik 1913)

6 Saint Christopher (E. Max 1857)

7 Saint Francis Borgia (F. M. Brokoff 1710)

8 Saint Ludmilla (sculptor unknown, probably from the workshop of Matthias Braun about 1720, erected in 1784 to replace the statue of Saint Wenceslas by Ottavio Most, 1695–1701, which was swept away by the flood of that year)

9 Saint Francis of Seraphin (Em. Max 1855)

10 Saint Vincent of Ferrara and Saint Prokop (F. M. Brokoff 1712)

11 Saint Nicholas of Tolentino (Jan Bedř. Kohl 1708).— Brunswick (Lud. Šimek 1884). Statue on the pillar erected in place of the original work in memory of the victory in the legal action brought by the citizens of the Old Town against the nobility about the payment of duties in 1506)

12 Saint Luitgarda (M. B. Braun 1710)

13 Saint Vojtěch (Jos. Michal Brokoff 1709)

14 Saint John of Mathy, Felix and Ivan with the Turk (F. M. Brokoff 1714)

15 Saint Wenceslas (Jos. Kamil Böhm 1858)

16 Madonna with Saint Bernard (Matthias Václav Jäkl 1709)

17 Madonna with Saint Dominic and Thomas Aquinas (M. V. Jäkl 1708)

18 Calvary (1657), statues by Em. Max 1861, the Hebraic inscription (1696) glorifying God (paid for by a fine imposed on a Jew who mocked at God)

19 Saint Anne (M. V. Jäkl 1707)

20 Saints Cyril and Methodius (Karel Dvořák 1928) in replacement of the statue of Saint Ignatius by F. M. Brokoff 1711, which now stands in the Lapidarium

21 Saint John the Baptist (Jos. Max 1857)

22 Saints Norbert, Wenceslas and Sigmund (J. Max 1853); also on the parapet a marble plaque at the spot where in 1393 Jan of Nepomuk is supposed to have been thrown into the Vltava

23 Saint John of Nepomuk (1683)

24 Saint Anthony of Padua (Jan Oldřich Mauer 1707)

25 Saint Jude Tadeus (J. O. Mayer 1708)

26 Saint Augustine (J. B. Kohl 1708)

27 Saint Gaetan (F. M. Brokoff 1709)

28 Saint Philip Benicius (Michel Bernard Mande 1714)

29 Saint Vitus (F. M. Brokoff 1714)

30 Saints Salvator, Cosmas and Damian (J. O. Mayer 1709)

PLAN OF CHARLES BRIDGE

Small side

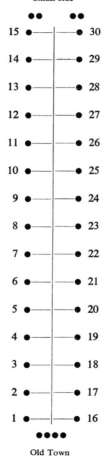

Old Town

The earliest statuary on the bridge dates from the 15th century when, besides a Cross we first hear of the Roland statue, called Brunswick, and later of a Martyrs' Pillar, at the spot where the Pietá stands today. It was not until 1683 that the statue of Saint John of Nepomuk was added; this was cast in metal in Nuremberg after a wooden model by the famous sculptor Jan Brokoff.

Between 1706 and 1714, 26 statues in all were erected on the pillars of the bridge, all of sandstone. The most artistically prized is the group of Saint Luitgarda, a work by the famous 18th-century sculptor, Matthias Braun. The best known is however Brokoff's Turk. These groups of statuary were erected in 1714 in honour of the Trinitarian Order whose mission it was to ransom Christians from imprisonment by the Turks. This Order apparently fulfilled its mission with great assiduity, for it freed altogether abour 400,000 captives. Hence the arrogant Turk, standing with an almost challenging callousness above the dungeon in which a Christian prisoner wrings his hands in anguish, additionally guarded by an imposing dog. Above the lower part of this part of the statue stand the founders of the Trinitarian Order, Saint Jan of Mathy, Saint Felix of Valois and Saint Ivan. Although not all the pillars were occupied in 1814, the work was interrupted, probably because the plague was raging throughout the country. Two pillars remained unoccupied and Saint Christopher did not appear in the middle of the bridge till 1857 and Saint Václav was erected at the Malá Strana end only in 1859. In the great flood of 1890 F. M. Brokoff's statue of Saint Ignatius (1710) was swept away by the water and shortly before the Second World War the statue of Saint Cyril and Saint Methodius (by Karel Dvořák) was erected in its place.

The Baroque style, for which the name "Prague Baroque" was coined both at home and abroad, marks the peak of native creativeness, and the names of the three Brokoffs, the two Brauns and Ignaz Platzer have never been surpassed. Their works, in so far as they have been preserved to the present time, are typically Baroque; powerful, robust figures, not dead and inanimate as in the middle of the 19th century, for example. On the contrary these figures strut and bear themselves with pride, as though breasting a gale, as can be seen from the movement of their flowing garments. There is a dramatic tension in their appearance. The modern Czech sculptor, Karel Dvořák, comes nearest to this conception in his above-mentioned statue of Saint Cyril and Saint Methodius.

E. THROUGH PRAGUE OLD TOWN ALONG THE KING'S ROAD (CORONATION WAY)

The thoroughfare which ran through the historic heart of the city and formed the main artery of communication was named the Coronation Way in the Middle Ages. It started at the Powder Tower, crossed the Vltava by the Charles Bridge and ended at the Castle. This road was used by the coronation processions of the Bohemian kings, setting out from the Royal Palace which stood on the site of the present Town Hall near the Powder Tower. It was followed also by soldiers on the march, prominent foreigners and merchants from abroad. Thus came into being, thanks to the efforts of many generations, one of the most important routes in the planning of Prague.

The **Powder Tower,** built by Matthias Rejsek of Prostějov between 1457–1508, formed the entrance to the Old Town. It was part of the fortifications of the Old Town and got the name "Powder" Tower in the late 17th century when it was used as a powder magazine. The present, partly pseudo-Gothic ornamentation is 19th century.

On the left side, at the corner of the Ovocný trh (Fruit Market) our eye is caught by the modern Cubist house (No 569), the "Black Mother of God" (1912), contrasting surprisingly with the Pachta Palace (No 587, 1759) opposite, with its façade dating from the period of Baroque efflorescence, with balconies and statues by Ignaz Platzer. Further on we note No 592 with its Madonna (about 1700) by an artist of Matthias Braun's workshop; then the Millesimo Palace (No 597, about 1750) with a beautiful doorway, the Hražán Palace (No 558), designed by Giovanni Bat. Alliprandi in 1702, and finally the "Three Kings" (No 601) with its original 14th-century gabled roof.

The Celetná leads into the **Staroměstké náměstí** (Old Town Square) where the history of the whole country has left its traces. It still remains the centre of the administration of the city and all important popular gatherings are held there.

The most remarkable building is the **Old-Town Town Hall** (erected in the 14th century and continuously built on to until the 19th century) which has always had great political importance in the history of Prague. Here were held the Diets, the assemblies and councils of the Hussites. Today it is the seat of the Prague Central National Committee. The new part was destroyed in May 1945, so that only its torso is left standing. The oldest parts were undamaged and the famous **clock** (made in 1490 and decorated in 1865 by the painter Josef Mánes) has been renovated. The neighbouring 14th century houses with Gothic adornments (windows and doorways) likewise escaped damage. These, with the Town Hall, form a whole attributed to the architect M. Rejsek. The corner house "U minuty" (Minute House, No 3), a Renaissance building with arcades, richly decorated with Sgraffito ornamentation of the 17th century, was spared.

The east side of the square is also picturesque and ancient. Here stands the **Church of the Virgin "in front of the Tyne"**, founded at the end of the 14th century, formerly the main church of the Hussites. The entrance leads through house No 604 the so-called Tyne School, with particularly beautiful 16th-century Renaissance double gables and with late 13th-century Gothic vaulting in the arcade. In the dazzling Baroque decoration of the church attention is caught by the stone baldaquin above one of the altars, the work of M. Rejsek. Facing the entrance into the Týnská Street, stands the house at "the Stone Bell" (No 607) with a 15th-century escutcheon of a bell. Close to it rises the splendid Kinský Palace (No 606), built in Rococo style between 1755 and 1765 (by K.J. Dienzenhofer and A. Lurago). The sculptural adornment is the work of Ignaz Platzer.

At the corner of the Železná (Iron Street) stands a remarkable, very old house (No 548), the "White Horse", where Frederick Smetana had his music school. This house has a very old doorway and a groined vaulted passage by M. Rejsek. Nor must we omit a visit to the Church of Saint Nicholas opposite (1732–35), a magnificent example of Baroque, designed by Kilian Ignaz Dienzenhofer and decorated with statuary by A. Braun, or to admire the **Magister Jan Hus Memorial** (1915) by Ladislav

Šaloun which stands in the middle of the square. But all the other houses of this square are no less rich in historical memories. We continue our way through the arcade of the Minute House and come into the picturesque Malé náměstí (Little Square), in the centre of which stands a well with a Renaissance wrought iron railing (1560).

We now turn into the narrow Karlova and there, where it joins the Husová we notice on the left side of the street the towering **Church of Saint Aegidius** (Sv Jiljí), late 14th century, and on the right side of the Husová the **Baroque Clam-Gallas Palace** (1713–19), built by J. B. Fischer von Erlach and decorated with statuary by Matthias Braun. As we proceed along the Karlova we pass the striking corner house, the "Golden Fountain" (No 175) and the entrance to the Welsh Chapel (1590–1600) and come to the Křižovnické náměstí.

From here we have a **splendid view** of the Malá Strana and the Hradčany with the "stone wonder" of the Charles Bridge in the foreground. On the east side of the square stands the finely decorated **Church of Saint Salvator** (1578–81); architect Carlo Lurago, statues by J. J. Bendl and Mathias Braun. There, too, is the entrance to the **Clementinum**, the largest Czech scientific library. The site of the Clementinum was formerly occupied by 32 houses, 4 churches, 1 monastery, 2 gardens and a few holes and corners. The building was erected by the Jesuits who came to Bohemia in 1556. Later the Clementinum became the seat of the University when it was unified with the Catholic Charles University in 1654.

The tower of the Clementinum houses an old **astronomy observatory** dating from 1721–23 and rebuilt in 1748. In the dome is a metal statue of Atlas, the work of an unknown artist, dating from 1722. Below the observatory is a museum of astronomic and mathematical instruments used by the famous Tycho Brahe, the personal astronomer of Rudolf II and the Habsburg family.

The biggest rooms are the old refectory (1670) with paintings by Christoph Tausch (1710) and a Rococo stove (1762); and the University library room with frescoes by Jan Hiebl.

On the north side of the square stands another magnificent building, the Church of the Knights of the Cross, dedicated to

Saint Francis (1679–89). The west side is partly occupied by the Old Town Bridge Tower, one of the finest bridge towers in Europe, built by Peter Parler, the architect of the Charles Bridge, in the second half of the 14th century. The tower gained tragic fame when, after the Battle of the White Mountains in 1621, for ten years eleven heads of Bohemian nobles decapitated on the Staroměstské náměstí were exposed on its battlements. Between the tower and Saint Francis' Church stands the **statue of Charles IV** (1848) by Ernst Hähnel of Dresden, erected to celebrate the quincentenary of the founding of the Charles University.

The Křižovnické náměstí is also memorable because it was here that the revolutionaries erected barricades in June 1848.

F. IN THE HEART OF PRAGUE
OLD TOWN

Still in the Old Town, we start this time from the busy end of **Václavské Avenue** along the **"Na Můstku"** (Little Bridge Street), which takes its name from the crossing of the fortification moat from the Old to the New Town, and come into the Rytířská.

In front of us we have the huge building which was formerly the Municipal Savings Bank, built 1892–94. Close to it stands the former **Carmelite Monastery** (No 539). This noble Baroque edifice was designed in 1671 by the Italian architect Domenico Orsi.

At the back of it is the splendid Baroque Church of Saint Gallus (Havel), founded in 1232. At the end of the 17th century it was reconstructed in Baroque style and its decoration is of that period. Here also is the tomb of the famous Czech painter Karel Škreta (17th century).

Opposite the east façade of house No 939 stand two of Prague's most important buildings; the **Carolinum** and the **Tyl Theatre**. In 1383 King Václav dedicated the Carolinum to Prague University, which still uses it. It has been restored both within and without. The large aula is used for festive occasions. The theatre was built for Count Nostitz in 1782. It was here that Mozart was received by the enthusiastic Prague public, and his opera, *Don Juan*, was performed for the first time. Every time he came to Prague, Mozart took part in the production.

We return to the Church of Saint Gallus and continue along the Melantrichova as far as the Kožní (Leather Street), where our attention is immediately caught by No 474, the famous "Two Golden Bears" with its Renaissance portal, dating from about mid-16th century. The house has an escutcheon with two bears and the bust of E. Kisch, nicknamed "the angry journalist". We turn off from the Kožní into the Železná, coming back along it to the Carolinum. From there we go left through the Kamzíková (Chamois Street) or alternatively through a passage leading into the Celetná, to the Tyne Rectory. Here, passing behind the Tyne Church, we come some yards farther on to the west of a sprawling building the so-called **Ungelt or Tyne Court** (No 640). Its history goes back to the 10th century. It was here that foreign merchants passed the goods they had brought to Prague through the customs. The neighbouring houses Nos 627 and 630 are also very old.

Through the Tyne Court we proceed along the Malá Štupartská to the Church and Monastery of **Saint James**. The church, which was founded in 1232, was damaged several times by fire, and twice rebuilt during the course of 700 years. Today it is one of the finest blocks of buildings in the Old Town. Inside the church the most notable thing is the tomb of Václav Vratislav of Mitrovitz, the chancellor of the Kingdom of Bohemia, by F. M. Brokoff. The church is illuminated at night, and concerts of sacred music are often held in it.

From the church we follow the Jakubská and the Templová back to the Powder Tower in the Celetná.

A walk through the Old Town would be incomplete without a visit to the district lying north-east of the Old-Town Square, in the direction of the Vltava. There, between the Šverma Bridge and Hatšalske náměstí, lies one of the most picturesque corners of the town, round the medieval **Rasnovka.**

From the small Anežská street we can get to the former **Convent of the Blessed Anežka**, a princess of the Premyslid family and the daughter of King Přemysl Otakar I. Founded as a retreat for women in 1234, the convent was enlarged in 1251 by the building of a monastery. At the same period two churches were built (Saint Francis and Saint Barbara). For its imposing aspect this group of buildings has no equal in any European country north of the Alps. Through the ages, the convent and the two churches have almost completely succumbed to the ravages of time. But lately methodical archaeological research has been devoted to the remains, and restoration work has begun. At present this is one of the most interesting historic sites in the town.

G. REMAINS OF THE OLD FORTIFICATIONS

It would certainly be very interesting to walk along the battlements of the fortification wall, but all that is left today are the ruins of old towers which mark the site of the Old Town walls. They run from the river to the present Revoluční třída (Revolution St), the Na Příkopě of 28 Řijna (28 October St) and Národní třida (National St) back to the river.

Let us begin our walk at the Powder Tower. We go along the Příkopě to the corner of the Havířská where, opposite the Children's House between two new buildings, stands the beautiful Baroque **Sylva Taroucca Palace** (No 852), built between 1743 and 1751. A Trade-Union Club now occupies the magnificent rooms of this palace. From the Havířska we pass the Tyl Theatre into the Rytířska and thence along the Melantrichová into the Havelská. The deep arcades of the west side of this broad street are evidence of the age of these houses. The two houses which principally attract our attention are No 510, "Brunswick", and No 511, the "Golden Scales", both of which have lovely Renaissance and Baroque decorations. We proceed to the **Uhelný trh** Coal Market where once stood a forge at which charcoal was sold in the 14th century. Of special interest here is No 420, the "Three Lions", at the corner of the Skořepka, which belonged to the composer F. Dušek and where Mozart stayed for a while as guest in 1787 (commemorative plaque).

Through the passage opposite we look into the courtyard of the first Prague apartment house "Platýz" (Národni třida No 416.) It was of course converted from a former noble's palace. Inside there are still remains of old 17th century frescoes. The façade overlooking the Národní třida is in Empire style (1817–25). If, on the other hand, we return to our original starting point via the Platýz, quite nearby is the ancient Church of Saint Martin in the Wall (the church was built into the city wall), founded at the beginning of the 12th century, enlarged in the 14th and 15th. Here for the first time in 1414 communion was celebrated in both faiths. The famous sculptor F. M. Brokoff was buried here in 1732. We proceed along the Skořepka to the corner of the Jilská where stands the 16th-century house "U Vejvodů" (No 353) and in which the "Mazhouse" (typical vestibule) is still preserved.

Only a few yards further on we are in front of the tall Church of Saint Aegidius (Jiljí), built between 1339 and 1371. The interior decoration is Baroque and especially worthy of note are the wood carvings and paintings by the famous painter V. V. Reiner, who lies buried here. From 1364 onwards the Czech Reformer Jan Milíč of Kroměřiž, a predecessor of Jan Hus, preached here. We return through the Husová and on the right side of the street arrive at the Betlémské náměstí (Bethlehem Square) where stands in its original form the recently renovated **Bethlehem Chapel**. It is one of the buildings most revered by the Czechs. Jan Hus preached there from 1402. The restoration of the chapel on the ruins of the foundation walls, completed in 1954, part of the scheme to preserve the city's ancient monuments, is an accomplishment unparalleled in Czechoslovakia. In the square there is also the house "U Halánků" (No 269) in which the Czech patron of the arts, Vojta Naprstek, founded a library and later, in 1863, an ethnographical museum with very valuable collections.

We now take the Konviktská into the Karoliny Světlé where at the left-hand corner of this street we come to the Romanesque **Rotunda of the Holy Cross**, one of the most ancient church buildings in Prague (about 1100); the remains of 14th-century Gothic frescoes decorate the interior. The railings surrounding the chapel, were designed by Joseph Mánes.

Continuing along the Karoliny Světlé, we turn into the Naprstek ulice and through the narrow "Silver Lane" come out into the Anenské náměsti. The former monastery and church of Saint Anne (originally of Saint Lawrence), early 13th century, cover the east side of the square. The façade is Baroque (1676). The building has been occupied by a printing works since 1795. From the square the Anenská leads to the Smetana embankment (Smetanovo nábřeži) where we stop at the quay above the dam not only to admire the enchanting view of the Charles Bridge, the Malá Strana and the Hradčany, but also to visit the Smetana Museum, housed in a charming Neo-Renaissance building by A. Wiehl (No 201), erected in 1883. We proceed upstream to the National Theatre. From here we could follow the line of the Old Town city wall along the Národní, but we should find only the ruins of 13th-century towers and those in the courtyards of houses Nos 313 and 341.

H. THE OLD GHETTO

Prague Ghetto, is of remote historical origin. It was already mentioned in the 9th century. It began as a colony of Jewish tradesmen who came to Prague and settled there permanently. In the 13th century on the order of the city administration and the church authorities an independent district was created and named the Jewish Quarter. In the 17th century the Ghetto grew considerably and was a Jewish metropolis in Central Europe. It ceased to exist as an independent whole in 1850 and at the end of the 19th century it was dissolved for hygienic and administrative reasons and became a District, the so-called **Josefov.** The Prague Ghetto was a complex quarter and some important historical monuments still remain to this day. In the Gothic period the Ghetto was shut off from the outside world by fortification walls with gates (1230–1530). In the Renaissance (1530–1630) the Jewish element spread even beyond the walls of the city. But simultaneously building went on inside the walls and dwelling houses arose round the synagogues, schools and cemeteries. There were also many changes in the Josefov in the Baroque period; new buildings were erected, old buildings reconstructed—mostly after the Great Fire of 1754. It retained its original form till the late 19th century.

Today the following historical buildings belong to the old Ghetto: the Old New School, the Pinkas and Klaus Synagogues and the Old Town Hall, beside which there is the world-famous old Jewish cemetery.

From the Old Town Square we go through the Pařížká and where the Červené ulice joins it we see on the left-hand side of the street the rear of the **Old-New Synagogue**. Its façade overlooks the Maislová ulice and its entrance is in the Červená. The Old-New School is a striking early Gothic building (about 1270) and is one of the most precious monuments of Prague. The interior hall, divided by two pillars into two naves with a beautiful groined ceiling, makes a strong impression on the visitor, and this impression is further enhanced by the entrance through the vestibule. Next door, in the Maislová, stands the old Jewish Town Hall (No 250), built at the same time as the Synagogue. Its present Rococo decoration is 18th century, period of the Hebraic clock whose hands moved anticlockwise.

We now proceed into the opposite street, at the corner of which, by the wall of the Jewish Cemetery, stands the Klaus Synagogue, built by an unknown Italian architect in 1680. In it and in the neighbouring pseudo-Romanesque building (1906) are housed collections of the **State Jewish Museum**, founded in 1906. Because of the catastrophe that befell the Jews in Czechoslovakia during the Hitler occupation this museum has become the most important institute of its kind, for everything of value from all the synagogues in Czechoslovakia was brought here, so that the inventory of the collection has risen from 1,000 in 1938 to 199,000 items. There were about 90,000 Jews living in the country in 1938; today there are only 18,000. The contents of the museum are immensely varied, showing not only the economic and social development of the Jews as an independent people, but also giving a picture of the life and customs of the Jews from birth to burial, as well as of the history of the Prague Ghetto. A part of the museum collections is housed in the old Jewish Town Hall.

The Klaus Synagogue stands on part of the ground around which the old Jewish cemetery was enlarged in the 17th century and is both historically and spiritually a unique complement to the museum. We reach this synagogue through the Pinkas Synagogue from the Josefská; its origin is even earlier than that of the Old-New Synagogue. This synagogue is much visited in memory of the 77,000 victims of the Nazi terror.

The old **Jewish Cemetery** (entrances from the street of the same name) was begun in the 15th century and the date of its oldest tombstone is 1439. This marks the grave of Avigdor Karos, the famous Rabbi and poet, who witnessed the Jewish massacre in 1389 and wrote a dirge about it. There are in all 200,000 graves in the cemetery. All important Jews who lived in the Ghetto lie buried here, among them notably Mordechai Maisl (died 1600) and Rabbi Jehuda Löw ben Bezalel (d. 1609), known from the

Golem legend. Visitors, even from abroad, still come to his grave and leave petitions there.

From the Ghetto we proceed to the náměsti Krasnoarmějců (**Red Army Square**) which is closely connected with it. From there we have a very magnificent view of the Hradčany, the Malá Strana, Strahov and the Petřín. Nor should we omit a visit to the Artists' House, built between 1876 and 1884 by Josef Zítek, the architect of the National Theatre. The Artist's House is the seat of the Czech Philharmonic Orchestra.

Also very interesting are the building of the **Faculty of Philology** (built 1928–29, architect Josef Sakař), of the Charles University on the east side of the square, and the **statue of Josef Mánes** the founder of modern Czech painting, by the sculptor Boh. Kafka. This statue stands in a little park in front of the Josef Mánes Bridge, on a site which affords one of the finest views of Prague Castle and the Hradschin district.

I. FROM THE NATIONAL MUSEUM
TO THE KAMPA

From the main railway station (Hlavní nádraží) we walk through a well-kept park to the top of the square **Václavské náměstí.** The station was built in 1901–09 by J. Fanta. On the way we note the **Smetana Theatre** (Neo-Renaissance, 1886–87). This was formerly the German Theatre and is today one of the stages of the National Theatre. Next to it stands the **National Assembly** building (1930–34), by the architect B. Bendelmayer.

The **Václavské náměstí** already existed in 1362 as the Horse Market. It got its name in 1848 from the statue of Saint Václav (Wenceslaus) which stood in the middle of the square: a stone equestrian statue with a well (now on the Vyšehrad). Today the **Saint Václav Memorial** by J. V. Myslbek, the founder of modern Czech sculpture, stands in front of the National Museum. The Václavské náměstí, which is no longer a square but a very broad avenue, is, with the Staroměstské náměstí, the main place of popular assembly where the citizens of Prague have always foregathered for celebrations (underground shops). The **National Museum,** built by J. Schulz as the Kingdom of Bohemia Museum (1884–91), stands on the site of the former "Horse Gate". The core of the building is formed by the vestibule, the staircase and Pantheon, the ceremonial hall used for the lying in state of the country's greatest sons. The collections in the National Museum are unique.

The National Museum was founded on 15 April 1818 and from its inception became the focal point of Czech culture, especially science, which had been expelled from the Germanized Prague University as a measure of political persecution. Thus the classic names of Czech science—Dobrovský, Šafařík and Palacký—are insolubly linked with the National Museum. The contribution they made to the growth of the National Museum also conferred on it a national character and a new political orientation, although its origins were coloured by the aristocratic character of its founders in the Age of Enlightenment. For this reason, too, the early collections which came mainly from the private collections of Prague aristocrats, especially the Šternberg family, were devoted predominantly to the natural sciences, but this was later compensated with the addition of historical collections.

The main building of the present National Museum (Václavské náměstí) is in a monumental Renaissance style, designed by the architect Josef Schulz (1885–90). The façade is decorated with allegorical and historic reliefs by Czech sculptors (end of the 19th century). The interior is decorated with both sculptures and paintings, especially the Pantheon room which has paintings (on themes from Czech history) by František Ženíšek and Václav Brožík, and sculptures by Czech artists (19th and 20th centuries). The galleries on the first floor and the stairway on the second floor have paintings of the historic Czech regions by Julius Mařák.

A. The department of natural sciences at the National Museum is divided into six sections containing two-thirds of the seventeen million items in the museum. Most of the collection is housed in the main building, except the botanic herbarium which is housed in the castle of Průhonice near Prague, and the African fauna at Březnice castle.

1. The section on paleontology and geology contains 500,000 rocks and fossils. It is housed in six rooms on the second floor (the items which are not exhibited are kept in the cellars of the main building).

The **Barrandeum** contains Czechoslovak paleozoic fossils; the collection bequeathed to the Museum by Joachim Barrande has been considerably augmented and completed so that there are now about 360,000 items of world-wide repute. The Barrandeum exhibition is housed in the large hall on the second floor in the main building.

2. The section on mineralogy was one of the first sections of the National Museum in 1818. The core of this section consisted of the mineralogic collection of Kašpar Šternberg. The collection contains more than 120,000 items—minerals, rocks, precious stones, and meteorites; a selection of 12,000 items is exhibited in five rooms on the first floor of the main building.

3. The section on botany contains a valuable herbarium with a noteworthy collection of mushrooms (1,300,000 items) and a collection numbering 13,000 items of pieces of wood, carpophores, drugs, etc. The bulk of the botany section is housed in the castle of Průhonice near Prague. There are some specimens in room 13 on the first floor of the main building.

4. The section on zoology is housed in four large rooms on the second floor of the main building. The collection of Bohemian birds (1,600 items) is particularly interesting. It was donated to the museum by the famous Czech ornithologist Dr A. Hořic and is the most valuable regional collection of its kind in Europe. A permanent exhibition of African fauna has been set up by the zoology section in several rooms of the castle of Březnice.

5. The section on entomology has more than six million insects. These collections are exhibited in one of the rooms on the second floor of the main building; the rest is kept in storage on the second floor of the building.

B. The history department has seven sections which illustrate the historic development of the Czech and Slovak people from prehistoric times to the present, the growth of their material culture and of their art, especially music and drama. One section (Náprstek Museum) is devoted to the ethnography of extra-European nations. Only four of these sections are housed in the main building in Wenceslas Square, the three others being in separate buildings.

1. The prehistoric section has the richest collection of prehistoric mementos in Czechoslovakia; it has Egyptologic collections, ancient collections and items from Asia Minor.

2. The section on historical archaeology has a rich collection, particularly of medieval items.

3. The numismatic section is the largest numismatic institute in the Republic. It contains some 250,000 Bohemian, Moravian, Silesian, Slovak and foreign coins and medals.

4. The section on drama contains collections illustrating the history of the Czech theatre: the archives of the National Theatre and the former Vinohrady Theatre, collections of stage art, a collection of the marionette theatre and manuscripts.

The following historic sections have their own buildings:

5. The ethnographic section is housed in the Empire-style building of the former Kinský villa in Petřínské Sady Park, but this building has become too small to accommodate the vast amount of material dealing with Slav—especially Czech and Slovak—ethnography. Only a part of the collections of national costumes, furniture, ceramics and documents dealing with popular occupations and costumes are shown on the ground floor and the single floor of the villa.

6. The musical section, housed in the Palace of the Great Prior (Prague III) has become the most important collection devoted to music in central Europe. Besides musical archives, the collection contains a wealth of musical instruments, 800 of which are exhibited in nine rooms. This section organizes popular concerts of ancient music in the former monastic gardens of the Palace of the Great Prior.

7. The Náprstek Museum (ethnography), founded in 1862 by Vojta Náprstek as a private museum now forms part of the National Museum (section of extra-European ethnography). The original name of the museum has been retained from respect for the founder and the popular tradition associated with his name. The large collections contain ethnographic material from all parts of the world, Asia (especially China and Japan), Africa (especially the western and southern regions), North America (Eskimos and Indians in the United States and Canada), Mexico, Central and Southern America, the South Sea islands and Australia.

8. The lapidary of the National Museum, administered by the historical archaeology section, is housed in a separate pavilion in the Julius Fučík Park of Culture and Recreation (Prague VII). It contains various mementos of buildings (romanesque fragments of the historic castle of Prague, remains of the Renaissance-style Krocín fountain, original sculptures of the Charles Bridge, etc).

The Library of the National Museum is devoted chiefly to manuscripts and literary documents. It now has some 1,230,000 volumes and 1,570,000 archive documents, and its collections are divided into collections of manuscripts, incunabula and old editions, editions dating from the Czech national Renaissance, newspapers, and finally literary correspondences and mementos of writers.

Descending the Václavske námesti, we see on the corner of Vodičkovast the interesting **Wiehl House** (No 792), today the property of the Czechoslovak Academy of Science, its façade decorated by murals designed by Nikolaus Aleš. At the bottom end of the avenue we continue right into the **Na Příkopě** once the city moat (hence its name).

Facing us we have the fine façade of the Exhibition Building "U Hybernů", the biggest Empire style edifice in Prague (1801–1811). A monastery and church of the Irish Order of Franciscans originally stood on this site (1652): in 1808 they were rebuilt as an Inland Revenue Office and after the Second World War as an Exhibition Hall.

We retrace our steps along the Príkopé to the Na Můstku at the bottom end of the Václavské námesti and continue straight on through the 28 řijna into the Národní třida. The **Jungmannová** runs into it on the left where in the little square of the same name stands the monument to the "Awakener of the Nation", the famous etymologist Joseph Jungmanns.

In the background is the interesting **Church of Our Lady of the Snow,** founded in 1346 by Charles IV after his coronation. It has the highest nave of all the Prague churches and the largest main altar. There is a fine view of the church and adjoining cloisters from the gardens through which one can walk from the corner of the Jungmannovo náměstí by way of the Alfa Cinema passage to the Václavské náměsti or the Světozor Cinema passage to the Vodičkova. The church is especially remarkable because it was one of the first churches in which Hussite services were held.

In the Národní we notice first the **Porges Palace** by Portheim (No 37–38) in Classical style with late 18th century portal. In 1946 a bronze bust of General Suvorov was erected here in memory of his stay in this house in 1799–1800. In the 18th century the famous sculptors Jan and Ferdinand Maximilian Brokoff had their atelier there. On the right side of the street is the house called "Platýs" which we have already visited on our walk along the line of the fortifications.

We are already at the **National Theatre**, the finest symbol of a nation's cultural rebirth and unique self-sacrifice. The Czech people built the theatre themselves between 1868 and 1881 and after its destruction by fire rebuilt it in 1883 from voluntary contributions. The building was designed by the well-known architect of the time, Joseph Zítek. All the important contemporary artists help to decorate it. The names of great musicians, Smetana, Dvořák and Fibich are inalienably associated with the National Theatre.

We now continue across the Bridge of the 1 May, the middle arches of which span Střelecký Island. The first May Day celebrations were held here in 1890. At the end of the bridge we turn right along the embankment and come to **Kampa Island,** separated from the Malá Strana by the arm of the Vltava known as the Čertovka. Today oarsmen and canoeists practice on the Čertovka. We can leave the island either by crossing the Charles Bridge to Klárov or to the centre of the Malá Stana.

K. From the Station through the New Town

From Prague **Central Station** we first turn right into the Hybernská in the direction of the Powder Tower. The second house on the right as we leave the station is the **Kinský Palace**, an early Baroque building by the architect C. Lurago (1660). This was the "Workers' House" and since 1953 has housed the Lenin Museum, containing material about the life and work of Lenin.

If we go along the Dlažděná ulice from the crossing by the station we come to the irregular **Maxim Gorki Square** above which towers the tall belfry of **Saint Henry's Church**. It is of the same date as the foundation of Prague New Town. The text of an epic poem celebrating the victory of the Hussites in 1426 was deposited in its cupola. We have now reached the Jindřišská which leads to the Václavské námĕsti and continues as the Vodičkova. In Palacký Street, a small street leading into Vodičkova, is the **former Mac-Newen Palace** (now No 719), built in 1790 by the architect Ignace Palliardi, where the great Czech historian and historiographer František Palacký lived and died. The house bears a commemorative plaque.

At the end of Vodičkova, on the left, we notice the school, a fine Czech Renaissance building (1866) with graffito decoration. We proceed to the Karlovo námĕstí, formerly a cattle market and parade ground. Today the whole area is laid out as a delightful park. On the north side stands the oldest monument in this square the **New Town Hall**, erected before 1367. Its present form dates from 1520–26, the tower from 1452. The signal for the outbreak of the Hussite Rebellion was given from here in 1419, and its occupation by conservative elements in 1434 marked the end of the Hussite movement.

On the west side looms the Czech Technical Institute (1877). The most artistically valuable building is the former Jesuit College with the **Church of Saint Ignatius** on the east side. This is the third edifice of its kind in Prague, for the colleges in the Old Town and in the Malá Strana were insufficient for the counter-Reformation activities of the Jesuits. Here too, as elsewhere, they instructed architects to create works which altered the panorama of Prague (as, for instance, the Saint Nicholas' Church in the Malá Strana). The tall façade of the Church of Saint Ignatius with the gilded statue of the founder of the Order dominates the whole neighbourhood. Church and monastery were built in the years 1658–87; today a hospital. Before continuing our inspection of the square, let us go down the Resslova in the direction of the river and visit the Czech Orthodox Church of Saints Cyril and Methodius (1730–36) by Dienzenhofer.

On the opposite side stands the Gothic 14th-century Church of Saint Václav na Zderaze (Czechoslovak Church) with traces of the original little Romanesque church (late 12th century). We now return to the Karlovo námĕstí, where on the south side, next to the lovely 18th-century Dienzenhofer portal, stands the Faust's House (No 502), a famous late 16th-century building, reconstructed in about 1740 in Baroque style. Its owner at the time it was built, Ferdinand Mladota of Solopysky, entertained his guests with such extraordinary chemical experiments that the house was soon notorious. Besides which its previous owner had dabbled in alchemy and natural science.

The garden of the house adjoins the Church of Saint John on the Rock (1730–39), a building that reveals the mastery of Kilian Ignaz Dienzenhofer, not only by the complicated ground plan of the church and its vaulted roof, but also by his interesting solution of the problem of arranging the steps from the street (today the Vyšehrad Steps). Opposite this church are the noteworthy church and monastery "Na Slovanech" or "Emaus", founded by Charles IV in 1347. The church was renovated in Baroque style in the 18th century and again restored in Gothic in the 19th, whereby from an artistic standpoint, except for the cloister, it has been spoilt. In February 1945 the building was razed to the ground in an air raid and restored in 1960.

We go along the Vyšehradská to where the street crosses the "Na Slupi" where on the left are the Botanical Gardens. On the left side of the "Na Slupí" we observe a group of buildings (today a hospital) which belonged to the Convent of the Order of Elizabeth with the Church of Our Lady at the corner of the Apollinářská (1724–1731), a Baroque edifice by K. I. Dienzenhofer. The second group, the Church of Our Lady "Na Slupi" with the former Servite convent is of Gothic origin, late 14th century. From here in 1420 the Hussite armies bombarded the Vyšehrad.

From the "Na Slupi" Church we go to the Albertov, the Children's Hospital quite close to which stands the magnificent **"Na Karlově" Church**, founded by Charles IV in 1350. The church has three cupolas with daring stellar vaulting; the story goes that the architect bound himself to the Devil in return for the success of his work. From here we return to the Inner Town along the "U Karlova" where, before the intersection with the Kateřinská stands one of the most attractive buildings in Prague Baroque (1712–1720) by K. I. Dienzenhofer: the Villa America, today the Antonín Dvořák Museum

In the Kateřinská itself is St. Catherine's Church, originally a gothic edifice, rebuilt in Baroque style, also by Dienzenhofer, in the years 1737–1741. We proceed along the Lípova as far as the Štěpánská, where we stop at the Church of St. Stephen which forms a picturesque corner with the Romanesque Rotunda of St. Longinus. The rotunda is late 12th century and has been several times restored. St. Stephen's Church is a legacy from the time of Charles IV and from 1351, the date of its foundation till 1866 it has undergone a succession of renovations. If we continue along the Štěpánská, we find ourselves back in the Václavské náměstí.

L. VYŠEHRAD

Vyšehrad is in the southern part of Prague, on the right bank of the Vltava.

The oldest chronicles of Vyšehrad are late 10th century, but it can be assumed from the results of archaeological research that there was a fortress-castle above the Vltava on the Vyšehrad Hill as early as the 9th, built under the Přemysl dynasty. In the middle of the 11th century Prince Vratislav II made it his court residence, building several churches contemporaneously. He lies buried with his wife in one of them: the chapter church of Saints Peter and Paul. As time went on the fame of this castle faded until the era of Charles IV, who renewed it and erected a royal castle there. At the same time he also founded a new Gothic church and Vyšehrad was connected with the New Town by battlements. In 1420 the Hussites destroyed the castle after a two-months' siege. The royal garrison defending the castle waited for help from the army of King Sigmund. Later, under the rule of George of Poděbrady and his successors, Vyšehrad became a self-contained settlement. The royal castle however was still no more than a ruin, and gradually open spaces were converted to gardens and vineyards.

At the time of the Thirty Years War, in 1654, Vyšehrad was made into a powerful fortress with stout walls as part of the fortification works of Prague. The outer gate "Táborská" on the Panrác side and the Leopold Gate, decorated with coat of arms and escutcheon, both date from this time. Vyšehrad received its present appearance only in the latter half of the 19th century when the Church of Saints Peter and Paul was also restored in neo-Gothic style. In the same period some other important improvements and renovations were undertaken. The altar in the chapter church was restored and the Romanesque rotunda of St. Martin (mid-11th century) was repaired. Also the statue of St. Václav by Bendl, which had stood in the Václavské námĕsti, was brought to Vyšehrad. Architectural repairs were also done to the cemetery and the "Slavín" founded, the common vault for all deserving men and women who have devoted their lives to the cultural advancement of the nation.

2. THE ENVIRONS OF PRAGUE

The landscape of central Bohemia is widely varied. The **middle Elbe valley,** the first region to be populated, is extremely fertile; even the vine flourishes there. The **Lower Vltava (Moldau) valley,** is fairly similar; it consists of a fertile plain on both sides of the Vltava; on the west it reaches the region of Kladno, an important industrial centre. The region of Křivoklát, in the past a hunting preserve of the Bohemian kings, stretches to the west of Prague along the Berounka river.

This area is geologically extraordinarily varied. The best-known part of it is the Bohemian Karst with its caves and curious rock formations. The Brdy Forest is the most timbered Bohemian plateau and the source of a number of rivers. The **Vltava region** has always been considered one of the poorest stretches of country in Bohemia. Even industry shunned this unfertile granite country with its often cheerless climate. It was not until the Vltava dam at Slapy was built that a material change occurred. The **Sázava basin** is the area most visited by the people of Prague. Here the water of the Sázava flows from east to west through wooded hills.

The **Bohemian Central Mountain region** is remarkable for the peculiar shape of the peaks formed by volcanic eruptions, and often referred to as a "lunar landscape". Here the climate is relatively warm, as is shown by the abundance endowity of the dense woods.

Fruit and vines thrive on the southern slopes. Large industrial towns have developed along the Elbe and the largest brown coal deposits in Czechoslovakia are located in the Ore Mountains.

List of sights and places of interest

State town reservations: Kutná Hora, Rakovník, Litoměřice.

State natural reservations: Bohemian Karst in the Beroun district; Medník (Prague East); Kammenná slunce (Bílina); Říp (Roudnice on the Elbe); Vrkoč (Usti on the Elbe).

Tourist regions: Bohemian Karst, Hřebeny, Křivoklát forest, Sázava region, middle Vltava region, Bohemian Central Mountains.

State-owned castles: Průhonice, Karlštejn, Křivoklát, Dobříš, Zbraslav, Konopiště, Veltrusy, Kačina.

Spas: Poděbrady, Teplice.

Other sights: Lidice (the village razed to the ground by the Nazis); Terezín (Theresienstadt), Nazi concentration camp; Sázava (monastery of St. Procopius); the botanical and dendrological museum in the state-owned castle at Průhonice; the dams at Slapy and Štěchovice.

Short half-day excursions round Prague

To the north: Levý Hradec, 16 km, the Church of Saint Clement, about 880 A.D., Slav liturgy.—**Nelahozeves,** 30 km, birthplace of the composer Antonín Dvořák (1841); fine Renaissance castle with Dvořák museum—**Veltrusy,** 33 km, magnificent Baroque park of 290 acres, laid out at the beginning of the 18th century.—**Říp,** about 50 km, a 1,514 feet high basalt hill, belvedere, Saint Georges Church (1126); here the magnetic needle of the compass deviates; legendary mountain.

To the north-west: Okoř, picturesque castle ruins, near-by the village of Neutonic, 20 km from Prague—**Budeč,** 25 km, Saint Peter's church (1055), former princely residence.

To the south: Zbraslav, 16 km, castle with collection of plastics by modern Czech artists.—**Slapy Dam** on the Vltava, 45 km, new Prague convalescent centre.—**Konopiště,** 50 km, castle with rich collections started by the former Austro-Hungarian heir to the throne, Ferdinand d'Este.

To the south-west: Karlštejn, 30 km, state-owned castle of Charles IV's time (1348) with valuable rooms.

To the south-east: Průhonice, 10 km, state-owned castle, park with rare timber, reservation.

To the east: Tismice, 35 km, 12th–century Romanesque basilica.—**Kouřim,** 45 km, a 13th–century walled town, extensive excavations of ancient Slav strongholds.

To the north: Stará Boleslav, 22 km, ancient seat of Bohemian princes and kings. In the 11th–century chapel of Saint Václav, one of the largest in Bohemia, Saint Wenceslas was murdered in 929. Near the town lies **Houštka Spa** (mud baths) with a sports stadium where the famous runner Emil Zátopek set up several world records.

Round Trips by car

1. To Karlštejn and Křivoklát:
Prague—Karlštein (30 km)—Beroun (40 km)—Zdice (50 km)—Žebrák (58 km)—Křivoklát (80 km)—Rakovník (96 km)—Kladno (130 km)—Lidice (138 km)—Prague (158 km).

2. To Konopište and the Sapy dam:
Prague—Benešov (42 km)—Konopiště (44 km)—Slapy dam (65 km)—Dobříš (85 km)—Mníšek (96 km)—Zbraslav (115 km)—Prague (127 km).

3. To Poděbrady and Kutná Hora:
Prague— Mochov (30 km)—Poděbrady (54 km)—Kolín (69 km)—Kačina (82 km)—Sedlec (85 km)—Kutná Hora (89 km)—Prague (156 km).

4. Into the Bohemian Central Mountains:
Prague—Veltrusy (31 km)—Budyně na Ohří (57 km)—Libochovice (63 km)—Hazmburk (69 km)—Třebenice (74 km)—Kozly (91 km)— Bílina (101 km)—Teplice (113 km)—Ústí nad

Labem (131 km)—Litoměřice (165 km)—Terezín (160 km)—
Roudnice nad Labem (172 km)—Mělník (190 km)—Prague
(221 km).

A. MIDDLE ELBE REGION
(the region east of Prague)

This is the most fertile stretch of Bohemia; grapes
ripen here, and other fruit are cultivated here. There
are many forests and the river banks are shaded by
oaks and pine trees.

Kolín (62 km east of Prague) is the busiest town
and the most important railway junction.

The town lies in the middle of a fertile plain where mainly
grain and sugarbeet are cultivated. Industry is represented by an
important coffee substitute manufacture and an oil refinery.
The town was founded in the 13th century. The Cathedral of St.
Bartholomew is worthy of note. It and the added Gothic sacristy
consisting of seven chapels from the time of Charles IV were
both built by Peter Parler of Gmünd, the architect of Gothic
Prague.

From the railway-line between Kolin and Prague, we can see
a raised monument near the Liblice broadcasting station. In
this neighbourhood in 1434 the Hussite revolutionary troops
were beaten by a ruse on the battlefield of Lipany.

Kutná Hora

12 km south-west of Kolín lies **Kutná Hora,** 65 km
south-east of Prague. Because of the number of
historical buildings in the town it has been placed
under the National Trust for the Preservation of
Ancient Monuments. These old buildings arose at a
time when Kutná Hora (Kuttenberg) by reason of
its silver mines and the Royal Mint, became the
first city of Bohemia after Prague. Its most flourishing
period was in the 13th century which is represented
by the **Court of the Italians (Vlasský)**, where in those

days the "Prague groschen" was minted, a coin valued all over Europe in that period. When the Emperor Charles IV built the Saint Vitus' Cathedral in Prague, the owners of the Kutná Hora silver mines decided to erect a magnificent **church of Saint Barbara,** the patron saint of the miners.

The **Church of Saint Barbara** was built between 1388–1548; it is a noteworthy building with a nave and four aisles, surrounded by a delightful square from which we have a very fine **view** of the valley and the town storeyed like an amphitheatre. Fine view of the buttresses of the church.

The **nave** was built by Benedikt Rejt and master Mikuláš (who created the famous Wenceslas room in Prague Castle); it is decorated with the arms of the city corporations and bourgeois families. Throne dating from 1566. The **choir** was built in 1499 by M. Rejsek (fresco of the Queen of Sheba, 1490, gothic stalls with three well-preserved statues).

Opposite St. Barbara are the 18th-century buildings of the **Jesuit College** (baroque sculptures; now secularized).

In the town, fine **fountain** and fine baroque and gothic **town houses.** The **Church of Saint James** (Sv. Jakuba) dates from the 14th century; it adjoins the **Court of the Italians** (Vlašský), begun towards 1300 and subsequently transformed on several occasions.

The Court of the Italians takes its name from the fact that the first craftsmen who came to Bohemia to mint coins were Italians; the **inner courtyard** offers a delightful view; remains of fortifications, **high House** (a wing of the palace of Wencelas IV), **royal chapel.** The building now houses the offices of the municipality and contains a museum.

The **castle** (Hrádek), dating from the beginning of the 14th century was rebuilt in the 15th (restoration works from 1954 to 1961 at the charge of the State). It contains the fine gothic "Knights' Hall" and frescoes dating from the end of the 15th century.

The **Church of the Holy Trinity** in a verdant suburb, was built between 1488 and 1504 by Jan Smisek of Vrchoviste. Another church, **Our Lady Na Námĕti**, dates from the end of the 15th century and has a fine gothic vault and a fine throne dating from 1520.

A **Plague Column** commemorates the epidemic of 1713 (in Šultys Square; workshop of F. Baugut). The baroque Church of Saint John Nepomuk dates from 1754 (by F. M. Kaňka).

Sedlec, a suburb of Kutná Hora, has an **abbey church** founded towards 1300, destroyed during the Hussite wars and subsequently converted to baroque. The building has a nave and four aisles and a fine portal; the stucco rib-vaults date from the beginning of the 18th century (by I. Bayer and J. Santini Aichl). Nearby is a strange **cemetery church** founded after the great plague of 1318 and decorated inside with bones (1877): this macabre decoration is notably used for pyramids, chandeliers, and the Schwarzenberg family crest.

In the nearby town of **Čáslav** (11 km south-east) the general of the Czech Hussite armies Jan Žižka of Trocnov lies buried in the **Gothic Cathedral**.

Between Čáslav and Kolín in the middle of a park stands the loveliest Bohemian Empire **chateau of Kačina**, especially delightful when the lilac trees are in bloom.

Podĕbrady

Podĕbrady Spa, 15 km north-west of Kolín and 50 km east of Prague, is one of the most frequented thermal baths for disorders of the heart. It has a whole number of historically interesting buildings, first and foremost the **Castle** with its centuries old history.

In the 11th century the town was an important posting-stage on the old road from Prague to Moravia. The town grew round the fortress. Nonetheless, Podĕbrady did not gain its reputation as a spa until the first years of the twentieth century. Its natural wealth consists of a spring of earthly mineral water containing a high percentage of carbonic gas and brought from 18 Artesian wells. The treatment consists mainly of natural carbonic-gas baths. A complete treatment also includes hydrotherapy, electrotherapy and auxiliary treatment with mud compresses.

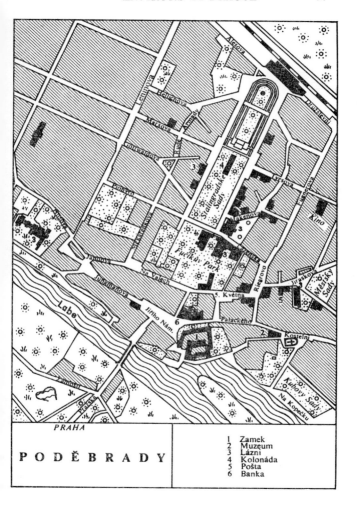

PRAHA

PODĚBRADY

1 Zamek
2 Muzeum
3 Lázni
4 Kolonáda
5 Pošta
6 Banka

Numerous, perfectly equipped establishments offer excellent medical care (open all the year round).

Indicated for heart diseases, hypertension, destruction of blood vessels, post-operative states.

Poděbrady lies in the Elbe plain, 577 feet above sea level. The fact that the town is in the plain is one of the chief features accounting for its efficacy in the treatment of heart diseases. The climate is very favourable for people suffering from this complaint. The sandy soil of the right bank of the Elbe where the baths have been built, assures a sufficiently dry atmosphere.

Poděbrady is a town of green meadows and groves, lime avenues and many parks and gardens. Everything is done for the patients, for their peace and their comfort (concerts, theatre performances by numerous ensembles).

The **Hellich Museum** is very interesting and gives a good idea of the history of the town and the region (numerous sections, on history, geology, zoology, etc, set out in an instructive manner).

Other things of interest: the **gothic church** containing the paintings by Brandl and Skréta, the **old parish church** and the **castle of Poděbrady** where the last Czech king Jiří (George) of Poděbrady was born in 1420; his statue stands in the square on the bank of the river. In the castle courtyard (Technical College) theatre performances are given in summer. Small **archaeological museum** in the rooms on the ground floor.

The town has an active cultural and social life. The Spa orchestra gives concerts, and Prague ensembles perform at the local theatre. There are cinema shows and musical evenings. There are water sports and fishing in the Elbe. The large swimming pool has a sandy beach. Visitors can ride and play tennis. In summer, motor-boat trips are organized on the Elbe as far as Kolín. There is a race course for horses. Quiet and beautifully kept, the "town without stairs" as Poděbrady used to be called, is one of the most pleasant holiday resorts in Bohemia.

Pleasant trips in the surroundings of Poděbrady, especially along the Elbe towards Nymburk. Farther on, in the direction (highway 38) of Český Ráj, we come to the town of **Mladad Boleslav**, 57 km north-west of Prague. It is chiefly notable for its Skoda automobile works. The Old Town is dominated by a mighty castle, built by Prince Boleslav II. The father of Czech music, Bedřich Smetana, lived here at Jabkenice from 1874 to 1884 and it was here that he composed his opera "Má Vlast" (My Country), and other works.

B. NORTH OF PRAGUE

Veltrusy Castle stands out on a height in the Vltava Valley south-west of Mělník (18 miles north of Prague by highway 8). A large park, decorated with several pavilions, surrounds this Baroque castle, which dates from the early 18th century. The park, laid out in 1754, is an example of Bohemian Empire landscape gardening.

East of Veltrusy (highway 16) one can see in the distance the slender church tower of **Mělník,** 33 km north of Prague, the town of Bohemian viticulture.

In the very earliest times of Bohemian history this place was inhabited by one of the tribes from which the Czech people later developed. The extensive viticulture was started by Charles IV in 1340 in which year he introduced the Burgundian vines. There are interesting cellars where excellent table wines are matured in the former Lobkowitz Château. The principal historical building is the Priory church, a fine example of late Gothic, particularly remarkable for its splendid ceiling paintings and frescoes. From the foot of the tower, and more especially from its gallery, we get a picturesque view of the confluence of the Vltava and the Elbe. The background of the Central Bohemian Mountains is dominated by the Říp, a peak 1,515 feet high; it is said that a tribe of the ancient Czechs scaled it and took possession of the surrounding region as a settlement.

Bohemian Central Mountains

As we continue down the Elbe valley, we come to a fruit-growing region dominated by the town of **Litoměřice,** 65 km north of Prague. It is under National Trust as an ancient monument.

This region was certainly inhabited in the earliest historical times. From way back there was busy traffic on the Elbe and as early as 1227 Litoměřice was granted trading rights and elevated to the status of a town.

Viticulture was started by Charles IV. The Utraquist sentiments of the town in the 16th century are visible in the historic **Patrician House "Pod báni"**. This has a roof shaped like a Hussite cup and the name means, roughly translated, "under the cupola". The re-Catholicisation of Litoměřice is recalled by the **Episcopal Palace** with a museum and by the **Saint Stephen's Cathedral** containing pictures of the school of Van Dyck.

The surrounding country, with its favourable climate, is truly the "garden of Bohemia". Richly productive apricot and cherry orchards thrive on the slopes round Litoměřice and there are vineyards of an improved Rhineland grape at **Žernoseky.** In the same fertile western part of the Bohemian Central Mountains on a cone-shaped height, towers the castle of **Hazmburk** offering a magnificent view of the surrounding country.

The old town of **Úštěk**, north-east of Litomerice, has a delightful setting and a pleasure lake. Near the town are the ruins of the stronghold of **Helfenburg** and **Mount Sedlo** from whose summit we have a panoramic view of the surrounding country.

A long bridge spanning the Elbe joins the town of Litoměřice with **Terezín**, of tragic memory. Terezín was built in 1780 as a prison. After the occupation of Czechoslovakia it was turned into a ghetto in 1939 and one of the most terrible concentration camps, Theresienstadt, was erected in the "Old Fortress". The National Cemetery of Terezín with its white cross bears eloquent testimony to the crimes that were committed there. On the Eger river, which flows into the Elbe near Litoměřice to the south, lies **Doksany** with a monastery founded in 1144. A crypt supported by 47 pillars is worthy of note.

Ústí nad Labem (Aussig on the Elbe) is the industrial centre of the Bohemian Central Mountains. The town is the hub of a highly developed chemical and metal-working industry and also a port for Elbe trade. Besides its industrial capacity, in its residential quarter the town enjoys such favourable climatic conditions that a number of sanatoriums have been built there.

Today there is nothing in Ústí nad Labem to remind us of the Middle Ages when Hussite armies captured it after a victorious battle in 1426. The memorial west of the town recalls the first of the great victories of Prokop Veliký, the successor of Žižka, when the Saxon armies numbering 70,000 men fled in panic from the field. Only the fortress of Střekov (Rock of Fear), which stands out on a steep rock, evokes these ancient times. Opposite Střekov, above a modern bathing beach, is a geological curiosity near the railway line: the Vrkoč Crag composed of fan-shaped basaltic pillars and prisms.

West of Ústí nad Labem at the foot of the Ore Mountains lies the wide basin of **Most** and **Duchcov** (Brüx and Dux). Brown coal production is concentrated in this basin and has laid the foundations of a prosperous industry. Most of the mines are near the industrial town of **Most** (88 km north-west of Prague). Coal was produced here as early as 1613.

Among the antiquities of the town first mention must be made of the late Gothic Diaconate Church. Heavy industry is represented by vast works extending as far as Horní Litvinov, where modern settlements have been built. This is the starting point of the railway to **Moldava**, a skiing centre in the Ore Mountains, and to the foot of **Mount Bouřňák** (tourist chalet at the top). The Fláje dam, whose waters are carried by a 12-km long tunnel to the industrialized outskirts of Most, has been erected on a windswept plateau.

Close to Most lies the town of **Duchcov**, a no less important industrial centre, although its importance dates only from the 19th century. The castle of Duchcov was the last domicile of the adventurer Casanova who died and was buried there in 1789.

The third town in the Northern Bohemian coal basin is **Teplice Spa** (90 km north-west of Prague) with hot and partly radio-active springs.

This charming watering place—formerly known as "Teplitz-Schönau"—lies at an altitude of 755 feet. It is indoubtedly one of the oldest in Czechoslovakia.

There is a legend that the Teplice springs were discovered by a herd of pigs from the domain of the
Knight of Kolostuj, on 29 August 762.

The beginnings of the spa in the time of Queen Judith, the
wife of Vladislav II, in about 1160 is steeped in history. She
founded a convent here where she lies buried. From 1813 onwards
Teplice was the headquarters of the Holy Alliance, a political
alliance of monarchs against Napoleon. The operations against
Marshal Vandamme in the battle near Chlumec, the prelude to
the Battle of Leipzig, were directed from here. A number of
eminent people have taken a cure at Teplice, such as Peter the
Great, Goethe, Beethoven, Richard Wagner and others.

The great curative virtues of the waters of Teplice are renowned; some interesting facts are told about the spring themselves. Thus, for instance, on 1 November 1755, during the great
Lisbon earthquake, the Teplice spring dried up for a few minutes.
In 1879, the thermal water flooded a number of galleries in the
"Döllinger" pits and then disappeared. Great efforts had to be
made to find the springs again.

Teplice has numerous radio-active springs whose water reaches
a temperature of 109° F, with a radio-activity of 130 Mach. The
total output of the springs amounts to 2,900,000 litres a day.
There are also peat deposits near the town.

Therapy consists of radio-active baths, radiation rooms, peat
baths, electrotherapy, hydrotherapy and rehabilitation exercises.

Indications: gouty or rheumatic arthritis, injuries of the bones,
muscles, joints and tendons, neuralgia, arterio-sclerosis of the
limbs, etc.

The majestic background of the Ore Mountains is dominated
by the **Komáří Hůrka** hill (tourist chalet) which affords a fine
view of the surrounding country. There is a chair-lift from
Bohosudov (whose baroque church attracts many pilgrims) and
Komáří Hůrka. The old mining town of **Krupka** nestles against
the slope of the hill. The winter sports resort of Cínovec lies in the
mountains above the bathing resort of Dubí (connexions with
Teplice).

If we return to Prague by highway 257, we go
through **Bílina** and **Louny.**

The western part of the Central Bohemian Mountains is dominated by Mount **Milešovka** (Milleschauer,

2,755 feet). From it there is a magnificent panorama of the distant surroundings.

Not far from Mount Milešovka is the commune of **Stadice,** the legendary cradle of the Czech royal Přemyslid dynasty. To emphasize the peasant origin of the legendary Prince Přemysl the Ploughman, the author of the Stadice monument has shown him beside a plough.

Near the town and spa of **Bílina,** where a fortress once stood on the site of the present castle and later a circular castle was built, rises the rocky **Mount Bořen.** This is a central European curiosity from the Tertiary Period, consisting of walls up to 300 feet high. South of here the range is continued by the bare heights of Louny. Some of these heights rise sheerly from the plain and so provide favourable conditions for gliding.

Louny (61 km north-west of Prague) has retained the ancient character of its old town. This is particularly true of the Gothic **Saint Nicholas Church** which contains many Renaissance motifs. Noteworthy also is the Renaissance building **Daliborka.**

Žatec (Saaz) lies about 24 km west of Louny and is a typical hop town.

The Žatec region provides approximately two thirds of the total hop yield of the Czechoslovak Republic. There are in existence historical documents relating to the cultivation of hops as far back as 1348, when Charles IV reigned. Bohemian hops were already exported in the 16th century. They gained a reputation as an indispensable ingredient for the finer kinds of bitter beer.

C. WEST OF PRAGUE
Kladno and its surroundings

The fertile plain on both banks of the lower Vltava, where beet is cultivated, extends to the west into a densely populated region, the importance of which increased especially in 1842 when seams of brown coal were discovered here.

Kladno, 29 km west of Prague, has grown in the course of the last hundred years into the foremost industrial centre. Thanks to the rich coal deposits, ironworks were opened in 1850 to which iron ore was brought and manufactured. Not far distant above Zákolany on the old fortress hill stands the Romanesque **Rotunda of Saint Peter and Saint Paul** (900). A Latin School was founded close to the church at the same date. Some miles south of Zákolany and east of Kladno is the famous site **Lidice.**

In spring 1942, the assistant "Protector" of the German Reich for Bohemia, SS Obergruppenführer and police chief R. Heydrich was killed by patriots. For a long time the authors of this assassination were not discovered by the occupation authorities, but the Nazis lost no time in undertaking a long series of reprisals to terrorize the Czech people. The village of Lidice became the focal point of these reprisals. Without any proof, the population of this small village was accused of having played a leading part in the planning and execution of the assassination of Heydrich, and the Nazis ordered its extermination.

In the evening of 9 June 1942, detachments of Nazi police surrounded Lidice. Before midnight, they forced their way into the small, sleeping houses and ordered the inmates to leave within ten minutes. The men were brutally driven into the cellars of the Horák farm, the women and children into the school building. At dawn on the following day, 10 June, 173 of the men of Lidice were mown down by the bullets of an execution squad. The oldest victim was a man of eighty-four, the youngest a boy who was not yet fifteen. The workers on the third shift who had been working at Kladno during that tragic night, were arrested and executed in their turn. The women and children were deported and most of them died. The farms and houses were burnt to the ground, the ruins mined and scattered by explosion. Then, for months, Nazi working parties systematically razed the village to the ground. Behind barbed wire and notices the Nazis threatened death to anyone who approached; the land of Lidice was completely transformed a by series of earthworks. The communes pond was filled in, the stream diverted from its natural course. On the site of Lidice appeared a devasted, arid and lonely plain. The name of Lidice was erased from maps, land registers and official documents.

During the Red Army's advance in May 1945, Soviet soldiers erected a monument with a poignant cross on the mass grave where the men of Lidice lay buried. The memorial bears an inscription in Russian and Czech: "To the victims of the German Fascist occupation—from the Soviet soldiers, N.C.O.'s and officers of the Unit of Heroes of the Soviet Union, Colonel Pankov".

After the war the Birmingham miners held a mass meeting at which they collected money for the rebuilding of Lidice. The initiative of the English miners gave birth to the great "Lidice shall live" movement. Some towns changed their name to Lidice (in Mexico, San Jeronimo; Stern Park Garden in Illinois in the United States; in Venezuela, a district of Caracas; Plaza de Lidice in Havana, Cuba; etc).

A small **museum**, on the south hill, commemorates the tragedy of 1942. To the north stands the **new Lidice** amidst beds of roses sent from all parts of the world, near a large **memorial** which dominates the small valley.

The woods of Křivoklát

South-west of Kladno, near the Berunka river, amid dense woods rises the state-owned **Křivoklát Castle** (52 km west of Prague).

The picturesque and restored castle with its round watch-tower and the palace in Vladislav Gothic style has rich historical associations. Křivoklát was built in the early 13th-century by King Václav I. Its present appearance dates from its reconstruction at the end of the 15th century; the unique gate to the castle itself is of that period. Křivoklát was used by the Kings of Bohemia as a pleasure palace and they hunted in the dense forest roundabout. In the reign of the Hapsburgs the castle was used as a prison in which, among others, the English alchemist Kelley was incarcerated.

The woods of Křivoklát extend north-westward as far as the town of **Rakovník** (56 km west of Prague).

Near the town are less productive anthracite coal deposits and also clay suitable for the manufacture of fire-proof china ware.

Consequently we find here the Rakovník Ceramic Works. There are also in the town soap factories and a brewery which was well-known in the Middle Ages. The brewery obtains the right raw material from the fertile hopfields of the surrounding country. The Inner Town of Rakovník numbers several important buildings. Two town gates in the shape of towers remain from the old fortifications; they give the town a characteristic appearance. Late Gothic is richly represented chiefly by the Saint Bartholomew's Cathedral. The sandstone pulpit, hewn out of a single block in the shape of a calyx, dates from 1504. A picturesque 16th-century wooden belfry stands in the cemetery.

Round about the Křivoklát woods we find a number of important places: in the north the state-owned **Lány Castle** on the edge of an extensive deer park stocked with big game. In the heart of lovely forests, between Lány and Křivoklát, is the **reservoir lake of Klíčava** which was made by the youth brigade and provides water for the mines and forges in the surroundings of Kladno.

South-west of Křivoklat, on the Berounka, is the village of Skryrje, which although insignificant in itself, is known for the excavation of fossilised trilobites (a species of crayfish). In the south, not far from the railway line which links Prague and Plzeň (Pilsen), stand two castles close to each other: **Žebrák** and **Točník.** King Václav I was fond of coming to them for hunting. We go back eastwards by highway 5. Northeast of here, in the wide valley of the Litavka river, is the town of **Králův Dvůr** with large cement and iron works.

The ancient town of **Beroun** (30 km south-west of Prague) is linked by modern settlements to the industrial Králův Dvůr. Beroun arose at the beginning of the 13th century. The old fortifications with two towers are still preserved in many places. The ancient alleyways near the fortifications are interesting.

In 1950, the **Koněprusy Caves** at **Zlatý kůň** were discovered in a disused limestone quarry 9 km south of Beroun. These underground structures, with a wealth of stalactites and stalagmites, are one mile long and divided into three storeys. Tools have been found there which had been used by the prehistoric men who inhabited this region, also bones of animals, especially those of a species of sabre-toothed tiger dating back some 500,000 years. The discovery in the "Robbers' Cave" of the workshop of 15th-century forgers where the false Hussite hellers called "flutky" had been struck, caused an international sensation. Zlatý kůň is connected with the Karst Kotýz plateau where ceramic articles from old Celtic dwellings have been found, and also with interesting karst formations whose shapes resemble a bridge.

Behind Beroun the river Berounka runs through the rocky valley of **Bohemian Karst,** followed by the railway and a small road.

The bones of prehistoric animals have been found in some caves in this area. There are also stalactite caves. Not far distant is **Svatý Jan** where, according to the legend, Saint Ivan is said to have lived as a hermit under the cliff. In **Tetín** on a high crag there are still the ruins of Tetín castle. Tetín was the scene of a long list of legendary and historical events in the earliest days of Czech history.

In the offing of the wooded hills along the Berounka there suddenly looms, like some castle out of a fairy story, the state-owned **Karlštejn** Castle (28 km southwest of Prague). A massive square tower rises above the stylishly restored buildings in the lower courtyard, the palace and the chapel in the upper courtyard. Because of its unique collections the castle has often been called the Bohemian Gralsburg.

Karlštejn was built by the Emperor Charles IV (1348–1355) and he frequently stayed there. Besides a lapidarium, there is in the palace a courtiers' chamber with pictures of the castle at various periods of reconstruction, a hall with cupboards and coats of arms of the lords of the castle and the **Luxemburger Hall** with the busts of kings, archbishops and the wives of Charles IV. The church of Our Lady is decorated with a 14th-century fresco of the apocalypse. It leads off into the bejewelled oratory of Charles IV. Crossing a covered bridge we come to the big **tower**, the subterranean vaults of which, with their 50 feet thick walls, were used as an exit from the castle. On the second floor is a sumptuous cruciform **chapel** with a gilded ceiling on which the sun, moon and stars are depicted. The walls of the lower part are adorned with carved semi-precious stones, the upper part with 132 vignettes by the painter Theoderich. The deepest part of the castle is the 250 feet deep well.

D. SOUTH OF PRAGUE

This region begins at **Zbraslav** (Königsaal), about 15 km south of Prague. The Kings of Bohemia were buried until the time of the Hussite wars in the **Monastery** of Zbraslav, today a State Museum with collections of modern Czech sculptures (in restoration).

Some of them lie today beneath the gravestones in the Saint James' Church. The National Gallery with a collection of modern Czech sculpture is housed in the old monastery. In the church we find valuable works by the two painters Škréta and Brandl. The extensive fortress above the town is believed to have been the seat of the Celtic chief Marobud.

The long ridge of hills (called Hřebeny, then Brdy, 3,150 feet) stretches south-west from Zbraslav, where on the edge of an expanse of woods stands the state-owned castle of **Dobříš** (42 km south-west of Prague). It is a Baroque chateau, built between 1745–65, surrounded by a French park, formally laid out with clipped hedges and figural bushes. The chateau is the convalescent home of the Czechoslovak Writers' Union. At **Mníšek** nearby at the foot of the Hřebeny, before Dobříš, iron ore is produced and modern settlements for the workers have been built. In the same region lies the town of **Příbram** (59 km south-west of Prague), where silver has been mined since the beginning of the 14th century. Today lead is also produced here. On the height above Příbram is a remarkable Baroque monument, the **Svatá Hora,** the greatest pilgrimage shrine of Our Lady in Bohemia. A covered stairway connects the town of Příbram with the shrine. It was built by the Jesuits in the second half of the 17th century.

South-west of Příbram on the slope of the hills is the little chateau of Vysoká. The Czech composer Antonín Dvořák liked staying here and it was here near the pond that he composed his fairy opera Rusalka ("Undine"). And the charming surroundings inspired him to a number of other works. The last buttress of the Brdywald is Mount Třemšín (2,722 feet). At its foot, round the well-preserved castle of the old Bohemian nobility, lies the little town of Rožmitál pod Třemišínem (76 km south-west of Prague).

The most remarkable thing on the Vltava is the **Slapy Dam** (40 km south of Prague), an important source of water power erected in recent years. It took four years to build the dam, which is 200 feet high. The dam retains an artificial lake 40 km long on the Vltava. A Kaplan turbine, weighing 700 tons, is mounted in the power house of the dam.

On the boat trip to Prague—Slapy Dam, we skirt, near the confluence of the Sázava and the Vltava—the **island of Saint Kilian** with the remains of the **monastery of Ostrov** founded in 999 by the Benedictines who there compiled the Annals which later became the source of the Dalimil Chronicle. There too, was composed the Czech liturgical chant called "About the Creation of the World".

Boats coming from Prague reach the Slapy dam through a lock and the Štěchovice dam. A number of picturesque little places have sprung up in the neighbourhood of the newly created lake where gradually a large modern rest centre has been set up. Transport on the newly created lake is provided by boats. The Slapy Dam is part of the so-called "Vltava Cascades" scheme, a project for the building of great waterworks to multiply the power derived from the river.

The middle-point of the last sector of the Sázava river, the right tributary of the Vltava, is the little town of **Jílové** (about 33 km south of Prague). There was a settlement in the 9th century; it was built up for the accommodation of gold prospectors. Then in the 13th century the royal hill-town of Jílové was founded on this oriferous soil. Its gold mines were known all over the Europe of that time. Ducats with the image of an owl were coined in the old mint, the present Town Hall. Not far from the town, in the Sázava ravine, towers the Mednik height, where valuable survivals of tertiary flora still grow. This is the **erythronium dens canis** (dog's tooth violet), which flowers in the spring.

In the gently rolling hill country towards Prague lies the state-ow.ed castle of **Průhonice,** some 15 km south-east of Prague. It is built in Gothic style. In the park, which covers an area of 625 acres, there is a botanical and dendrological museum containing hundreds of flowers and shrubs from all over the world. Some fishponds have been laid out along the course of the river which flows through the park. In the chateau itself are housed horticultural, meteorological and acclimatisation research departments.

On the line Prague-Tábor in the Sázava region is the town of **Benešov,** 52 km south-east of Prague, with ruins of a Minorite monastery. 3 km west of Benešov is the state-owned **castle of Konopiště** with a vast park.

The original castle belonged in the 14th century to the Sternberg family, whose coat of arms was a golden star in an azure field. It was bought in the late 19th century by the Austrian Archduke and heir to the throne, Francis Ferdinand d'Este, who was assassinated at Sarajevo in 1914. It was sumptuously rebuilt in 1894 and thereby aroused a political controversy. The German Emperor Wilhelm II and the Austrian Archduke Franz Ferdinand met in the adjacent Choral Pavilion in 1914. Here they agreed on a common campaign in the First World War.

In the 82 rooms of the Castle, crammed with unique collections, the spacious Weapons Hall, the Picture Gallery and a Museum of Plastics of Saint George are especially notable. Ferdinand d'Este was an untiring collector of the latter. All the corridors are decorated with hunting trophies. On the garden-terrace of the park is the statue of a huntsmen. Bears are bred in the moat. The castle is dominated by the round tower in which the Bohemian King Wenceslas IV was held prisoner by the rebellious nobility.

Behind the heights overlooking the Sázava is hidden a historic monastery in the village of **Sázava** about 55 km south-east of Prague.

The story goes that the hermit Procopius met the Bohemian Prince Oldřich here. At the request of the hermit Prince Oldřich founded a Benedictine monastery with Slav liturgy in 1032. When the services were changed to Latin the **church** was rebuilt in Gothic; the reconstruction was not however completed. Today there is only one nave, left standing without vaulting and tower, and a Baroque church containing a **Procopius museum** with a wooden chalice and relics of the saint. On the other bank of the river are the well-known glassworks which specialise in blown glassware produced by a special method.

3.   WESTERN BOHEMIA

This region occupies almost a third of the whole of Bohemia and is characterised by three different types of landscape.

1. Mountains of volcanic origin, the **Imperial Forest**, the **Tepler and the Duppauer mountains**, a massif run, in contrast to the uninterrupted chain of the **Ore Mountains**, along the **north bank of the Eger and the Czechoslovakian frontier**. Apart from the brown coal-pits of Sokolov and the Jáchymov uranium area the local industry is confined to the Karlovy Vary porcelain works. The world-famous spa triangle Karlsbad-Marienbad-Franzensbad is of great economic importance.

2. West Bohemia consists of the **Plzeň region** with districts known both for industrial and coal production. First and foremost are the Plzeň anthracite mines. The ore-mining areas made possible the erection of some iron-works, especially near Rokycan. North of Plzeň there are also excellent china clay pits which form the basis of the development of the local porcelain industry. The Pilsener brewery is also world-famous.

3. The Plzeň region is continued southwards by moderately hilly country until the foot of the **Bohemian Forest**. The Bohemian Forest Český Les zone follows the frontier from Mariánské Lázně (Marienbad) to the Všerubský Pass with Mount Čerchov, 3,430 feet. Then follows the most extensive range in Bohemia, the Šumavas. The massif runs along the frontier N.W.–S.E. and ends in the southern-most foothills of Bohemia. The mountains are covered with dense woods and even a remnant of primeval forest still exists here. The retreating glaciers left behind a number of interesting mountain tarns and some highland moor reservations are protected. The local industry is chiefly concerned with timber manufacture (paper and match factories).

Communications

To Karlovy Vary (Karlsbad); railway line Prague-Cheb (Eger); distance from Prague to Karlovy Vary 187 km. Motor highway Prague–Karlovy Vary (125 km). During the summer months there is a direct air service between Prague and Karlovy Vary. The connection with Máriánské Lázně (Marienbad) is maintained by the express service Prague–Plzeň–Cheb. Distance from the capital is 166 km. The West Bohemian Spa triangle can be reached from the German Federal Republic by the frontier post at Rozvadov. The whole region of West Bohemia is criss-crossed by a dense network of roads and railways.

Express trains in the Plzeň area run frequently every day.

Sights and places of interest

Towns under State protection as Ancient Monuments: Loket (Ellbogen), district of Karlovy Vary, Cheb, Domažlice (Taus), Klatovy, Prachatice, Horšovský Týn.

Natural reservations (State protected): Černé jezero (Black Lake), Čertovo jezero (Devil's Lake), Boubín primeval forest (Vimperk district).

State-owned castles and chateaux: Kynžvart (Königswart), Loket castle, Radyně, Plzeň; Švihov (Klatovy); Velhartice (Klatovy); Rábí, Sušice.

Spas: Karlovy Vary, Mariánské Lázně, Františkovy Lázně, Jáchymov (Joachimstal), Lázně Kynžvart.

Other sights: The Teplá Monastery (Mariánské Lázně), Plasy Monastery, buildings in Volary (Prachatice), Husinec—birthplace of Jan Hus (Prachatice), Chodsko—a place rich in folklore near Domažlice.

Round trips by car

1. West Bohemian spas: Plzeň-Stříbro (31 km)—Planá (56 km)—Mariánské Lázně (72 km)—Kynžvart (83 km)—Cheb (103 km)—Františkovy Lázně (108 km)—Sokolov (133 km)—Loket (143 km)—Karlovy Vary (154 km)—Bečov nad Teplá (176 km)—Plzeň (145 km). This trip can also be done in two days, staying overnight in Karlovy Vary.

2. Chodsko and Klatovy: Plzeň-Stod (19 km)—Horšovský Týn (42 km)—Domažlice (52 km)—Kdyně (62 km)—Klatovy (83 km)—Švihov (93 km)—Přeštice (104 km)—Plzeň (124 km).

3. Bohemian Forest: Plzeň—Klatovy (44 km)—Železná Ruda (86 km)—Nýrsko (110 km)—Klatovy (127 km)—Plzeň (171 km).

4. Bohemian Forest (2 days tour): Plzeň-Klatovy (44 km)—Velhartice (61 km)—Sušice (72 km)—Rejštejn (84 km)—Kvilda (102 km)—Vimperk (122 km)—overnight in Horní Vltavice (134 km)—Volary (148 km)—Prachatice (164 km)—Husinec (172 km)—Strakonice (200 km)—Horaždovice (217 km)—Nepomuk (241 km)—Plzeň (277 km).

Karlovy Vary (Karlsbad)

Karlsbad was founded between the years 1347–58 at the instigation of the Emperor Charles IV, who had visited the health resorts of Italy during his travels.

There is a legend that King Charles IV of Bohemia discovered the hot springs accidentally during a hunt, when his dog was scalded by the boiling water while pursuing a stag. It is not known if this is true, but it is certain that Charles IV knew of the springs and founded the town called Karlovy Vary there because he appreciated their importance.

The first baths to make use of the hot geyser water were built in the little village of Wary, the site now occupied by the Křížová, Vřídelni, Pražská and Tržiště streets in present-day Karlovy Vary. Soon the importance of these baths increased to such an extent that the Cure Tax was introduced in 1351. The first analysis of the hot springs was undertaken by Dr. Payer in 1522 and was unanimously recognised by scientists of note until the 17th century. The introduction of new methods by Dr Springfield, who published a monograph about Karlsbad giving the temperatures of all the springs and initiated the drinking of water straight from the geyser, marked a turning point. Dr Hoffmann was the first to introduce the daily dosage and the production of Karlsbad Salts. From a strictly scientific standpoint however Dr Becher was the first to prescribe special cures for the disorders of his day. In the 19th century Karlsbad developed enormously. Colonnades and comfortable hotels were built. In 1945 Karlovy Vary (the name to which it was changed in 1918) was nationalised.

The principal illnesses treated at Karlovy Vary are digestive disorders. There are 12 thermal springs:

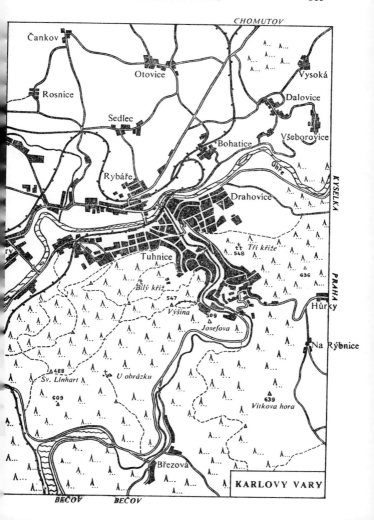

KARLOVY VARY

Geyser (72° C), Hygies (72° C), the Castle Spring (52° C), the Mill Spring (52° C), the Nixen Spring (46° C), Prince Václav's Spring (59° C), Libussa Spring (43° C), the Rock Spring (56° C), the Liberty Spring (63° C), the Park Spring (48° C).

In the past Karlsbad has been visited by famous persons, among them, for instance, the Russian Czar Peter the Great, the poets J. W. Goethe, Friedrich Schiller, Adam Mickiewicz, Alexander Pushkin and the composers Ludwig van Beethoven, Frederik Chopin, Joh. Brahms and Bedřich Smetana.

The route of those taking the cure, their walks and water-drinking is centred round the Czechoslovak-Soviet Friendship Colonnade (formerly the **Mill Colonnade**), built by the Prague architect J. Zítek. Most of the springs are in this colonnade. It is continued by the Tržiště Colonnade (Marketplace) with other springs and the relief depicting the discovery of the Karlsbad hot water springs.

From here a stairway leads to the **Castle Colonnade,** above which on a crag stands a tower built as a hunting lodge by Charles IV. A narrow lane leads on from the colonnades, across the bridge spanning the Teplá, to the uncovered pavilion where the bubbling geyser shoots up 40 feet into the air. The continuous stream of hot mineral water yields 61,600 gallons in 24 hours at a temperature of 72° C. The rest of the water flows into the Teplá stream where it produces curious sedimentary stone formations.

Opposite the geyser is the Baroque **Cathedral,** built between 1732–36 by Kilian Ignaz Dienzenhofer, the Prague Baroque architect. The last part of the spa is occupied by world-famous hotels and clinics. The largest is the Grand Hotel Moskva (formerly Pupp's Hotel).

On the portal of the **Municipal Theatre** we read the names of all the doctors concerned with the study of the Karlsbad springs.

The Puškin walk runs along the Tepla, and even in the river bed stone slabs bearing inscriptions in all languages testify to the gratitude of sick people healed by the cures.

The direction of the curative procedure is located in the five buildings of the National Spas; these extend the whole length of the spa quarter. This ends on the north side of the town part of Karlovy Vary, in which the offices of the town administration are located.

The **main railway station** is on the far side of the Ohře, into which the Teplá flows. It is surrounded by factories. Noteworthy is the carving of the stone deposited by the geyser water which, polished and shaped into various ornaments, is one of the typical souvenirs of Karlovy Vary.

The local ceramic industry and porcelain manufacture, depending on the china clay-pits in the neighbouring towns of **Slavkov, Chodov, Loket** and **Ostrov,** have the highest reputation throughout the world. The porcelain factories, and especially those manufacturing the "Epiag" chinaware, are at **Stará Role** (Alt-Rohlau), **Slavkov, Březová, Chodov, Loket, Merklín, Klášterec nad Ohří** and other places roundabout.

Gloves are also manufactured at Karlovy Vary and there is a food industry (the production of Karlsbad wafer and "zwieback"). In the spa we can inspect the interesting production of Karlsbad Salts. There is also the **Moser** glass factory (on the Cheb road).

The whole of Karlovy Vary is enclosed by green wooded hills. The most remarkable view from the promenade paths is that of the **Stag's Leap.** This is a high crag with the statue of a stag (the place from

which, according to the legend mentioned above, the
stag when at bay leapt into the geyser). A cog-wheel
railway runs up to a summer restaurant and a look-out
tower. Opposite on the so-called "Mount of Eternal
Life", stands a similar tower from which can be seen
the whole panorama of the Ore Mountains with the
Klínovec (Keilberg), 4,039 feet high.

B. THE NORTH-WESTERN CORNER
OF BOHEMIA

Jáchymov

Jáchymov (Joachimsthal) lies 20 km north of
Karlovy Vary, nestling among the mountains at the
foot of the Klínovec, the highest peak of the Ore
Mountains. It owes its world-wide reputation to the
discoveries of M. and Mme Curie who found in the
local ore new elements with surprising healing properties; namely, polonium and radium. The production
of uranium ore was started here in 1908. Radium
springs were discovered in old local mines and con-
ducted into the radium palace. Here nervous disorders,
rheumatism, circulatory illnesses, among others, were
cured.

For a long time silver was mined in Jáchymov, and at Jáchymov were struck the famous Jáchymov "tollars" from which the
name of the American dollar is derived. When the mines were
worked out it seemed as if the town would sink into oblivion. But
the discovery of radium has revived interest in this old mining
town.

It was also noticed that the water from the Jáchymov mines
contained an element of gasified radium, a kind of radio-active
emanation with curative properties in some cases, especially
rheumatism, gout, arterio-sclerosis of the peripheral veins, etc.

Within a very short time a spa with modern baths was created.

The lovely situation of Jáchymov, at an altitude of 2,130 feet,
in a wooded valley on the southern slopes of the Krušné hory

enhances not only the charm but also the curative value of this spa. The pure mountain air and the wealth of ultra-violet rays have a propitious effect on the health of the patients.

Above Jáchymov is the wooded **Mount Klínovec** (4,081 feet) where there is a tourist hotel and a belvedere. The mountain road to Klínovec goes through the commune of **Boží Dar** (3,280 feet). In the surroundings are vast peat bogs covered with mountain flowers, especially on Spičák hill.

Jáchymov is near the mining town of **Ostrov** which is a model of a modern industrial town. An 18th-century park near the old castle is called "The Eighth Wonder of the World".

Nejdek

A railway running through the Rolava valley links Karlovy Vary with the town of Nejdek. Nejdek has a large yarn-carding workshop and a modern workshop for sorting local ores. The railway skirts a picturesque slope with a fine view on the surrounding country and then goes up to **Pernink,** a well-known winter-sports centre where—as in the neighbouring commune of **Horní Blatná**—silver and tin used to be mined. Later other industries grew up, notably lace-making, toy and musical-instrument making (very widespread in the Ore Mountains). Pernink is the starting point for **Mount Plešiveke** (tourist chalet, ski-lift, fine panorama).

Going up the Ohře

1. A picturesque road along the river Ohře leads to **Lázně Kyselka** Spa (Kysibl), famous for its "Mattoni's Kysibl" mineral water which has been exported since 1829 to numerous countries. In a tufa rock above this watering place small caves called "Dwarfs' Holes" have been discovered. They are formed by the volcanic gases which rise from the depth of the subsoil and escape freely in the air.

2. The road continues through the delightful Ohře (Eger) valley, then leads through a narrow pass where we come to the

small spa of **Korunni (Krondorf)** whose alkaline acidulous mineral waters are famous and in great demand even in foreign countries. At this point the river Eger crosses a deep valley, enclosed on both sides by mighty phonolite rocks surmounted by the ruins of the strongholds of Hilmštejn, Perštejn, Egrburk and Šumburk. The valley widens near the town of **Klášterec nad Ohří** which is known not only for its medicinal spring but also for its very old porcelain factory (founded in 1793) and its castle which has now been converted into the Museum of Bohemian Porcelain.

3. **Kadaň,** surrounded on all sides by powerful ramparts, is another town of historic value in the region round the Eger. **The Market Square** is bordered by arcaded houses and the **Town Hall** surmounted by gothic spire without roofing. The narrow little **Katovská** (Hangman's) Street is also very interesting. In a deep valley 10 km north of Kadaň are the restored ruins of the great feudal **Hasištejn** castle where the Czech humanist Bohuslav Hasištejnsky of Lobkovice composed the first classic ode in praise of the "Sprudel" of Karlovy Vary (beginning of the 16th century). In 1827, this ode—called "In Thermas Caroli Quarti"—was translated into 28 languages and published in the press.

At the end of the North Bohemian lignite basin lies the town of **Chomutov** whose industrial character is emphasized by the presence of large metallurgical works, rolling mills, and railway-carriage building works. Above the town is the Kamencové jezero recreation centre on the banks of an emerald lake.

Loket

Loket (the "elbow"), under National Trust as an Ancient Monument—lies 12 km south-west of Karlovy Vary and can be reached either by road or by the footpath along the Ohře under the pillar-like cliff walls. The ancient little town, built on terraces, is dominated by the well-preserved 12th–century royal **castle.** The finest view of the castle can be had from the river, spanned by the oldest **suspension bridge** in Bohemia.

The castle was considered the strongest in all Bohemia and was a favourite residence of King John of Luxemburg. Architecturally, it is a mixture of different styles.

When the castle well was cleaned out in 1775 a meteorite, weighing 108 kilograms (nearly a ton) was found there and given the name of the "Petrified Burgrave". In the Burgrave's house, in a room with an unusually curious vaulted roof, are kept valuable archives.

The strongest part of the castle is the **tower**; its walls are 11½ feet thick. In the town, which still preserves its medieval character, the **Saint Václav's Church** (13th century) stands out. In it is a priceless picture of the patron saint by the master Peter Brandl.

Sokolov

Sokolov, in the heart of the North Bohemian lignite basin, has numerous glassworks and textile factories which make it, together with the kaolin mines and surrounding porcelain factories, an important industrial centre. Coal is sorted in a modern workshop and burnt in Tisová power station, the largest in Czechoslovakia.

A railway along the river Svatava leads to **Kraslice**, which is universally famous for its manufacture of musical instruments (its beginnings go back to 1778), its laces and its textile factories. Peat bogs lie hidden in the dense frontier forests, e.g. at **Velké jeřábí jezero** (Great Lake of Cranes) where there is a rare species of pine called "blatka".

Cheb

Cheb (Eger) lies up-stream from Loket (47 km from Karlovy Vary). The town's industries include bicycle factories. (30,000 inhab.).

On the **main square** of Cheb stands a group of interesting houses, recently restored. The steep, tall roofs of these houses, and their congeries of by and dormer windows, make a very typical impression. At No 14 a **Folklore Museum** is housed. At No 17 the German Poet-dramatist Schiller wrote his "Wallenstein".

In the middle of the square stands the uncompleted **Town Hall** (by G. B. Alliprandi) and two fountains with the **Roland Column.** In 1634 the famous general

Albrecht von Wallenstein, Duke of Friedland, who led the imperial troops in the Thirty Years War, was assassinated in Cheb. Only the ruins are left of the **Imperial Castle,** three parts of them still interesting: the **"Black Tower"** (70 feet high), the **"Palatine"** **chapel** (12th century), with vaulted roof, Romanesque in the lower part and early Gothic higher up. The remains of the 12th–century palace recall the tragedy of Eger, the murder of the generals who had remained loyal to Wallenstein. Among the churches the **Cathedral Church** with its spiral staircase and the **Church of Saint Francis** with its many-shaped Gothic windows are worthy of mention.

Other things to be seen in Cheb are several fountains of different periods in various parts of the town.

Not far from Cheb is the only remaining volcano in Bohemia, called **Komorní Hůrka** (1,650 feet), under natural reservation. From the top the adjacent Františkovy Lázně can be seen.

East of the town is a reservoir covering an area of 700 hectares. To the north-west is the town of Aš well known for its numerous textile factories. In the same direction, in a central basin with a pond, are the stronghold of **Ostroh** (Seeberg) which has preserved its original form to this day, and an interesting church with perfectly flat wooden ceiling.

Františkovy Lázně

Františkovy Lázně (Franzensbad),—some 50 km south-west of Karlovy Vary—is, apart from the latter, the oldest spa in western Bohemia.

The first mention of the mineral water of Cheb goes back to the 12th century. In 1526 Paracelsus mentioned it and spoke of its healing properties. But the inhabitants of Cheb did not take advantage of their important spring. It was not until the end of the 18th century, in the reign of Francis II, that a pavilion was built over the spring and a plan made for building the watering place. The spring was called František Spring and the town **Franzensbad**, which became **Františkovy Lázně**. The Swedish

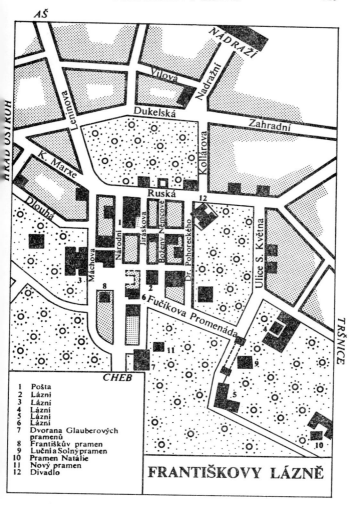

1 Pošta
2 Lázní
3 Lázní
4 Lázní
5 Lázní
6 Lázní
7 Dvorana Glauberových
   pramenů
8 Františkův pramen
9 Luční a Solný pramen
10 Pramen Natálie
11 Nový pramen
12 Divadlo

FRANTIŠKOVY LÁZNĚ

chemist J. J. Berzelius made a close chemical analysis of the waters; the real originator of its prosperity was however Dr D. Adler. Goethe and Beethoven were among its visitors.

The present Františkovy Lázně has nothing of historic interest. The town spreads amid green parks (400 acres) which surround it on every side. The block of the Baths with four clinics forms the centre of the spa. The 23 alkaline-muriatic-saline springs, which contain a considerable amount of Glauber salt, are used for the cure. Specially notable is the Glauber Spring IV which, almost one third Glauber salt, is reckoned the strongest spring of this kind in the world.

The expanse of radio-active moorland of volcanic origin consists of 30 million cubic metres, with a surface area of 10×2 km. It is on the boundary of the town and the park.

The principal diseases treated here are gynaecological (including sterility) and the cure is effected by means of mud baths and the drinking of mineral water.

Quite close to Františkovy Lázně is the **Vonšovské peat moor** (or **Soos**), a unique phenomenon in Europe. The vast layer of peat, estimated at seven million cubic metres, is perforated by many aerated mineral springs and free carbonic acid. This is the cause of the so-called bog-geysers in many places. One can only go on the moor without danger in dry weather.

Mariánské Lázně (Marienbad)

Mariánské Lázně (Marienbad), south-west of Karlovy Vary, 32 km south-east of Cheb—is the most recent spa of this region. Only 170 years ago its surroundings were still covered with primeval forest.

The development of the spa was subsidised by the **Teplá** monastery. Hence the name of Marienbad. In 1818 the baths were opened to the public and the protected spring area was defined. Among the best-

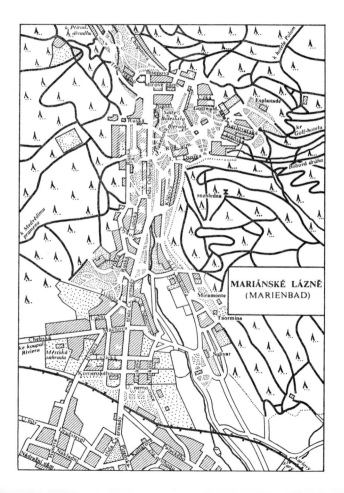

MARIÁNSKÉ LÁZNĚ
(MARIENBAD)

known visitors who have taken the cure there are King Edward VII, Richard Wagner and Goethe.

More than forty alcaline, ferruginous and plain acid springs are used for the cure. The treatment is efficacious for disorders of the digestive system, rheumatism, etc. The cure consists of drinking water, taking baths, inhalations and walks (touristic therapy). The parks laid out round the town, which gradually give place to woods, are criss-crossed by numerous walks, prescribed according to the medical diagnosis, for, as has been said, walking exercise is an important part of the cure.

The town part of Mariánské Lázně gradually merges with the spa, in the middle of which is the Cross Well with a covered colonnade. Architecturally, the town is of the Empire period. The Church, with a regular octagonal ground plan, was built in the style of the Munich Basilica.

Situated as it is in a wooded and enclosed basin at an altitude of 2,200 feet, the place enjoys a bracing, almost sub-alpine climate. The same applies also to the distant surroundings, especially on the north-west, where at the foot of the Imperial Forest, about 10 km away, lies:

Kynžvart

Kynžvart (Königswart), a spa used chiefly today for the treatment of children. The best-known of the six springs is the "Richard-Spring" and its water is even exported. The spa itself was once the private property of the princely Metternich family, which built a chateau not far from here.

In the last century Goethe, Alexander Dumas the Elder, Beethoven and Aldabert Stifter were guests at the **chateau.** The adjacent park is decorated with arbours and groups of statues.

Teplá

Teplá Monastery, about 15 km east of Mariánské Lázně, was founded in 1193. It belonged to the Premonstratensian Order and in 1472 a chair of philosophy, physics and mathematics was founded there.

The finest part of the building is the Romanesque Basilica with nave and two aisles (1197). Later reconstruction gave the church a temporary Gothic form, but its present appearance dates from 1720, in which year it was rebuilt to the plans of Kilian Ignaz Dienzenhofer who designed the Prague Baroque style.

C. THE PLZEŇ REGION

Plzeň (Pilsen)

Plzeň (88 km south-west of Prague) is the administrative, cultural and industrial capital of western Bohemia (pop. 160,000).

Its favourable position in the middle of a regular wide basin, with four largish rivers flowing into it, made it as early as the 10th century a lively trade centre. Pilsen was founded by King Václav II in 1295 as a fortified town on a rectangular ground plan. In the town, where German colonists settled, are two monasteries and the Saint Bartholomew's Church on the sites where they can still be seen today. Plzeň still preserves the unspoilt ground plan of a medieval fortified town.

The square Republiky náměstí forms the centre of the town. There rises the **Saint Bartholomew's Church** (1444) with its 343–foot tower, a landmark typical of Plzeň and visible from far away. In this church, built in monumental Gothic when the town was founded, the well-known Gothic tufa figure of the **Pilsener Madonna** is preserved on the altar.

The square is surrounded by houses with Renaissance, Baroque and Empire gables or neo-Gothic façades. On the north side the eye is caught by the **Renaissance Town Hall**. In its top storey is a **Picture Gallery** of works by artists connected with the landscape of Plzeň. In the Dřevěná ulice, which runs into the middle of the east side of the main square, at No 4 stands the patrician residence of the **Gerlach** family (1557); in it is housed a **Folklore Museum** with rich collections. Four different architectural styles can be discerned on the building.

In the Frantiskánská ulice, which also runs into the square, stands the 13th-century **Monastery Church of the Virgin Mary.** Noteworthy here are the cloisters and the 15th-century Saint Barbara Chapel with its beautiful frescoes. Behind the monastery, in the direction of the park which now occupies the square of the old town walls, stands the corner house of the **Town Museum** with a historical section, arts and crafts collections and library. Equally interesting architecturally is the **Saint Anne's Church** (1711). The Smetanova ulice runs from the south side of the square through the so-called little Smetana Gate into the Smetana Park.

Bedřich Smetana was once a pupil at the adjacent Premonstratensian Grammar School.

Plzeň boasts a whole number of houses, the façades of which are adorned by artistic friezes by the Czech master Mikoláš Aleš. Most of the graffiti with historical subjects are on the houses in the Kollárova and the Nerudoa, west and south-west of the main square. Professor Skupa's puppet theatre with the puppets Spejbl and Hurvinek which are famous today all over Europe was also first opened in Plzeň.

Plzeň is a town of heavy industry; its most important works are the V. I. Lenin Works (formerly "Škoda"). These occupy the whole west side of the town.

On the other bank of the Radbuza river stretch the factory buildings of the Pilsner Breweries. Pilsen beer won its universal reputation way back in the Middle Ages. The brewery achieved the peak of this development at the beginning of the last century when the first limited company, later "Urquell", was formed, Because of the countless factory chimneys, which often envelop the whole town in their smoke, Plzeň has been given the epithet "Black".

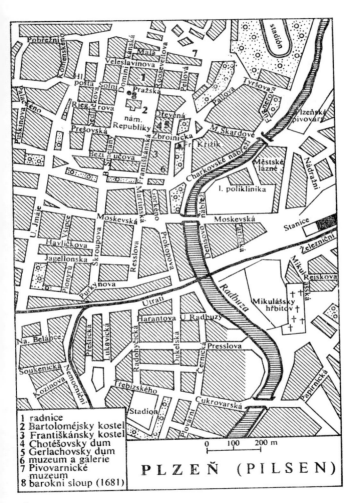

1 radnice
2 Bartoloméjsky kostel
3 Františkánsky kostel
4 Chotěšovsky dum
5 Gerlachovsky dum
6 muzeum a galerie
7 Pivovarnické muzeum
8 barokni sloup (1681)

0   100   200 m

PLZEŇ (PILSEN)

Walks and excursions from Plzeň

Radyně (about 12 km south-west of Plzeň) is a castle ruin. The castle was built in 1348 by the Emperor Charles IV. From the top of the crag (1,864 feet) there is one of the finest views towards the whole of western Bohemia.

At **Hůrka** (1,405 feet), about 12 km from Plzeň, with remains of the oldest Romanesque rotunda in western Bohemia, the Church of Saints Peter and Paul, the foundation walls of two other churches have been exposed.

Buben (about 13 km east), ruins of a stronghold rising above the river Mže near a large dam which forms a 30 km-long reservoir as far as **Stříbro,** a town founded in the 12th–century in the vicinity of silver mines. **Kladruby Monastery,** restored by J. Santini in baroque-gothic style, was founded in 1108. North of Stříbro lies a mountainous region and in its centre is the spa of **Konstantinovy Lázně** whose waters are rich in carbonic gas and have restored thousands of invalids to health. The thermal springs of Konstantinovy Lázně were discovered in the 17th century.

Nepomuk (about 30 km south of Plzeň) is the birthplace of the Vicar General of the Prague Episcopal Court, John of Nepomuk, who was hurled into the Vltava from the Charles Bridge. After the Battle of the White Mountain (1620) the cult of John of Nepomuk was made the main plank of the Jesuits' programme to re-Catholicise the Bohemian people. Kilian Ignaz Dienzenhofer built a **pilgrimage church** on the site of the former birthplace of the Blessed John of Nepomuk (later canonised). In the blackground, on a height, above the town of Nepomuk stands the castle of **Zelená Hora.** 11 km south-west of Nepomuk lies the market town of **Plánice,** where the world-famed inventor of the arc lamp, František Křižík, was born.

Švihov (some 30 km south of Plzeň) is a Water Castle. The mighty castle in the plain was surrounded by the waters of the Uhlava river in times of flood. The castle buildings, the palace and the chapel adorned with a fresco of Saint George are grouped round the high Gothic tower.

Horšovský Týn (about 40 km south-west of Plzeň), a town which, with its **castles,** is under National Trust as an Ancient Monument, is a most interesting place, both culturally and historically. The original castle above the Radbuza river, which stood sentinel on the old trade route from Regensburg to Pilsen, belonged to the Bishops of Prague. The situation of the castle shows that it was probably built in the 13th century on the site of the original 8th–10th century fortress. At the same date the town below the castle began to develop. Castle and town are very well preserved; and here can be found some pre-eminent monuments of the Gothic and Renaissance periods. This applies in particular to the old **Episcopal Palace** with its unique chapel and castle with valuable sgraffiti, built in Renaissance style; the interior is richly decorated with sculpture and wood carving.

Horní Bříza lies about 20 km north of Plzeň on the railway line Plzeň-Duchcov and has the richest deposit of china clay in all Europe. In 1880 the manufacture of fire-proof chamotte bricks and tiles was started here.

Plasy (about 24 km north of Plzeň) is a little town whose centre is the Cistercian **Monastery** founded by Prince Vladislav II in 1144. The finest building is the old **Convent,** designed by Kilian Ignaz Dienzenhofer.

Its foundation walls stand in the current of an arm of the river Střela and are strengthened by 5,000 oak pillars. In the Church of Our Lady are valuable pictures by the Prague Baroque painters K. Škréta and Peter Brandl, besides many excellent wood carvings.

D.   THE BOHEMIAN FOREST

The Bohemian Forest is part of the Sudeten Mountains, which girdle Bohemia and Moravia. The Bohemian Forest is the biggest mountain system of the Sudetes. It is formed by a mountain chain close to the frontier and also by some inland mountain groups running N.W. to S.E. The geological bed of the Bohemian Forest is composed of gneiss above which lie strata of granite and mica. Geographically, the Bohemian Forest begins at the Všerubský Pass and ends in the easternmost part of Bohemia, at Horní Dvořiště.

Some rivers, including the Vltava, have their source in the middle of luxuriant coniferous forests, mainly of pines and firs, which retain moisture; they are also fed by the streams of vast heats and peat-bogs.

Once the Bohemian Forest was impenetrable except by the trade route passes. These however often served an enemy in war. Royal towns where trade was concentrated sprang up along these routes, frontier castles were built to strengthen the defences of the country; free peasants also settled there. Their task was to guard the State frontiers and to bar the invasion of enemies. In early Christian times gold was already buddled in primitive fashion on the banks of the rivers of the Bohemian Forest. Later, in the 13th century, mining was started here. Prospecting for precious and semi-precious metals led to the foundation of settlements in the midst of the frontier forest.

Then in the 18th century the erection of glass works led to further development.

Roads into the Bohemian Forest start from Plzeň and České Budějovice. From these towns there are also good railway and road connections with the most interesting towns in the Bohemian Forest.

Domažlice (50 km south-west of Plzeň, 140 km from Prague) is a town under National Trust as an Ancient

Monument and the geographical centre of the characteristic Chode country.

The town, not far from the Všerubsky průmsk (the Wscherauer
Pass), has witnessed many battles down the centuries. In 1040,
for instance, the Bohemian Prince Břetislav I defeated the army
of the German Emperor Heinrich III. In 1431 the Catholic army
fled with the Papal nuncio at the sound of the Hussite hymn
chanted by the troops, a tenth of their number, led by Prokop
Holý, the successor of Jan Žižka of Trocnov.

The entrance to the town on the east side is through
the gate on which one can read the inscription:
"Domažlice, stout wall of the Fatherland, what thou
hast once been shalt thou be again in the future".

The elongated main square is surrounded on both
sides by historically interesting houses with arcades
and Renaissance, Baroque and Empire gables. The
north side is dominated by the Baroque **Cathedral**
(built in 1747 by Christoph Dienzenhofer) and the
185–foot tower, from which there is a view over the
town. Not far from the Town Hall opposite is another,
similar tower, the remains of the **Chode Castle.** Here
were once kept the valuable documents known as the
"Chode Privileges", which were the reason for the
historic rebellion of the Chodes against Prince
Laminger in the 17th century. The town of Domažlice
is one of the most beautiful towns in Bohemia. It is
principal town of the

Chodsko, a region interesting for its folk lore and one which
has played its part in the national history and been often mentioned in literature. From Hrádek downwards, where stands the
statue of Jan Kozina, the defender of the Chode Privileges and
leader of the rebellion against injustice mentioned above, a
panorama opens over the villages of the Chodsko. Another,
equally fine view can be had from "Výhledy", where the memorial to Jindřich Šimon Baar, the Chode writer, stands.

Mount Čerchov (3,432 feet) which belongs to the Bohemian
Forest massif forms the background to the whole Chode landscape.

Klatovy (Klattau). The town lies 30 km east of Domažlice, 45 km south of Plzeň and 135 km south-west of Prague. It is dominated by the 247 ft Black Tower (built in 1557); the tower clock dates from 1759. From the top of the tower there is a fine expansive view of the surrounding country. Opposite the tower stands the Jesuit Church (1655–1679), built in Baroque style by Kilian Ignaz Dienzenhofer. Under the church are the well-known catacombs with the mummies of members of the Jesuit Order. East of the square rises the so-called White Tower and next to it a Gothic church, a row of historic and well-preserved houses and the Town Hall.

The town of Klatovy is specially noted for its cultivation of carnations. It is also called the "Gate of the Bohemian Forest" because it is the best starting point in the direction of the Bohemian Forest region round Železná Ruda.

Železná Ruda (45 km south of Klatovy) was founded near the now disused iron ore mines. Its only historical monument is the typically Baroque Church in the main square; it has a hexagonal cupola shaped like an onion.

Železná Ruda is a much frequented starting point for hikers far and wide in the surrounding country, one of the most favoured parts of the Bohemian Forest.

In the woods along the highway, high above the town of Železná Ruda, is the summer resort of **Spičák** and it is but a short distance to the mountain tarns left by the retreating glaciers; notably the Black Lake, which can also be reached by automobile.

The climb to the top of Mount Pancíř (4,006 feet) is also enjoyable, with a view of the highest peak of the Bohemian Forest, Mount Javor (4,775 feet), which is already in Bavarian territory.

Velhartice lies on the railway line Klatovy-Sušice. Among its sights the Castle and an interesting weir bridge, supported by five pillars and joining two isolated towers, is worthy of mention.

Sušice, 27 km south-east of Klatovy, lies picturesquely in a valley basin at the foot of Mt. Svatobor (2,772 ft). All buildings of interest are to be found in the main square. These are especially the 16th-century Museum, built in the style of the Italian Renaissance, and near it the Baroque house with Renaissance gable and a fresco. The finest view of the surrounding country can be had from the near-by "Hill of the Guardian Angel" (1,818 ft), from the chapel on the top. The town of Sušice is known as the centre of the "Solo" match production. It is the starting point for roads into the middle of the Bohemian Forest.

Kašperské Hory (11 km south-west of Sušice) is an ancient mining town below the Castle of Kašperk. Here the Otava river flows through a romantic valley. The Otava is fed by two streams, the Křemelná and the Vydre, which flow into the river up-stream from Rejštejn. The Vydra valley is specially wild and romantic. It begins upstream at the "Antigel" farm and ends downstream at the Čeňkova sawmill. The bed of the river is full of granite blocks in which whirlpools have eroded hollows.

The ruined **Rábí** Castle (about 10 km from Sušice) is the biggest ruined castle in Bohemia. The entrance is by the Žižka Gate. The interior of the castle is buttressed by 20 ft thick walls. From the fourth castle gate a passage leads into the three-storied cellar, built into the limestone rock. The centre of the castle is a rectangular tower which offers a magnificent view of the surrounding country.

Strakonice (70 km south-west of Plzeň, 110 km south-west of Prague) began as a little town below a castle, founded by the Maltese Knights of the Cross (the Order of St. John).

A round tower rears above the old part of the castle; it is known as the "Rumpál" tower. The projecting "Jelenka" tower embellishes the castle palace. In the castle church are valuable pictures by the Baroque masters Peter Brandl and Karel Škréta.

Vimperk (33 km south-west of Strakonice along the Volyňka river), crowned by an ancient castle, lies picturesquely at the foot of the mountain. In the narrow valley stands a printing works in which prayer-books of all religions are printed in every language.

At **Kubova Huť,** 17 km from Vimperk, the railway line climbs to 3,310 ft; starting point for a walk to Mt. Boubín (4,494 ft) where the remains of a virgin forest cover 100 acres.

The little mountain town of **Volary** (20 km south-east of Vimperk) lies in a broad pastureland valley basin; there are typical mountain barns in the meadows. Peculiar to the place are the wooden houses with wide, obtuse-angled roofs weighted with stones They were built in the 15th century by the settlers from Styria.

Prachatice (15 km north-east of Volary, 145 km south of Prague and 38 km west of České Budějovice) is famous not only for its picturesque situation, but also chiefly for the medieval character of its main square and buildings.

It lies at the foot of Mount Libín (3,600 feet) from which an enchanting view of the Bohemian Forest panorama can be had from the belvedere.

The royal town of Prachatice arose in 1322 on the site of a former reloading station for merchandise. It was chiefly the "Golden Road of Prachatice", running from Bavaria to Bohemia across the Bohemian Forest, that was responsible for the growth of the town. In particular salt was carried into Bohemia along this route. We still have a reminder today of the mule caravans in the "Caravan Bell", the sound of which told errant merchants the position of the town. Even now the bell is rung every day at 10 p.m.

From the north the **Rosenberg Gate**, with inscriptions and a fresco depicting a mounted horseman, leads into the old embattled town.

Inside the gate the medieval **Horní třída** runs off to the right. On the left side of it stands the old school at which Jan Hus was supposed to have been a pupil. The noblest monument of Prachatice is the **St. James's Church** which was already standing here in the 11th century. Its present appearance dates from 1507, in which year the building of the taller of the two Renaissance towers was finished. Gothic stonemasonry decoration is particularly effective in the richly decorated portal, in the church vestibule, in the lofty cross vaulting of the nave and in the presbytery. Artistic wood-carving is especially to be noticed on the Gothic tabernacle of the High Altar.

A short street leads into the main square, on the west side of which the **Old** and the **New Town Halls** stand side by side. The frescoes of the New Town Hall represent the busy traffic on the "Golden Road". The old Town Hall, built in 1571, is artistically the most interesting edifice in Prachatice.

The two-storied building is decorated all over with frescoes accompanied by rhymed inscriptions. On the band just below the eaves of the roof the eight Virtues are depicted. Lower down we see scenes from the Old Testament. Two of these, the most striking, represent a corrupt judge with legal formulae beneath. On the opposite side of the square is a house with frescoes depicting an ancient battle.

Husinec (6 km north of Prachatice) is a little town where Magister Jan Hus was born on 6 July 1369.

Only one small room with a worn floor, a table, some book-shelves and a tiny red kitchen are preserved of the original house. In the other rooms is housed a revered museum of the martyr of Constance.

The town of **Vodňany** (24 km north-east of Prachatice) lies in the South Bohemian basin. Round about the town are numerous ponds. Vodňany is the seat of the School of Fishery. The slender Gothic Church in the main square is decorated by artistically executed sgraffiti representing the "Bohemian Heaven" (they depict the patron saint of Bohemia) by the Czech master Mikoláš Aleš.

Not far from Vodňany is the village of **Chelčice**, where in the 15th century the religious thinker and spiritual founder of the Bohemian Brotherhood, Petr Chelčický, lived.

18 km north of Vodňany on the highway we come to the town of Písek.

Round trip through the Bohemian Forest

Domažlice—Klenčí-Výhledy (14 km)—Domažlice (28 km)—Klatovy (61 km)—Železná Ruda (105 km)—Špičák (110 km)—Walk for pedestrians following the red signs on Mount Pancíř (3 km) or along the road to the Black Lake (6 km)—Železná Ruda-Běšiny (142 km)—Velahrtice (150 km)—Sušice (160 km)—Rábí (178 km)—Sušice-Rejštejn-Čeňkova sawmill (197 km)—along the Vydra to the Turner Hut (202 km)—Antigl Mount Quilda-Vimperk (230 km)—Kubova Hut (240 km)—Zátoň (248 km)—from here follow the blue sign on foot into the primitive forest of Boubín-Lanora-Volary (261 km)—Prachatice (277 km)—Husinec (286 km)—Bavorov-Vodňany (310 km)—Strakonice (336 km).

Hiking through the Bohemian Forest
(using means of transport)

Domažlice, following the path with red signs, via Hrádek to Výhledy (11 km) on the road to Klenčí (4 km). By rail to Domažlice. By rail to Klatovy. By rail to Zelená Lhota, by the green-marked footpath to Prenet (3 km), by the red-marked path to Železná Ruda (5 km). By train to Špičák, by a side-road to the Black Lake and back (12 km). By train via Klatovy to Sušice. By train to Žichovice, from there on foot to Rábí (ruined castle) and back (6 km). By train to Sušice. By car to Velhartice and back. By motor bus via Rejštejn to Čeňkova sawmill. By side-roads along the Vydra to the Turner hostel and back (10 km). By motor bus to Sušice. By train via Horažďovice to Strakonice. By train via Vimperk to Kubova Huť. By the blue-marked footpath to Boubín; halt on the blue-marked path through the Boubín primitive forest on the railway line at Zátoň (8 km). By train to Volary. By train in the direction of Prachatice to the halt at Rohanov. By the blue-marked path up Mount Libín (3 km). Down the red-marked path to Prachatice (5 km). By the red-marked footpath to Husinec (6 km). By the highroad to Husinec (3 km). By train to Vodňany.

4. SOUTH BOHEMIA

For centuries, this region has been Czech territory *par excellence*, and it has a rich and eventful past. It was here that the Hussite revolutionary movement, influenced by the Reformation ideas of Magister Jan Hus, broke out, with repercussions far beyond the frontiers of Bohemia.

This undulating, wooded region has several ponds which are used for fishbreeding. South Bohemia might be divided into five parts, centred respectively round the towns of **Tábor, Písek, Třeboň, České Budějovice** and **Český Krumlov.**

List of sights and places of interest

National Trust Towns: Tábor, Jindřichův Hradec, Český Krumlov, České Budějovice.

National Parks: Stará řeka, Velký and Malý Tiský fishponds (Třeboň district).

State-owned castles and forts: Český Krumlov, Rožmberk Hluboká (České Budějovice), Jindřichův Hradec, Blatná, Zvíkov Castle (Písek), Orlík Castle.

Tourist regions: Surroundings of Písek and Otava valley, Lužniec valley, fish-ponds near Třeboň, roundabout Český Krumlov.

Other places of interest: Zlatá Koruna monastery (Č. Krumlov), Římov (Č. Budějovice), Trocnov (birthplace of Jan Žižka in the district of Trhové Sviny), Bechyně, Podolsko (Písek).— Fishponds at Rožmberk, Svět (Třeboň), Bezdrev (Č. Budějovice), Orlík and Lipno.

Round trips by car

1. To the castles Zvíkov and Orlík: České Budějovice-Hluboká (10 km)—Týn nad Vltava (33 km)—Albrechtice (43 km) Písek (61 km)—Zvíkov (79 km)—Varvažov (84 km)—Orlík (94 km)—Zalužany (102 km)—Mýšlovice, junction (110 km)—

Orlík dam (123 km)—Čimelice (163 km)—Mirotice (168 km)—
Písek (186 km)—Vodňany (207 km)—České Budějovice (247 km).

2. *To Tábor and Písek:* České Budějovice-Hluboká (10 km)—
Veselí on the Lužnice (37 km)—Soběslav (45 km)—Tábor (65
km)—Bechyně (95 km)—Bernartice (106 km)—Podolsko (Bridge
115 km)—Písek (126 km)— Vodňany (147 km)—České Budějovice (177 km).

3. *To Jindřichův Hradec, Český Krumlov, Třeboň and sur-
roundings:* Český Budějovice-Lišov (11 km)—Lomnice on the
Lužnice (22 km)—Veselí on the Lužnice (35 km)—Jindřichův
Hradec (61 km)—Třeboň (90 km)—Borovany (110 km)—Trocnov
(112 km)—Velešín (130 km)—Český Krumlov (142 km)—Zlatá
Koruna (147 km)—České Budějovice (166 km); or from Třeboň
(90 km); České Velenice (115 km)—Nove Hrady (125 km)—
Žumberk (131 km)—Trhové Sviny (137 km)—Trocnov (151 km)
—České Budějovice (167 km).

4. *To the Lipno dam* (Lake of the Bohemian Forest): České
Budějovice—Řimov (21 km)—Zlatá Koruna (32 km)—Český
Krumlov (39 km)—Rožmberk (64 km) Vyšši Brod (73 km)—
Lippa Dam (81 km)—Frymburk (90 km)—Cerná (100 km)—
Hořice in the Bohemian Forest (107 km)—Česky Krumlov (122
km)—České Budějovice (147 km).

A. TÁBOR

History: Tábor lies 88 km south of Prague. It was founded in
the 15th century as the regional centre where the Hussite Revolution, started off by the teachings of Magister Jan Hus, broke
out. In 1420 the people of Tábor introduced a communistic
society. Their motto was: "In Tábor nothing belongs to me or
to you, for every one has an equal share in everything". That is
why large tuns stood in the market place, into which newcomers
dropped all their personal possessions and then went to work
wherever they were sent. The people settled their theological
problems for themselves; hence the familiar remark of the Papal
Legate in 1451: "a simple woman in Tábor knows more than an
Italian priest". Militarily, Tábor's defence was in the hands of
three elected captains; one of them was Jan Žižka of Trocnov.
The people's army would make a sortie from Tábor and return
to it after victorious battles. Apparently, the Hussite religious-
social experiment ended with the Battle of Lipan in 1434 which
was won by the nobility. But the Hussite ideas lived on and
the Bohemian Brotherhood was founded on them. The red

chalice still flew on the black flags under which the peasant serfs fought against their lords in the 16th and 17th centuries. Later the town took part in the armed rebellion against the Hapsburgs and in 1621 Tábor was the last of the towns captured by the victors of the Battle of the White Mountain. But even the enforced Catholicisation and oppression of later times failed to break the town (20,000 inhab.).

The **Old Town** of Tábor, surrounded by battlements, has remained as it was alongside the New Town. It stands on a bulwark below which flows the Lužnice. Its typically narrow, window streets where deliberately designed to facilitate the defence of the town, in the event of a forced entry by the enemy. In the Žižková Square stands a **monument** to Jan Žižka of Trocnov and the original **stone table** on which communion was celebrated with bread and wine. Underneath the whole square and the Town Hall extend vast subterranean passages and cellars, which were used as hiding places from the enemy. In the **Town Hall,** built in 1521 in late Gothic style, the **Hussite Museum** is housed. Another **museum** devoted to the settlement of Tábor, is in the Tábor castle of Kotnov.

North-east of Tábor lies the pond called Jordan, in which the inhabitants used to baptise their children.

Excursions from Tábor

Sezimovo Ústí (4 km south of Tábor) stands on the site of a small 14th century town preceding Tábor. Today there are large works belonging to the "Svit" metal industry with modern settlements.

Kozí Hrádek (6 km south-east of Tábor), a ruined castle, where Jan Hus stayed at the beginning of the 14th century. This place means to the Czechs very much what the Wartburg, where Martin Luther stayed, means to the Germans.

Bechyně (31 km by electric train, 18 km by road, south-west of Tábor) is a town with a very beautiful chateau, picturesquely situated on the Lužnice river. Today the chateau is used as a convalescent home by the Czechoslovak Academy of Sciences. Not far from the chateau in a monastery church there is a remarkable Gothic vaulted ceiling (diamond vaulting). The **church** in the square of Bechyně contains a priceless picture of the three Magi by Peter Brandl. Typical of Bechyně, interesting and of historical value, are the 16th-century **tiled roofs**. There is also a well-known School of Ceramics in the town and outside it mud baths. The Lužnice is spanned by a high ferro-concrete bridge of daring construction.

B. PÍSEK

The river Otava, on the banks of which gold was buddled in bygone times, flows through the town. Písek sprang up when a castle was built here in the 13th century. The 13th-century stone bridge is the oldest **stone bridge** in Bohemia. Among the old houses in the large central square we see, next to the Baroque **Town Hall,** the courtyard of **Pisek castle.** In the Gothic castle hall are valuable 15th-century **frescoes** representing a jousting tournament.

The **Church** with its 244 ft high tower was built in the 13th century in early Gothic style. On a side altar is a 15th-century picture of the Madonna of Písek. The view of the town walls and the church tower from an island in the river is very picturesque. The buildings of Písek castle are also most effectively seen from the river. The **Town Museum** contains a great number of historical objects, especially miniatures painted on porcelain by Jan Zacharias Quast.

The violinist and teacher Otakar Ševčík and the poet Frána Šrámek lived at Písek. **Mirotice**, not far from Písek, was the birthplace of the painter Mikoláš Aleš.

Because of its agreeable climate, influenced by its situation with deep woods all round, Písek was a favourite health resort in the last century for those in search of rest. Today there is also industrial activity, chiefly the Jiter Textile concern and a harmonica factory.

Excursions from Písek

1. Zvíkov Castle (24 km north of Písek) on account of its majestic situation above the river amid densy woods has been called the "queen of the castles of Bohemia". One enters the castle with its three gates through a high round watch-tower, bearing the escutcheon of its owner of that time—a white swan and a red rose. The oldest part of the castle is the square Marcomanni tower, so called because possible the Marcomanni were originally installed there. The adjacent palace with a courtyard enclosed by arcades, is typical early Gothic. Its frescoes are famous.

Since the building of the Orlík dam, Zvíkov has become a lake stronghold; the magnificent Otava and Vltava valleys have been transformed into a large lake whose bays run deep into the interior of the plateau. Opposite Zvíkovské Podhradí two bridges have been built, one across the Otava, the other across the Vltava.

2. Orlík is a castle that used to belong to the Schwarzenberg family and is surrounded by an extensive park. Its rooms have been turned into a Museum which contains valuable collections. On the ground floor of the castle is a collection of souvenirs given by the Emperor Napoleon to Prince Schwarzenberg, the victor of the Battle of Leipzig. Among the most interesting is a plastic map of the Battle of Austerlitz.

Orlík castle is surrounded by the picturesque bays of the lake; steam launches can go as far as Zvíkov.

Orlík dam, the largest hydraulic work in Czechoslovakia, measures 328 feet in height and 1,510 feet in length. It was built in 1961, with the aid of 1,200,000 cubic metres of concrete. Behind the dam lies a 68-km long reservoir with an area of 126 square kilometres. The hydroelectric power station has four Kaplan turbines. Thanks to a boat-lift, navigation on the Vltava can be continued without interruption (from the Slapy dam). Passenger transport to Zvíkov and Orlík castles is by steam launches.

3. Blatná 30 km south-west of Orlík, 25 km north-west of Písek. The town lies in a hollow between wooded hills with many fish-ponds and is known for its rose gardens. It is embellished by a castle that was once a flood refuge; it was built on a small island between two arms of the little Lomnice river.

4. Albrechtice (18 km east of Písek). Baroque church decorated with romanesque frescoes, in the middle of the local cemetery; the latter is surrounded by chapels whose walls are decorated with paintings by regional artists and with original verses.

5. Sudoměř (15 km south-west of Písek). Set in the midst of pools, a granite monument to Jan Žižka, the Hussite leader who defeated the troops of the "iron lords" on this spot in 1420. To the north, near the Řežabinec lake (zoological and botanical reservation), at a place called "Pikárna", a workshop has been discovered containing primitive quartz tools from the Mesolithic Age. Above the Otava behind "Pikárna", is the commune of Staré Kestřany with its well-preserved medieval bastions (13th–15th centuries).

6. Cervena (12 km north-east of Pisek). Holiday centre and health resort. 223-ft high railway bridge built in 1889, the highest structure of the kind in the former Austrian monarchy. Before the reservoir lake was filled, the Gothic church was moved above the level of the water.

7. Podolsko. In 1939 the old chain bridge was replaced with a new road bridge supported by a single arch.

C. TŘEBOŇ

The town, in the centre of the South Bohemia basin which abounds in fishponds, was founded in the 13th century. The mediaeval character of the town inland has given Třeboň status as an ancient monument protected by the state.

Three **gates** in the **town walls,** which are very well-preserved, lead to the square. In the **Market Place,** adorned by houses with Renaissance and Baroque gables, stands a plain **castle** where the famous archives of Třebon are kept. The Long Corridor is associated with legends of the White Chatelaine. Next to the **Augustinian monastery,** in which is the altar by the Třebon master of 1380, considered the greatest work of Czech Gothic painting. The altarpieces are in the Prague National Gallery. In the adjoining cloister are 14th- and 15th-century **murals.**

The once unhealthy marshland round Třeboň was exploited as early as the Middle Ages for the planning of extensive fishponds, which completely altered the character of the landscape and created the conditions for a profitable pisciculture. Třeboň is still known as the centre of the Czech fish-breeding economy. Quite close to the town, to the south, covering an area of 540 acres, lies the **Svět fish-pond**, on the shores of which a model sports centre has been erected. It is used for training in water sports.

North of the town lies the largest Bohemian **fish-pond Rožmberk**, laid out between 1584 and 1590. The surface of water, comprising 1,790 acres, retained by a centuries-old oaken dam, measures 2,600 m long, 80 m wide and 12 m deep. When the ponds are emptied every three years, it is a great event throughout the district. The fishing lasts three days and the catch is over 1,000 quintals of excellent Třeboň carp. Besides these fish-ponds there are many smaller ones in the region, occupying altogether an area of more than 750 acres. The fish-ponds are linked by many canals which were already constructed in the Middle Ages.

Excursions from Třeboň

1. Stráž on the Nežárka (14 km north-east of Třeboň) is situated in wooded country. The opera singer, Emma Destin, lived and died in its chateau and was known as the "black lady of Stráž".

2. Jindřichův Hradec (28 km north-east of Třeboň, 133 km south of Prague). The chief sight of the town is the State-owned **castle**, once a fortress, built in the 13th century. The best place to see it from is the fish-pond bridge. Many legends are associated with this castle in connection with the White Chatelaine, Perchta von Rosenberg. The castle has three court-yards. The square **Menhart tower** is a valuable monument of Vladislav Gothic. In the 16th century Italian architects and builders erected the so-called **New Building** with its Renaissance gables and chimneys, arcades in the main palace and a charming pavilion in the gardens. In the **Chapel of St. George** is a well-known fresco of the legend of the saint (1338). Among the collections of the castle are pictures by the famous Baroque painters Peter Brandl and Karel Škréta; also a 14th-century **Madonna** painted on wood. In the castle archives is the biggest collection of autographs in Central Europe. Bedřich Smetana lived in the brewery below the castle. In the near-by museum there are various collections; of particular interest is the unique crib by Kryr with some hundred mechanically mobile figures.

From the main square a street leads to the **Church of St. John the Baptist** near the Minorite Monastery. The nave has a vaulted ceiling in Vladislav Gothic style. The walls and the roof of the side-aisles and the cloister are painted with 14th-century frescoes (restored). The adjacent St. Nicholas' Chapel is also architecturally interesting.

3. Veselská Blata, a region in the environs of the town of **Veselí** on the Lužnice (25 km north of Třeboň, 120 km south of Prague) is a vast region of pastureland, with characteristic, luxuriant flora, dotted with peatbogs. The surrounding villages are remarkable for their "Blata farmsteads", buildings with typical Baroque gables.

4. Landštejn (30 km south-east of Jindřichův Hradec by Nová Bystřice). Imposing ruins of a stronghold which belonged, in turn, to the Rožmberk family, the lords of Hradec and the Krajířové of Krajek. From the top of the tower we have a splendid panoramic view of the frontier region, to the borders of Bohemia, Moravia and Austria.

5. Červená Lhota (15 km south-west of Jindřichův Hradec). A small Renaissance castle built on an island in the middle of a lake.

D. ČESKÉ BUDĚJOVICE

České Budějovice is the metropolis of South Bohemia, the regional capital, railway junction on the line from Prague to Vienna and an important centre of light industry. The town arose in 1265 and has a rich history, specially from Hussite times. It has preserved its special atmosphere and architectural beauty until today. (70,000 inhab.).

Most remarkable is the square **Market Place** with its regular arcades on all sides of the square and the Baroque **Samson fountain** in the centre. The **Town Hall** is adorned by allegorical figures. The oldest church building is the **Dominican Church** in early Gothic style, built at the same time as the town itself. In the north-east corner of the square stands the 327-foot belfry, the **Black Tower.** Its bottom part is Gothic, with a passage round it supported on Tuscan pillars and a Renaissance cupola. The near-by **Saint Nicholas Church** after many conversions remains Baroque. Among the remains of the Middle Ages we also notice the high gables of 16th-century butchers' shops.

Not far off, near the former town wall, the tall roof of the **Salt Chamber** stands out, with its jagged gable. This building was used as a storage for salt brought from the Salzkammergut and sent on to Prague by the Vltava. Near the salt store is a Gothic **armoury.** Three **towers** which were part of the fortifications remain on different sides of the town. An arm of the river encircles the historic centre of the town.

In the **Linz suburb** a plaque marks the terminus of the old horse-drawn tram, the first on the continent linking Linz in Austria with České Budějovice.

Today České Budějovice is chiefly important for its industry: principally the pencil works (Hardtmuth) and the wood industry. In the food industry South Bohemia is known for its mills and lemonade works.

Excursions from České Budějovice

1. Hluboká on the Vltava (10 km north-west of České Budějovice), magnificent castle with a history going back to the 11th century. It took on its present form only in 1840 when it was reconstructed in Tudor-Gothic style. There are hardly any collections to compare with those at Hluboká. The façade of the castle is richly decorated with ornamentation. In the hall hang famous **tapestries** and in the corridor our attention is riveted by a Baroque sledge and the **Eggenberg carriage** (1638). Of the 900 **pictures** in the 144 rooms of the castle the most valuable are the 15th- and 16th-century religious pictures, the "Twelve Months" by the school of Van Dyck, eleven hunting scenes by **Snyders** and five landscapes with game by John George Hamilton, court painter to the Emperor Charles IV. In the armoury stand the statues of Adolf Schwarzenberg, conqueror of the Turks at the Battle of Raab in 1598, and of Karl Schwarzenberg, the victor of Leipzig in 1813.

In the former riding-school of the castle is the monumental South Bohemian **Aleš Gallery** which shows at a glance the works of **South Bohemian artists,** sculptors and painters from the early Middle Ages down to the present day. The collection is particularly rich in works by Mikuláš Aleš with numerous subjects drawn from South Bohemian history, chiefly the Hussite period.

The castle itself is picturesquely situated in the middle of an **English park** on a slight eminence above the little town of the same name. The Vltava flows round it to the east and then on through extensive woods and country well-stocked with game. The surroundings of Hluboká resemble a well-kept park-like zoo and there are many fish-ponds. The **Bezdrev** fish-pond occupying 1,300 acres is the second largest Czechoslovak pond after Rožmberk. There is a harbour for sailing boats at Bezdrev. Not far from there is the hunting lodge **Ohrada,** reached by a long avenue of oak-trees. The rooms of this lodge are used as a Hunting Museum. In the hall are ten pictures by Hamilton with hunting subjects of incalculable value. The ceiling is decorated with frescoes by Werle depicting the legend of Diana. Notable are the chairs made of antlers and carved with scenes of the chase. In the zoological collections are grotesquely mounted stuffed animals.

2. **Trocnov** (30 km south-east of České Budějovice), originally the court of a landed nobleman, was the birthplace of the Czech national hero, Jan Žižka of Trocnov. The story goes that the Hussite leader was born during a thunderstorm under an oaktree north-west of here in the forest. A granite obelisk has been erected on this legendary spot.

3. **Římov** (20 km south of České Budějovice) is a place of pilgrimage with Stations of the Cross along the way to the shrine. These unique lifesize scenes and groups of statuary (early 17th century) were set up against the natural background of the surrounding landscape.

4. Zlatá Koruna (26 km south of České Budějovice), a Cistercian monastery right on the bank of the Vltava, founded by the Czech King Přemysl Otakar II in 1269 in memory of the victory at Kressenbrunn. A thorn from the crown of thorns, a gift from the French King Saint Louis, is preserved here as a relic. The imposing **abbey church,** the third largest in Bohemia, is built in early Gothic style. Inside the cathedral our attention is caught by the copies of statuary by Maximilian Brokoff and the tomb of Přemysl Otakar II. The most interesting painting is a 14th-century panel of the **Madonna.** Noteworthy is the circular window in the transept; also the chapter hall with the corbels of the cross-vaulting carved as portraits of Přemysl Otakar II and Queen Kunhuta. The gravestones of the abbots of the monastery can be seen in the wall.

5. Žumberk (30 km south-east of České Budějovice) is a village surrounded by medieval fortifications and keeps.

E. ČESKÝ KRUMLOV

The town lies on the Vltava on the slopes of **Mount Kleť** (Schöninger), 3,577 feet. The course of the river divides the town into several parts, one of which is dominated by the massive **castle.** Krumlov is one of the most picturesquely situated places in Czechoslovakia, 25 km south of České Budějovice.

Český Krumlov started in the 12th century as a town below the mighty fortress. In the 16th century Italian architects converted the castle into a Renaissance noble's seat. The whole property including the town and the castle was bought in 1600 by the Hapsburg Emperor Rudolf II. He gave the castle as a residence to his irresponsible natural son, Don Julius of Austria, who caused a number of scandals here; among them was the bestial murder of Margarethe, his bathkeeper's daughter. In 1719

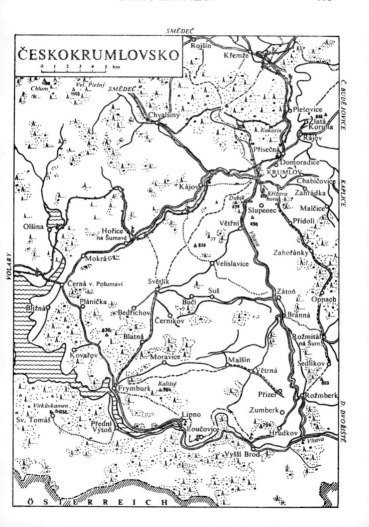

the Schwarzenberg family acquired Krumlov and made Český Krumlov the centre of their domain.

The historically interesting town is divided by the river into the **Old Town** and the **Latrán suburb,** in bygone days the town below the fortress. There are in Latrán ancient houses with many medieval remains of masonry and coats of arms. The **Minorite Monastery** with the **Corpus Christi Church** complete the beauty of the town. Near the bridge across the Vltava the typical Krumlov **watch-tower** stands on a crag.

The **Town Hall street,** from which we enjoy a lovely view of the castle, leads into the **Market Place.** On one side of this stands the Renaissance **Town Hall** with its Gothic vestibule. A number of narrow lanes with architecturally notable houses lead off from the street and the market place in different directions. The Horní ulice runs past the **Church of Saint Vitus,** built in the 14th century with Gothic ornamentation. The last buildings in the Horní ulice are the former Prelate's Palace and the Jesuit Seminary.

We enter the **castle** through the Latrán Gate, above which is the inscription: "Audi, vide et tace, si vis vivere in pace" (listen, look and keep silent if you wish to live in peace). In the second courtyard we notice the mythological decoration of the administrative building, the guard-room and in a corner on a rock the **Hrádek tower.** We can see the town in all its details from the passage round the tower. We enter the first of two courtyards of the upper castle, which is also decorated with frescoes, through a passage. From here we come to the **castle's art collections.** Several rooms are filled with various objects, tapestries, pictures and carvings. The last courtyard is surrounded by angular buildings with bays, decorated with coats of arms. The high **stone bridge** (1764), from which there is a good view of the town, is composed of three covered passages, one above the other. Two of these lead into the curious, well-preserved 18th century **theatre** and the third into the gardens of the little pleasure palace "Bellaria" (1706–1708). The fish-pond was constructed in 1686 and the Riding School in 1745.

South of Krumlov

Rožmberk on the Vltava (25 km south of Český Krumlov), a state-owned castle, formerly a stronghold. It consists of the new 16th-century **castle** and the original 13th century **stronghold,** which still preserves its Gothic appearance. In the rooms of this remarkable castle are rare collections and a gallery with pictures of Crusaders. The most notable room is certainly the large armoury with a panelled ceiling. The old town below the castle has also some interesting ancient buildings.

Vyšší Brod (40 km south of Česky Krumlov) is notable for its **monastery,** founded in 1259 for the Cistercian Order. The monastery was under the protection of the Rožmberk family and members of the family were buried there. The monastery buildings are surrounded by a wall like a fortress.

The **Monastery Church** (1259) has a slender tower, 274 feet high, on the façade side. The ground plan of the church is in the shape of a cross and there are a nave and two aisles. In the wall is the marble tombstone of the founder, Peter Vok of Rožmberk. Formerly in the Byzantine chapel of the presbytery the 14th-century picture of the **Madonna of Vyšší Brod** (by Wurmser) was transferred a few years ago to the National Gallery in Prague Castle. The **chapter hall** with diamond vaulting and richly ornate windows adjoins the sacristy. The **cloister** with variously shaped windows is a splendid work of mature Gothic.

The monastery **library** is surprising; it has many first impressions, a globe, a 1720 map of Bohemia and murals illustrating "The Judgment of Solomon". There are particularly valuable works in the **picture gallery**, such as a "Holy Family" by Raphael, works by Rembrandt, Karel Škréta, Peter Brandl, a series of paintings by Vyšší Brod masters, besides many carvings and curiosities. The most precious jewel in the **treasure chamber** is a 22 cm high cross of gold and silver, set with 205 pearls and 100 oriental gems; this is presumed to be an 8th-century Byzantine work.

Upstream from Vyšší Brod in the bed of the Vltava lies a great heap of granite blocks with cliff walls rising above them. Still further upstream the **Lipno Dam** was built, at the highest point of the "Vltava cascades", with a reservoir 40 km long and 15 km wide.

The lake has an area of 5,000 hectares. The underground hydroelectric power station, with a 650 foot long slanting tunnel leading to it, results in a saving of 46 waggons of coal a day. Splendid boat excursion on the reservoir lake to the graphite mines of Černá or to Horní Planá, the birthplace of the poet Adalbert Stifter. A modern road goes from Lipno to **Černá** (one can return by Krumlov) and **Volary** (page 136) in the heart of a beautiful forest landscape.

F. NAVIGATION ON THE LUŽNICE AND THE VLTAVA

The whole stretch is 266 km long, 121 km on the Lužnice and 145 km on the Vltava. Boats are transported by rail from **Veselí** on the Lužnice to **Suchdol** on the Lužnice, from here the river is navigable even at low water level, as it feeds many fish-ponds with water.

Boating on the Lužnice

The first section is through beautiful pasture-land as far as Pilař farm where the Zlatá stoka (Golden Canal) branches off to the left. At Magdalene the Nová řeka (New River) canal runs off to the right from the Lužnice to the Nežárka. The continuation of the Lužnice flows through charming scenery, but this section is difficult to navigate; it ends where the river empties into the Rožmberk fish-pond. This section is full of natural obstacles, such as fallen tree-trunks, reeds and sandbanks. This part of the river is actually a natural park, known as the Stará řeka (Old river). Crossing the Rožmberk pond is most enjoyable, especially when a fresh breeze makes waves on the water. The crossing ends at the Electricity Works. The Lužnice winds through meadows to the town of **Soběslav** (with many buildings of interest); the slender tower is visible from far away. Beyond Soběslav the pine-clad slopes descend to the river and accompany us to **Tábor**. The river is part of the beautiful panorama of the town. The Lužnice flows under the New Bridge below Kotnov Castle into a deep, wooded valley which follows the river to its confluence with the Vltava. At the Klokoty pilgrimage shrine the river is choppy because of rapids. From here a tourist path runs beside the river to where it flows into the Vltava. The path passes the ruined castle of Příbenice. In the widening valley above a tiny village are the ruins of Castle Dobronice. The river flows quietly under a ferro-concrete bridge, from which point the town of **Bechyně** with its picturesque castle can be seen.

The Lužnice flows into the Vltava near the village of Koloděj. There is a typical Martyrs' Column at the confluence. There is a relatively feeble current all the way along the Lužnice and a number of weirs, 36 in all, over which boats have to be carried at low water, are something of a hindrance.

Navigation on the Vltava

The Lužnice flows into the Vltava at the highest point of the Orlík dam whose lake extends as far as the town of Týn on the Vltava; there, in the Middle Ages, salt and other goods brought by boat, were trans-shipped. Shipping was done mostly by rafts which travelled along the waters of the Lužnice and the Vltava from the Bohemian Forest to Prague. To facilitate the passage of boats, rafts and other craft of this kind, locks and dams were placed at various points of the Vltava. On the return trip, the empty boats were towed by horses along the tow-paths which skirt the two banks in places. The first horse-tram in the world was built between Linz and České Budějovice for the transport of salt. The building of a series of hydroelectric dams on the Vltava will make that river navigable along practically the whole of its course.

So far, motor boats only navigate some sectors (for instance, on the lake of Slapy, between Slapy and Kamýk; on the lake of Orlík, between Orlík dam and Orlík and Zvíkov castles; and on the lake of Lipno, between Lipno and Horní Planá).

Description of the trip: at the confluence of the Lužnice and the Vltava we see, on our left, the pilgrimage place of **Nezdášov**. The lake extends from below the small church of Saint John to the bridge of Podolsko and the railway bridge of Červená. Behind the solitary church of Červená the Vltava describes a number of large bends and then runs through dense forests. On the left, behind the bridge across the Vltava, we glimpse the slender tower of **Zvíkov castle**. The river port is in front of the rocky spur on which the castle stands. At this spot the Oltava flows into the Vltava and the Orlík dam forms a large artificial lake, 20 km in length, in the heart of the picturesque forests surrounding Zvíkov.

On the left, at the foot of picturesque rocks, Orlík castle stands proudly in the midst of a vast park which extends to the edge of the water. Behind Orlík castle corn fields alternate with wooded stretches abounding in granite quarries. Many villages in this area were submerged under the waters of the lake. On the right is the pointed spur of Bořín and then we approach the Orlík dam. Below the dam we can see—until the planned second reservoir is built—a stretch of the former river whose bed shows the typical deposits of pebbles.

Below Mount Chlum, near the former "Šefrovna" inn of the timber raftsmen, the Vltava describes the lovely "Podkova" (horseshoe) bend. Then we come to Kamýk on the Vltava where the **artificial Slapy lake** ends. Gliding along the calm waters of the reservoir, our boat passes along a rural landscape dotted with many villages and recreation centres, such as Cholin (bridge) and Živohošt (bridge). Behind the Ždáň peninsula is the Nová Rabyně holiday resort and, farther on, the outline of the **Slapy dam**. Beneath the Slapy hydroelectric power station is the monument dedicated to Saint John Nepomuk, a historic figure after whom the largest and most dangerous of the Vltava rapids, the Rapids of Saint John, used to be named.

Our boat takes us over Lake Štěchovice, along steep rocks, to the lock of the Štěchovice dam. Our boat passes through the chambers in the Stechovice dam, past Stechovice, the "Na Šlemíně" boathouses and the floating inn "na Mandátu", to the **Island of Saint Kilián** with ruins of the 10th-century island monastery. The Sázava flows into the Vltava on the right at Davle close by. We pass Davle and come to the **Vrané Dam**,

spanned by a railway bridge at Měchenice. The Vrané lock sinks
the water level of the barrage on which there is a busy traffic in
the summer. We carry on past Zbraslav to the confluence of the
Berounka on the left and we are already in Greater Prague, in
the suburbs of Chuchle and Modřany. The waterway ends in the
harbours for sporting boats at Braník, Zlíchov or Podolí.

The river trip may be broken and accommodation found at the
following places: Červená (22 km), Zvíkov (32 km), Orlík (45
km), Kamýk (70 km), Nová Rabyně (109 km) and Davle (126
km).

To travel by boat on the Lužnice from Suchdol to Prague
takes 10 to 14 days.

The Vltava is navigable not only from the confluence of the
Lužnice, but also from Lenora in the Bohemian Forest, and the
stretch from Lenora to the confluence of the Lužnice is particularly romantic all the way. The distance to České Budějovice is
165.8 km and from there to the Lužnice another 40 km. There are
36 weirs in this section of the river.

The lower stretch of the Vltava, from Prague to Mělník, where
the Elbe joins the Vltava, is also navigable. But these 60 km are
not nearly as beautiful as the trip upstream from Prague. There
are eight weirs in this section.

5. NORTH BOHEMIA

General Features

North Bohemia is one of the most beautiful and most frequently visited regions in Czechoslovakia. The great variety of its natural beauty can be attributed to its geological structure, formed at different periods in the evolution of the earth's crust by the flexure of strata, chalky ocean deposits and volcanic eruptions during the Tertiary period, on the one hand, and, on the other, the erosion of the rivers.

The mountain chains which shut off North Bohemia also form the political frontiers which separate Czechoslovakia from the German Democratic Socialist Republic and Poland. They start with the Lužické hory (the Lusatian Mts.) which split into two ridges in the Jizerské hory (Iser Mts.), east of which rise the highest mountains of Bohemia, the Krkonoše (Giant Mts.) with its tallest peak, the Snezka (5,290 ft).

Picturesque rock formations, separated by fertile plains downstream on the tributaries of the Elbe, lie at the heart of North Bohemia.

As we approach the mountains, the highly developed agriculture of the plains gives way to a no less prosperous industry. The eastern part of the country, lying directly below the line of the Giant Mountains, has long enjoyed an excellent repute for its weaving, the beginnings of which go back to the Middle Ages. Also right up in the north we find important centres of the textile industry (Varnsdorf, Rumburk). Characteristic and known far beyond the frontiers is the production of jewellery and the cutting of precious and semi-precious stones, of which the centre is Turnov. As far back as the Middle Ages the wealth of timber in the frontier forest give rise to Bohemian glass manufacture and later promoted the creation of numerous paper factories. The great variety of industrial undertakings in North

Bohemia completes a widespread engineering and food-stuff industry and other branches of production.

From the tourist standpoint North Bohemia is divided into the following regions: **Krkonoše** (the **Giant Mountains**), the highest mountains in Bohemia, their slopes covered with deep woods and the meadows on the ridge offering magnificent distant views; Jizerské hory (the **Iser Mountains**) and the Ještědské pohoří (**Jeschken**) with beautiful valleys and plenty of stags and other game. The region of the **Český ráj** (the **Bohemian Paradise**), with its strange rock groups, looking like towns; the Máchův kraj (**Mácha Lake District**), full of romantic valleys and extensive meres which invite one to all kinds of water sports, **Českosaské Švýcarsko** (the **Bohemian-Saxon Switzerland**), with wild canyon-like rock formations cleft by the torrents of rivers, especially on the lower Elbe and Kamenice. Finally, the **Lužické hory** (the **Lusatian Mountains**), an inland range with beautiful woods with abundant game in which stags, deer chamois and mountain go at are indigenous.

Communications

The chief railway junctions are Turnov, Česká Lîpa and above all Liberec (Reichenberg), where three main lines meet. The distance from Liberec by rail to Prague is 137 km, to Děčín 95 km (Dresden 256 km), to Pardubice 161 km. Zittau in the East German Republic is 25 km from Liberec. A line runs through East German territory to the industrial town of Varnsdorf (45 km).

There are numerous well-kept roads, notably the good State highways. Distances: from Prague to Liberec 108 km, Karlovy Vary (Karlsbad) 224 km, from Brno (Brünn) 242 km, from Bratislava 410 km.

Sights and places of interest

National Trust Towns: Jičín, Úštěk.

Natural reservations: a) Giant and Iser Mountains—the Jizera National Park with strict protection of the mountain meadows and surviving primitive forest; this includes the whole Giant and Iser Mountains region.

b) The Bohemian Paradise (Český ráj), protected in the districts of Turnov, Jičín, Mnichovo Hradiště, a total area of 125 square km.

c) The gorges and the Pravčická brána, the gateway into Bohemian-Saxon Switzerland, Děčín district. Area 215 acres. ▨

d) Kokořín valley in the districts Mělník and Doksy. Area 4,200 acres.

State-owned castles and chateaux: Kost, Bezděz, Trosky, Sloup, Humprecht near Sobotka, Hrubý Rohozec and Sychrov near Turnov, Mnichovo Hradiště, Frýdlant, Lemberk near Liberec Zákupy near Česká Lípa.

Spas: Janské Lázně (Johannisbad) in the Giant Mountains, Lázně Bělohrad, Libverda in the Iser Mounts.

Holiday centres: In the Giant Mountains Janské lázně, Pec, Špindlerův Mlýn, Harrachov. In the Iser Mountains Hejnice. In the Český ráj Prachovské skály and Malá Skála. In Bohemian-Saxon Switzerland Hřensko and Jetřichovice near Děčín. Máchovo Jezero near Doksy. Kokořínský důl Mělník. Hamr on the lake, Stráž-by-Ralsko (lake with beaches), Úštěk (large pond of 35 hectares with beaches), Bělá-by-Ještěd, Dubá (Černý pond).

Worth seeing: The highest peak of the Giant Mountains, the Sněžka (5,290 feet; cable railway). The Ještěd near Liberec (3,333 feet; cable railway). The Kozákov (2,452 feet), Trosky (1,696 feet), Bezděz (1,996 feet), Nedvězí near Dosky (1,505 feet). Panská skála (1,952 feet), a geology reservation near Kamenicky Šenov.

A. LIBEREC (REICHENBERG)

Liberec (75,000 pop.) is the centre of North Bohemia. It lies in the picturesque valley of the Neisse, enclosed by a border of mountains, the Ještědské pohoři in the south and the dense woods of the Iser Mts. in the north. Liberec is a beautiful garden city; its outskirts reach the mountains. In early spring its gardens and parks are bright with blooming rhododendrons and azaleas. But Liberec is at its loveliest in autumn, when on the mountain slopes around it the brilliant colouring of the deciduous trees blends with the rich green of the pine woods.

Liberec is the seat of many North Bohemian industrial concerns and numerous cultural institutions. It is also the industrial, economic and cultural centre of the whole of North Bohemia.

In the field of industry special mention must be made of constructional engineering (foundries and bus building), the food industry (pork curing and sweets), breweries, but chiefly of the textile industry with its centuries-old tradition. It is not without reason that Liberec has been called the "Bohemian Manchester". The cotton and silk fabrics, cloth, carpets and tapestries manufactured here enjoy a world wide reputation. The well-known and much frequented Liberec Fairs are held here annually in August and September and local industrial products, specially textiles and glass, are exhibited.

At Liberec are the **Plastimat** factory, employing 6,000 workers, and the College of Engineering Construction and the College of Textiles. It is also the headquarters of **Glassexport,** a foreign trading company for the export of glass (except jewellery).

The town of Liberec was founded in the 13th century. Clothweaving had already begun to prosper in the 16th, especially linen and woollen weaving. In 1577 the place was elevated to a city by the Emperor Rudolf II. The peak of its prosperity in the Middle Ages was reached under Albrecht of Wallenstein, Duke of Friedland. In the 18th century the old guild and handicraft production was superseded by the first textile factories which gave Liberec its world-fame.

Electric trams and numerous motorbus services provide communication between the Ještědské pohoří and the Iser Mountains. The inner town, a maze of old winding lanes and alleys, has been gradually changed into a friendly modern town by planned sanitation and rebuilding.

Walks through the town

From the railway station the broad 1 Májé třída (1 May Street) with the Glassexport building and the modern and comfortable **Imperial** Hotel leads into the Gottwaldovo náměstí. Following the Revoluční and the Moskevská ulice, where the Music and Poetry Theatre is, we come to the **Mírové náměstí** (Peace Square), the actual centre of the town. In the middle of this square stands the splendid pseudo-Renaissance **Town Hall**, with its 185 ft tower; behind it the **Theatre** with permanent opera and ballet performances. In some of the houses of this square the old arcades are still preserved.

Two fine modern streets run off from the Mírové náměstí in the direction of the Iser Mountains. The older, where remarkable patrician houses attract the eye, is **Leninova Street** in which we find several schools, the Park of the Fair and the Town Baths (Městské lázně); this has a covered swimming pool. Here also is the **North Bohemian Museum (Severočeské museum)**; its treasures comprise natural curiosities, archaeological finds and chiefly glass and textile collections. The outstanding one is the tapestry collection with 22 medieval tapestries (principally Flemish).

The Leninova třída ends at the **Bezručovy sady** (park); the park continues straight on into the woods of the Iser Mts. Above the park is a vast **Open-Air Theatre** with seating accommodation for 30,000 persons and not far away is the **Zoo** (zoologická zahrada), the oldest in Bohemia, and the **Botanical Gardens,** famous for its tropical flora and typical North Bohemian flora (especially from the Iser Mountains); specially worth seeing is the rich collection of orchids.

Beyond the park the **Liberecká výšina** (Liberec Height) rises above the woods (20 minutes by a well-kept path). There we can regale ourselves at a restaurant built in the style of a medieval castle, from the tower of which there is a fine view of the town and its setting of gracious mountains.

From the Leninova třída we turn right into the Alšova ulice, and passing the **Broadcasting Station** into the modern Husova Street, where we find a museum of **Nazi barbarism**. In the same street is the **Engineering High School**, with modern boarding accommodation for students and a large national health institution.

Past the "Zlatý lev" (Golden Lion) Hotel we come to the **Castle** with a fine Renaissance chapel, one of the finest architectural monuments of Liberec. It was built onto the castle in 1604. Altar, oratory, choir and the coffered ceiling bear testimony to the high level of the art of carving of that period.

In the little park of the castle is the **Museum of Fine Arts** (Galerie výtvarnýck umění), with pictures of the famous Barbizon school and paintings and sculpture by Bohemian artists.

Interesting from an artistic point of view are also many **private houses** built in the late 18th century; their façades have elaborate stucco ornamentation in the shape of flowers, garlands, bouquets, foliage and fruits, and also reliefs with religious, biblical and mythological subjects. The graceful gables are characteristic. The peculiarity of a certain type of these houses led to its being given the name "Reichenberg house"; the best example is No. 15 in the Mírové náměstí, which was built in 1795. Behind the Mírové náměstí lies a small square, the Sokolovské náměstí, from which the narrow medieval Větrná ulice runs off. This little street is one of the most striking structural curiosities of the town. Its ancient wooden buildings with porches date from 1632.

Of the other architectural works of art mention must at least be made of the **Church of the Holy Cross** (Kostel sv. kříže), a Baroque building (1753–1761). The interior is decorated with paintings by prominent Baroque artists. The monument to the Virgin in front of the church, by Matthias Braun (1719), is also worth noting.

Excursions from Liberec

Ještěd, 3,330 ft above sea level, 30 minutes from the centre of the town by electric tram and cable railway. A mountain road for motor vehicles goes to the top where is a modern hotel. The Ještěd offers a magnificent panorama of a third of Bohemia.

We warmly recommend an excursion taking the route Jěstěd—Pláně (tourist chalet)—Javorník (tourist chalet) whence we have a magnificent view of all the surrounding region. A trip to the **Kryštof Valley**, which cuts deeply into the Jěstěd range and has a charming medieval wooden church, is also very interesting. In the immediate surroundings of Liberec is **Rudolfov**, a well-known summer and winter resort, with the Česká chalupa (Czech hut) and Jizerská chata (Iser chalet) tourist chalets.

B. Jizerské hory (Iser Mountains)

Frýdlant (Friedland) in Bohemia (23 km north of Liberec by highway 35). An ancient town with the remains of medieval fortifications. The late Gothic Church of the Holy Cross, built in 1551, contains the unique Renaissance tomb of the lords of Redern (1615). Above the town on a high rock stands the walled town and castle of Frýdlant. The castle was built in the 13th century, the courtyard (Indica) however dates from as far back as 1014. In 1550 the castle was rebuilt and Renaissance elements were added. There are copious collections in all the rooms. Portrait galleries of the former owners of the castle (among them the portrait of Albrecht of Wallenstein painted in 1626), collections of weapons, etc. A Renaissance chateau was built directly below the castle between

1598 and 1602; in it are some unusual paintings of the Baroque period by V. V. Rainer, P. Brandl and K. Škréta. The original furnishing of a noble's residence is still preserved here.

Lázně Libverda (17 km east of Frýdlant, on the road running through Nové Město pod Smrkem). The carbon dioxide and mud baths of Libverda were already known in the Middle Ages. The spa now specialises in the treatment of heart and gynaecological diseases. Accommodation: Park Hotel.

Hejnice (2 km south of Libverda), a holiday center in a lovely mountain valley. A fine Baroque **Pilgrimage church** dedicated to the Mother of God, with an altar adorned by a Gothic statue carved out of wood of great artistic merit. Hotels: Jizera, Perun.

From the town of Hejnice pleasant walks lead into the valleys where the mountain streams descend in cascades and waterfalls; one such (following a marked path, 15 km) leads to the Štolpich waterfall on the Černý Potok. Karl Maria von Weber composed his "Freischütz" there.

Other interesting sites in the surroundings of Libverda and Hejnice include Bílý Potok (the White Brook) on the western slopes of the Iser Mountains (Bartl chalet and colony of wooden chalets), Smědava (excursion of 10 km in the direction of Jizera, 3,678 feet, virgin forests, fine panorama), the Souš dam (water sports, camping), and the waterfalls of Černá Desná below Souš.

From Hejnice the road climbs southwards through deep woods, prolific in game (stag, wild boar, capercailzie) to the **Smědava** Hostel; from here on to the high-lying **Souš Dam** and by way of **Tanvald** into the town of **Jablonec nad Nisou**: Gablonz (pop. 28,000).

Jablonec (Gablonz) gained a world-wide reputation for its jewellery. It is the seat of the **Jablonec** Foreign Trade Company which exports Czech jewellery to all parts of the world. Everything of interest in this new town is modern: a dam, the monumental Town Hall and the Church. In the **National Museum** (Národní technické museum) there is a collection of rare glass.

Communications: An electric tram runs through the town, connecting with the main line Prague–Liberec, and then on into the Iser Mountains. Jablonec has direct communication with Liberec by rail and by electric tram. Accommodation: Hotel Corso.

Above the town rises the wooded mountain ridge of the **Černá Studnice** (2,760 feet above sea level) with a tourist hostel and a lookout tower. A very attractive road, bordered by picturesque rock formations, leads along the crest to **Tanvald** (10 km); splendid view over the whole region. In winter good skiing terrain and toboggan run. A motor road goes up to the hostel (7 km from Jablonec).

A route back from Liberec to Jablonec (12 km) runs through **Vratislavice** (sparkling mineral springs, brewery, carpet factory).

C. MÁCHŮV KRAJ
(MÁCHA LAKE DISTRICT)

Leave Liberec by highway 13 to Děčín.

State-owned **Lemberk** Castle. On the highway from Liberec which runs north-west to **Lvová** (24 km). On a wooded hill above the village stands the Renaissance castle on the site of the original 13th century stronghold. Of the latter only the first gate and the tower remain. It was reconstructed in Renaissance style in the 17th century. Specially beautiful are the stucco decorations of the inside rooms. The wood ceiling of the so-called "Fables Hall" is decorated by 77 painted scenes from Aesop's fables. In the castle are

collections of the Prague **Museum of Applied Arts,**
so far as these represent the living habits of the
15th to the 19th century. We find here castle kitchens,
besides furniture of the following periods: late Gothic,
Italian Renaissance, early Baroque, high Baroque,
Classicism, Empire, Biedermeier, pseudo-Rococo,
neo-Renaissance.

Jablonné v Podještědí (3 km from Lemberk). The
Church of Saint Laurence is one of the outstanding
church edificed of the High Baroque period in North
Bohemia (a miniature Saint Peter's in Rome). Underground crypts with mummies.

Zákupy (from Jablonné 12 km southward to
Mimoň, then turn off right—going by highway 268
north-east—7 km to **Zákupy**). The castle, originally
built in Renaissance style, has been modified several
times, most recently between 1850 and 1853, when the
Emperor Ferdinand chose it as a summer residence.
The rich murals of the rooms were done then. The
caryatids of the terrace are also worth seeing.

Česká Lípa (8 km west of Zákupy by highway 262).
A town with a predominant engineering industry.
The **small hunting lodge,** in which a museum is now
housed, is of interest.

Nové Zámky (7 km south of Česká Lípa by highway 9). Below the beautiful old park stretches the
sandstone canyon "Peklo" with rare vegetation. Near
to it lies the **Nové Zámky** mere (625 acres), a sanctuary
for waterfowl (200 nesting species). On the other side
of the mere rises the geological reservation "Provo-
dínské kameny", where the **Lysá skála** offers a
beautiful view. Rare minerals have been found in the
protected area. On the marshy meadows the Siberian
ragwort (Ligularia sibirica) grows; this is far the
most westerly spot where this plant appears. An

isolated sandstone rock with the ruined castle of **Jestřebí** is the limit of the panorama.

On the main road from Nóve Zámky to Litoměřice lies **Úštěk** (17 km west) a town scheduled as a historic site and containing remains of ramparts and town houses dating from the 15th century. Near the town is a superb natural swimming pool, the **Chmelař pool,** bordered by sandy beaches; about 5 km east are the ruins of Hrádek (Helfenburk) stronghold. The surroundings have a wealth of picturesque sandstone formations with steep precipices.

Doksy (10 km south-east of Jestřebí). The town lies in the centre of the wide North Bohemian lake basin in a sunny, gently undulating country on the shore of the Máchovo jezero; the Mácha Lake covers an area of 875 acres. The **bathing beach** extends for some distance on the sandy shores of the lake; all facilities for the practice of every kind of water sport especially for sailing, are provided. There is a motorboat service across the lake.

Bezděz (2,145 feet above sea level, on the road. 9 km south-east of Doksy). The pointed cone of a mountain of volcanic origin is crowned by the sprawling ruin of a **royal castle,** which was built in the 13th century by King Přemysl II. Exceptionally interesting is the Gothic **chapel** (1260).

By car from Doksy through the Mácha Lake District

Leaving Doksy towards the West, we go past the ruins of Starý Berštejn, and reach the small agricultural town of **Duba** (9 km), in the middle of a hopgrowing district. We then go through picturesque forets until the isolated village of *Raj* (11 km to the South), and then by the national park of the beautiful Kokořín valley, to the castle of Kokořín (which is state-owned).

(Cars stop on the highway about 1 km above the tunnel; from here 5 minutes' walk to the castle.) The ruins of this Gothic 13th-century castle on a sandstone rock were restored between 1811 and 1918 under the supervision of leading Bohemian historians and, apart from minor alterations, they restored it to its original form.

The Kokořín valley, above which the castle proudly towers, is a favourite place of excursion with several hotels. Fine sandstone formations cut by ravines.

Another stopping place is the mountain village of **Horní Vidim.** Here the first thing to catch the eye is the Baroque castle, recently converted for use as a Home for Old People. Behind the castle extends a vast natural park with a view over wildly romantic mountain scenery. A road round the castle crosses thirty small bridges over chasms and gorges, amid cleft rock and cliffs (45 minutes, only with guide).

We come back to the highway along a narrow mountain road through a wooded valley; from here through Dubá to Doksy 26 km.

From Doksy back to Liberec, passing Lake Břehyňský, via Mimoň 54 km.

D. THE GLASS INDUSTRY DISTRICT

Nový Bor (45 km west of Liberec by highway 13 via **Jablonné v Podještědí**). Centre of the famous Bohemian glass production; here we find glass straining workshops, refineries and glass grinding shops. The most remarkable is the production of glass ornaments of all kinds, especially chandeliers. Particularly worth seeing is the extensive park-like cemetery in the woods.

Sloup (by highway 268, 3 km south-east of Nový Bor) is a favourite summer holiday resort in the midst of wooded sandstone mountains. On an isolated rock above the valley stand the interesting ruins of a medieval castle. In the castle and round about the church are some statues by the most eminent Baroque sculptor Matthias Braun.

Kamenický Šenov (Steinschönau) (6 km to the west by highway 13), famous for its glass chandeliers.

Near the town is a geological reservation: **Panská skála.** The hexagonal basalt rocks, in the shape of organ pipes, offer one of the most curious sights in Europe. From them one has a fine view of the mountain chain **Chřibské pohoří,** the ridge of which is covered with deep woods, and an abundance of game (chamois, stag, deer, wild boar).

Česká Kamenice (5 km north-west of Kamenický Šenov). Large paper factory. The ruins of Kamenice castle dominate the town. The immediate surroundings are rich in picturesque rocky scenery. Also noteworthy are the Gothic and Renaissance **Saint James's Church** dating from 1555, and the Rococo **Saint Mary Chapel** (end of the 18th century).

E. BOHEMIAN-SAXON SWITZERLAND (DĚČÍNSKÉ STĚNY)

In the great sandstone deposits left behind after the recession of the cretaceous ocean, the Elbe with its tributaries has forced its way to the sea through a deep valley. Through thousands of years the action of water, wind and weather completed the modelling of the gigantic ravines, solitary towers and rock cities of sandstone, to which the Romanticism of the last century gave the name "Bohemian-Saxon Switzerland". This description applies to the whole region, part of which is in Czechoslovakia and part in East Germany. The Bohemian part begins at Děčín (Tetschen) from which place it takes its name Děčínské stěny (the Tetschen Walls). The Děčínské stěny form part of the sandstone rock-cities which are also in the Český ráj and Adersbach (see East Bohemia). In height and extent they surpass the other rock-cities of Czechoslovakia. The larger, wilder and more romantic part stretches along the frontier on the right bank of the Elbe, where the last Bohemian tributaries, the Ploučnice and the Kamenice, flow into it. On the left bank of the Elbe the sandstone peak, the Děčínský Sněžník (2,379 ft above sea level) towers above the woods, the highest point of this region. Behind it lies the lonely island of the rock-labryinth, the Tiské skály, beyond which lie the foothills of the Ore Mountains

(Krušné hory). The natural entrance to both parts of the Dě-
činské stěny is the town of Děčín (Tetschen) which lies astride
the Elbe. Upstream, to the south, the landscape opens into the
wide Elbe valley; to the north, on the left bank of the river the
Pastýřská stěna, a great wall of rock, stands sentinel while, on
the right bank, looms the Stolniční vrch (930 feet above sea level).

Děčín

The town, which was founded way back on the
important trade waterway, is dominated by the
castle, built on a 165 foot crag on the right bank of
the Elbe. The stronghold of the Slav tribe, the Děčané,
is believed to have stood there in the year 993. The
castle was rebuilt in its present form between 1788
and 1790. Especially striking is the mighty square
tower.

The local industries are engineering and foodstuffs
(chocolate factories). On the Elbe is a harbour for
freight and passenger traffic.

Communications: Direct express line from Prague (132 km)
to Dresden and Berlin. Railway line Liberec-Děčín 95 km. By
road to Prague (119 km), Liberec (95 km), Lázně Teplice
(Teplitz) in Bohemia (34 km). To the industrial and regional
capital Ústí nad Labem (Aussig on the Elbe) 24 km.

Excursions from Děčín

Děčínské stěny (motor trip, 50 km). Westwards
from Děčín to **Sněžník,** where a narrow road runs off
up the mountain **Děčínské stěny.** From the belvedere
a fine view.

Another stopping-place before the tourist hostel at
the entrance to the rock-labyrinth of the Tiské stěny
(Tissaer Walls). The tour of the rocks from the hostel
and back takes about two hours. The rocks are
remarkable for their strange formations of the most
various shapes. From the steep, narrow path round
them one has a wonderful view of the Jílovský valley.

After our visit we return to Děčín by way of **Tisá** and **Libouchec.**

Hřensko, 14 km north of Děčín, either by the road along the right bank of the Elbe or by steamer. The river trip through the deep valley, enclosed by steep, wooded slopes, above which rise mighty crags, is especially interesting.

For thousands of visitors, particularly in summer, the favourite goal is the **Cz. Army** and **Divoká soutěska** (formerly the Edmundsklamm, now the Cz. Army Ravine, and the Wild Ravine) and the formation of rocks called the **Pravčická brána** (Prebisch Gate). From the landing-stage we proceed through the town (by car we go as far as the side-road into the ravine). A narrow footbridge to the pier in the Cz. Arm Ravine. The boat glides through a dark gorge, shut in by the tangled greenery of the most strangely shaped rocks. We reach the Wild Ravine along the Kamenice river by a narrow footpath which runs partly across the riverbed. Equally interesting is the passage through the Wild Ravine. At the end of it, after following the marked path through the woods, we reach the tourist hotel **Mezní louka** (frontier meadow), from where the truly beautiful Fučik path—with red signs—branches off, seemingly buried in the gigantic woods. The reddish sandstone walls open up to the eye new and astounding rock-groups at every step, culminating in the mighty work of Nature, the **Pravčická brána.** From its "bridge" one has an unforgettable view, not only of the rock-towers round about, but also into the valley of the Elbe far beyond the frontier of Bohemia. We come down from the Pravčická brána by a steep path through the woods into **Hřensko.**

Jetřichovice (22 km from Děčín by road) is a much frequented holiday resort at the back of the Děčínské stěny. In a three-hour walking tour on a route marked with direction-signs one wanders through the most interesting part of Jetřichovice rocks: the **Mariina skála,** the **Vílemínina stěna** and the **Rudolfův kámen,** all bizarre sandstone formations.

F.   ČESKÝ RÁJ (THE BOHEMIAN PARADISE)

The town of **Turnov** (28 km from Liberec) is the Northern Gate to the picturesque foothills of the Giant Mountains, which have been called "Bohemian Paradise" (Český ráj) because of its beauty and historical associations.

Numerous ruins of medieval castles on rocky heights, sumptuously furnished chateaux, peasant villages whose typical buildings testify to the folk-culture of the last century, quiet towns, but especially the remarkable labyrinths of piled-up sandstone blocks, hidden in pinewoods, all combine to create the peculiarly interesting character of the centre of North Bohemia.

This region, covering an area of 125 square km, is under both natural and ancient monument protection. The so-called rock-towns of the **Český ráj** are of course the greatest attraction: the sandstone rocks near the town of Jičín, the rock-town of Hrubá Skála near Turnov, the rock labyrinth of Malá skála near Železný Brod (Eisenbord) and the cliffs below Mount Mužský near Mnichovo Hradiště (Münchengrätz).

Turnov railway junction, fast train stop, distance from Prague 100 km, from Liberec 37 km, from Hradec Králové 101 km, from Pardubice 124 km. By road: from Prague via Mladá Boleslav (Jungbunzlau) 85 km, from Liberec 28 km, from Hradec Kralové 69 km.

Turnov is known for the cutting of precious stones, and, for some time now, as the producer of pieces of jewellery mounted with the semi-precious stones from

Mount Kozákov, notably Bohemian garnets. In the town itself is the State **School of Jewellery.**

7 km north of Turnov (Liberec road, 1 km on the left), is the **castle of Sychrov** built in 1693 on the site of an old stronghold. It received its present form between 1822 and 1862 when, after the French Revolution, it had become the property of a French exile, Prince Camille de Rohan. The castle, an extensive building with six towers, built in the noble style of Norman Gothic, is surrounded by a magnificent park with exotic trees and shrubs. It is furnished in princely fashion. The Gothic style furniture, ceilings, portals and doors are the work of native artists who were also responsible for the rest of the decorations. The Rohans brought from France the valuable portrait gallery of their ancestors and of the French kings of the 16th and 17th centuries.

For several years the famous Czech composer Antonín Dvořák spent his summer holidays at Sychrov castle.

Jičín, fast train stop on the Prague—Giant Mountains line, distance from Prague 97 km. By road: from Prague via Mladá Boleslav 89 km, via Lázně Poděbrady 95 km, from Hradec Králové 46 km, from Liberec 51 km.

National Trust protected area. Jičín lies in a fertile plain on the little river Cidlina. Its day of glory was in the transitional period from the Middle Ages to modern times. Albrecht von Wallenstein, the famous general of the Thirty Years War, chose Jičín as the principal seat of his dukedom. Some notable architectural monuments of the period still remain: in the centre of the town the mighty **Valdická brána,** a gate 170 feet high, dating from 1568, and nearby an interesting **church** without a spire, built by Wallenstein in 1627. The whole front of the extensive central square, Baroque and Renaissance with arcades, which lend the town its ancient charm, is enclosed by the **Wallenstein** (Valdštejn) **Palace,** built by Italian architects between 1624 and 1634. The Conference Hall on the first floor is still preserved, in which in 1813 the Holy Alliance, a League of Austria, Russia and Prussia against Napoleon, was signed. Today Jičín has no lack of industries (chiefly engineering works concerned with the manufacture of agricultural machinery).

Excursion: an avenue with four rows of hundred year old linden trees, 2 km long, leads out of the town to the former Wallenstein park **Libosad** with Renaissance loggia. Jičín is the starting point for excursions into the **Prachovské skály** (sandstone rocks).

Mnichovo Hradiště (**Münchengrätz**). Fast train stop on the Prague—Liberec line. Distance from Prague 86 km, from Liberec 51 km. By road: from Prague 68 km, from Liberec 42 km.

The town's chief landmark is the State-owned **Castle,** built at the end of the 17th century by Wallenstein. The sumptuous furnishing of a noble's residence was preserved in the castle rooms. Here one finds, besides rich collections of rare porcelain, an old **library** of 22,000 volumes which include 293 manuscripts and 33 incunabula. In the Saint Anne's Chapel in the castle park is the vault of Albrecht of Wallenstein. In the **castle museum** are exhibited prehistoric excavations and the model of a prehistoric settlement—the most important in Bohemia, which lay at the foot of **Mount Mužský.**

Mnichovo Hradiště is the starting point for excursions into the rocks at the foot of mountains (7 km away).

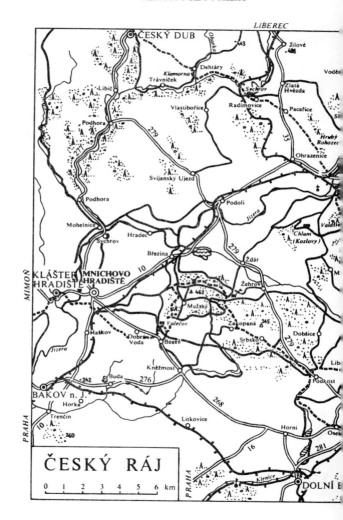

ČESKÝ RÁJ

0   1   2   3   4   5   6 km

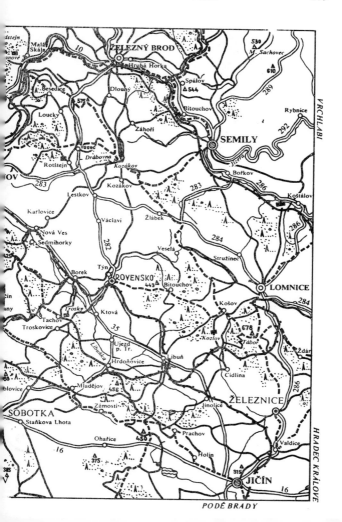

Železný Brod, express stop on the line from Prague to the Giant Mountains. Distance from Prague 114 km, from Krkonoše (Giant Mountains) 34 km, from Liberec 51 km, from Pardubice 110 km. Distance by road from Prague 99 km, from Liberec 42 km, from Harrachov (in the Giant Mountains) 33 km.

This town, much frequented by tourists and holiday makers, lies in the picturesque Iser valley. It is known far beyond the frontiers of Czechoslovakia because of its artistic glass, particularly cut and engraved glass and little ornaments (figurines, flowers, etc.). There is a **Glass Technical School** with a permanent exhibition of glass in the town.

Accommodation in Železný Brod: the Hotel Cristal.

Excursions from Železný Brod into the Bohemian Paradise (Good rail connections everywhere. From any station roads lead further to places of interest to tourists).

(a) **Malá skála** (6 km south-west of Železný Brod) in a deep section of the Iser valley with many orchards. On foot to the **Pantheon** and the ruins of Frýdštejn castle. A path with red signs leads over the sharp ridge with rock-caves and astonishing views into the valley as far as **Frýdštejn**, from where a narrow road below the cliffs runs to **Malá skála**.

(b) From Malá Skála to **Besedice** 6 km. From the "U Kalicha" hostel a path with red markings leads to the **Kalich caves** in which in the Middle Ages the persecuted Protestants held their religious services; from there on to the belvedere. **Kde domov můj** and to the **Sokol**. From here back to the Kalich inn (6 km in all).

(c) **The Kozákov,** 2,452 feet above sea level (13 km south of Železný Brod), is a black porphyry mountain, esteemed for its distant view of the Český ráj to the Giant Mounts and also known as the place of discovery of the Kozákov semi-precious stones (agate, jasper, calcedony, garnet, amethyst). These stones are cut at Turnov and shaped as objets d'art. Kozákov has a tourist chalet which is chiefly intended for foreign visitors and which forms a sort of complement to the Cristal Hotel at Železný Brod.

The "rock-town" of **Hrubá skála** reaches from Železný Brod above Malá Skála as far as the castle of

Hrubý Rohozec, which stands on a steep crag high above the Iser. The castle is a reconstruction, carried out in the 16th century, of a medieval stronghold, built in 1300 and is sumptuously furnished. The old weapon collection and the picture gallery merit special attention.

Continue through **Turnov** (16 km south-west of Železný Brod) and then onto a side-road until before **Hrubá Skála** castle. From there a worth-while footpath with red signs—to **Mariánská vyhlídka** (belvedere) and further on to the medieval ruins of **Valdštejn castle.** On the way back—blue signs—we pass through the rock labyrinth to **Sedmihorky** and from there through the **Myší díra** (Mousehole) to Hrubá Skála.

Farther on towards Jičín, highway 35 leads to the parish of **Borek** and the ruins of **Trosky** castle, visible from far away. The mighty rock formations **Panna** and **Bába** (the Maiden and the Grandmother) rise from the volcanic basalt mountain (1696 feet); the remains of castle towers can still be seen on them. From the belvedere one can enjoy a wonderful panorama. Following the road through **Libuň,** we reach the tourist hostel in the **Prachovské skály.**

The **Prachovske skály** (sandstone rocks), a historic and natural reservation (6th to 11th-century settlements), cover an area of 3 square km and are a great labyrinth of sandstone rocks of weird shapes with countless narrow grottos, passages and view-points, interconnected by well-kept and well-marked circular paths.

The most interesting circular tour from the hostel is the following (it takes 2 to 3 hours): Šikmá věž (Leaning Tower)—Hraběčina vyhlídka (the Countess belvedere)—Denisova steska (Denis footbridge)—Císařská chodba (Imperial Walk)—Hlaholská vyhlídka (Hlahol belvedere)—Bratrská modlitebna (Brotherhood Prayerhouse)—Všetečkova vyhlídka (Všetečka belvedere)—Javorový důl (Maple Valley)—na Vodách (on the waters)—Pelíškův most (Pelíšek Bridge, summer resort)—tourist hostel.

On the south-western side the pine-woods continue to **Kost Castle.** The well-preserved 14th-century castle stands on a mighty sandstone crag rising above the romantic valley, dotted with tarns. Not far away lies the small town of **Sobotka** with characteristic wooden buildings. **Humprecht** castle above Sobotka was built in 1677 by the Italian master C. Luragho. Today it houses the **Museum** of National Literature (Památník národního písemnictví).

Further on through **Kněžmost** to the interesting ruins of **Valečov** castle, standing on and surrounded by rocks. From there 2 km further along the road to Mount **Mužský** with a magnificent view all round. Following a footpath for another 2 km we come to a prehistoric burial ground, called **Hrada,** and to the craggy rock-town of the **Drábské světničky,** where we are rewarded with a view.—Then on to **Mnichovo Hradiště** (the whole tour till there 58 km). The sights of this town have already been detailed above.

G. KRKONOŠE (THE GIANT MOUNTAINS)

After the Alps and the Carpathians, the large mountain mass which forms the frontier of Bohemia (and belongs in part to the Sudetes) is the highest in Central Europe.

Geography

The main ridge, 28 km long, reaches an average height of 4,000 feet above sea level. Above that altitude rise the granite peaks of huge blocks and groups of granite rock, often strangely shaped, which with the tallest peak, the Sněžka (Schneekoppe) attain a height of 5,290 feet. The frontier ridge is 200–400 yards wide, in parts even 2 km. The Elbe and its tributaries have their source in this group of mountains. In the distant past, these rivers, eroding deep valleys, separated the ridge from the less resistant micaceous slopes of Bohemia. That is why the Bohemian ridge has a different character from the frontier ridge because it is not uniform but broken in the middle by the Elbe and numerous valleys.

The frontier ridge rises from the saddle of Nový svět above mountain woods to the Luboch (4,277 feet). From here as far as the Špindlerovo sedlo (Spindler saddle) the continuation of the ridge is bare of vegetation. Between the Luboch and the Polish mountain Szrzenica (4,494 feet) lies the dip of the marshy Hraniční louka (Frontier Meadow), from which the Tvarožník (4,495 ft.) rises. Below it is the Vosecká bouda (hostel). The ridge dips to a grassland with dwarf pines, in which the Elbe rises in the Labská studánka (Elbe spring). Below the Labská bouda the Elbe cascades into the Labský důl (Elbe valley) in a 165 feet waterfall. Beyond the Schronisko Wawel the frontier ridge climbs across the Sněžné jámy chasm to the Vysoké kolo belvedere (4,969 feet); from here it drops down to the granite rocks of the Mužské kameny (2,640 feet) and the Dívčí kameny to the Špindlerovo sedlo. The altitude of the saddle is 3,953 feet; there is the chalet-hotel Špindlerova and a colony of other shelters belonging to it. A mountain roads climbs to the saddle (9 km) from **Špindlerův mlýn**. The ridge now ascends again to the Malý Šišák (4,758 feet) and the Střibrný hřeben (4,914 feet); below it, at the bottom of a 600 foot precipice, on the Polish side of the frontier, glisten the beautiful glacier lakes Malý and Velký Staw. The declining ridge here broadens to the Bílá louka plateau, a grassland with dwarf pines. Here stands the big Mountain Hotel, Luční Bouda. Further on, at the Obří bouda, the ridge narrows again and climbs steeply to the highest peak in Bohemia, the **Sněžka** (Schneekoppe, 5,290 feet). There is a Polish and a Czechoslovak hostel at the top; also a meteorological station and the rotunda-like Chapel of Saint Laurence (1668–81). From the Bohemian side a chair-lift runs up from the Obří důl over the Růžová hora to the top. From here there is a magnificent panorama looking towards Bohemia and Poland. The ridge now dips to the Pomezní bouda saddle (road from Úpa) and further on to Rýchory and finally Žacléř (Schatzlar).

The Bohemian ridge ascends over the wooded Plešivec (3,971 feet) to the belvedere of the bald Lysá hora (4,431 feet) and then across the Labská and Pančická louka, grassland which links the frontier and Bohemian ridges. Across these meadows rises the great Mount Kotel (Kesselkoppe, 4,732 feet) with wide views of Bohemia. On its eastern slope can be seen the Kotelné jámy

a favourite hunting place for rare mountain flowers. From the
Kotel the ridge drops slightly to the Krkonoš (4,607 feet),
approached by the new mountain road from Jilemnice. Then
follows the deep cutting of the Elbe valley. Beyond it the ridge
continues above Špindlerův Mlýn on the hogsback Kozí hřbety
(4,700 feet), the rocky surface of which then changes to the meadows of the Bílá louka, where the Bohemian ridge again meets
the frontier ridge. To the south other ridges branch off the main
ridge, the biggest running over Mount Studničná (5,115 feet) and
the Luční hora (5,131 feet) to the Černá hora, to where a cable
railway runs up from Jánské Lázně.

The whole mountain has legendary associations; most of the
legends are concerned with the mountain gnome Krakonoš,
the powerful old man with the long beard, the guardian of the
mountain treasure. Hence people often bring home souvenirs
from the Giant Mountains in the shape of a little Krakonoš figure
made of bark and wicker from the woods on the mountain.

The flora and fauna

The flora of the Giant Mountains makes a separate chapter
in the botany of Czechoslovakia. Mountain slopes and valleys
are covered with magnificent pine woods which at higher altitudes
give place to large areas of fir and flowering meadows. In the
gorges, especially in the glacier ravines, rare Alpine flowers
appear, the last vestige of the Ice Age. Among the most uncom-
mon flora of the Giant Mountains are: Veratrum lobelianum,
Viola biflora, Gentiana asclepladdea, Pulsatilla alpina, Primula
minima, Cryptogramma crispa and Salix lapponum.

Sedge (Carex), cotton grass (Eriophorum), Rubus chamae-
morus, Axycoccos palustris, Vaccinium uliginosum and Drosera
rotundifolia grow in the mountain bogs.

The fauna of the Giant Mountains are also characteristic.
Among specially rare species of birds are found the Apternus
tridactylus, the Bonasia silvestris, the capercailzie (Tetrao uro-
gallus) and the Tetrao tetrix.

The whole of the Giant Mountains and Iser Mountains is a
natural reservation. It is part of the Giant and Iser Mountains
National Park with the following sanctuaries:

Černohorská rašelina (Schwarzenberg Bog) with rare flora,
covering an area of 1,050 acres; Obří důl (Giant valley) below the
Sněžka with mountain flora and fauna (4,750 acres); Labský
důl (Elbe valley) above Špindlerův Mlýn with rare mountain flora

and fauna (3,750 acres); Pančická louka (Pantsche meadow), a
marshy tract with relics of glacial flora and fauna (1,200 acres);
Úpská rašelina (Aupaer Bog) on the Bílá louka (White meadow,
700 acres); Kotelné jámy with rare alpine flora, 375 acres.

Tourism in the Giant Mountains

After the High Tatra the Giant Mountains are the most
popular and important holiday and touring region in Czechoslovakia. This imposing mountain world exerts a considerable
attraction for visitors; thanks to a well-thought out system of
communications, they can be sure of spending a pleasant holiday in comfortable hostels and inns.

Tourism in Czechoslovakia is by no means new. Travel in the
Giant Mountains was already of importance in the 17th century
when non-Catholic emigrants, persecuted for their faith, crossed
the frontier on their way into exile (among these was Jan Amos
Komenský). For them a wooden hut ("bouda") was put up in
the Bílá louka on the ridge in 1620, on the site of which the Hotel
Luční bouda now stands. That is why all tourist hotels and
hostels in the Giant Mountains have the name "bouda". Later
these and constantly newly built chalets were used as shelters by
shepherds and pilgrims. Tourism in the present-day sense of the
word, developed in the Giant Mountains towards the end of the
18th century.

Today, in summer countless, tourists wander about on the
ridges and in the valleys of this superb mountain world comfortably and on well-marked, well-kept roads and paths. In
winter tourism is of equal, if not of even greater importance, for
the Giant Mountains is one of the finest skiing terrains, almost
without rival in European mountains. For greater security for
winter sports, poles have been erected to indicate the way from
the various tourist boudas to the villages at the foot of the mountain. There is a rescue service for tourists who have lost their way
or had an accident; it has units in every bouda of any size and in
different holiday resorts.

Communications with the interior: In addition to the normal
express, railway and motor-coach connections with Prague,
Hradec Králové (Königgrätz) and Liberec (Reichenberg),
special fast train and automobile excursion services are run by
the Čedok Travel Bureau in the summer and winter seasons to
the chief tourist centres: Jánské Lázně (Johannisbad)-Pec-Špindl-
lerův Mlýn-Harrachov.

Three days on the ridges of the Giant Mountains

1st day: by fast train from Prague to Jánské Lázně, by motorbus to Pec and then cable railway to the top of the Sněžka. On
foot by way of the Luční bouda and over the Kozí hřběty to
Špindlerův Mlýn. Stay there overnight.

2nd day: Špindlerova bouda—Petrova bouda—Vysoké kolo—
Labská bouda. Detour to the source of the Elbe and to the Pan-
čice waterfall by way of the Elbe valley. Spend the night at the
Labská bouda.

3rd day: the Kotel—Dvoračky—Harrachov. Motorbus to
Polubný, fast train to Prague.

Car trip in the Giant Mountains (2 days)

1st day: From Prague 166 km (from Liberec 117 km) to Pec at
the foot of the Sněžka and to the lower station of the chairlift.
Lift to the top. From there on foot either:

a) from the Obří bouda—blue signs—through the Obří důl
reservation to Pec or

b) following the red signs from the Sněžka as far as the Luční
bouda and—yellow signs—through the Modrý důl (Blue Valley)
to Pec.

By car to Špindlerův Mlýn (44 km). Stay overnight.

2nd day: 44 km via Vrchlabí to Jilemnice, up the mountain
road to the Krkonoš. Walk through the Labský důl to the Elbe
waterfall near the Labská bouda—the source of the Elbe—eventually up Mount Kotel. By car 66 km to Harrachov. Visit to the
glass factories. Walk to the Mumlava waterfall. Return to Prague
130 km, to Liberec 43 km.

Trutnov (Trautenau), express stop on the lines:
Prague—Turnov—Trutnov, 187 km; Prague—Jičín—
Trutnov (the so-called "Krakonoš" line), 177 km;
Prague—Hradec Králové—Trutnov, 183 km.

Distance by road from Prague 162 km, from
Liberec 107 km.

Trutnov is a typical mountain town (textile industry).

Jánské Lázně; through fast trains from Prague.
From Trutnov to Jánské Lázně by rail 10 km; by

road from Prague 156 km, from Liberec 107 km. Altitude 1,900–2,300 feet. Accommodation is provided by 18 hotels and as many pensions.

Jánské Lázně **(Johannisbad)** is a world famous spa for the treatment of paralysis and especially for polio; it is the only health resort of its kind in Europe equipped for this cure. It derives its repute from hot water springs, 23 of which reach a temperature of 30° C., apart from another ten springs of a different character. According to legend the first spring was already known in 1006. The first Baths were built here in the 17th century, but there was no modern equipment until 1875. The spa is visited not only by patients, but also by tourists. It lies in a sheltered hollow below the **Černá hora** (4,287 feet above sea level). An overhead railway runs up the mountain since 1928. The Černá hora, where there is a whole colony of mountain hotels, first and foremost the Čedok Hotel, is a wonderful skiing terrain.

Mountain tour: From the Černá hora we descend to the Lesní bouda and from there climb up to the Lyžařská and the Hradecká bouda. Above towers the Liščí hora (4,498 feet); further on the Výrovka and from there to the hotel Liščí bouda. The path with red markings leads on along the Czechoslovak-Polish frontier to the Obří bouda and up a stiff climb to the Sněžka where the Česká bouda stands. We come down to Pec by chair-lift and then on by motor-bus to Janské Lázně (Round trip on foot 20 km; 5–6 hours).

Pec pod Sněžkou (Petzer) is another health resort. The settlement was started by ore-smelters in the 18th century. There is a fine road to Pec from Jánské Lázně through the deep valley of the Úpa; it is used by numerous coach services (distance from Prague 166 km, from Liberec 117 km)—Accommodation is provided in several hotels and also in private houses.

Pec is the starting point for walking tours (marked paths) into the surrounding mountains: Sněžka, Studnični hora, etc. The lower station for the chair-lift to the top of the Sněžka is 2 km above Pec at the juncture of the valleys Růžový důl and Obří důl.

Excursion from Pec: to the top of the Sněžka by cable railway, from there 8 km back to the Obří bouda and from there—blue signs—through the Obří důl. An easy half-day excursion.

Vrchlabí (Hohenelbe), district town (1,597 feet) in the Elbe valley. In the town, which has a highly developed textile industry, there are characteristic wooden buildings. The castle (1548) with four towers is of interest.

To Vrchlabí there is a direct fast train service from Prague via Jičín (154 km) or via Turnov (164 km).— Distance by road from Prague 130 km, from Liberec 75 km.

Vrchlabi is the starting point for the most important holiday centre of the Giant Mountains, **Špindlerův Mlýn** reached by a road through the Elbe valley (14 km).

Direct motor coach services from Prague, Liberec and Hradec Králové.

The town lies in a beautiful mountain basin where the **Sedmidolí** (seven valleys) converge. The altitude in the centre is 2,310 feet above sea level. It is sheltered on all sides by mountains; the **Mechovinec** (3,540 feet), the **Medvědín** (4,075 feet), **Kozí hřbety** (4,702 feet) and the **Pláň** (3,927 feet).

In the Middle Ages (until 1704) there were silver mines here. During the Austrian period the town was called **Spindlermühle.** Today the place is a colony of hotels and pensions (the Čedok Savoy Hotel and a number of other hotels and boarding houses). A busy centre for summer and winter sports of every kind, a summer swimming pool with electrically heated water. Nor are toboggan and ski runs and ski jumps lacking. International Skiing contests are held at Špindlerův Mlýn.

Ten minutes walk from the centre of the town is the lower station of the chair-lift to the top of the **Pláň** (3,929 feet). The mountain road runs up to the ridge as far as the **Špindlerovo sedlo,** where Spindlerova bouda stands (9 km).

Mountain tours from Špindlerův Mlýn

1. over the Pláň to the Sněžka, back over the **Kozí hřbety** (Goat's Back); by chair lift up to the top of the Pláň, from here—green signs—through the woods to the Klínová bouda. A path with blue signs leads to the Výrovka and then on—red signs—to the Luční bouda. Along the frontier up to the Sněžka. Back to the Luční bouda and following the red-marked path from the Bílá louka to where the path forks; the path running right and marked yellow leads to the narrow ridge Kozí hřbety (altogether 24 km).

2. through the mountain valleys: green signs to the village of Sv. Petr na Výrovka, from where red signs lead uphill to the Luční bouda. Then follows—blue signs—the descent through the lovely valley of the Bílé Labe (White Elbe), shut off on the north by the Stříbrný hřeben and on the south by the Kozí hřbety, into the Elbe valley and back to Špindlerův Mlýn; 22 km.

3. Pohraniční hřeben (frontier ridge): By car to the Špindlerovo sedlo (9 km). A path with red signs leads to the Petrova bouda and a bit higher up to the ruin-like groups of granite known as the Dívčí and Mužské kameny. Here begins a series of distant views, culminating in the finest on the Vysoké kolo (4,970 feet). Descent over the abysses of the glacial Sněžné jámy to near the Polish Wawel bouda and from there to the Labská bouda. On to the source of the Elbe, past the waterfall (165 feet); through magnificent scenery, still along the Elbe, we come down into the Labský důl natural reservation and to Špindlerův Mlýn. Altogether 18 km.

4. Mountain views: To the Labská bouda, as in the previous tour, only this time instead of descending from the bouda we keep on, following the red signs, with a continuous view of the valley bottom as far as the Krkonoše (a road from Jilemnice runs up here, see later), from where, still keeping to the red signs, we come down, at first gently, then steeply through the woods to Špindlerův Mlýn. 18 km.

Jilemnice on the local railway line from **Martinice** (express stop on the line Prague—Giant Mountains). Distance by rail from Prague via Jičín 154 km, via Turnov 164 km. Direct motor coach services to and from Prague. Distance by road from Prague 130 km, from Liberec 75 km.

An old district capital, on the former trade route across the Giant Mountains, with a textile industry and ski and toboggan production. The **castle,** built in 1716, contains outstanding collections of local folk-art.

Jilemnice is the cradle of skiing in the Giant Mountains. In 1892 Count Jan Harrach, the pioneer of tourism in the Giant Mountains, sent his game-keepers here for training.

Two mountain roads lead from Jilemnice to the top of the ridge, one the main **Krkonoše** ridge (23 km), the other up Mount Žalý (where there is a belvedere) and to the hotel colony of **Benecko** (14 km).

Excursions from Jilemnice: 1. Mountain road to the Krkonoše (regular motorbus service in summer) and from here to the source of the Elbe, the Elbe waterfall and up to the top of the Kotel with another panorama (half-day trip).

2. again to the Krkonoše, from here descent—red signs—to the Bucharova stezka, a narrow path over the Mechovinec (3,560 feet view), the Černá skála (3,452 feet) and the Šeřín (3,409 feet) to the belvedere on the Žalý (3,419 feet). Descent to Benecko, from here to Jilemnice either by motorbus or on foot (the whole tour 25 km).

From Jilemnice an excellent mountain road runs through the Iser valley to **Harrachov,** after **Špindlerův Mlýn** the most important tourist centre in the Giant Mountains.

Harrachov lies deep in the woods in the western part of the Giant Mountains (2,145 feet). In the neighbouring village of **Rýžoviště** the Czechoslovak

Physical Culture Association has a large gymnastic centre. A ski jump with an artificial track, which makes summer training also possible, is available.

Communications with Prague via Polubný-Kořenov, to which place there is a direct fast train service (139 km). From Liberec to Polubný-Kořenov by rail 34 km. A motorbus service meets every train to Harrachov.—Distance by road Prague-Harrachov 130 km, Liberec-Harrachov 43 km (regular motor-bus connection). From Harrachov a ski lift to the top of the Čertova Hora (3,323 feet). A number of hotels and pensions cater for visitors to Harrachov.

Excursions from Harrachov to the ridges of the Giant Mountains: a green-marked path leads past the Physical Training grounds to the Dvoračka bouda (well-known ski terrain), from there—red signs—up to the top of the Kotel (4,732 feet) with a beautiful view; below the mountain lies the Kotelné jámy natural reservation with rare alpine flora. We follow the red signs on to the top of the Krkonoš above the Elbe valley, pass the Pančice waterfall to the Labska bouda at the fall and return to Harrachov either following the:

a) blue signs—through the lovely Mumlava valley, with mountain flora. Just before we reach Harrachov is the well-known Mumlava waterfall, formed like steps, or—

b) red signs—to the source of the Elbe, then across meadows and through dwarf pine woods to the Vosecká bouda and from there into the Mumlava valley to the waterfall and on to Harrachov.

c) by the Iser valley (red signs) as far as the peak of Bukovec (3,277 feet the largest basalt formation in central Europe, a botanic reservation with remains of a magnificent beech forest and some 120 varieties of high mountain flora; fine panorama) and to the village of **Jizerka** (9 km, "Pyramida" tourist chalet) in the heart of the dense forests of the Iser Mountains. In the surroundings, the vast "Velká and Malá jizerska louká" (the Large and Small Meadow of the Iser) peat moors, of a rare beauty but accessible only with an experienced guide. Return route (yellow signs): 9,5 km. A mountain road leads also to Jizerka by Kořenov-Polubný (14 km).

6.   EAST BOHEMIA

The region of East Bohemia is clearly separated from the rest of Bohemia by the following rivers: the **Úpa,** the upper course of the **Elbe** and the **Chrudimka.** The character of the whole region is dictated, on the one hand, by these rivers and, on the other, by the mountain chains which separate it on the north-east from Poland and on the east from Moravia.

General Features

The difference of natural scenery gives East Bohemia its variety. It has also a great wealth of monuments in the most different architectural styles. The Elbe valley is the beginning of one of the most fertile regions of Czechoslovakia, which extends from here into Central Bohemia and because of its fertility is called the "Golden Strip of Bohemia". On the other hand, East Bohemia is remarkable for a varied and extensive industry. Some East Bohemian enterprises have long been the pride of the country. Pre-eminent here is the cotton textile industry. Among the towns with a highly developed textile industry are Dvůr Králové, Náchod, Nové Město nad Metují, Police nad Metují, Rychnov nad Kněžnou, Hořice, Vamberk and others. The leather industry is chiefly concerned in Hradec Králové, Chrudim, Třebechovice pod Orebem, Týniště on the Elbe and Jaroměř. The metal industry, the woodworking industry (the manufacture of furniture), the agricultural industry (alcohol production) and the chemical industry are principally represented at Hradec Králové and Pardubice. By and large the denser industrial network is concentrated in the northern half of East Bohemia; the southern part around Pardubice, because of the great expanse of arable country, has more of an agricultural character.

Geographically, the surroundings of Hradec Kralové form part of the following river basins: Metuje, Divoká and Tichá Orlice. However, the special character of the Pardubice region is due to its position at the centre of the Chrudimka and Loučná basins. Along these two waterways lie the most interesting tourist regions, including, to the north, the strange and ragged sandstone formations near the town of Police on the Metuje, and the Eagle Mountains and, to the south, the last northern foothills of the

Českomoravská vyšocina (Czecho-Moravian Plateau); for the last-named region, see Chapter 7. These two mountain regions are extremely rich in coniferous forests which abound in all kinds of game.

East Bohemia has much to interest the tourist: let us only mention the great number of strongholds and feudal residences which are now administered by the State, and the multitude of towns—now scheduled as historic sites because of their remarkable architectural features—which extend to the foot of the Eagle Mountains.

Almost next to one another in a relatively small area the old towns Náchod, Nové Město nad Metují, Opočno, Rychnov nad Kněžnou and others grew up, their architectural charm offset by wonderful castles and ancient citadels, which are today used as museums or art galleries.

Communications: East Bohemia is connected with the capital both by rail and by a network of numerous roads with many motor coach services. The distance from Prague to Pardubice and Hradec Králové is 104 km.

Sights and places of interest

Scheduled Towns: Pardubice, Litomyšl, Nové Město nad Metují.

Natural reservations: The Adršpach and Teplice Rocks, the Broumov Rocks, the rock group Ostaš near Police nad Metují, Babiččino údolí near Česká Skalice.

Tourist regions: The Bohemian-Moravian highland plateau, the Orlické hory, the Adršpach and Teplice Rocks, the Broumov and Police Rocks between the towns of Broumov and Police Metují.

Castles: Pardubice, Litomyšl, Náchod, Nové Město nad Metují, Opočno, Rychnov nad Kněžnou, Častolovice, Doudleby nad Orlicí.

Other sights: Kuks and Betlem (Jaroměř district), the battlefield of Hradec Králové (Königgrätz), 1866, the Seč Dams (Chrudim), Bílá Třemešná (Dvůr Králové), Pastviny (Žamberk).

Spas: Bohdaneč (Pardubice district).

A circular tour of East Bohemia

Pardubice-Litomyšl (57 km), Rychnov nad Kněžnou (103 km), Deštné in the Orlické hory (127 km) (the tourist hotel on the

Šerlich, 133 km), Deštné (129 km), Opočno (163 km), Nové
Město nad Metují (175 km), Náchod (190 km), Dobrošov
(196 km), Náchod (202 km), Police nad Metují (217 km), the
rock-town of Adršpach (233 km), Police nad Metují (249 km),
Náchod (264 km), Jaroměř (286 km), Kuks (293 km), Jaroměř
(300 km), Hradec Králové (321 km), Pardubice (345 km).

The largest towns and main centres of the economic and cultural life of East Bohemia, which makes up one of the administrative divisions of Czechoslovakia, namely the "Department of
East Bohemia", are Hradec Králové and Pardubice. Hradec
Králové is the seat of the National Departmental Committee
and thus the capital of the entire region.

A. HRADEC KRÁLOVÉ

Hradec Králové is the largest town in East Bohemia.
It has a population of about 65,000 and is one of
the oldest cities in Bohemia.

History: Hradec Králové lies at the junction of the Elbe and
the Orlice, where in the 10th century there arose a settlement, a
fortress with a market on the trade route from the Danube to the
Baltic and from Prague to the Polish city of Cracow. In about
1225 the market grew into a town. A royal stronghold was built
there. In the 14th century Hradec became the residence of the
Bohemian queens and the name of the town derives from that
time. At the same time the cathedral of the Holy Ghost was built
here. It is still an ornament of the town although it has suffered
some alterations since it was built, as it has been repeatedly
reconstructed and restored.

In the 14th century the free city of Hradec Králové became the
greatest and most important city after Prague and had a decisive
influence on the history of the country. In the most important
era of Czech history, in the time of the Hussite Revolution,
Hradec Králové remained loyal on the side of the Hussites,
whose famous general Jan Žižka of Trocnov, today honoured as
a national hero, was buried for a time in the cathedral of the
Holy Ghost. In later years the city regained its prosperity and
always remained loyal to the Bohemian kings. Councils of
significance for the fate of the whole of Bohemia were held at
Hradec Králové. Disaster did not overtake the city until the
Thirty Years War when the catastrophe involved the confiscation
of property and the destruction of some 500 houses, and religious

conflicts, caused by the return to Catholicism, which was imposed by force on the whole region, and made possible only by the flight into exile of the intellectual Protestant élite.

In the 18th century Hradec Králové suffered from the war between Prussia and Austria. The town was several times occupied and in 1762 it was pillaged and razed to the ground by Prussian troops. This sealed the fate of the town from then on. Between 1766 and 1789 Hradec Králové was rebuilt as a powerful fortress. Only the historic core of the town was preserved, enclosed by impressive fortifications, trenches and breastworks. Nevertheless the town developed as a lively centre of culture which was fostered to a remarkable extent by the activity of Prague, especially in the 19th century when the Czech nation experienced its renascence. The fortress of Hradec Králové was destroyed in 1884 and the removal of the fortifications was begun in 1893. Soon afterwards the town started to develop thanks to experienced administrators; it was planned on a rational basis, and new buildings were designed to meet the demands both of modern urban environment, and of aesthetic principles.

Architecturally, Hradec Králové holds a privileged position among Bohemian towns: in fact, the new districts were built with the aid of the most eminent Czechoslovak artists, including the architects Jan Kotěra, Josef Gočár, Jan Reichl, Oldřich Liška, etc. and the best modern sculptors, e.g., Jan Štursa and Otto Guttfreund. Thanks to the combined efforts of all these experienced experts, the various tasks of renovation and restoration of the remains of the former fortress were accomplished most skilfully, and numerous original palaces and buildings were erected such as few Czech towns can boast.

Let us only mention here the Zdeněk Nejedlý National History Museum, the Ambrož choir, the diocesan buildings, the tanning school, the hospital, the gymnasium, the Town Baths, the railway station, the Jirásek Park, among others. Today Hradec Králové consists of two clearly differentiated parts: the Old Town standing on the so-called "Hill" at the junction of the Elbe and the Orlice and the modern New Town which lies between the Elbe and the railway station.

Sights and places of interest

Žižka Square (Žižkovo náměstí) is the town centre. The **Cathedral of the Holy Ghost** or Epicospal Church (Hradec Králové was raised to an episcopal see in 1653) is an outstanding monument in Gothic style, the only perfect early Gothic edifice in all Bohemia. The church was built in 1307 and in the choir, for the first time in Bohemia, an unbroken verticality was adhered to without articulated vaulting. The cathedral strikes the eye because of its red-brick walls, for bricks were not generally used in Bohemia in ecclesiastical buildings. In the cathedral itself are a very beautiful shrine in the form of a Gothic turret (1497), a pewter font (1407), a 15th–century aisle altar and a picture of Saint Anthony by the famous Baroque painter Peter Brandl.

The **White Tower** dates from 1574–90; it is built of sandstone, is 220 feet high and its Augustine bell (1509) is the second largest in all Bohemia. The letter "G" on the top of the tower stands for George (Jiří) of Poděbrad, who was a great patron of the town.

The **Saint Clement's chapel** under the White Tower, a baroque building erected on the site of the original wooden church, is dedicated to the saint of that name. It dates from the time when Christianity began to spread from Moravia into Bohemia. The cupola of the chapel is adorned by a papal tiara (1716).

The **old Town Hall** was built in the 15th century. It was reconstructed in the 16th, 18th and 19th centuries and has two proud towers.

The house "**U Špulaků**", No 51, an unconventional Baroque building, was once used by the Bohemian Brotherhood, an evangelical religious community to which the pedagogue Jan Amos Komenský (Comenius) also belonged, the space at the back being their chapel and choir.

The **episcopal residence** has the house number 52. It dates from 1709–16, has a private chapel, a collection of antiquities and a small gallery of old and valuable pictures, among which the portraits of the Hradec bishops are especially noteworthy.

The **Church of Our Lady** (1654–66)—also called the Jesuit church—is a veritable treasure of Baroque architecture and painting. The church was built by the Italian architect Carlo Luragho. The large pictures of Saint Ignatius and Saint John of Nepomuk were painted by Peter Brandl. The **statue of the Madonna** is Baroque (1717). The sculptor was an unknown Italian master.

The best view of Hradec Králové Old Town can be had from the arcades on the north side of the big market square, the five towers of the buildings in the market place being visible from No. 155.

All the sights hitherto mentioned are in the Žižkovo náměstí.

We enter the **Castle Yard,** an intimate square dotted with Baroque buildings, in which stands the former Episcopal Seminary with the **Nepomuk Church** (1714) on the same site as once stood the castle of the Bohemian queens and later the residence of the burgrave, decorated with 15th century graffiti. Part of it is still preserved.

The **small market place** with its arcades. The **town Museum,** designed by Jan Kotěra, the founder of modern Czech architecture, and built in 1909–12, has fine exhibition rooms, lecture halls, reading rooms and a library. It consists of two parts: the handicrafts museum and the historical museum which includes a lapidarium.

The Town Baths have a swimming pool with artificially created waves.

The **Greek Orthodox church** (1759) was transferred to the Jirásek Park from Malá Polana in East Slovakia.

Accommodation in Hradec Králové can be found in the Hotel Bystrica and others.

The surroundings of Hradec Králové

1. To the north-west: The **battlefield** where in the Prusso-Austrian War of 1866 the opposing armies met decisively on the soil of **Königgrätz** and **Sadowa,** about 15 km north-west of Hradec Králové. The centre of the battlefield is Mount **Chlum** (1,108 feet) with a look-out tower. The place can be reached directly by road or by rail. Station: **Dlouhé Dvory.**

Hořice. Direct rail connection with Hradec Králové; distance by road, running north-west is 27 km. The Special School of Sculpture, in which the **Giant Mountains Museum** is also housed, is in the town. In the museum is a "Plastics Gallery" with originals and copies of almost all outstanding works by Czech sculptors. The school buildings are also adorned by statuary.

2. To the west. Hrádek near Nechanice, about 15 km west of Hradec Králové, a State-owned **chateau** (1841–54) built in Tudor style to the plans of the English architect Lamb. The little chateau stands in a park; the ornamentation, mostly in late Renaissance style, is the work of native artists.

Chlumec nad Cidlinou, some 29 km west of Hradec Králové, has a **castle** known as the "Charles's Crown". The plan of the castle was designed by the Italian architect Giovanni Santini and carried out by the Czech builder Maximílian Kaňka in 1721–23. An interesting centre block with three wings, with an overarched middle section and a perron leading up to the great hall on the first floor.

3. To the north. Kuks and Betlem, about 30 km north of Hradec Králové. Both places are monuments of Baroque art. A spa was started here in the late 16th and early 17th century and a noble's residence, besides a hospital with a church and a garden, were built. The work was done by Italian architects and masons (G. B. Alliprandi, P. Netola, P. della Torre) and completed by Matthias Braun, one of the most famous Baroque sculptors who worked for a long time in Bohemia. Braun left here about 55 works which are still the pride of Kuks and Betlem although they have been affected by time and weather.

B. THE NÁCHOD-BROUMOV REGION

The **Vale of Ratiboř**—also called the Grandmother valley—is a natural reservation in the valley of the Úpa river. On the right bank of the Úpa a **castle** was built on a hill in 1708, which is sentimentally associated in the minds of the Czech people with the immortal work "The Grandmother" by the Czech writer Božena Němcová.

In 1813, at the initiative of the chatelaine of that time, Princess Zaháňská, Friedrich Wilhelm, King of Prussia and the Austrian chancellor Metternich met here for a consultation. Not only the castle, but the whole surroundings (the "Old Bleaching-house", the mill, the Viktorka weir, the Panklovna, etc) are perpetually admired by the thousands of visitors who come here all the year through. The sculpture group "The Grandmother" by the contemporary Czech sculptor Otto Guttfreund merits special attention. The nearest town is **Česká Skalice,** about 30 km north-east of Hradec Králové.

Broumov, about 70 km north-east of Hradec Králové (by road 33–303). This ancient town on the Bohemian frontier has some important monuments. The imposing **Benedictine Monastery** was founded in 1322. The present building was designed by Kilian

Ignaz Dienzenhofer. It was built in 1727–35. It contains a unique **library** with numerous manuscripts, some of which are as old as 800. The monastery church is also the work of the same architect and is decorated with frescoes by J. Stenens of Steifels and pictures by Václav Vavřinec Reiner. The main altar is the work of another famous Prague artist, the sculptor Maximilian Brokoff. In the churchyard stands a tiny **wooden church** dating from 1450.

Police nad Metují, a little town about 65 km northeast of Hradec Králové, on the road to Broumov. It is a favourite starting point for excursions to the romantic **Police** or **Broumov** cliffs (about 2,310 feet above sea level). These are sandstone rocks, split by many deep chasms and precipes. Near-by are the rock groups **Ostaš** (2,300 feet), Mount **Hvězda** (2,222 feet) with a stellate Baroque chapel by Kilian Ignaz Dienzenhofer, the Slavný Rocks with Mount **Koruna** (2,382 feet) and Mount **Špičák** (2,477 feet). On the **Skály** stands a ruined castle and another small castle. In the town itself are a number of things of architectural interest, e.g. various details in the former **monastery** (built by K.I. Dienzenhofer), old wooden houses, etc.

Hronov nad Metují, an industrial town, some 50 km north-east of Hradec Králové, also on the road to Broumov, has a special significance for the Czech people. It was the birthplace of the famous classic Czech novelist, **Alois Jirásek.** He lies buried in his birthplace. A great amateur theatrical competition, a so-called "Jiráskův Hronov Theatrical Harvest", is held every year at Hronov.

Noteworthy is the construction of the old **Belfry** with a wooden cupola, the **Jirásek Theatre** built in

1930 and **Jírásek's tomb** with modern sculpture in the new cemetery.

The Teplice and Adršpach Rocks. This is a region dominated by two magnificent rock-labyrinths. They consist of strange sandstone formations, the remains of the Cretaceous Ocean. The "rock-towns" are not inter-connected. Each has its own entrance. The mass of rocks are 6 km long and 4 km wide, they are shaped like an elliptical sandstone stratum, rising to 1980 feet, and covered with magnificent forests. Starting point for the rocks is the small town of **Teplice nad Metují** (about 60 km north of Hradec Králové), a favourite excursion in the valley of the river Metuji and well-known as a spa with mineral springs of repute.

Náchod, an important East Bohemian town, about 45 km north-east of Hradec Králové. It is close to the frontier. The town is an industrial centre and has a wonderful **castle** with large collections; outstanding is a series of Brussels tapestries of old designs (1650). The original castle was obviously built to guard the road into Bohemia from Silesia and was reconstructed in 1556. At a later period a number of Italian Baroque masters (C. Luragho, C. Serena, D. Rossi, G. B. Spinetta, G. Vanetti, etc.) contributed to the decoration of the castle. In the market place stands a **Gothic church** built in 1310 on a ground plan resembling a cross.

6 km east of Náchod lies Mount **Dobrošov** (2,052 feet above sea level) from where one can enjoy a magnificent panorama of the region, particularly of the Eagle Mountains.

Nové Město nad Metují, about 9 km south of Náchod, is a remarkable memorial of Renaissance architecture in Bohemia with an oval market place; all the little houses have porches. The town also has a superb 17th-century **Renaissance chateau,** built by the Italian architect Duretti. It is one of the most picturesque towns in Bohemia, also because of its beautiful surroundings in the foothills of the Eagle Mountains.

The **Eagle Mountains (Orlické hory)** are a tourist region about 60 km north-east of Hradec Králové along the Czechoslovak–Polish frontier. The ridge of the Eagle Mountains reaches a height of over 3,600 feet (Velká Deštná) and is almost entirely covered by pinewoods, which in places have a primitive forest character. The Eagle Mountains are visited all the year round, for, apart from its natural beauties, many opportunities for excursions and good accommodation, it is one of the most frequented holiday resorts in Czechoslovakia. The most popular places to stay are the tourist hotels on the Šerlich (3,344 feet), Deštné (2,142 feet), Zdobnice (2,195 feet), Číhák (1,980 feet) and at the Pastviny Dam.

C. RYCHNOV NAD KNĚŽNOU

Opočno, about 25 km north-east of Hradec Králové, is famous for its **castle,** built in 1567. This has an arcaded fore-court, a chapel, a picture gallery and a collection of weapons which gives an idea of the development of the military arms and accoutrements of all Europe from the Middle Ages till the end of the 19th century.

Rychnov nad Kněžnou, a district capital roughly 40 km east (highway 11) from Hradec Králové, which was once famous for its cloth manufacture. Today the town is the economic and cultural centre of the district of the Orlické hory foothills. Rychnov nad Kněžnou has an interesting history and possesses notable artistic monuments, chiefly the State-owned **castle,** an early Baroque edifice (1676–90).

It is one of the great stately homes of the nobility, has many splendid rooms, three fore-courts and a **picture gallery,** consisting preponderantly of 18th and 19th-century pictures, besides valuable still life paintings and portraits. In the Castle picture gallery one can follow the evolution of artistic portraiture from the beginning of the 16th century to the mid-19th. Alongside numerous pictures by unknown masters and copyists, there are paintings by artists with famous names (e.g. Correggio, Jordaens, Halbac, Škréta). The collection of pictures is completed by carvings by old Bohemian masters and some tapestries from Brussels and Flemish workshops. Recently the district picture gallery was transferred from Hradec Králové to Rychnov castle. Also there is a copious **library** with manuscripts, many of which date from the 13th century. The **Gothic Church of the Holy Trinity**, with an ornate Baroque vaulted roof (1713) by Giovanni Santini, also belongs to the castle. The church assumed its present appearance after reconstructions carried out in 1798 and between 1837 and 1843.

On the so-called Jews' Hill above the town lies an interesting Jewish cemetery. At the foot of the castle hill the old cloth-makers' houses have been preserved.

Častolovice nad Orlicí, a State-owned castle, about 10 km west of Rychnov nad Kneznou, originally a Renaissance building (c 1600), later rebuilt, is interesting for its murals, coffered ceilings richly decorated with paintings, the collection of pictures of the Bohemian kings, its library and finally its English park.

Doudleby nad Orlicí, likewise a State-owned castle in Renaissance style of about 1590 (7 km south of Rychnov by Vamberk). Noteworthy are the graffiti decorations in the corridors, an arcaded fore-court and an interesting huge glazed stove (Baroque, 1690) richly ornamented with sculpture. The castle is surrounded by an English park.

D. PARDUBICE AND ITS ENVIRONS

Pardubice lies 24 km south of Hradec Králové so that this town can also be easily reached from there both by rail and by road. Pardubice is the second largest town in East Bohemia with a population of about 51,000 and is situated at the junction of the Elbe and the Chrudimka at the western end of East Bohemia. It is the seat of many administrative departments. The town has many schools, among them a **High School,** as well as other important cultural institutions including a permanent **theatre,** an **opera,** a **museum,** a public **library,** etc. Pardubice has been declared a State reservation and is an important road and railway junction. Pardubice is renowned throughout Czechoslovakia for its excellent gingerbread called "Pardubický perník".

History. The town has a centuries-old history, for its origins go back to the 13th century when it was built as a trade mart near a fortress which was later transformed into a refuge in case of invasion. There was an old Cyriecian Monastery close by. Pradubice was raised to the status of a city as early as 1340. 1490 however brought decisive changes for the development of the town, for in this year it became the property of the Czech family Pernštejn and at the instigation of this noble family was rebuilt at the beginning of the 16th century to exact plans in Renaissance style. Almost all the houses of the inner town near the new castle and three small churches were rebuilt on the old, late Gothic ground plans. Unfortunately little remains today of this work carried out by Italian and native masters. In the Thirty Years War Pardubice was razed to the ground by Swedish troops. Nevertheless so many artistic monuments still remain—some of course of later date—that Pardubice rightly belongs to the most treasured historical towns of Bohemia. That is also why it has been placed under State protection as a national site.

The sights of Pardubice

The Vilém of Pernštejn square, despite various reconstructions and new buildings, is one of the architectural show-pieces of the town, with a row of beautiful patrician houses, as for example No. 50 "U Jonáše" and No. 60.

The **street of the same name** can also boast a number of fine buildings: ancient Renaissance houses with late Gothic features (Nos 7, 8, 10 and 11).

The **Zámecká Street** with similar buildings (Nos 20, 21, 23, 41, 42, 46). The **Kostelní Street,** which because of the former castle water dykes is architecturally very interesting.

The State-owned **castle,** the biggest and artistically most valuable building in the town, built on the ground plan of an early 16th century Gothic stronghold, is typical of an early Renaissance noble's residence. It has four wings with arcades on the ground and first floors. The entrance to the castle is framed by a magnificent portal (1529). The interior furnishing is remarkable for 120 murals and panelled ceilings. From the castle bridge between the first and second forecourts is an interesting view of medieval Pardubice, looking towards the back of houses No 93 to 103.

The **Green Gate** (1507). Extensive reconstruction in 1886 restored this gate to its original appearance. It was once used to protect another town gate. Today it affords the best view of the town and its immediate surroundings.

The **church of Saint Bartholomew,** the **churches of the Annunciation** and of **Saint John the Baptist** date from 1510 to 1515 and are important memorials of the time when the town belonged to the Pernštejns. In the church of Saint Bartholomew are unusual Baroque paintings, as for instance the "The Torture of Saint Bartholomew" by L. Willmann.

Further, mention must be made of the **race track** where ever since 1874 the well-known "Grand Pardubice Steeplechase" is run every year over 4¼ miles. Many foreign motor cycle enthusiasts also know the local **motor cycle track** where the contest for the "Golden Helmet of Czechoslovakia" is regularly held.

Accommodation: Hotel Veselka, Hotel Zlatá Štika.

Excursions from Pardubice

1. Mount Kunětice 6 km north-east of Pardubice 1,006 feet above sea level. A high sugarloaf hill on the top of which stands a 15th-century ruined **castle.** A superb view in every direction. A **prehistoric burial ground** was discovered below the hill. The discoveries are in the Municipal Museum at Pardubice (in the castle).

Bohdaneč Spa, 9½ km north-west of Pardubice, with a mineral spring (21° C) and mud baths. Treatment is given for rheumatism, gynaecological, nervous and heart disorders and venereal diseases. Noteworthy are the Renaissance Town Hall and the Baroque church.

2. Chrudím (12 km south of Pardubice). A historical town with a castle mentioned as early as the middle of the 11th century. The town has some interesting monuments: e.g. the **Soap-boilers' House** (No 74) (1573), the Rozvadov house (No 76), Gothic and Renaissance portals, Baroque details and Empire buildings. The old 17th–century **Town Hall,** the **Church of the Assumption** (founded in 1291), the **Saint Michael's church** (16th century), the old Town Gates and the remains of the **castle.** Chrudím is the birthplace of the inventor of the ship's propeller, J. V. Ressel. A puppet-player's congress, known as the Chrudim Marionette Festival is organised here every year.

Interesting walks and excursions can be taken from Chrudím; to **Kočí**, 6 km east of Chrudím, for one. There is an interesting little **church** at Kočí and a **plebeian building** (1397) with a 17th-century wooden turret and 16th and 18th-century frescoes. Near the village of **Hradiste** are the remains of a Celtic oppidum.

18 km south-west of Chrudím a dam has been built on the small river Chrudímka with a surface area of 450 acres in the middle of the woods of the "Iron Mountains" (Železné hory) with excellent facilities for fishing. Ruins of a 14th-century castle.

E. LITOMYŠL

Litomyšl, 147 km south-east of Pardubice. An ancient town which sprang up around a stronghold built before 891. Litomyšl was raised to the status of a town as early as 1259. The town lies on the main highway 35 from Hradec Králové to Brno on the borders of Moravia. Under State protection as an Ancient Monument Litomyšl is the birthplace of the composer **Bedřich Smetana.** The room in which he was born is in the former brewery of the castle. It is also the home town of Zdeněk Nejedlý, the historian of music, historiographer of the town of Litomyšl, and first President of the Czechoslovak Academy of Science after 1945.

Things of interest in the town include: the **small Renaissance castle,** now administered by the State. It was built by the Italian architect Giovanni Battista Avostalis of Sala, and has attractive gables and an interesting interior.

The **Piarist College** and its church, built in 1730 by B. Alliprandi; now it houses the Municipal Museum with the valuable "Litomyšl Gradual", a collection of liturgical chants dating from 1563.

The **square with the Town Hall** and arcaded houses, one of the loveliest in Czechoslovakia.

The surroundings of Litomyšl and of Chrudím directly adjoin the "Českomoravská vysočina" (Czecho-Moravian Plateau), a region which abounds in natural beauty spots and cultural, economic and historic mementos.

7. THE HIGHLANDS OF BOHEMIA—MORAVIA

ČESKOMORAVSKÁ VYSOČINA

Českomoravská Vysočina (the Bohemian-Moravian highlands or Central Mountains) is an extensive plateau, not very high, in the frontier region of Bohemia and Moravia, two provinces which in the past formed a unity and were generally called the lands of Saint Václav's crown. This complex is part of the great mountain system, known as the Bohemian massif, which includes the whole of Bohemia and West Moravia and stretches as far as the Danube towards Austria and Bavaria and as far as the Oder towards Saxony and Silesia in the north.

The geological structure of the Bohemian-Moravian highlands is very old and probably goes back to the primary era. The plateau which extends to the Czecho–Moravian frontier is, for the most part, the vestige of a very old range which was transformed through the ages by erosion and denudation into a relatively high plateau. The average altitude of the ridge varies from 1,950 to 2,300 feet.

Originally the range was wooded and even today is rich in forests. The settling of this region began in the 13th century, and the first inhabitants of these parts burnt vast wooded areas to turn them into arable fields.

The Highlands of Bohemia–Moravia form an important watershed. In fact, the rivers running down the western slopes are carried by the Elbe to the North Sea, while those on the eastern slopes flow down to the Black Sea (Danube). At the foot of Mount Žákova hora—only some ten yards apart—are the sources of the Sázava which flows into the Vltava and then the Elbe, and of the Svratka which flows into the Dyje south of Brno and subsequently into the Morava and the Danube.

The highest part of the plateau is called **Zdárské vrchy,** the summit of which attains an altitude of 2,770 feet above sea level. This region is one of the most beautiful parts of Czechoslovakia. The whole ridge and its branches are densely covered by woods. Many excellent trout-streams and brooks add to the natural charm of the scenery. There are also many places, both towns and numerous castles and ruins with historic associations. Not least among the historic monuments are the works of popular architecture in the mountains, in the highest and most interesting part of them round Žďár on the Sázava river. No part of the Českomoravská vysočina fails to reward the tourist. It is also a paradise for shooting and fishing. The abundant flora and fauna are worth seeing. The local game include stag, roebuck and especially hares, partridges and pheasants galore. This beautiful scenery has long been an attraction for many artists who have found inspiration and peace there. An undulating, densely forested country with wide prospects and many historical sights, a long winter with a plentiful covering of snow and a hospitable people attract more and more tourists into the Central Mountains. In Žďárské vrchy in the country round Žďár on the Sázava, Polička and Nové Město na Moravě there has developed an important tourist and holiday area which is frequented at every season of the year. Natural bathing beaches have sprung up on the numerous lakes (e.g. Dářko, Sykovec, Milovy); all kinds of water sports, including sailing, are catered for here (Medlov).

In the finest town in the range, **Žďár** on the Sázava, an important industrial centre has been built up which has transformed the life of the local inhabitants. From way back this beautiful, but not very fertile mountainous country has been inhabited by an industrious, frugal people who have generally suffered hardship in the past. The poor soil could not provide them with sufficient nourishment and therefore the woods were the chief source of their livelihood. It has been aptly said that in the Českomoravská vysočina the bread was of wood. After the Second World War however consideration was given to this formerly forgotten region. In a few years Žďár, a small town with a population of 3,000, has become a hive of industry with modern equipment and installations. In a couple of years the town has increased its population to such an extent that it is reckoned that it will very shortly become an important industrial centre with 40,000 inhabitants. The visitor can see for himself from day to day the change in the character of the town and the region and in the people who live there. Alongside little wooden shacks, mostly with home-made clapboard roofs, tiny rooms modestly furnished with home-made furniture, have arisen not only modern houses, but also whole towns with new communications. The dwellings are equipped with modern facilities and so, because of the speed with which this new building has been carried out, it is possible to see here the old and the new world side by side. This applies not only to buildings but chiefly to the people and their dress. Here one can encounter old women who have lived here all their life, and who but a few decades ago weaved their own clothes and next to them workers dressed in the latest fashion and driving their own cars. In the cottages you will still find the typical fare of the mountain-dweller, as for example breakfast soup and peculiar potato dishes unknown elsewhere. A self-made, painted chest stands besides modern furniture, the wireless or television set, the washing machine or the refrigerator.

Communications

The Českomoravská vysočina can be reached by several roads, by rail and motor coach services. There are also some aerodromes (Křižanov, Přibyslav, Havlíčkův Brod) suitable for small air-taxis. Two highways run through the Bohemian–Moravian Central Mountains, connecting Prague with Brno. The southern connection runs from Prague through Kolín, Čáslav, Havlíčkův Brod or through Benešov and Vlaším to Jíhlava, and from there via Velké Meziříčí to Brno. The northern highway from Prague via Poděbrady, Hradec Králové, Litomyšl, Svitavy, Letovice and Blansko to Brno. Both highways are connected by several asphalt roads which facilitate access to all important places in this tourist region for motor vehicles. In the south one must also consider the main road connecting South Bohemia (České Budějovice) with Brno, via Jindřichův Hradec, Telč and Třebíč, and also the main highway from Jihlava running southeast through Moravské Budějovice and Znojmo (Znaim) where it branches to Vienna (frontier post Hatě-Klein Haugsdorf).

The Českomoravská vysočina has good railway connections with Prague and Brno, on the one hand through Jihlava, on the other through Havlíčkův Brod, Žďár on the Sázava, Tišnov or via Pardubice, from where the line to Havlíčkův Brod runs through Skuteč and Hlinsko, and also by the branch line from Svitavy (off the main Prague-Brno line) via Polička and Skuteč. The local service between Žďár on the Sázava and Tišnov via Nové Město na Moravé and Nedvědice is also important; it runs past the pearl of Czech castles, Pernštejn.

Sights and places of interest

Scheduled Towns: Telč.
State-owned castles: Telč castle, Pernštejn.
Dam: Vír.
Holiday centres: Jimramov, Sněžné, Svratka (golf course), the shore of the Dářko, Sykovec and Milovy lakes.

Other places of interest: the book museum at Žďár on the Sázava, the Štursa room in the museum at Nové Město na Moravě, the single-roofed bridge at Unčín, the burial mound of the Hussite general Jan Žižka of Trocnov near Přibyslav, the Porta Coeli at Předklášteří u Tišnova.

Excursions and tours in the Bohemian-Moravian Central Mountains

Polička, about 16 km south of Litomyšl (see East Bohemia) or 60 km east of Havlíčkův Brod by road; railway station on the Svitavy-Skuteč line. The famous composer **Bohuslav Martinů** was born here.

Bohuslav Martinů (born in 1890 at Polička, died in 1959 in Switzerland) was born in the tower of Polička church where his father worked as a watchman. At first he studied in Prague and later continued his studies with Professor Albert Roussel in Paris. Martinů ranks with the best composers of the twentieth century. Although he spent most of his time in France, the United States and Switzerland, his symphonies, concertos and vocal compositions abound in the traditional melodies of his native country.

The town also has a museum with interesting souvenirs of this famous son of Polička, especially of his artistic beginnings. The museum also contains outstanding ethnographical collections, namely a unique collection of wooden toys and of stained cut glass.

Svratka is about 25 km west of Polička on the road through Borová, and about 10 km from Hlinsko on the main line Prague-Havlíčkův Brod-Brno. An important holiday centre with the modern Hotel Mánes, a golf course, a swimming pool, excellent skiing terrain, a ski-jump and a racing rink for ice-skating. Permanent art exhibitions are also installed here.

Žďár nad Sázavou, about 30 km east of Havlíčkův Brod; a fast train stop on the Prague-Havlíčkův

Brod-Brno line. A new industrial centre of the Českomoravská vysočina. In the near-by **castle** of Žďár is an interesting section of the National Museum, the **Book Museum,** in which rare examples of the rich history of Bohemian book-printing are collected. The architecture of the old castle and the former Cistercian monastery are also of interest; further, the museum and the not distant **Pilgrimage Church** built to an unusual pentagonal ground plan by the architect Giovanni Santini.

Nové Město na Moravě, 11 km east of Žďár nad Sázava by road; on the railway line Žďár—Tišnov. An ancient town built by the noble Czech family Pernštejn. In the local **museum** are many interesting ethnographical collections and the remarkable Štursa room (Jan Štursa, one of the best modern Czech sculptors, pupil of Rodin and contemporary of Mestrovič, was born here).

Přibyslav on the road between Havlíčkův Brod (about 15 km away) and Žďár nad Sázava; on the railway line connecting these two towns. The famous general of the Hussite troops, Jan Žižka of Trocnov, died here in 1424. Žižka's burial mound close to the highway is one of the most important memorials of Czech history. In the middle of the 13th–century there were silver mines in the town. The 14th–century Gothic church and the 16th century castle stand on the site where the fortress for the protection of the mines once stood.

The **Dářko** lake on the road running north from Žďár (about 10 km distant) to **Ždírec and Chotěboř**. The lake with a surface area of 625 acres is a natural reservation. It is part of a system of iron mill ponds which, built one above the other, provided power for local industry in the 19th century. They date from the 15th century. Many interesting botanical rarities grow on the peat soil, as for example the marsh dwarf pine (pinus montana religinosa), creeping sedge (cares glauca), cotton grass (eriophorum) and many other curious plants. There is a bathing beach and many good camping places on the Dářko lake.

On the east bank of Lake Dářko is the important **Škrdlovice glassworks**, renowned particularly for its glass which is moulded directly in the oven and used for the manufacture of various finely coloured objects with modern lines, e.g., vases, dishes, etc which are now fashionable throughout the world and are exported in large quantities from Škrdlovice to many international markets.

Jihlava on the main highway Prague (144 km)—Brno (91 km); fast train stop. Jihlava is the political, cultural and economic centre of the Českomoravská vysočina. Silver was mined in the town in the past. In 1249 the first mining rights in Europe were granted *(jus regale montanorum)*. In the town one can also visit an interesting **picture gallery** and the **museum.**

Telč on the road from Jindřichův Hradec (41 km) to Třebíč (35 km). It lies about 30 km south of Jihlava (by road). Telč is a town protected by the National Trust. Here has been preserved a magnificent main square with arcades which is one of the most notable monuments of simple Renaissance architecture. The good condition not only of single houses, but also of the whole square is remarkable. One of the finest State-owned castles is in Telč, built in its present state in the 16th century by Italian architects and luxuriously decorated with pictures and stucco. The murals are particularly striking. Telč castle is one of the three most beautiful castles of the Rožmberk (Český Krumlov, Jindřichův Hradec, Telč). Foreign visitors to Czechoslovakia should not miss seeing this architectural and artistic gem.

The foothills of the Bohemian-Moravian
Central Mountains

They have the same character as the Českomoravská vysočina, described above and are immediately connected with it. The most typical part is round the course of the river Svratka, its valley being the most interesting and beautiful region, highly recommended, especially for walking tours. The best place to start from is either **Nové Město na Moravě** (see above) or **Bystřice pod Pernštejnem** (about 16 km east of Nové Město by road; railway station on the line Žďár nad Sázavou-Tišnov).

Jimramov (about 17 km north-west of Bystřice pod Pernštejnem) because of its beautiful situation has been called the Moravian Merano. In the past the little town lay on an important trade route linking Bohemia and Moravia. In the 13th century a noble's castle Skály was built here, but nothing remains of it. Jimramov was badly damaged in the Thirty Years War when General Torstensen's Swedish army passed through it. There are two notable places on the road from Bystřice to Jimramov. On a steep declivity above the **Vítochov** (about 8 km from Byštrice) a little 13th–century **church** dominates the surrounding country. Then nearer to Jimramov, one passes through **Unčín** where there is one of the latest important monuments of popular architecture, the single-roofed **wooden bridge.** At this place the river is dammed by a large waterworks, built a few years ago.

The Vír Dam. The huge dam, with a power station, completed in 1955, forms a lovely lake surrounded by woods. In the immediate neighbourhood we can study popular architecture. First mention must be made of **Fryšava** and **Krátká** near Sněžné and secondly of **Telecí** near Politička with its wooden church.

Sněžné, on the road between Jimramov and Nové Město na Moravé, is a small holiday resort visited all the year round. It has a comfortable hotel with a notable collection of pictures. The place is much frequented because of its good opportunities for walking and its excellent skiing terrain. There is also a swimming pool.

Pernštejn Castle, about 12 km south-east of Bystřice pod Pernštejnem (in the direction of Brno). The name of the castle derives from the famous noble family of the lords of Pernštejn. It is an outstanding edifice which was built on an inaccessible craggy projection above the Svratka river in the 13th century. After a fire in the middle of the 15th century the castle was rebuilt in Renaissance style without pulling down the original walls. The reconstruction was carried out with a view to the harmonising of the newly built Renaissance part with the original Gothic. Although at the time of its reconstruction comfortable chateaux were already being built in the parks of the larger towns, the Pernštejns had become so attached to their home that they not only stayed there, but went as far as to furnish it superbly and laid out a charming garden, so that the castle became not only a fortress, but also a comfortable aristocratic residence. The safety of the castle was assured by moats and ramparts, five gates and five towers. As the castle has remained essentially unaltered since the time its reconstruction was completed at the end of the 15th and the beginning of the 16th century, it is one of the most valuable architectural monuments. In the castle we find many reminders of the history of the family which formerly owned it, big collections of minerals and collections of hunting trophies and weapons. The furniture of various periods and the picture gallery are also noteworthy.

A few small castles belonging to the minor nobility were built near Pernštejn, e.g. at **Mitrov** which is now used as a Home for Old People.

Doubravník (further on in the direction of Brno) is a town chiefly interesting for its Gothic church, a daring edifice containing the vaults of the Pernštejn and Mitrovsky families. A monastery was founded here as early as 1208; it was destroyed in the 13th century when the Tartars invaded Moravia.

Předklášteří u Tišnova, on the road from Bystřice pod Pernštejnem to Brno (24 km); railway connection with the fast train station of Tišnov. In 1243 the Přemyslid Queen Konstanza founded a Cistercian Convent here which with its chapter hall and cloisters is one of the most important architectural monuments in the Czech provinces. A real gem is the church portal—Porta Coeli (heaven's gate)—, a superb, well-preserved Gothic memorial, richly ornamented with Gothic figures and bas-reliefs.

The region, especially the district near Žďár nad Sázavou, Polička and Svratka, is criss-crossed by a dense network of footpaths. It is advisable to start walking tours from Svratka, which is very favourably situated.

8. BRNO (BRÜNN) AND SURROUNDINGS

Brno and the department of Brno are among the most economically important districts of Czechoslovakia. Their importance is enhanced by the organisation of trade fairs in the fair grounds of Brno. The present-day fairs carry on the tradition of collective exhibitions of Czechoslovak engineering which also used to attract numerous interested visitors from abroad.

The region is of course also an important centre of tourism with many natural beauties and historical monuments. To give a better idea of it from a touristic point of view it may be divided into three smaller areas: the foothills of the Českomoravská vysočina; the course of three rivers, namely the Oslava, the Jihlavka and the Rokytná; and finally Podyjí, a wine-growing district in the Pavlov Mountains. Brno and its immediate surroundings may be considered as a separate unit, principally the Moravian Karst north of the town with its marvellous stalactite caves and the famous Macocha Gorge. It includes the district of Slavkov with the Napoleonic battlefield and the district of Bučovice, east of Brno, quite close to the most interesting region of Moravian Slovakia, renowned for its wealth of folklore where the prettiest local costumes are worn and fragrant wines are produced. As is shown by archaeological discoveries, the environs of Brno were settled in prehistoric times and the first traces, remains of ovens, ancient utensils, etc. found near Brno, indicate that 100,000 years B.C. the so-called bear-hunters who lived at the beginning of the Ice Age dwelt here. In later times these Neandertal people were replaced by the immediate predecessors of homo sapiens, the so-called Cromagnons or mammoth-hunters. Among the richest excavation sites is Dolní Věstonice. The Věstonice Venus, a figurine modelled out of clay and ashes, has become world-famous. From then on the population has steadily increased, from the reindeer-hunters, and other races to the protoslavs and Slav tribes. The visitor to Brno can get a good idea of this distant past in the excellently arranged archaeological section of the municipal museum.

Brno also has an anthropologic museum devoted to prehistoric Man. It is unique of its kind and contains precious items discovered not only on Czechoslovak territory but also in other European and overseas countries.

Communications

Brno lies on the railway line connecting Prague with Bratislava. It is an important junction with direct connections to Ostrava, to Warsaw and Jíhlava, České Budějovice and Plzeň. Brno has also a direct air service to Prague and Bratislava. The national highway connects Brno with every important centre in Czechoslovakia and with Vienna (approx. 130 km, frontier post Mikulov-Drassenhofen).

Sights and places of interest in the Brno region

Town reservations: Mikulov, Slavonice, Znojmo.
Natural reservations: Serpentit Steppe near Mohelno (Jíhlava district), the Bird Sanctuary at Lednice.
State-owned castles: Bítov, Lednice, Náměšt nad Oslavou, Slavkov near Brno, Vranov on the Dyje, Židlochovice.
Dams: Kníničky near Brno, Vranov on the Dyje.
Stalactite caves: The Moravian Karst with the Macocha.
Folklore: Břeclav, Podluží.
Other objects of interest: the Králice Bible Museum at Králice, the Romanesque basilica at Třebíč, the game park at Židlochovice, the Věstonice Venus in the Municipal Museum at Brno and the Napoleonic battlefield near Slavkov (Austerlitz).

A. BRNO

Brno, departmental capital, pop. 325,000, is the historic and economic centre of Moravia.

Its industry, particularly its engineering and textile industries (machines, tractors, bridges, complete factory installations—produced in some local machine shops) earned the town a worldwide reputation. Its special electro-technical products and its well-known cloth are also in demand in many countries all over the world.

In the town, which was once the seat of Moravian margrave, there are many monuments of various eras. Before coming to Brno, especially on the road from Prague, the traveller is struck by two buildings; Brno castle on the Špílberk and the cathedral on the Petrov (St. Peter). The two hills on which these buildings stand, are familiar silhouettes in Brno. The Petrov is the oldest part of this historic town.

The castle, the seat of a branch of the Přemyslid dynasty, once stood on the site of the present Gothic cathedral. The present **cathedral** stands on the foundation walls of the original Romanesque basilica. On this foundation stone also stood a 15th–century Gothic church. But of this edifice, too, only the walls and an additional tower remain whereas the cathedral itself was restored in Baroque style in the 17th century after the end of the siege by the Swedes. It was later re-Gothicised to its present appearance. Inside the cathedral are many interesting memorials, pictures and statues.

The little park below the cathedral was laid out on the old fortifications, as were the wide circular roads running into it. There is a fine view to the south and south-west from the park.

The **castle** is chiefly worth seeing for its dungeons with casemates and torture chambers. Among others the Italian Carbonari were imprisoned here, one of whom was the poet Silvio Pellico. The subterranean casemates are accessible. Instruments of torture are still preserved there. Although the prison on the Špilberk was liquidated and closed in 1855, it was used again during the Hitler occupation. And once more not only Czech but also Polish and Italian patriots suffered in its dank dungeons.

The other side of the Husova Street is formed by a row of great buildings, the back part of the New Town Hall with the remains of the castle ramparts, the Applied Arts Museum with its admirable collections, (recently the ultra-modern "International" Hotel has been built in the vicinity; it was designed and furnished by the best architects and decorators and has every comfort) and the Beseda House, which towards the end of the Hapsburg monarchy was the Czech headquarters in Brno. It is a remarkable cultural monument with a large concert hall. The entrance to the New Town Hall is in the náměstí Družby Národů (International Friendship Square), dominated by the **Dominican church of St. Michael**, a 17th-century Baroque edifice which replaced the former Gothic church. The cathedral contains valuable pictures and chiefly bas-reliefs by Winterthal, besides a pulpit and altar by Černý.

The neighbouring houses, Baroque buildings by the architect Grimm, are today the headquarters of the National Committee. Remarkable is the old refectory in Gothic style, once used by the Diet, an old Romanesque-Gothic cloister and the assembly room richly adorned by frescoes. The adjoining Knights' Hall, in which traces of Renaissance style can be found, is used today for the celebration of marriages.

The Dominikánská runs the length of St. Michael's cathedral; the outstanding house in this street is one of the most picturesque and historic palaces, the so-called **Podebradsky dvur.** Its origins date from the 14th century.

The Mečová Street, connects the large náměstí 25 unora (25th February square), with a beautiful old fountain in the centre, with the náměstí Družby národů, from where a passage leads to the Old Town Hall (Stará radnice). There in the well of an ancient staircase hangs the so-called **Dragon of Brno**, a reptile

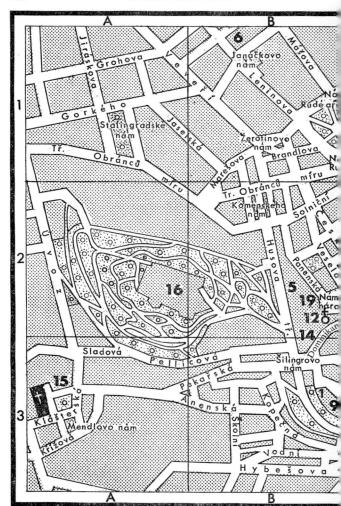

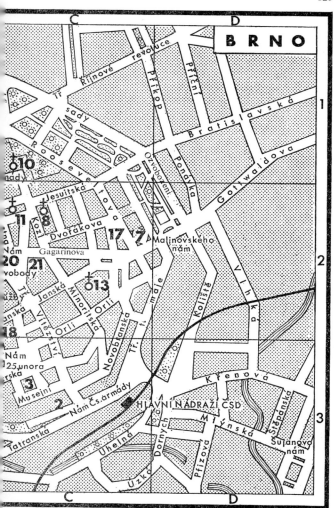

which according to an old legend devoured the maidens of the town. Although the facts are indisputably different, the Dragon of Brno still remains the principal sight of the town together with the **Brno Wheel,** which was made in a day long ago by a skilful apprentice in South Moravia and brought to Brno. The Dragon of Brno is often used as the emblem of the town.

Through the ancient house with picturesque nooks and numerous Renaissance and Baroque additions we come into the Radniční ulice and to the Old Town Hall tower. The original Gothic tower is still embellished by a late Gothic portal. The **Radnicni Street** leads into the náměstí 25 unora, in the centre of which stands a beautiful fountain, a work by Johann Bernard Fischer of Erlach. On the far side of the square the eye is held by the imposing **Moravian Museum,** formerly the Dietrichstein palace.

In its fore-court stands a charming Baroque Mercury fountain. In the picture gallery the connoisseur will find not only works by **Etgens,** but also paintings by **Rubens, Cranach** and other masters as well as pictures by young Moravian artists.

On the opposite side of the market place is the Redoute where theatrical performances were given at the end of the 17th century. From there the narrow Kapucínská ulice leads to the old Capuchin church

---

Key to the plan of Brno (pages 222/223)

1 Bishop's Palace, B3	2 Capucins Church, C3
3 Moravian Museum, C3	4 Municipal Museum, B2
5 Industry Museum, B2	6 Leoš Janáček Museum, B1
7 House of Arts, C2	8 Jesuit Church, C2
9 Saint Peter's Cathedral, B3	10 Saint Thomas' Church, C1
11 Saint James's Church, C2	12 Saint Michael's Church, B2
13 Minorite Church, C2	14 Court of Poděbrady, B2
15 Cloister of Old Brno, A3	16 Stronghold (Špilberk), A2
17 Leoš Janáček Opera House, C2	18 Old Town Hall, C2
19 New Town Hall, B2	20 State Bank (Exchange), C2
21 Ethnological Museum	

with a vault in which the mummies of dead monks lie and which also contains the tomb of Baron Trenck.

We continue our walk from the Capuchin church through the Josefská into the narrow alleys of the Old Town. There we find some interesting Baroque buildings, especially the **Minorite church.** The original Gothic edifice was reconstructed in Baroque style and in the first half of the 18th century its vaulting was decorated with imposing frescoes. In the adjacent building which was once a monastery we admire valuable carvings, Baroque statues and paintings. The **St. James's Church** (kostel sv. Jakuba) has a 300 ft tower, the highest in the whole of Brno. In its apparent simplicity it is one of the finest Gothic buildings. Plain pillars support a delicately reticulated vault. In the church itself are valuable Romanesque-Gothic statues, notably a cross, then statues of the Renaissance and Baroque periods and a remarkable organ. Behind the altar stands the sarcophagus of Raduit de Souches, the defender of the town in the Thirty Years War when it was besieged by the Swedes.

Immediately behind the St. James's church, the **Jesuit church** (Jesuitský kostel) merits attention, an important early Baroque monument with notable treasures in statuary and pictures within its walls. The ceiling frescoes were damaged in the Second World War, but have already been restored. The Jesuitská leads on to a large park with some cafés and kiosks. Turning left, at the park we pass the Red Army Memorial on the way into the Red Army Square (náměstí Rudé Armády), laid out as gardens. The block of buildings on the left is a former 18th-century monastery, later used as the Statthalter's residence. The **St. Thomas's church** near-by (Kostel sv. Tomáše) with its early Baroque portal facing the square is chiefly interesting for the very beautiful painting above the high altar, a work by Maulpertsch.

Through the ulice 9. května (9th May street), past the main door of the church, we come to **Freedom Square** (náměsti svobody), the actual centre of Brno. There is an early Baroque **Plague Column** in the square, which is surrounded by many palaces, richly ornamented with statues and sgraffiti. Noteworthy is the early Renaissance house of the **Lords of Lipa.** At the corner of the Gagarina in the north-east corner of the square interesting Baroque buildings have been restored and are today as an **ethnographic used museum.**

This museum, which was opened at the end of 1961, has an interesting exhibition of objects relating to the **old, traditional Moravian culture** (traditional architecture, costumes, embroideries), and also shows the cultural life of the people today. Especially interesting is the collection of **ceramics** which contains unique pieces from all periods. There are also vast store places near the museum, because the exhibition can only contain a fraction of the items. The collection of ceramics has a worldwide importance, and the wide range of traditional designs make it interesting even to the layman.

The Kobližná, one of the most animated of the old business streets, leads into a square with **Janáček Opera House** in the centre. Leoš Janáček, a world-famous name in contemporary music, lived at the end of the 19th and the beginning of the 20th century in Brno where he composed his greatest works. The broad trída 1 máje leads past the modern motorbus station to the main railway station and continues from there through the nádražni ulice to the Brno Fair Grounds. On the way we should not overlook the **Augustinian Monastery** in the Old Town with a beautiful Gothic church. The church was built in 1322. In the past science and art thrived in the monastery;

many famous philosophers and artists worked there, among them composers. The world-famous naturalist Gregor Mendel, the founder of Mendelism, also made his experiments in this Augustine monastery.

The **Fair Exhibition Grounds** draw plenty of visitors when the fairs and exhibitions are on, but all year round a cultural and recreation park is open to the public with many restaurants, a theatre, a cinema and other places of amusement.

The main Exhibition Palace was erected in 1926–1928. The Brno Fair Grounds are undoubtedly among the most interesting fair grounds in Europe, from an architectural standpoint. The whole pavilion is dominated by a glass tower from which one can enjoy a wonderful view of the grounds and a large part of the town.

New, architecturally interesting pavilions have been built in the last few years in the precincts of Brno Fair (e.g., the circular "Z" pavilion, and others). The Fair grounds, surrounded by wooded slopes, are among the loveliest parts of the town.

The boundary on the south side of the grounds is the river Svratka, and the visitor now reaches a little wood with well-kept walks and a restaurant with a view. At the foot of the wood runs the circular road where every year at the end of August the car and motor-cycle race for the "Grand Prix of Czechoslovakia" is held.

There are also many other things to see in Brno. Numerous parks add to the amenities of the town. There is an active cultural and social life. Brno has four permanent theatres; first and foremost, the Janáček Opera House where operas and ballets are presented. Other cultural institutions are several museums and exhibition rooms and some concert halls. The Technical High Schools and chiefly the Engineering High School are the leading educational establishments. Brno also has a University, an

Agricultural High School and the Janáček Academy of Music. There are in addition an amplitude of sports grounds. Amongst the several playing fields and stadiums pride of place must be given to the Winter Stadium where ice hockey matches and skating contests are held from October to March. In the summer the Winter Stadium is used as a cultural and recreation centre.

In the suburbs, particularly in the eastern part of the town, are several industrial concerns.

Brno has many places of amusement and night clubs; the most popular are the "Club", the "Typos", the "Roxy", the "Boccaccio" and the Rozmarýn Cabaret and there are plenty of cheerful bodegas and restaurants.

Accommodation: The International, Čedok Grand Hotel near the main railway station, the Hotels Slovan, Slavia, Avion, etc.

Excursions from Brno

The visitor will find the beautiful surroundings of Brno easily accessible. The ground plan of the town is shaped like a star and lovely pine woods infiltrate almost into the centre of the town between the points of this star, especially on the west and north. These woods cover the last foothills of the Bohemian-Moravian plateau. Starting points for the most enjoyable excursions into the environs of the town are near the roads leading out towards Jíhlava, Ostrovačice, Veverská Bitýška, Tišnov, Bílovice and Vyškov; you can also set off from the tram or bus terminus in Bystré, or at the Knínice Dam, at Pisárky, Královo Pole, Rečkovice, Soběšice and Obřany.

The Knínice Dam, about 5 km from the centre of the town, is the most popular excursion for the towns-folk. The 8 km long reservoir provides ample opportunities for various water sports. Contests and races are often held here. There are swimming pools and playing fields in different places along the reservoir. The picturesque castle of **Veveří** can be reached by motor-boat.

The Zoological Gardens are situated in the middle of a wood, specially set aside for this purpose, not far from the terminus at Bystré.

The Myslivna (Forest House) with its restaurant stands on a hill overlooking the town. From there one has a wonderful view of the Fair Grounds and a part of Brno. At night, especially, the view of the brightly lighted town is superb. A road leads up to the restaurant. From the terminus at Pisáky one can walk along well-kept paths through the woods to the restaurant in about three quarters of an hour.

Vranov is about 11 km north of Brno on the highway that runs north through Soběšice or Česká to Svitava. Vranov is a place of pilgrimage with a little Baroque church in which is the vault of the noble Liechtenstein family. The place is beautifully situated in the midst of deep pine-woods. A fairly long walk through the woods either from the terminus at Řečkovice or at Soběšice takes one there. There is plenty of game in the woods, especially deer in great numbers.

The **Svitava Valley** already begins from the tram terminus in Obořany. In addition to many natural beauties the little church in **Adamov** with a wonderful wood-carved altar deserves special attention. The most important of the castles round about is the **New Castle** not far from the industrial centre of Adamov (railway station on the Prague—Brno line). The Svitava valley is a good starting point for the southern part of the **Moravian Karst,** where on the left bank of the river Svitava and the Ricka brook; one comes upon some interesting **stalactite caves.** Of these mention must be made of the "Pekárna"

(Bakery) Býčí skála (the Bull's Rock) and the "Švédův Stůl" (the Swedish Table) which are famous for the remarkable archaeological remains discovered here. The Valley of the Říčka brook can also be reached conveniently from the tram terminus in Líšeň.

Slavkov (Austerlitz) and the Peace Memorial on the Napoleonic battlefield: here in December 1805 the famous battle of the three emperors was fought in which Napoleon defeated the Austrian and Russian generals. In Slavkov (about 21 km east of Brno) is a very beautiful Baroque-style **castle** with a museum. On the **Pracký** (Pratzen) hill we find the **cenotaph** and **a museum** containing various exhibits of the Napoleonic period.

Some 10 km further on the road from Slavkov is **Bučovice,** which has a **castle** with a unique arcaded courtyard, an outstanding example of Czech Renaissance architecture. 18 km from there we find another architectural curiosity, a Baroque cemetery in the village of **Střilky.**

Rajhrad and Židlochovice. About 12 km south of Brno the **Monastery** of **Rajhrad** with its famous library merits the visitor's attention. And 7 km further on the road to Břeclav lies the village of **Židlochovice** with a **castle** and a large pheasant breeding establishment. Shooting parties are organised there every autumn in which sportsmen from all over the world take part. It is not exceptional for these to achieve a bag of 1,000 birds. Further south the vinegrowing district of South Moravia begins. There old popular traditions and old popular costumes still exist. Every tiny village has its own richly embroidered costume. Every Sunday in autumn interesting folk festivals are celebrated.

B. SOUTHERN MORAVIA

The Moravian Karst and the Macocha

The northern part of the Moravian Karst, the most interesting for tourists, can best be visited by starting from **Blansko** (about 30 km north of Brno). It lies on the highway to Svitavy. From there one turns off after 18 km to the right into **Lipůvka.** From there a dust-free road with stretches of very romantic scenery leads to Blansko, where in the so-called "Suchý Zleb" the remarkable karst formations of the **Catherine Cave** begin.

The Catherine Cave is nearly 100 yds long, over 40 yds wide and roughly 60 ft high. From this subterranean cathedral steps lead to even more fantastic and fabulously beautiful karst formations. One of the grandest natural phenomena is the Punkva cave. Through a tunnel passage one comes out onto the bed of the **Macocha Gorge,** which is 455 ft deep. At the bottom of the Macocha are two lakes from which a passage leads to the underground river Punkva. On the Punkva one can proceed by boat across three more lakes into the magnificent grotto which resembles some fantastic cathedral. In the northern part of the Karst we find still more groups of caves, of which the most notable is the Sloup-Šošůvky **Labyrinth.**

These caves are by no means the only beauties of the Moravian Karst. The limestone formations have also an interesting flora. It is a good game country, with some attractive sites. In the surroundings there are several cultural and historic sights, e.g. the church in **Křtiny,** the castle at **Rajec** with wonderful inlaid furniture and a picture gallery.

The course of the rivers Oslava, Jíhlávka and Rokytná

The many tourist hostels and the romantic scenery are the chief attraction for hikers. Yet there is also in this region a whole number of historical sights which can be visited on a circular tour from Brno in the direction of Prague. This tour takes us round the circuit used for the "Grand Prix of Czechoslovakia" car and motor cycle race, via **Ostrovačice** to **Domášov, Velká Bíteš** to **Velké Meziříčí** (56 km north-west of Brno), where there is a fine castle with remarkable collections (furniture, costumes, pictures painted on glass, artistic wrought-iron work, etc.). 21 km further south we come to **Třebíč.** The local museum has a unique collection of carved Christmas cribs. Also well worth seeing is the Romanesque-Gothic **Basilica** of Saint Procopius, built in 1101. It is one of the oldest monuments in Moravia.

East of Třebíč, on the way back to Brno, lies **Náměšť nad Oslavou** (21 km from Brno), a remarkable little town with a fine, well-preserved castle, built in 1578. There was once in the town one of the first printing presses in the Bohemian provinces which was later removed to the neighbouring town of **Kralice.** There, among other things, the press won fame for the Kralice Bible, a masterpiece of Czech literature. The river Oslava, above which stands Náměšť **castle,** with beautiful hanging gardens and an old park, on a crag, is spanned by an old stone bridge embellished by 20 statues. The surroundings of Náměšť are also distinguished for their natural beauties. The near-by ponds are a bird sanctuary. In the woods round about there are some well-kept preserves with large numbers of game (hart, roe and fallow deer) where hunting parties are often organised. The castle has also been adapted for the accommodation of visitors.

Further east in the direction of Brno, about 2 km away, lies the above-mentioned little town of **Kralice.** There one can visit the Kralice Bible museum. Apart from the six-volume Bible, translated from the original language by the most learned brains of the Moravian Brethren and printed in 1579–93, the most notable exhibit is the Czech translation of the Psalms by Jan Amos Komenský (Comenius).—**Ivančice** is another place in this district with important associations with the Hussite period and the Moravian Brethren (24 km south-east of Náměšt). In Hussite times the place was a bastion of the Reformation. Many monuments still remain, such as the 14th-century **cathedral,** among others. In Ivančice in the 16th century there were many Moravian Brethren schools. A visit to the near-by **Serpentit Steppe,** with its interesting flora and fauna, is recommended. It is close to Mohelno. The course of the three rivers is dotted with old castles, but they are now mostly ruins (Ketkovice, Holoubek, Rábštýn, Templštýn, among others). The scenery of the district is extremely attractive.

Among other objects of historic interest is the Romanesque basilica in the little town of **Řeznovice.**

The way back from Ivančice to Brno runs through the important Rosice-Oslava coal-mining district via **Rosice** and further on rejoins the "Grand Prix of Czechoslovakia" motor race circuit.

Podyjí (The Thaya river region)

The south-west tip of Moravia with the river Thaya (Dyje) is a favourite place of excursion. Its centre is a great lake belonging to the dam not far from Vranov nad Dyjí. There are however also numerous important cultural and historic sights. We mention here the town of Slavonice (a National Trust reservation), the castle of Jemnice and Jevišovice, the old strongholds of Bítov and Vranov, some ruined castles and the ancient town of Znojmo with its outstanding artistic monuments of the Přemyslid period. The lower course of the Dyje with its wonderful scenery is a magnet for tourists. Here there are many opportunities for bathing and beautiful camping sites. An excellent wine is produced in the region.

Not far from the source of the Dyje in the western part of Moravia, almost on the Austrian frontier, lies the town of **Slavonice,** a State reservation. It is one of the most impressive National Trust units in Czechoslovakia. In the past Slavonice was an important town on the road from Prague to Vienna. Recent discoveries have brought to light many beauties, especially on the patrician houses on the south side of the market place. These houses date from the 15th to the middle of the 16th century. They are all decorated with frescoes. They are all in good state of preservation and extensive reconstruction work is now being undertaken on them. Besides the portals and the exterior of the houses many valuable features of the interior remain, e.g. porches ("Maz House") with vaulting and coloured lunettes. The inside of these houses have many architecturally valuable details. Slavonice can be reached from Jíhlava by the road to Telč and Dačice (about 55 km from Jíhlava). A visit to Slavonice can comfortably be combined with a visit to **Telč.**

There is also a convenient road connection from Jindřichův Hradec (about 40 km). Slavonice can also be reached from Jíhlava rail, changing at Cejle-Kostelec. Starting from Brno, one may combine a visit to Slavonice with a trip through the Dyje valley, through Třebíč, Telč, Dačice or via Znojmo and Jemnice.

Jemnice lies about 20 km east of Slavonice and is one of the oldest Moravian towns. In the distant past gold was extracted near by, so that the town was very wealthy. Worth seeing are the old Saint George's church, the ruins of a monastery and the castle.

Bítov Castle is 18 km south-east of Jemnice on a height above the western bay of the Vranov reservoir. Bítov was originally a medieval fortress, probably built at the beginning of the 11th century, of which a 13th–century tower and fortifications remain. In the 16th century a Renaissance addition was made to this Gothic part of the building. The last reconstruction was done in the 19th century when it was rebuilt in neo-Gothic, e.g. the hall on the first floor was decorated with paintings to give it a Gothic effect. To-day the castle is open to the public. It contains rare scientific collections and a collection of weapons. Near Bítov in Dyje valley are some other old castles which even in their ruined condition still proclaim the region's glorious past. By far the most important is the ruined **Cornštejn** castle, not far from Bítov, which was once a mighty, impregnable fortress. Seven gates give admission to the inner courtyard.

Vranov nad Dyjí. In the town, which lies on the eastern edge of the reservoir, there is a huge dam with a large power station, supplying a wide area round about. Vranov is dominated by a very beautiful **castle** on a high crag. It was originally built as a stronghold in Gothic style before the 13th century. It was reconstructed in later years and received its present appearance only after 1687. Later again some Baroque-Empire and other alterations were made. Specially noteworthy are the oval hall, richly decorated with murals with mythological subjects and the chapel with frescoes by Ceinits on the cupola and other elaborately decorated rooms. There is also an interesting collection of Moravian ceramics, recently installed in the castle. Today Vranov is also a summer holiday resort, the chief attraction being the reservoir with its plenitude of fish. Here there are excellent conditions for every kind of water sport. During the season motor-boats ply regularly on the lake carrying excursionists to the different sights in the neighbourhood, e.g. to **Bítov** castle.

The town of **Znojmo** (Znaim) lies 20 km east of Vranov, 64 km south-west of Brno. It is on the main highway from Prague to Vienna; the frontier post is at Hatě-Klein Haugsdorf. It enjoys excellent railway services with fast trains to Prague, Brno, Břeclav and Bratislava. This old town, which is now under protection as an Ancient Monument, is first mentioned in ancient documents in 1084 as a strong and fortified residence. The environs of the town were however settled very much earlier, as it is evident from many archaeological discoveries. Of the numerous historic sights the most valuable is certainly the fresco painting in the Romanesque rotunda of **Saint Catherine.** The frescoes were discovered only recently and when they were being cleaned it became apparent that they were portraits of members of the Přemyslid dynasty by contemporary painters. There used to be several monasteries in the town, e.g. the **Dominican monastery,** with the church of the Holy Cross (early 13th century). The original Romanesque **Saint Nicholas church** received its present Gothic appearance in the 14th century. The Saint Michael's church was also originally Romanesque. The Saint Václav's church is interesting for the ingenious tracery of its vaulting. Znojmo has besides no lack of patrician houses of the Renaissance and Baroque periods. The original ground plan of the Romanesque twisting little street below the castle is preserved. The last emperor of the House of Luxemburg Sigismund died at Znojmo in 1437.

A new dam is now being built on the Dyje (Thaya) near the town of Znojmo. The dam is to be part of an electrification scheme which will have great importance not only for the southern part of Moravia but also for the neighbouring regions of Austria.

There are also numerous food processing concerns, especially world-renowned fruit and vegetable preserve factories. Without bitter-sweet cucumbers, one of the gastronomic specialities of the Znojmo region, a true gourmet cannot properly appreciate the delicious taste and exquisite flavour of the famous Prague ham.

The Pavlov Hills

This gently rolling country rising from the plain is recognisable by its sandstone formations which are visible from far away. The sandstone cliffs that suddenly start up from the plain are often frequented by mountain climbers. On the slopes, covered with massive layers of sand, important settlements of primitive people have been discovered. This is also an important wine-growing district and there are many historic buildings and sights besides.

Mikulov is connected with Znojmo by a dust-free road running along the Austrian frontier to Břeclav and on to Bratislava. In addition there is the old Imperial Road which is still an important link between Brno and Vienna. Mikulov is under National Trust protection. Especially interesting is the grandiose **Dietrichstein castle.** It contains a number of natural science and archaeological collections. The great castle library has many items of interest. One should not miss seeing the enormous wine tun which contains 1,010 hectolitres and dates from 1643.

There are also some churches of architectural interest and a Piarist monastery in which were once a seminary and a college.

Dolní Věstonice lies about 10 km north of Mikulov and is the most remarkable excavation site in the whole of Czechoslovakia. The world famous Věstonice Venus (c. 20,000 years B.C.), was found here.

Lednice lies some 10 km east of Mikulov and is a beautiful natural park with interesting flora and fauna.

The park is embellished by some pleasure lodges, gloriettes and even a minaret. The State-owned **castle,** which once belonged to the noble Liechtenstein family, built in neo-Gothic style, is surrounded by huge conservatories with numerous tropical plants. For this reason it is often visited by botanists and with its lovely surroundings is a favourite excursion for tourists. A state bird sanctuary has been created on the fishponds near Lednice. Besides thousands of laughing gulls (larus ridibundus) many other very interesting and extremely rare species of birds make their nests here, e.g. the red-crested duck (netta ruffina), heron (ardea cinera), various birds of the Passerine order (himantropus, recurvirostra) and others.

Valtice lies on the road between Mikulov and Břeclav. From way back there has been a vintner school here and the castle is famous for its wine-cellars. There is moreover an interesting church, a monastery and the old alm-house of the monks hospitallers.

Břeclav, about 22 km south-east of Mikulov, is the railway junction between Vienna, Budapest and Bratislava, Prague and Warsaw. Břeclav is the frontier station on the Prague-Vienna and Prague-Vienna-Ostrava lines. The town is the centre of an interesting region called **Podluží** where folk art, costumes, songs, dances and old usages are still cherished. Every year in the nearby town of **Strážnice** a festival of popular art is organised. Every small village here has its own different costumes, its own customs, songs and dances. The ethnographical wealth of this region with its traditional folklore and its fiery wine pressed locally make it particularly attractive and interesting to tourists.

Mikulčice, about 15 km north-east of Břeclav in the direction of Hodonín, was in 1957 the centre of attention for archaeologists, for it was here that remains of a Slav fortified settlement with the foundations of ten 9th-century churches, including a 118-foot long basilica, a burial ground and many objects of gold and silver, such as weapons and coins, were discovered, besides the foundation walls of houses of a settlement with stone brickwork below and also vestiges of a later 11th–12th-century settlement.

9. OLOMOUC AND THE JESENÍKY

Tourist region Jeseníky (Gesenke)

The Olomouc region covers a part of Central Moravia and almost the whole of Northern Moravia. The area is bounded on the north-east by the great **Hrubé Jeseníky** massif, on the north by the **Králický Sněžník** group of mountains which form the frontier with Poland, on the west by the **Drahanská vysočina** ridge, on the south by the small river **Haná** and the influence of the river **Bečva** and on the east by the **Oderské Vrchy**, a chain of mountains which joins the **Nízký Jeseník.** The **Morava** (March) river, which rises on the slopes of the Králický Sněžník (4,692 feet) and feeds to the Danube most of the waters of this region, is the axis of this whole country. Here the north and the south form two quite different landscapes.

The southern part includes the whole Haná plain, a part of the Hornomoravský úval (Upper Moravian Basin) and the Drahanská vysočina. The wide expanse of the Haná plain in the region of the Morava river is the most fertile part. Sugar-beet, wheat, corn and barley are the chief crops grown in the Haná. That is why it has the biggest towns of the region with an extensive sugar milling and brewing industry. There are few woods in the Haná; a fair-sized area of timberland lies between Olomouc and Litovel. The plain is of interest on account of its folklore. The people there still wear local costumes and speak a local dialect.

The northern territory of the Olomouc regions includes the Nízký and Hrubý Jeseník, the Králický Sněžník group and the high ridge of the Rychlebskě hory. The raw climate there has characterised not only the mostly wooded country but also the towns and villages which more often than not hug the south and east mountain slopes where they are sheltered to some extent from the cold north winds. The soil of this region is poor; only potatoes, oats and flax do well. Most of the last is covered with pinewoods, in some places (Orlík, Šerák, Keprník) still with primitive forest. The woods have abundant game (deer, stag, and in the reservations, chamois) and wild boar. The highly developed timber industry offers good working conditions for the local population. The textile and paper industries are also widespread; in recent years the engineering industry has also made great strides. The mineral wealth of the region is a promising guarantee for contemplated extraction of granite, marble and metal ores. Numerous spas, e.g. Lázně Jeseník (Gräfenberg), Dolní Lípová (Niederlindewiese), Karlova Studánka (Karlsbrunn) among others came into being because of their mineral springs.

Jeseníky is the most attractive spot for tourists in the region of the Hrubý Jeseník, the highest part of the whole massif. The varyingly wooded country which rises to a height of 1,650–2,000 ft affords a view of great variety. The poor fields with their crumbling soil gradually give place to large, extensive woods—exclusively conifers—up to 3,000 ft above sea level where the ridge of the Hrubý Jeseník is crossed on the saddle Skřítek by the road from Rýmařov to Šumperk (Schönberg). The main ridge continues in a long ascent over the Ztracené skály (3,798 ft), Pec (4,330 ft), Břidličná (4,481 ft), Jelení hřbet (4,511 ft) and Vysoká Hole (4,842 ft) to the summit of the Praděd (Altvater 4,923 ft). At the Praděd the mountain chain divides in two directions; north-west over the Červenohorské sedlo (Rotheberg saddle, 3,333 ft), Keprník (4,689 ft) and Šerák (4,458 ft) to the Ramzov sedlo (Ramsauer saddle) and north-east over Velké Bradlo (3,475 ft), Orlík (3,973 ft) and Rejvíz to Mikulovice on the Polish frontier. This massif is nearly 70 km long and 12-30 km wide.

30 km north-west of the Praděd rises the massif Králický Sněžník to a height of 4,692 ft. This with the Malý Sněžník (4,384 ft) and Sušina (4,362 ft) ends the massif towards the Glatzbasin.

In summer and in winter the scenery of these mountain chains is enchantingly romantic. At an altitude of 3,600 to 3,900 feet alpine conditions prevail. The trees are stunted by wind and cold; some bow so low as to develop horizontally. The region is most suitable for excursions and holidays.

Communications: The Olomouc and Jeseník region is crisscrossed by many railway lines and a dense network of roads. Five lines run through Olomouc. The main line from Prague (250 km) to Olomouc runs through Česká Třebová. Other important railway connections: with Brno (100 km), Ostrava (105 km), Bratislava (via Brno, 280 km) or via Břeclav (200 km), with Slovakia (475 km to Košice) and with Vienna via Břeclav (212 km).

The Jeseníky region is connected with Prague by the railway line from Poland via Jeseník (Gräfenberg)-Hanušovice-Hradec Králové (270 km). Distance by rail from Olomouc to Jeseník 120 km.

Important motor coach services from Olomouc to Brno (75 km), to Ostrava (90 km), to Jeseník (120 km), to Rýmařov (55 km), to Bruntál (63 km).

Sights and places of interest

State town reservation: Olomouc.

State natural reservations: Rejvíz (Jeseník district), Divoký Důl (Kouty nad Desnou), Šumperk, Velká kotlina (parish of Malá Morávka, Bruntál district), Malá Kotlina (parish of Karlov, Bruntál district).

Castles: Bouzov (Olomouc), Úsov (Olomouc), Náměsť na Hané (Olomouc), Čechy pod Kosířem (Prostějov), Plumlov (Prostějov), Javorník (Jeseník).

Spas: Lázně Jeseník, Dolní Lípová, Velké Losiny (Šumperk district), Karlova Studánka (Bruntál district).

Dam: near Stichovice (Prostějov district).

Caves: Javoříčko and Mladeč (Olomouc district).

Chief view-points: Olomouc Kopeček (Olomouc district), Mravenečnik (4,432 feet above sea level) east of Loučná nad Desnou (Šumperk district). On the main Jeseníky ridge: Šerák (4,348 feet), Keprník (4,696 feet), Vozka (4,544 feet), Praděd (4,923 feet).

Motoring circuits

In the environs of Olomouc (Olmütz):

1) Olomouc-Litovel (19 km)—Javoříčko (35 km)—Bouzov (45 km)—Mohelnice (57 km)—Úsov (65 km)—Uničov (74 km)—Šternberk (Sternberg 90 km)—Olomouc (107 km).

2) Olomouc-Čechy pod Kosířem (30 km)—Prostějov (40 km)—Přerov (66 km; castle, optical instruments factory)—Lípník nad Bečvou (79 km; match factory)—Hranice na Moravě (91 km)—Teplice nad Bečvou (98 km; health resort for heart diseases;

limestone (aragonite) caves)—back to Lípník nad Bečvou (117 km)—Svatý Kopeček (143 km)—Olomouc (150 km).

Jeseníky—two days:

1st day: Either **a)** Olomouc-Šternberk (15 km)—Bruntál (54 km)—Vrbno (76 km)—Karlova Studánka (83 km)—Ovčárna (90 km)—Karlova Studánka (97 km)—Vrbno (104 km)—Jeseník (130 km). Stay overnight at Jeseník; or **b)** Olomouc-Šternberk (15 km)—Paseka-Sovinec-Rýmařov (51 km)—Karlova Studánka (71 km) and on as above under **a**).

2nd day: Jeseník-Lázně Jeseník (3 km)—Dolní Lipová (9 km) —na Pomezí-Žulová (20 km)—Javorník (33 km)—Dolní Lipová (57 km)—Jeseník (61 km)—Domašov (70 km)—Červenohorské sedlo (85 km)—Kouty nad Desnou (92 km)—Velké Losiny (101 km)—Šumperk (111 km)—Bloudov (116 km)—Zábřeh (124 km)—Mohelnice (138 km)—Loštice (141 km)—Litovel (155 km)—Olomouc (174 km).

Passes—roads for motor vehicles:

Červenohorské sedlo (Rotheberg saddle, 3,333 feet above sea level), 1st class road, open all the year round: Šumperk-Jeseník.

Ramzovské sedlo (Ramsauer saddle, 2,504 feet), 2nd class road, may be closed in winter; Šumperk-Hanušovice-Jeseník.

Skřítek (2,838 feet), 1st class road, open all the year round: Rýmařov-Šumperk.

A. Olomouc (Olmütz)

History: The first settlements in the region of Olomouc go back to over two thousand years ago when the Celts, Quadi and Marcomanni made their homes here on the river Morava (March). It was not until about the 5th century A.D. that Slav tribes settled here. The real history of Olomouc does not begin until the second half of the 11th century, when it was made an episcopal see in 1063. Thanks to the great power of the bishops and princes of Olmütz the place eventually became the capital of Moravia. The wealth of the noble and clerical hierarchy is still visible in the mighty church building and noblemen's palaces.

During the reign of Přemysl Otakar II, Olomouc became a royal city with a number of privileges; at the same time the gates were thrown open to the Germans. In 1380 and 1388 outbreaks of fire temporarily hindered the further development of the town. In the reign of Ferdinand I Protestantism grew in Olomouc despite executions to deter the new faith. The Jesuit Order, introduced in 1566, exterminated the Protestants. In 1641, the

Moravian tribunal was transferred to Brno (Brünn) and in 1642 the town captured by the Swedes. In the same year it surrendered its pride of place to the new capital Brno. During the Prussian War Olomouc was fortified (1742–54) and the development of the town was thereby stopped. The University was transferred to Brno in 1778. Here took place in 1850 the famous Olomouc retreat. The fortifications were not demolished until 1886. The town experienced its hardest times when it was occupied by Hitler's troops and police. The whole northern part of the Olomouc region was incorporated in the Sudeten and the frontier pushed forward to within 9 km of the town.

Olomouc is the seat of a National Committee, a district court and a number of other administrative departments, the **Palacký University,** a university library, technical and secondary schools, cultural institutions, a **theatre,** an **opera house,** a **philharmonic orchestra,** etc. The town is also an important railway and road junction, connecting Bohemia with East Moravia and Slovakia. **Steel works,** machine tools, chocolate and sugar factories, a brewery with malt factory, low cooling plant, rope-making and salt-milling are the most important industries of the town. 80,000 inhabitants.

Sights

The oldest Romanesque architectural feature is above the cloister in the **Saint Wenceslaus cathedral** (Chrám sv. Václava); a window case in the former castle of the Přemyslid princely family. A Romanesque basilica was built into this originally wooden and later stone castle. The window columns with Corinthian capitals are among the most interesting sights of Olomouc.

The cathedral stands on a jutting rock in front of the castle proper. The original cathedral, built by the Olomouc princes in 1131, has undergone great changes in the course of the centuries, partly owing to fires, partly through reconstructions. The original

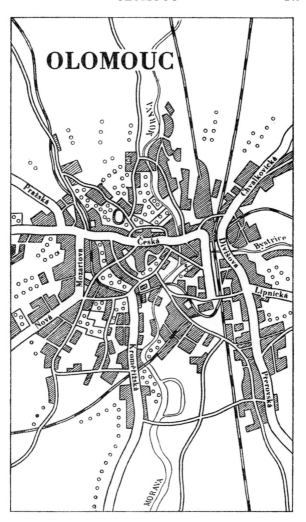

Romanesque stone walls are preserved, as are the Gothic nave (1365) and the large presbytery. It was only in 1880 that the cathedral was rebuilt in neo-Gothic style. The decoration of the cathedral with statues and paintings is completed by superb wood-carvings (the canon's stalls in the presbytery and the choir). The cathedral treasure, the most notable item of which is a gold Baroque monstrance, is also remarkable.

The **cathedral deanery** (domské děkanství) near the Saint Wenceslaus church, a 17th–century building with ornate arcades, today houses the **Historical Institute** (Historický ústav) of the Palacký University. A late 13th–century grave-stone and a memorial tablet commemorating the murder of King Václav III, the last of the Přemyslids, in the house of the Cathedral dean on the 4th August 1306, merit special notice.

The **Episcopal palace.** The whole east side of the Wurmova ulice is formed by the very beautiful portals of the episcopal and canons' residences. The extensive episcopal palace, where many rulers, ministers and princes stayed on festive occasions, was built in the seventieth year of the 17th century on the site of the oldest episcopal residence by the Wallachian architect Balthasar Fontana. The **armoury** (1771) stands near the episcopal palace. In the Křižkovského ulice (behind the armoury) the renovated Palacký University catches the eye.

The Our Lady of the Snow church (Chrám Panny Marie Sněžné) in the Square Náměstí Republiky was built between 1712 and 1719. The Baroque portal is one of the sights of Olomouc. The stucco work and frescoes on the ceiling and also a number of artistic wood carvings, are strikingly beautiful.

The **Municipal Museum** (Krajské museum) converted into an Institute for Regional Research, in the Námesti Republiky, founded in 1875, contains rich collections of minerals, plants and animals. The herbarium of European and extra-European flowers (65,000 plants), the Egyptological collections and the collections of insects are of special interest. Another section of the museum is at No. 2 Purkrabská ulice, in the former house of the Karel starší ze Žerotína (note the coat of arms in the courtyard).

The **St. Michael's church** (Kostel sv. Michala) in the Žerotínské náměstí, originally Gothic, was rebuilt in 1674 in early Baroque. The interior is a gem of Baroque Moravian art. Above the Gothic portal of the Alexius chapel is the only Czech inscription in any Olomouc church. The county court once stood on the site of the present church.

The **Town Hall** in the Rudé Armády náměstí (Red Army Square) dates from the end of the 14th century. The portal, the Gothic bay and the Renaissance loggia are very beautiful; noteworthy are the waterspouts, the 230 ft high tower (1607) and the old clock (Orloj). It was made before 1572 and was almost completely destroyed in the fighting for Olomouc in May 1945. After being repaired the clock was decorated by the modern Czech painter Karel Svolinský. The interior of the Town Hall, the so-called 15th–century Knights' Hall (Gothic vaulting, murals) also deserves mention.

The pillars of the Holy Trinity church in the Red Army Square are 118 ft high and a picturesque pendant to the Town Hall. It has 18 gilt copper statues, the work of native artists.

Buildings worth seeing in Red Army Square: No. 1, the former **palace of Count Julius Salm** (1747); No. 5, a Renaissance building (1572); No. 25 has a Renaissance courtyard; No. 26 was the former residence of Karl von Liechtenstein (1598).

The **church of St. Maurice** (Chrám sv. Mořice) in the **square** Mořické náměstí was built circa 1275. The exterior is plain Gothic. The south tower, reminiscent of an 11th or 12th century fortress tower, is interesting. The interior of the church is the only Gothic survival of its kind in Olomouc. The church covers the largest area of any church in Moravia. The Baroque organ with 2,311 pipes deserves special attention.

The fountains of Olomouc because of their beauty arouse the wonder of every visitor, especially tourists and art-lovers:

the Triton fountain in the Náměstí Republiky dates from 1707;

the Caesar's fountain in the Rudé Armády náměstí south-west of the Town Hall dates from 1715. A statue of Caesar with horse and hound, hewn from a single sandstone block;

the Hercules fountain (1668) on the north side of the Town Hall square;

the Mercury fountain (1730) in the Ulice 28. října;

the Neptune fountain (1695) and

the Jupiter fountain (1707), both in the Náměstí Rudé Armády.

A Plague memorial column, dedicated to the Virgin Mary (1720) stands in the middle of the Náměstí Rudé Armády.

Klášterní Hradisko a monastery, 2 km from the Náměstí Rudé Armády. A huge building, founded in 1078. The interior is decorated with statues and frescoes by native and foreign artists. The monastery is now used as a hospital.

Accommodation: Hotel Družba (68 Jeremenkova ulice, opposite the railway station, Telephone 2367), Hotel Národní dům (21 ulice 8. května, Tel: 4806, 4966), and Hotel Palác (tř. 1. máje 27, Tel: 3283, 3284, 4096).

Excursions from Olomouc

Kopeček (1,250 ft above sea level). 7 km by motor bus from Red Army Square. An old place of pilgrimage with the earliest Baroque church of Olomouc (1669–1679). The edifice bears the stamp of the Italian influence of Baltasar Fontana, who participated with other native and foreign artists in the decoration of this church. The façade with statues of the Twelve Apostles is interesting. There is a magnificent view from the church over the Haná and the town of Olomouc.

The extensive **zoological gardens** begin at the back of the church.

Náměšť na Hané (about 25 km west of Olomouc) lies at the foot of the **Drahanská vysočina** (ridge); the castle, surrounded by a large garden and woods, is situated above the town. Quite near is the modern **amphitheatre** for the well-known "Hanácké dožínky" (the Haná harvest festival).

Čechý pod Kosířem. The castle (about 30 km south-west of Olomouc), built in 1716, was the property of Counts Sylva Taroucca from 1768 to 1945. From 1846 to 1847 the founder of modern Czech painting, Josef Mánes, a friend of the family, worked here.

Šternberk (about 17 km north of Olomouc), departmental town with a beautiful castle and rich collections. The church (1775–83) is of interest. Clock factory. The international motor race circuit Ecce Homo runs through the town.

Prostějov (21 km south-west of Olomouc on the railway and road from Olomouc to Brno). The principal old cultural monuments are: the **castle** with a Renaissance portal, built 1522–26, the old **Town Hall** (1521) with a Renaissance portal. Today it houses the museum with a unique collection of clocks, the biggest in Czechoslovakia. Interesting also is the Baroque Plague Column (1714).

Economically Prostějov is one of the most important towns in Moravia. Clothing industry, agricultural machines factory, ironworks, chicory and manufacture of buttons.

Accommodation: Grand Hotel, 35 Palackého ulice. Tel: 4257.

In the surroundings:

Plumlov castle (10 km west), built 1680–92. The castle, about 130 feet high, rises above the mere. One of its façades is richly decorated with stucco and ornamentation and divided by columns. Stucco decoration also inside. The castle is now used as a museum.

The Dam near Stichovice (about 8 km west of Prostějov). Splendid opportunities for bathing and for the practice of all kinds of water sport.

Malé Hradisko (25 km west of Prostějov). On the site of the so-called Staré Hradisko the ramparts and town moat can still be seen (former total length 2½ km). Staré Hradisko was a Gallic settlement two thousand years ago. Objects, mostly iron tools, have been unearthed here and are now in the National Museum in Prague and in the museums at Prostějov and Boskovice. Pieces of amber are still found today, evidence that the former inhabitants traded in it.

Litovel (19 km north-west of Olomouc). The municipal museum contains rich collections of costumes and embroideries peculiar to the Haná and discoveries from the Karst caves of Mladeč (Diluvial Age—primitive cave-dwellers).

The State-owned castle of **Bouzov** (21 km west of Litovel). This late 13th-century fortress was renovated between 1895 and 1909. It contains rich collections got together by native and foreign nobility. Ten towers and a 200 feet high watch tower embellish the castle. With some other strongholds Bouzov was once part of a system of defence.

The caves of **Javoříčko** (17 km west of Litovel or 5 km southeast of Bouzov by a footpath with blue signs). The caves were discovered in 1938; the largest of them is the Giant Cathedral (53 yards long, 34 yards wide and 60 feet high). There is a new tourist hostel at the entrance to the caves. One km away is the village of Javoříčko, which was razed to the ground by the Germans on the 5th May 1945 when a part of the population, chiefly men, were shot. The village has been rebuilt. A memorial to the victims of Nazism has been erected in the square near the school.

Úsov (about 45 km north of Olomouc by road). The 11th–century castle was last renovated in the 17th century. Today Úsov is frequently visited because of its Natural Science and Forestry Museum founded at the end of the 19th century and then the only one of its kind in Central Europe. Valuable altar pictures in the church.

Zábřeh na Moravě (46 km on the main Olomouc—Prague line). The town was founded before the 13th century. Highly developed textile and silk industry. The environs of Zábřeh border the principal tourist region of the Jeseníky.

B. THE JESENÍKY

Šumperk (57 km north-west of Olomouc), district town with a highly developed textile industry.

To the ruined castle of Berníčko—blue signs—12 km footpath. By train to Nový Malín (5 km south-east), on foot—green signs—to Skály and Skřítek (16 km), then over the ridge—green signs—to Jelení studánka (23 km) and from there—red signs—to the Alfredova chata (mountain shelter, 26 km).

By rail to Velké Losiny (10 km north-east). Visit to the sulphur baths and the castle. Beautiful castle park, especially in the spring when the rhododendrons are in bloom.

Ramzová (2,504 feet above sea level, 103 km north of Olomouc), fast train stop on the line from Olomouc. There are two mountain inns.

Excursions:
Green signs: through the valley of the Vražedný Potok stream to Obří skály (3,570 feet), then on—blue signs—to the Šerák. About 7 km.

Red signs: over the Černava slopes to the Šerák. About 7 km.

Yellow signs: direct up to the Šerák (5½ km). From the Šerák magnificent view. On the slope about 300 yards south-east a mountain inn. From here—red signs—to the Keprník (4,696 feet). The woods through which this path leads are a natural reservation 4 km long and 1 km wide. From the Keprník a grand view over the whole of North Moravia. After about 1½ km the path forks—yellow signs—to a group of rocks, called Vozka (4,544 feet); then return. Red signs on to Trojmezí and Vřesová studánka (inn) and through the woods to the Červenohorské sedlo (Rothberg saddle). The road from Olomouc via Šumperk to Jeseník runs over the saddle. Two mountain inns on the saddle. The total length of the trip from the Šerák is about 10 km (3½ hours). From the Červenohorské sedlo either by motorbus to Jeseník (20 km) or on foot to Kouty nad Desnou to the railway station (7 km).

Dolní Lipová (Niederlindewiese, 114 km north of Olomouc), health resort for metabolic diseases.

Jeseník (Gräfenberg, 119 km north of Olomouc). Historical records of the town from the 12th century. Noteworthy are the oldest building—the **Water Tower**—(12th century) in which the museum is housed, the 15th-century **Church of Our Lady,** rebuilt in the 19th century in Renaissance-Baroque style and the Town Hall on the main square. This is 250 years old. In the Smetana Park the memorial to the founder of the near-by health resort, Vinzenz Priessnitz.

Excursions round Jeseník

Lázně Jeseník (Bad Gräfenberg). Either by the so-called Musicians' Path—blue signs—(35 minutes) or by motorbus from the Náměstí Svobody. The spa lies 2,145 feet above sea level and was founded in 1826 by the young peasant Vinzenz Priessnitz. In 1910 a large sanatorium was erected here with more than 300 rooms. At the spa the principal ailments treated are nervous disorders, internal diseases, arthritis, circulatory disorders and organic neuroses.

Four Priessnitz memorials (Czech, Polish, Hungarian and French) are noteworthy. A burial mound with a cross (magnificent view) recalls that here, on the so-called Přední Vršek between the spa and the town, in 1682 women and girls accused of witchcraft were burned.

Rejvíz, 13 km east of Jeseník. The unusual wood-carving on the chairs of the **Noskova chata** (mountain inn) merit attention. 2 km south—blue signs—we come into the marshy area on the little lake Mechové Jezírko with rare flora. From Rejvíz—red signs—on foot over the **Bleskovec** (2,914 feet above sea level), the **Bílé kameny** (2,056 feet) and the **Zlatý chlum** (2,696 feet)—belvedere—and back to Jeseník (total distance from Rejvíz 9–10 km).

Jeskynní bludiště (cave labyrinth) on the **Špičák.** By train to the station **Písečná** (8 km north-east), from here 1½ km on foot—blue signs—to the rock city Skalní město with dwarf pines and juniper trees. Wonderful prospect over the Jeseníky and the high ridge of the Rychlepské hory from the rocks.

Krasové jeskyně na Pomezí (karst caves), yellow signs—5 km west of Jeseník. The Vstupní dom s kazatelnou (cathedral entrance with chancel) on several storeys is well worth seeing. 2 km from here—yellow signs—is the mountain inn Na Smrčníku. Blue signs mark the way from the caves to the railway station at Dolní Lipová (3 km).

Javorník. 30 km north-west of Jeseník. Rail and motorbus connection via Dolní Lipová. The town lies below the Rychlebské hory ridge and is dominated by a Renaissance castle with rich collections

Červenohorské sedlo—Starting-point for the Praděd (Altvater).—From Jeseník 20 km, from Šumperk 30 km by motorbus. From here on foot walking north-west—red signs—to the **Klínovec** (3,861 feet), the path ascends at a gradient of about 1 in 10, over the **Výrovka** (3,805 feet), the **Malý Jezerník** (3,940 feet) and the **Velký Jezerník** (4,303 feet) to the connecting route to **Kouty**—green signs. On across open country, following the red signs, to the summit of the **Praděd** with belvedere.—Descent—red signs—by serpentine path to the **Chata Barborka** (mountain inn, 4,339 feet). Continuing east—blue signs—and later yellow signs along the little river Bílá Opava (high waterfall) to **Karlova Studánka** spa (Karlsbrunn). From the Červenohorské sedlo to here altogether about 18 km. From Karlova Studánka to Jeseník or Bruntál by motorbus.

Kouty nad Desnou (72 km. north of Olomouc. Terminus of the railway line Zábřeh-Šumperk-Kouty).

7 km walk northwards—green signs—over the Šindelná (3,706 feet) and Vřesová studánka. Then on over the Keprník, Šerák and Obří skály to Ramzová.

Through the valley of the little river Hučivá Desná—yellow signs—7 km to the so-called Trohmezi and on as in the previous walk.

Following the blue signs eastwards through the valley of the little river Dívoká Desná and Dívoký důl (natural reservation) up to the Praděd (Altvater) 13–14 km. From the Praděd to Karlova Studánka.

Following the green signs eastwards to the mountain inn Švýcárna (4,323 feet) about 11 km. Further—red signs—up the Praděd and on to Karlova Studánka.

Rýmařov (Römerstadt), 73 km north of Olomouc, railway connections: Olomouc—Valšov, from there branch line to Rýmařov. Well-known silk industry in the town.

From Rýmařov by motorbus 10 km north-east up to the Skřítek (saddle), from here—green signs—on foot over the Ztracené skály (3,798 feet), Pec (4,330 feet), Pecny (4,362 feet), Břidličná (4,481 feet), Jelení hřbet (4,511 feet), Máj (4,570 feet), Kamzičník (4,686 feet), from here—red signs—by way of Vysoká

hole (4,831 feet) and the Petrovy kameny (4,772 feet) up the
Praděd. Altogether about 15 km. Return from the Praděd by
way of the Chata Barborka (mountain inn) to Karlova Studánka
(Karlsbrunn) to the motorbus.

Two days:

From Rýmařov—red signs—15 km north-west up to the
Alfredova chata (mountain inn), then on—without signs—3 km
northwards to Malá Kotlina (below the Máj)—natural reservation—back to the Alfredova chata.

The next day either to the ridge—red signs—and on to the
summit of the Praděd or—green signs—eastwards to Karlov and
to the railway station at Malá Morávka (11 km).

Malá Morávka, 81 km north of Olomouc. Terminus of the local railway line from Bruntal (Freudenthal).

Blue signs: via **Karlov** through the Moravice valley to Velká
Kotlina and on over the Petrovy kameny up to the Chata
Barborka (mountain inn, about 12 km). In Karlov there is a
Youth Hostel. In Velká Kotlina there is a natural reservation
rare flowers and shrubs which grow near the natural springs;
(chamois, moufflons). In winter a ski descent and a slalom course.

From Malá Morávka north-west—yellow signs—up to the
Chata Barborka (inn) below the Praděd (about 12 km).

Karlova Studánka, 20 km north-west of Bruntal (2,640 feet above sea level). The climatic resort with mineral springs is a cure and holiday centre for the mountain people of Ostrava.

Following the yellow signs westwards through the valley of
the Bílá Opava river past the romantic High Waterfall (Vysoký
vodapád) and then—blue signs—to the Chata Barborka (mountain inn) below the Praděd (7 km). Red signs southward to Malá
Morávka to the railway station.

Vrbno pod Pradědem (95 km north of Olomouc), railway connection Olomouc—Milotice. From here by branch line to Vrbno.

Westward following the green signs through the valley of the
Střední Opava and on through the valley of the Bílý Potok to
where the path crosses the yellow signs; then follow this path to
the Orlík massif (3,973 feet)—primitive forest—. Over the Kaza-
telny (3,034 feet) to the bog-land near the lake Mechové Jezírko
and to Rejvíz (22 km). From here by motorbus to Jeseník (Gräfenberg).

From Vrbno—red signs—northward through the valley of the Černá Opava via Brandlův mlýn and Wurzlův mlýn to Rejvíz (18 km) and from there either by motorbus via Zlatý chlum to Jeseník or on—red signs—via Zlatý chlum to Jeseník.

Staré Město pod Sněžníkem, 93 km north-west of Olomouc, railway connection with Hanušovice by branch line.

North-west from the railway station—blue signs—to Nový Rumburk (4 km) and on to the frontier (7 km), along the frontier westward to the Adelin pramen (spring) (9 km). From here—red signs—north-west to the mountain inn on the Králický Sněžnik, 11 km. The whole climb from Staré Město is 2,640 feet. The belvedere tower is in Polish territory.

Vysoké Žibřidovice, railway station on the Hanušovice—Staré Město line.

First along the road running north-west—yellow signs—then through the valley of the Prudký Potok with picturesque waterfalls at the juncture of the road with the blue-marked path (at Podbělek). From here northward—blue signs—over Mount Sušina (4,359 feet)—bog-land to the Adelin pramen (spring) 15 km and on—red signs—north-west to the hostel on the Králický Sněžník (17 km).

Červený Potok, railway station on the Hanušovice—Hradec Králové line (14 km from Hanušovice).

From the halt—yellow signs—northward to Velká Morava (4 km), then on through the valley of the Morava (March) river over the Tvarožné díry—red signs—to the frontier (15 km) and—red signs—north-east to the hostel on the Králický Sněžník (16 km).

Oštružná, station on the Olomouc—Jeseník line, 103 km from Olomouc.

From the railway station—green signs—north-west over the Trn (3,501 feet), past the Císařská bouda (inn) to the junction of the path with the red markings (5½ km), then on westward—red signs—to the Výhled mountain inn (3,366 feet). Red signs to the Mědvědí bouda (10 km), to the Kladská brána (15 km) and by way of the Adelin pramen (spring) back to the inn on the Králický Sněžník (26 km). From the Králický Sněžník magnificent view into the Glatz basin, south-west to the Praděd (Altvater), northwest to the Sněžka (Schneekoppe) in the Giant Mountains. The source of the Morava is near the mountain inn.

10. THE SURROUNDINGS OF OSTRAVA AND THE BESKIDS

The largest concentration of Czechoslovak heavy industry is to be found at Ostrava and its surroundings. The whole region forms a vast coal basin where large quantities of high quality coking coal are mined. This is the reason why the large Steelworks of Vítkovice and of Třinec were built there in the 19th century, and why so many foundries, forges, iron works and sheet-iron rolling mills have been built in this area. The pit-heads and blast furnaces give this whole region a special character. The Ostrava region is in a way the steel core of the whole Republic.

The surrounding country is extremely beautiful and the **Beskids** range is a most popular tourist region. Dense forests alternate with vast pasture-lands where juniper trees grow. The forest includes deciduous trees on the lower slopes, spruce and pine higher up. Although the Lysá hora barely rises above 4300 feet, the region's physical features do not lack variety. The Beskids abound in hunting and fishing possibilities. In winter the Beskids are alive again thanks to the snow. There are many excellent skiing grounds to please the most exacting enthusiasts.

The majority of the population work in local industrial enterprises; agriculture is not very highly developed in this mountain country, except for sheep rearing which has some economic importance. The ethnographic region of Walachia lies between the towns of Gottwaldov and Vsetín to the south, and the Beskids to the north; its chief centres are the towns of Rožnov pod Radhoštěm and Valašské Meziříčí.

The Walachian mountain villages, with their characteristic appearance, are scattered on the slopes of the hills where there are also many isolated huts and hamlets with shingle roofs; they are a valuable memento of the old traditional architecture. The most northerly part of the Ostrava region, in the surroundings of Karviná and Těšín, has a strong Polish minority which lives peaceably beside the Czech population.

Things of interest

Town scheduled as a historic site: Štramberk near Nový Jičín.

Nature reservations: Mionší in the Těšín Beskids, virgin forest of the Carpathians (pines and beeches); Hořina near Opava, a stream abounding in trout and a region where Heuffel saffron grows; Vesník near Vestín, a meadow of orchids with an abundance of tropical flora; and 17 further reservations which are of particular interest to the specialist.

Strongholds and State-owned castles: Hradec Castle, near Opava, a regional centre of culture; ruins of Hukvaldy stronghold, near Místek; "Štramberska trúba", the round tower at Štramberk, near Nový Jičín.

Tourist regions: The Beskids, the Javorníky Mountains, the Highlands of Vsetín, the Highlands of the Oder.

Important wooden buildings in a traditional architectural style: Tichá near Frenštát pod Radhoštěm, the old Church of Saint Nicholas, a wooden building dating from 1510; Hodslavice near Nový Jičín, the old Church of Saint Andrew, wood, dating from 1551; Velké Karlovice, near Vsetín, a small wooden church and other interesting buildings; Rožnov pod Radhoštěm, open-air museum of Walachian architecture, laid out on the lines of the Swedish Skansen.

Museums: The Municipal Museum of Ostrava; the Silesian Museum of Opava; the J. A. Komenský (Comenius) Pantheon of Fulnek; the Natural History Museum of Rožnov; the Motor Car Museum of Kopřivnice (Tatra Works); the Emil Žatopek Museum of Kopřivnice; the Hatters' Museum (Tonak factory) of Nový Jičín; Hukvaldy, the birthplace of the famous Moravian composer Leoš Janáček (1854–1928); Příbor near Nový Jičín, the birthplace of Sigmund Freud, the founder of the famous school of psychoanalysis (1856–1938).

Folk art and traditions: Valašské Meziříčí, Vsetín, Rožnov, Velké Karlovice, Nový Hrozenkov, Horní Bečva, Jablunkov (site of the "Highlanders' Festival"). "The Walachian Year" is held alternately in the various towns of the region.

Things of archaeological interest: The "Šipka" Cave near Štramberk where remains of Neandertal man were discovered.

Cable cars: Chairlift of Frenštát at Pustevny under the Radhošt; chairlift of Oldřichovice near Český Těšín at the top of the Javorový.

Dams: Bystřička near Valašské Meziříčí (good bathing); the Kružberk dam west of Opava supplies Ostrava with drinking water.

Hotels: Ostrava and **Palace** Hotels at Ostrava; Vlčina Mountain Hotel near Frenštát under the Radhošt.

Communications: The chief route through the region is the railway line Prague-Olomouc-Ostrava-Bohumín-Karviná-Český-Těšín-Třinec-Jablunkov Pass-Žilina-Upper Tatra-Košice-Černá near Čop (frontier station between Czechoslovakia and the Soviet Union). Another important railway line, used by express trains, goes from Ostrava through Valašské Meziříčí, Vsetín and Horní Lideč to Púchov where it branches off in the direction of Žilina (eastern branch line) and Bratislava (southern branch line). The region is also served by other, smaller railway lines, two of which are very important to the tourist trade (Frydlant-Bílá line and Vsetín-Velké Karlovice line).

The dense road network consists mainly of first-class roads in a perfect state of upkeep. The roads from the west include highway No 11 which joins the road linking Prague with the eastern part of the country. From Šumperk that road enters the Jeseníký mountains and leads through a magnificent mountain landscape through Rýmařov and Bruntál to Ostrava whence it turns towards Slovakia, passing through Český Těšín and the Jablunkov Pass. Another road goes through Olomouc, Lipník and Hranice; then one of its branch-roads runs east through Valašské Meziříčí, Rožnov and the edge of the Beskids to Makov, and on to Slovakia. Another branch-road goes north-east from Hranice, crosses Fulnek and Bílovec, and ends at Ostrava. We can also take the road which goes from Nový Jičín through Příbor and Místek to Český Těšín. Very important, too, is the main north-south road (highway No 57, Opava-Hradec near Opava-Fulnek-Nový Jičín-Valašské Meziříčí and beyond, or Vizovice and Gottwaldov, or Valašské Klobúky and Trenčín). The roads are generally well kept up. A winding mountain road which, however, affords magnificent views of the whole region, runs from Rožnov through Soláň to Velké Karlovice. There are also many bus lines so that tourists can easily visit even the most remote corners of the country.

There is also an air service between Ostrava and Prague; there are several flights a day. At Ostrava, as in some other towns of the region, air taxis are available.

A. OSTRAVA

Distances by road: Prague, 349 km; Brno, 176 km; Bratislava 312 km; Gottwaldov, 111 km. Distance from Prague **by rail**

358 km. A special express—the "**Ostravan**"—runs between the two towns in 5 hours.

Ostrava, a departmental capital (more than 250,000 inhabitants) is the centre of the most important industrial region of the Czechoslovak Republic.

The town was founded in 1267 by Bishop Bruno of Olomouc as a fortress commanding the approach to te whole of Moravia. The citadel was destroyed in 1495, but the town ramparts survived until last century. In 1767 rich coking coal deposits were discovered in the area, and in 1830 the first blast-furnace was put in operation at the Vitkovice Steelworks which became, in a relatively short time, the most important ironworks and also the largest rolling mill in the former Austro-Hungarian monarchy. Subsequently, new mining and iron works made their appearance at Ostrava, and a whole series of large mines were opened whose pit-heads now are in the very centre of the town. In 1950 the "new Klement Gottwald Forge"—the most up-to-date ironworks and rolling mill in the country—was completed. Ostrava also has numerous cokeries, engineering works and chemical establishments. The constantly growing number of workers has led to the development of new workers' towns in the region, e.g., Havířov and Poruba, which are inhabited by tens of thousands of miners' and iron workers' families.

The town itself has not very many historic buildings. There is, however, the **Church of Saint Wenceslas,** dating from the 13th century, and the former **Town Hall** with a single tower, built in 1687 and now converted into a municipal museum. The collection in the latter illustrates the growth of the town and the progressive industrialization of the region. Ostrava has its own professional opera and ballet, several theatres, a large House of Culture, a House of Arts and its own philharmonic orchestra. There is also a vast winter stadium and many other sports grounds (playing fields, swimming pools, gymnastics halls, etc.). Ostrava also has a fine zoo set in the midst of pits and forges.

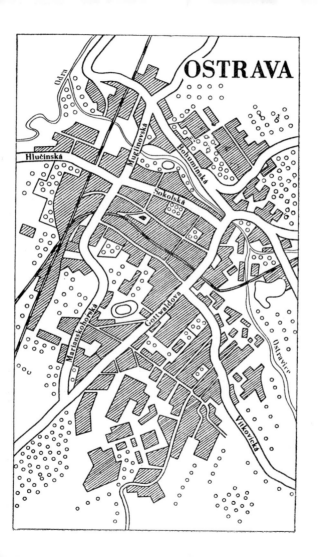

Besides numerous establishments of secondary and professional education, Ostrava has a **Mining College,** divided into a faculty of engineering and a faculty of metallurgy which are attended by both Czechoslovak and foreign students.

B. WEST AND SOUTH OF OSTRAVA

Opava (32 km west of Ostrava).

In the most distant past, important trading routes passed through the Opava region; the best known, the "Amber Route", connected the Baltic countries with Vienna and Italy. According to surviving historic documents, the town was founded in the 12th century, but the region was inhabited long before then, as is shown by the wealth of archaeological discoveries (e.g., at Holasice, on Kylešov hill, and elsewhere). Unlike Ostrava, the black coal town, Opava is a clean, quiet town, with many well-tended schools, parks and gardens. For some time it was the capital of the Principality of Silesia which came under the suzerainty of the Bohemian crown in 1318.

During the Second World War many buildings were destroyed, notably the gothic **Town Hall** of which only the "Clock Tower"— built in 1618 and 236 feet high—remained intact. Other buildings worth noting include the gothic **Cathedral of St. Mary,** dating from the 13th century and decorated inside with magnificent baroque paintings by Ignác Raab; a group of monastic buildings with the **Church of the Holy Spirit,** built in 1234, and other similar ecclesiastic buildings. The former **Minorite monastery** is renowned for the room in which the Diet of the Estates met from the 16th century on. There, too, met the Austrian, Russian and Prussian diplomats and military leaders after the Napoleonic Wars.

The **Silesian Museum,** destroyed during the Second World War and rebuilt since, contains interesting collections devoted to the historic evolution, the natural features and traditions of Silesia. The **Petr Bezruč** memorial Museum, dedicated to the famous poet who was born at Opava, contains numerous mementos of the life and work of that unforgettable bard of the Silesian people. Opava is the seat of the Silesian Institute of the Czechoslovak Academy of Sciences, a scientific centre studying the history and culture of the Ostrava region.

Hradec near Opava (9 km south of Opava).

The first manuscript mentioning Hradec dates from the second half of the 11th century. The castle belonged to many feudal families, in turn, including the kings and queens of Bohemia. At the end of the 18th century, when it became the property of the princes Lichnowsky, who were great patrons of music, many eminent composers visited Hradec, including Ludwig van Beethoven (1806), Niccolo Paganini (1828) and Franz Liszt (1846). Now the castle has been converted into a regional centre of culture and contains a picture gallery, and a concert hall where music festivals are organized in honour of the famous visitors to Hradec.

The rooms of the castle are arranged as a museum. Young couples from all the surrounding region come to get married in the **Wedding Room,** one of the loveliest in the castle. The castle is noteworthy for its contrasting architectural styles dating from various periods. The main building contains the vestiges of gothic and Renaissance arches; stranger still are the romanesque-gothic stone buildings which are reminiscent of English castles with their ramparts, keeps and riding hall. The castle park, which has a wealth of exotic wood and shrubs, has an outstandingly delightful atmosphere.

Fulnek (28 km south of Opava)

The famous educationalist and last bishop of the Moravian Church, Jan Amos Komenský (Comenius) lived at Fulnek and worked there as the principal of the school of the Moravian Brethren. After a stay of 4 years (1618–1621) he went into exile for his religious ideas and was never to return to his native country. His library was burnt in 1623 in the Fulnek Market square by the Jesuit inquisitors. The former house of the Moravian Brethren, built in a flamboyant gothic, now contains a Jan Amos Komenský memorial museum with a complete collection of his works.

Nový Jičín (16 km farther south).

An old town with a large, square **Market Place** bordered by old arcaded houses, the oldest of which— the "Old Post"—is decorated with Renaissance arcades and dates from the 16th century. The 17th-century **castle** has now been converted into a museum which contains ethnographic collections and a picture gallery.

There is also a very interesting **Hatters' Museum** which shows not only the various methods and techniques used by hatters, but also the countless changes which the shape of hats has undergone through the centuries. There is also an interesting collection of coiffures from all parts of the world and a collection of hats worn by famous people. Now the local "Tonak" hat factory exports its products to all parts of the world.

Near Nový Jičín is the commune of Hynčice, the birthplace of the famous botanist and biologist Gregor Mendel (1822–1884) who devoted his studies to the problems of heredity which led to Mendel's laws on the subject.

Hodslavice (7 km south of Nový Jičín).

This is the birthplace of the famous Czech historian and historiographer **František Palacký** (1798–1876). The commune is also known for its wooden **Church of Saint Andrew** (1551) which contains a valuable statue of the Virgin dating from the 16th century.

Štramberk (10 km north-east of Hodslavice).

A town with a decidedly medieval character, now scheduled as a historic site. The first documents mentioning the town date from 1211. **Kotouč hill** which dominates the town, has a small belfry at the summit; from the top of the belfry we have a magnificent view of the whole town, its narrow streets, its small houses nestling under the bastions of the castle, and of the **castle** itself which is surmounted by the "Štramberská trúba" keep. Near the road leading to the Kotouč is a chapel which contains a Walachian crib carved in wood. Those who are interested in archaeology should not miss the Šipka Cave where a child's jaw dating from the Neandertal era has been found, as have been weapons and decorative objects of the archaic period of the Celts.

Kopřivnice (2 km from Štramberk).

In this town is the well-known large **Tatra** car factory whose products—especially heavy vehicles and eight cylinder luxury cars—can be seen on many roads.

The factory's present appearance dates from the reconstruction of the old coach and carriage builders, founded in 1853. At the Kopřivnice museum, visitors can see all the types of cars which have been made at the factory, as well as various spare parts and engine models.

Kopřivnice is the birthplace of the most famous Czechoslovak athlete and world champion, Emil Žátopek, whose trophies include 4 Olympic gold medals which are exhibited in the museum named after him.

Příbor (about 5 km north of Kopřivnice on the main highway to Ostrava).

An old town, founded in the 13th century, with an attractive market place bordered by arcaded houses and embellished with a wealth of statues. In Příbor Cathedral note the very fine statue of the Virgin dating from 1490. Příbor was the birthplace (1856) of the famous founder of psychoanalysis, **Sigmund Freud.**

Not far from Příbor is **Hukvaldy**, the birthplace of one of the greatest Czech composers, Leoš Janáček (1854–1928). His best known operas include "Jenufa" and "The Cunning Little Fox", his symphonic compositions "Sinfonietta" and "Tarass Boulba"; Janáček also composed numerous choral works and several pieces of chamber music. His work was deeply influenced by the traditions of folk music which provided him with an inexhaustible source of inspiration.

C. THE BESKIDS

These mountains are particularly popular with tourists and skiers. The most important centres are **Frenštát pod Radhoštěm, Radhošt, Rožnov, Valašské Meziříčí, Vsetín** and **Velké Karlovice.**

Frenštát is the main starting point for the Beskids range. We can go to the **top of the Pustevny** by cable car or by a mountain road. There are several hotels and mountain chalets, the largest being the **Tanečnica** (Dancing Girl) Hotel. There is also a swimming pool and an excellent skiing ground with downhill runs, slalom runs and even a jump-board.

From Pustevny we can continue on foot to Radhošt (4 km, 3,280 feet) whence we have a splendid view of the surrounding country. Near the road stands the statue of the pagan god Radegast after which Mount Radhošt was named; at the top of Mount Radhošt is the chapel of St Cyril and St Methodius, with a painting of the Walachian Virgin by K. Liebscher.

Rožnov pod Radhoštěm (at the foot of the southern slope of the Radhošt) is a small, typically Walachian town with a noteworthy ethnographic museum, weaving workshops producing a Gobelin-type cloth, and a very modern astronomy observatory which is very popular with the people of the region.

Valašské Meziříčí (14 km west of Rožnov) is well known for its interesting open-air museum which shows typical Walachian wooden buildings which contain a museum of traditional Walachian culture.

Vsetín (33 km north-east of Gottwaldov) is a tourist centre and an important industrial town. The town is the starting point of a road and railway line which runs through the Becva valley and the picturesque villages of **Hovězí, Halenkov** and **Nový Hrozenkov** to **Velké Karlovice,** a commune which is famous for its wooden church and many other buildings in a traditional architectural style (small farms, bells, huts). The commune was founded as early as the 15th century.

The following are the main starting points for ski trips or excursions on foot in the Beskids: Tanečnica (3,556 feet), Čertův Mlýn (3,960 feet), Kněhyně (4,124 feet), Martiňák (2,720 feet), Vysoká (3,346 feet). To the south: Javorník (5,580 feet), Portáš (3,159 feet). In the Beskids of Vsacké: Benešky (2,766 feet), Soláň (2,825 feet), Tanečnica (2,992 feet) and Vsacký Cáb (2,759 feet).

Another starting point is the Ostravica valley below Lysá hora, the highest peak in the Beskids (4,347 feet). On Lysá hora skiing is possible until the spring. There is a tourist chalet for skiers.

Several hundred kilometres of marked paths run through the Beskids range (red markings for paths along the ridge, white, green and yellow markings for approach roads and transverse paths). Food and lodging can be obtained in the many mountain chalets and hotels, of which the best equipped is the Vlčina hotel which can be reached by road from Frenštát pod Radhoštěm (3 km).

11. SOUTH-EASTERN MORAVIA

This part of Moravia, which is formed mostly by the basin of the Morava (March) and which adjoins the Austrian Republic to the south, is separated from Slovakia by the densely wooded range of the White Carpathians; it has many very interesting features which help visitors to appreciate the beauties of Czechoslovakia and the life of its people. Administratively, this region is part of the department of southern Moravia, with its capital at Brno.

As we have said, the region abounds in natural beauties, especially in the Chřiby mountains and the White Carpathians, in all kinds of historic mementos and archaeological excavations (for instance, Staré Město, probably the capital of the famous Empire of Great Moravia from the 7th to the 9th century). It is also a region of highly developed agriculture and flourishing industry with its centre at Gottwaldov (formerly Zlin), famous for its shoe and leather industries for more than 40 years. Foreign tourists who come to this region never tire of the local crafts and traditions, which are still very much alive in these parts. Each village has its own dances and songs, its richly embroidered traditional costumes, its houses embellished with brilliant ornaments by local painters, and its characteristic pottery; the rich gamut of gaudy colours make this a very gay and welcoming country.

Vines grow on the fertile slopes of the hills, but the farmers of the region also grow tobacco, cereals, maize and especially some vegetables, mainly cucumber and paprika. Fruitgrowing is also very wide-spread and this accounts for the numerous fruit-preserve factories.

The climate in southern Moravia is one of the hottest in Czechoslovakia, but unfortunately the region suffers from a great lack of water. The Chřiby mountains, the Vizovice hills and the White Carpathians are densely wooded, and although the region is below 3,280 feet in altitude, it has its own mountain features which favour the growth of the tourist trade. Numerous hot springs with great curative properties gush from the bowels of the earth; the most important ones are at Luhačovice, a spa which specializes in the treatment of respiratory ailments and which exports the famous "Vincentka" mineral water for sufferers from bronchitis or asthma (it is usually drunk mixed with hot milk).

The people of south-eastern Moravia are ethnographically very interesting. In fact, they are even now divided into three distinct ethnographic groups, each with its own language, its own way of life, its culture and traditions; they have survived in spite of the fact that economic conditions, intensive agricultural development and the industrialization of the 20th century have considerably changed the way of life of the people in the region. The southern part, from Břeclav and Hodonín to Uherské Hradiště and Uherský Brod, is called "Moravian Slovakia"; its people speak a language which closely resembles literary Slovakian. In the fertile plains along the banks of the Morava where vine-growing flourishes, rich local traditions find expression in lively folk-songs and the brightly-coloured ornaments which decorate the walls and façades of the village houses. In the immediate surroundings of the forests and at the foot of the mountains potatoes and fruits—especially plums— are cultivated intensively. In these parts local traditions are perhaps less rich than in the fertile plains, but they are nonetheless interesting and attractive.

By far the most famous drink in these parts is not the wine of the plains, but "Slivovice", a spirit made by distilling a special type of large plum ("quetsche").

Places and things of interest

Town scheduled as a historic site: Kroměříž.

Castles and strongholds: Buchlov, a State-owned stronghold; Buchlovice, a State-owned castle surrounded by a superb park; Milotice Castle; Vizovice Castle; Kroměříž episcopal palace.

Local crafts and traditions: Strážnice, where the International Festivals of songs and dancing are held; Vlčnov, famous for the "Cavalcade of Kings" on Whit-Monday; Velká nad Veličkou; pilgrimage places where in summer many pilgrims come from all over the country, usually dressed in traditional old costumes, include: Velehrad, St Anthony near Blatnice, Hostýn near Holešov.

Museums: Gottwaldov (Shoe Museum, Art Gallery), Lešná, botanical collection, Zoo, Kroměříž, Uherské Hradiště (local traditions), Jan Amos Komenský (Comenius) Museum at Uherský Brod.

Tourist regions: the Chřiby Mountains with numerous ruins of medieval strongholds in the depth of dense forests (mush-

rooms, strawberries, raspberries); Lázně Luhačovice, spa
(bathing cures, recreation facilities on the banks of a large dam
reservoir); White Carpathians (Holuby chalet on the Javorina,
ski grounds).

Archaeological sites: Staré Město, Velehrad, Mikulčice.

Communes with interesting local traditions and architecture:
Hroznová Lhota, Tasov, Ostrožská Ves, Hrubá Vrbka, Ratíš-
kovice, Tvrdonice, Lanžhot, Kyjov, Milotice, Rohatec and many
other villages. Traditional costumes can best be seen at Strážnice where a great festival of traditional craft is held annually,
at Hrozenkov and Velká nad Veličkou, and also during the great
pilgrimages to Velehrad (5 July) and St Anthony (13 June).

Hotels: Gottwaldov: Moskva Hotel. Luhačovice: Alexandria
Hotel and others, houses for cures and hospitals.

Communications: There is a regular **air-service** (several flights
a day) between Gottwaldov and Prague (Holešov airport).
There is also a small air-taxi rank. **Railways** run between practically all the large places in the region. Especially important
is the old railway line connecting the western parts of the Republic with Slovakia, going through Brno via Slavkov (Austerlitz), Kyjov, Uherské Hradiště (branch-line to Gottwaldov),
Uherský Brod, (branch-line to Luhačovice; express trains have
through carriages from Brno and Prague), and by the Vlára
Pass (over which important trade routes have passed from
times immemorial), to Trenčianska Teplá where it joins the
railway system of Slovakia. Another very important railway line
for express trains to Warsaw and Vienna runs through Czechoslovak territory via Ostrava, Přerov, Hulín (branch-line to
Kroměříž), Otrokovice (branch-line to Gottwaldov), Uherskě
Hradiště, Hodonin and Břeclav to Vienna. South-eastern
Moravia can also be approached by the railway line between
Prague and Budapest passing through Brno and Bratislava.

The **road network** is also very dense. The most interesting
road, because it goes through a very fine, well cared for landscape, is highway No 50 which runs from Brno through Slavkov
(Austerlitz), Bučovice, Střílky, across the wooded range of the
Chřiby Mountains (near Buchlov, a modern "Motorest" restaurant in the midst of splendid country) and goes through
Buchlovice to Uherské Hradiště, an important junction of main
roads. The road then goes on to Uherský Brod and Starý
Hrozenkov, crosses the wooded range of the White Carpathians
and ends at Trenčín in the Váh plain.

Other roads leading to the region include highway No 2 from
Brno through Židlochovice, Břeclav and Lanžhot to Bratislava,

and highway No 55 from Olomouc to Břeclav via Přerov, Otrokovice (highway No 59 to Gottwaldov, Vizovice and the Beskids), Uherské Hradiště, Strážnice and Hodonín.

There are bus connections between practically all the communes. The main bus centres are, on the one hand, Gottwaldov, and on the other Uherské Hradiště. There are also long-distance services between Brno and Gottwaldov and Gottwaldov and Slovakia.

A. GOTTWALDOV

Distances by road: Prague, 139 km; Brno, 106 km; Ostrava, 111 km; Bratislava, 169 km. Distances from Prague **by rail:** 314 km.

Greater Gottwaldov, which comprises numerous communes on the outskirts of the town, now has some 80,000 inhabitants. It is an important cultural and, above all, industrial centre of the region. To the rest of the world, Gottwaldov (formerly **Zlín**) is known as a large "shoe town", but it is also one of the most modern urban centres in Czechoslovakia. Modern sky-scrapers, a hotel equipped with the latest comfort, a cinema for 2,000 spectators, a sports stadium, a swimming pool, numerous playgrounds, parks abounding with greenery, attractive new residential districts comprising both blocks of flat and family bungalows surrounded by pretty gardens—all this proves that Gottwaldov rightly ranks among the best planned Czechoslovak towns. Besides its theatre, philharmonic orchestra and various other forms of entertainment, the town is also renowned for its film studios which specialize in marionette films and cartoons; the film of "The Devil's Invention" which was made at Gottwaldov by the producer Karel Zeman from the well-known novel by Jules Verne, won a Grand Prix at the Brussels World Fair in 1958. The film of

"Münchhausen", which enjoyed a brilliant success at numerous world film festivals, was also made at Gottwaldov.

The large shoe factories which employ some tens of thousands of persons, have also led to the growth of a new branch of the industry in the town and its surroundings, namely the manufacture of shoe-making and tanning machines which, together with the shoes themselves, constitute a much demanded export to various markets of the world. Every summer Gottwaldov organizes an "Exhibition of Modern Shoes" which always draws large numbers of foreign specialists. Various fashion accessories are also manufactured at Gottwaldov, as are stockings in conventional and synthetic materials, especially in **silon**, a Czechoslovak nylon.

Lázně Luhačovice (28 km south of Gottwaldov) is a spa set in the midst of deep forests and is very popular because of the great curative properties of its springs and its climate. It is indicated especially for illnesses of the respiratory tract (e.g., chronic bronchitis, asthma, pulmonary emphysema, silicoses, etc.) and for chronic gastric catarrhs and disturbances of the metabolism.

There are eleven springs of healing mineral waters at Luhačovice, containing potassium, sodium, chlorine, magnesium, calcium and, above all, carbonic acid and carbonic gas in a free state. The alkaline waters of the country—called "salt water" by the local people—have been known since the 12th–century. The first buildings were erected by the Brno doctor Jan Hertold von Todtenhof in 1668, at a time when the mineral waters of the region—the most famous of which is called "Vincentka"—were first analysed and their curative properties examined.

There are many hotels: foreign visitors will find every possible comfort at the Alexandria Hotel (Class A) which is very modern and has a café, terraces and a dance floor.

B. KROMĚŘÍŽ

The first mention of this town (38 km north-west of Gottwaldov), which is now a scheduled historic town, goes back to the year 1100. A very attractive and picturesque town, Kroměříž still has numerous historic buildings of great artistic value. The old gothic stronghold, the cathedral, and a part of the Old Town were ravaged by a great fire at the time of the Thirty Years' War, when the town was besieged by Swedish troops under General Torstensen. Between 1664 and 1695, Bishop Charles of Liechtenstein built, on the site of the old stronghold, a baroque **castle** surrounded by a magnificent park and a "Flower Garden", and containing a picture gallery and a library. In the 18th century a part of the castle was again burnt down, but by 1752 Bishop Maximilian Hamilton had completed the repairs and rebuilding.

The most noteworthy of the sumptuously decorated rooms of the castle is doubtlessly the Diet Hall in which the Constituent Assembly of the peoples of Austria sat in 1848. The rooms are richly decorated with valuable **frescoes.**

The **Picture Gallery** contains valuable works by flamboyant gothic, Renaissance and baroque painters. It is one of the richest art treasures in Czechoslovakia.

It contains Titian's famous "Flaying of Marsyas", the portrait of King Charles I of England and Queen Henrietta by Van Dyck, the "Beheading of St John the Baptist", St Catherine and St Barbara by Lucas Cranach, and paintings by Veronese, Peter and Jan Breughel, Lucas Cranach the Elder, by Brandl, Francisco and Giacomo Bassano, and others, and numerous sketches by the artist Max Švabinský who was born at Kroměříž.

The **library** contains some 40,000 volumes, including many unique historic specimens, incunabula (e.g., a Bible dating from 1488-1489) and manuscripts, the oldest of which dates back to the 9th century. The library also houses the archiepiscopal archives which have a tremendous historic value, with documents dating back to the 11th century (the oldest dates from 1063). The bishopric was raised to the rank of an archbishopric in 1777. The music archives of the library contain valuable manuscripts by composers of the baroque period. Also interesting are the collections in the museum, the most valuable being undoubtedly the numismatic items (more than 10,000 different items and models, including coins struck by the bishops of Olomouc at the Kroměříž Mint in 1608–1760).

Kroměříž also prides itself on its superb park whose designers were greatly influenced by Versailles. Kroměříž park is embellished by a 1,000-foot long colonnade, called "Great Colonnade", and lined with statues of mythological scenes. The avenues of the park converge on the "Rotunda", a gothic-style music pavilion built in 1669. To this day, concerts of ancient music and summer festivals are held under the colonnade and in the park's vast conservatory, and even dramatic performances are given there.

The park below the castle is noteworthy for its Pompeian Colonnade embellished with antique statues which were brought directly from Pompeii.

At present Kroměříž is an important cultural centre. One of the finest male choirs in the country, the "Male Choir of Moravian Teachers", was founded within its walls, and has since gained brilliant successes at many international festivals. Kroměříž, too, was the birthplace of the unforgettable conductor Václav Talich, whose fame is known. The town as a whole makes an excellent impression: its buildings as well as its decorative features bear witness to the unsurpassed mastery of the architects of bygone days. Sculptures include works by Paganini, Maulpertsch, Hirnl, Fontana, Joseph Stern, Dieussart and other eminent sculptors of the time. The town has always attracted artists from all parts of Europe, especially painters, sculptors and musicians who loved to work in this welcoming and hospitable place. The archbishop's residence even welcomed crowned heads, e.g., the King of Bohemia and German Emperor Charles IV, the

Empress Maria Theresa of Austria, Czar Alexander III and other sovereigns and ecclesiastical dignitaries.

The buildings of the town include the **cathedral of Saint Maurice** built in 1260 in a sober gothic style, and later completed with a baroque chapel; this building also contains the tombs of the cardinals and bishops of the period. One of the most superb baroque creations in Bohemia and Moravia is the oval-shaped **Piarist Church of Saint John** at Kroměříž, surmounted by an imposing dome decorated with frescoes by Etgens and Stern.

Equally interesting, from the architectural point of view, besides the other less important ecclesiastic buildings, are the municipal buildings, e.g., the **Town Hall** dating from 1611, the old patrician houses in the **Market Place**, etc.

Other places of interest

Buchlov (61 km from Brno on the Brno-Uherské Hradiště road).

The **fortified castle** of Buchlov was built in the 13th century as a citadel controlling the southern routes of access to Brno and Olomouc. It was built on the site of an old fortress as is shown by the numerous archaeological finds dating from the period of the Great Moravian Empire.

Buchlov castle is a very interesting building, with a happy combination of different architectural styles. The romanesque vestiges are found chiefly on the main entrance. The second gate, however, is characterized by gothic arches. The rebuilding and renovations were carried out in Renaissance and baroque styles. Originally, Buchlov stronghold was a royal castle which subsequently became the property of several noble families, as is shown by various valuable mementos that have survived to this day. Particularly noteworthy are the **collections of weapons** (the castle was often used as a hunting lodge), the collections of porcelain and earthenware dinner services, and especially the glasses which are very rare and of great historic value (the oldest ones date from between 1582 and 1600). Also very valuable are some carved furniture and the old library.

Buchlovice (8 km from Uherské Hradiště).

A baroque castle with a "Sala terrena", richly decorated and furnished in the 17th century and inhabited until fairly recently.

In 1908, negotiations between the Ministers of Foreign Affairs of Czarist Russia and the Austro-Hungarian Monarchy were held there; the owner of the castle, Count Berchtold, was the Minister of Foreign Affairs of Austria-Hungary at the time of the outbreak of the First World War. More interesting than the castle itself is the vast park, which is beautifully tended and contains rare trees from all over the world.

Uherské Hradiště (75 km from Brno, 26 km from Gottwaldov).

This is a very old town, founded in 1257 as a royal fortress, which has preserved its original medieval appearance to this day. Especially interesting is the architecture of the **Town Hall** which is surmounted by a tower. The most noteworthy churches are the **Jesuit Church,** dating from the 17th century and embellished with paintings by T. Supper, J. Heintsch, and J. Raab, and statues by O. Schweigel, and the **Franciscan Church** with its monastery, founded in 1490. When the church was rebuilt in baroque style in 1709, a valuable refectory was added.

In the market square is a **chemist's shop** with remarkable rococo paintings dating from 1754. Another noteworthy historic building is the former **Salt-tax Office** and **Salt Storehouse** dating from 1578. The **Slovak Museum**, with its wealth of traditional, historic and archaeological collections, discovered in the excavations of Staré Město and Velehrad, should also be visited. Museum devoted to regional **folk traditions.**

Staré Město, a kind of suburb of Uherské Hradiště, lies on the other side of the river.

The first mention of the locality occurs in old documents dating from 1131, when the town was still called **Veligrad**. It was an important junction of the trade routes between the Black Sea and the Baltic, and between the countries of the West and those of the East. According to recent archaeological discoveries, Veligrad was one of the main centres of the Great Moravian Empire; in fact, tombs in the region have yielded discoveries of gold, silver and bronze jewels, artistically decorated daggers, and a multitude of decorative items and ornaments which were, for the most part, manufactured in the workshops of Byzantine and Eastern craftsmen. On the other hand, numerous ceramic objects of typically Slav influence, decorated with wavy lines and horizontal incisions, have also been discovered, as have the remains of large churches. The discoveries made to date have shown that the culture of the old Moravians, which bore a marked Byzantine influence, achieved a very high standard as early as the 9th century.

Velehrad (9 km from Uherské Hradiště).

Now it is a famous pilgrimage centre, recalling the work of Cyril and Methodius the apostles of the Slavs, who converted Bohemia and Moravia to Christianity. It used to be thought that Velehrad was the capital of the Great Moravian Empire, but it was subsequently proved that the site of the present Velehrad did not correspond with that of the old Veligrad. Nonetheless, numerous valuable objects of the romanesque period were found there, especially near the church and the cross-shaped passage. The **church,** to which crowds of pilgrims come each year, is a large baroque building, rebuilt towards the end of the 17th century and outstanding for its nave which is the longest in Moravia (282 feet); the church is decorated with **stuccoes** and paintings, and has richly carved **choir stalls** dating from 1695.

Milotice (35 km south-west of Uherské Hradiště).

This unusually charming **castle** was built on the site of the former lake citadel of which only vestiges of the ramparts and moat survive. The present castle was built in baroque style at the beginning of the 18th century by a member of the Sérényi family. The castle is approached by a **stone** bridge decorated with baroque sandstone statues, with winged Pegasi, sphinxes, and children of Hercules. It is also noteworthy for its large state room which is two storeys high and whose walls and ceilings are embellished with baroque paintings on mythological themes by **Francis Eckstein.**

Vizovice (12 km east of Gottwaldov).

This town is well known for its fine **castle built** between 1750 and 1770; the left wing houses an original, richly decorated chapel. The sculptures are by Ondřej Schweigel.

The **Picture Gallery of the castle** used to be one of the most important galleries in the whole of Moravia. Its founders aimed at assembling important works by Dutch, Italian and French masters and thus creating a great collection of European painting of the period. Although they did not succeed, they nonetheless assembled some very valuable paintings. The rooms of the castle also contain numerous **objets d'art** and interesting collections of French tapestries with scenes from Aesop's fables, China, Japanese and Meissen porcelain, hunting weapons and trophies, etc.

A part of the castle has been transformed into a **History** Museum of regional **folk traditions.**

Vizovice exports the famous "Slivovice"—a very strong spirit distilled from special plums—to all parts of the world.

Uherský Brod (20 km east of Uherské Hradiště, 39 km south of Gottwaldov).

This was probably the birthplace, in 1592, of Jan Amos Komenský (Comenius), the most famous educational reformer of the period. His works on education, e.g., "Orbis Pictus", "Schola Ludus", etc., have long been regarded as authoritative documents on the subject.

This old town has a whole series of interesting features, including, above all, the **Jan Amos Komenský (Comenius) Museum** which contains many mementos of this exceptional genius, one of the greatest figures sprung from the Czech people. The museum also has valuable editions of Comenius's books which appeared abroad, and other mementos of his outstanding life and work.

Folk art and traditions

Lovers of traditional costumes, of embroideries, ceramics and pottery, of works of architecture and, above all, of songs and dances will find many expressions of local traditions in this region. As we noted above, the region round Gottwaldov is the meeting place of three very distinct ethnographic zones, namely Moravian Slovakia (the region round Břeclav, Lanžhot, Hodonín, Strážnice, Uherské Hradiště, Uherský Brod, and the surroundings of Velká nad Veličkou although the last-named already is somewhat different), the southern part of Walachia (the surroundings of Gottwaldov, Vizovice, Valašské Klobùky and of Starý Hrozenkov, all with a regional culture and local traditions which differ from the first-named zone), and the eastern part of Hannakia (the surroundings of Kroměříž, a very fertile country, abounding in traditional costume with magnificently embroidered sleeves).

The richness of costumes in this area is really exceptional: for instance, during the Exhibition of 1895, Moravian Slovakia alone showed 28 different kinds of costumes, each more beautiful than the preceding one. It is no exaggeration to say that each village in this region has its own special charm. Folk art is an inexhaustible source of beauty which has long inspired Czechoslovak and foreign artists, whether it be sculptors, musicians or actors, including the famous French sculptor Rodin, the eminent Czech composer Vitězslav Novák, Václav Talich, the well-known conductor of the Czech Philharmonic Orchestra who was a native of Kroměříž, and many others.

The visitor to this delightful and picturesque corner is doubtlessly most impressed by the brightly coloured costumes, the music and the songs. Orchestras of folk music have their special instruments: first and second violins, violas, double bass and drums. The other special features of the region include also painted Easter eggs, called "kraslice", pottery and objects made of wood and maize spikes, etc. The doors, passages and windows of many village houses are decorated with mangificent traditional paintings. Especially at Easter the whole countryside is decked out in its most festive garb.

Nowadays traditional costumes are only rarely worn on weekdays. Nonetheless, the State devoted great care to the development of folk art. In almost every commune there are groups who see to it that future generations should know the old folk customs. Each year, festivals and contests are organized in different parts of the country, and during the village festivals in autumn one can still see many old customs and magnificent regional costumes.

SLOVAKIA

Archaeological discoveries have proved that the territory occupied by the present Slovakia was inhabited from the earliest times. The Slav peoples began to settle in this region by stages in the fourth century A.D., at the time of the decline of the Roman Empire and of the Migration of Peoples. At the beginning of the 10th century the Slav tribes of Slovakia were gradually subjected to the Magyars and for a thousand years were incorporated in the Hungarian kingdom, particularly in the feudal state.

Slovakia played an important part in the Hungarian state. As early as in the 11th and 12th centuries many market centres and settlements of handicraftsmen had arisen which later developed into towns. Mining gave rise to new urban settlements. Bratislava (Pressburg), Kremnica, Banská Štiavnica, Banská Bystrica, Košice, Levoča, Prešov, Bardejov and other towns became free royal towns; the King often made trading cities free towns, and it was chiefly in these towns that the most valuable monuments of Romanesque, Gothic, Renaissance and Baroque architecture, sculpture and painting were preserved. In the age of feudalism two great wars were carried into Slovakian territory. In the middle of the 13th century the country was overrun by Tartar hordes. In the 16th and 17th centuries the Turks invaded southern Slovakia. At that time Bratislava was the capital of Hungary. At the time of the Turkish wars Hungary, and Slovakia with it, were incorporated in the polyglot Hapsburg monarchy.

The life of the subject Slovak population was hard. Throughout that era the fight against feudal subjection often broke out into open rebellion. Latin was at that time the official language in Slovakia, but in writings and also in economic life Czech in its Slovak form was used as well. This fact and the lively economic and cultural relations between Slovakia and the Bohemian provinces kept alive the consciousness of the common ties which united the Czechs and the Slovaks. The formation of the Slovak language began with the 18th century. The national consciousness grew in the 19th century to a national movement, primarily as a reaction against Hungarian suppression. The interval between 1849 and 1918 is one of the saddest periods of Slovak history. Every national expression was brutally suppressed. Up to 1819 the Slovaks had no cultural institution, no secondary schools and even almost no primary schools of their own.

This national suppression was profoundly interwoven with the economic and social repression of the Slovak people. The hard economic and social conditions were the cause of mass emigration. In the struggle for the maintenance of the national consciousness the Czechs and the Slovaks came closer together. The result of the efforts of the people and of progressive politicians was the creation of the Czechoslovak Republic at the end of the First World War.

The Slovak people were deprived of all democratic rights, and never reconciled themselves to the enforced separation from the Czechs. The national resistance movement culminated in the Slovak National Insurrection which broke out on the 29th August 1944.

Before the war, Slovakia was hardly industrialized and very little developed in general. Since 1945, the area has been the object of special care, and the gap between Slovakia and the Czech countries has diminished. Now Slovakia, which has 4,5 million inhabitants (almost a third of the total of the Republic), takes one fifth share of total industrial production (twice as much as in 1938); a quarter of the population works in industry as much as in agriculture; the number of University graduates is three times as great as before the war; in one year, 65,000 television sets, 33,000 refrigerators, and 63,000 washing machines were sold there. These figures illustrate the rapid development of today's Slovakia.

When Hitler ordered Bohemia and Slovakia occupied, he imposed on the latter infeudation to Nazi Germany.

12. SOUTH-WEST AND WEST SLOVAKIA

Geography: The territory of west and south-west Slovakia geographically forms a compact unit, separated from the neighbouring countries by rivers and mountains. The Morava river marks the frontier with Austria, the Danube with Hungary, the Hron and the Žitava with the Vtáčník Mounains and the Stražovská Heights with central Slovakia and the White Carpathians with Moravia.

The region is mainly characterized by the fertile plains along the courses of the Danube and the Little Danube, the Váh (Waag), the Nitra, the Žitava, the Hron and the Morava; the granary of Slovakia and also of the whole of Czechoslovakia. The border regions, especially the north and the north-east, are interspersed with hills and mountains, which quite suddenly rise up from the plain to considerable heights.

South-west and South Slovakia can be divided into a few typical units, each with its own characteristic natural and economic conditions. First, the low plain of the river courses. In the west the plain from Záhoria on the left bank of the Morava to Bratislava. It is divided from the plain of the lower Povážia (the Waag valley) by the White Carpathians, the valley stretching as far as the Trnava plateau, the Danube plain and the plain of the Nitra river. The Danube together with the Little Danube forms the Danube plain, known as the Rye Island. Finally the north-eastern part of this region is characterized by the fertile valley of the Nitra and its tributaries, between which the Triveč Mountains are wedged.

Economy: The greater part of the above-mentioned region is covered with fertile fields. It is the granary of Czechoslovakia; wheat, rye, maize, sugar-beet, vegetables and even tobacco and rice are cultivated. The most developed of the various branches of industry is food; the manufacture of the agricultural products of the region. This refers primarily to the sugar factories of Trnava, Sládkovičovo, Šurany, Pohronský Ruskov and Trenčianska Teplá, the fruit and vegetable canneries at Záhorie and the Corn Island; then spirit distilleries and mills. The engineering industry is also specially developed with large works at Bratislava, Trnava, Nové Mesto on the Váh, Trenčín, Dubnica on the Váh, Nové Zámky and Komárno; likewise the chemical industry at Bratislava, Senica, Púchov, leather factories at Partizánské and

Bošany, the textile industry at Trenčín and mining (naphta) at Gbely. The manufacture of building materials is also showing a remarkable upward trend, principally with brick and cement works and prefabricated elements. A number of modern hydro-electric power stations dot the Váh valley from the Youth Dam as far as Madunica south of Piešťany and others are under construction, so that 21 stations in all work successively in cascades. The region's originality lies in the countless vineyards bearing good grapes, particularly on the sunny slopes of the White Carpathians from Bratislava to Modra. Here the best Slovak wine is cultivated.

Geographically the whole region of South-west and West Slovakia is determined by the Carpathians and the river plains, chiefly the great Danube plain.

Regarded from a **tourist standpoint**, this part of Slovakia is remarkable for its wealth of cultural-historical monuments, especially for the well-preserved interesting architecture of church and secular buildings in the medieval towns **Bratislava, Modra, Pezinok, Trnava, Trenčín** and **Nitra**; for its remains from the Roman period; for its period fortresses and castles, many of which having now been converted into cultural institutions, such as Červený Kameň, Topolčianky; for the enormous amount of hunting-groups, specially plentiful in stags, deer and wild boar, moufflons (wild sheep) in the enclosures of Topolčianky and the Little Carpathians, in pheasants, waterfowl and hares round Palárikovo and Bajč near Nové Zámky and in fish in the tributaries of the Danube. And lastly, also situated in this part of Slovakia, are the world-famous spas Piešťany and Trenčianské Teplice.

Communications: Connections between South-west and West Slovakia and the whole of Czechoslovakia are maintained by railways, motorways and air lines. The most important town in the province—**Bratislava**, the capital of Slovakia—has a direct air service to and from Prague, Brno, and within Slovakia Sliač, Piešťany, Poprad (High Tatra), Košice and Prešov. There is a direct service to London and New York either directly or via Prague. International railways connections are assured by direct through carriages from Prague via Brno and Břeclav (Gmünd, 396 km), from Vienna via Marchegg, from Budapest via Komárno or Szob, from Wroclaw (Breslau) via Bohumín and Žilina. The most important towns lie on the rail and road network from Bratislava via Trnava, Piešťany and Trenčín in North Slovakia and in Central Slovakia via Nítra. The main lines connecting this region with the whole of Czechoslovakia and the rest of

Slovakia are: Prague—Brno—Břeclav—Bratislava, Bratislava—Žilina—Poprad (High Tatra)—Košice, Bratislava—Nové Zámky—Zvolen. The main motor highway in this region runs from Gmünd to Bratislava. From there it continues either north-east through Trnava in North Slovakia or east via Trnava into Central and East Slovakia and through Nítra into the High Tatra. The autobahn from Vienna runs through Hainburg and Berg, from Budapest through Komárno or through Rajka-Rusovce to Bratislava.

The most important cultural, economic and political centres of South-west and West Slovakia are: the capital of Slovakia Bratislava and the towns Trenčín, Nitra, Komárno, Trnava and Piešťany.

Sights and places of interest

National Trust town: Bratislava.

Natural reservations: the "Cormorant Island" Podunajské Biskupice, Šúr Jelenec, Arborétum Mlyňany, Pata, Zlatná on the Isle (bustard), Žibrica Lupka and Roštún (rare flora), Tôn, Apáli island Komárno, Chotín, Kovačovské kopce (Kovačov Hill), the Island Baka.

Castles: Červený Kameň, Budmerice, Smolenice, Beckov, Čachtice, Trenčín, Vršatec, Nitra, Topolčany, Bojnice, Jelenec, Topolčianky, Smolenice, Borinka, Pajštún, Tematin, Bernolákovo and Adamovské Kochanovce.

Hunting grounds: Podunajská Biskupice, Jelenec, Topolčianky, Bajc, Čičov, Polarikovo, Zlatna on the Isle, Šala, Jelenec, Stupava, Smolenice and Dunajska Streda.

Spas: Piešťany, Trenč, Teplice, Smrdáky, Bojnice, Nosice near Púchov.

Folklore: Vajnory, Vinične, Moravany, Krakovany, Dolná and Horná Suča, Trenč. Teplá, Chotin, Modra, Cajkov, Rybník, Bošáka, Moravská Liesková.

Other notable sights: Senec—lake, Dolná Krupá (Beethoven), Čachtice (cave labyrinth), Horná Streda Jankov (hill with monument), Youth Dam at Púchov, Dražovec—little Romanesque church, Bojnice (zoo and castle), Iža—Roman fortress, Bíňa—Romanesque church, Piešťany (Lake Síňava), Stará Turá (Lake Dubník).

Circuit in south-west and west Slovakia:
Bratislava—Pezinok (22 km)—Modra (30 km)—Červený Kameň (40 km)—Trnava (61 km)—Piešťany (104 km)—Beckov (129 km)—Trenčín (150 km)—Trenč. Teplice (165 km)—Trenčín

(180 km)—Janov Vršok (229 km)—Nitra (289 km)—Topolčianky (321 km)—Arboretum Mlyňany (333 km)—Nitra (362 km)—Bratislava (451 km).

A. BRATISLAVA

Bratislava (pop. 300,000), a town under National Trust protection, is in the south-west tip of Slovakia where the frontiers with Austria and Hungary meet, on the southern foothills of the Little Carpathians. It lies on both banks of the Danube (540 feet above sea level) and is an important rail and road junction.

The history of the settlement of Bratislava, once Pressburg, goes back to Roman times. At the beginning of our chronology Roman outposts were stationed here and in the 5th century finally came the Slavs. In the 13th century the town was already an important trade centre and in 1465 the first university on Hungarian soil was founded here. After the occupation of Budín by the Turks in 1536, Bratislava became the capital of Hungary. Until 1848 the Hungarian Diet sat here and the Kings of Hungary were also crowned here. At the end of the 18th century the town began to grow thanks to industrial development. With the foundation and, more especially, with the rebirth of the Czechoslovak Republic, in 1918 and 1945 respectively, the town achieved a fresh prosperity. Bratislava became the capital of Slovakia and the centre of all its political, economic and cultural life.

We are able to follow the importance of Bratislava in political, economic and cultural life from the many historical monuments which the town possesses in abundance, from the Middle Ages down to the present day.

Among the architectural beauties of the town are many historical valuable buildings, places, houses and churches on the foundations of the Old Town. First and foremost of these is the old **Bratislava castle**— which dominates the town. From it one gets the finest view of the town and its surroundings; beyond the shining surface of the Danube one can see clearly into the neighbouring Austria and Hungary.

The earliest history of the castle goes back to the days when castles were built as fortresses. Later it became a clerical and administrative centre. It got its appearance resembling an "overturned table" (which it still has) in the 17th century when the old fortress was reconstructed as it substantially stands today. Reconstructions done in the 17th and 18th centuries were essential. Thus in 1632–49 the Gothic edifice was converted into a Renaissance palace. The last rebuilding in the time of Maria Theresa gave the castle a Baroque appearance. In 1811 it was burnt down. Restauration is well advanced and the entire building was opened to the public in summer 1968. The Knights' Hall is also open to visitors. The castle is to house the National Slovak Museum. An amphitheatre capable of seating 10,000 spectators has already been erected in its grounds for the purpose of providing recreation and entertainment to the people of Bratislava. The entrance to the Castle still radiates a medieval, romantic magic. The buildings of the outer part are relatively well preserved. The castle, together with the Old Town and the part in front of the castle are under National Trust protection as Ancient Monuments.

The **Old Town Hall.** The oldest part dates from the 15th century and is used today for cultural purposes as a municipal museum, with archives and a scientific library. The Town Hall tower was added in 1734.

The **Primate's Palace** (Archiepiscopal palace), erected in the years 1778–80 as an annex to the Town Hall, is one of the finest monuments of early, stylistically very mature, Baroque Classicism. The decoration of the palace is remarkable, especially the Hall of Mirrors, in which in 1805 after the Battle of Austerlitz the so-called Peace of Pressburg was signed by Napoleon and the Austrian Emperor Franz I. The reception rooms are adorned by valuable English tapestries. The palace is used by the town Gallery.

The **University Library** in the Michalská No 1 was built in 1753. The Hungarian Diet sat here until 1848.

The **Michalská brána** (gate and tower) are part of the town's fortifications. The road to the town gate

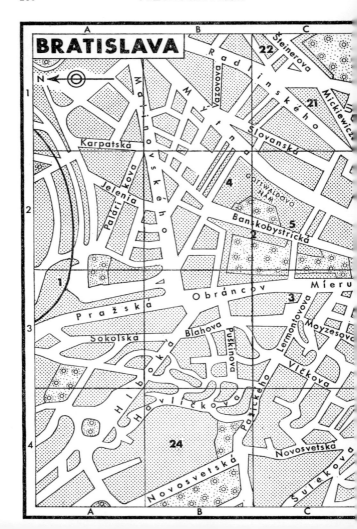

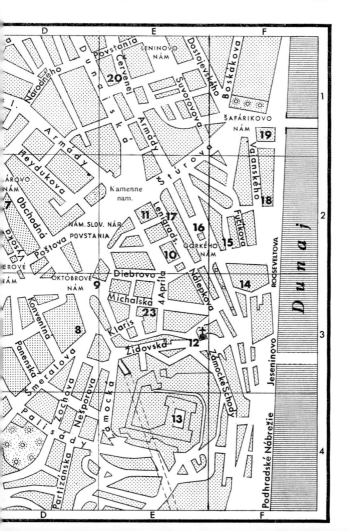

leads over a bridge. The 15th–century tower is 168 feet high. A Gothic gate-house tower stands on Gothic foundations and was completed in 1758 by a Baroque copper dome in the shape of a double turban. The statue of Saint Michael surmounts the gable of the tower. Between the gate and the tower stands the oldest apothecary's shop in Bratislava "At the sign of Cancer" (Zum Krebs) dating from the 14th century and which houses the pharmacological Museum. In Michalská brána is also a fine collection of medieval arms.

The **Pionerský palác Klementa Gottwalda** in the square Mierové námestie No 1 is the finest Baroque palace with garden, built in the time of Maria Theresa (mid-18th century). It was built as the Grassalkovich Palace in 1760. In the hall, statues by the sculptor Rafael Donner, representing the Four Seasons, are worth noting. Another of these Baroque palaces, the former **Archiepiscopal Summer Palace,** in the Gottwaldovo námestie is now the headquarters of the Slovak National Council and in the **Aspermontov Palace** in the street ulice Čsl. Armády is the deanery of the faculty of medicine of the Komenský University.

KEY TO THE PLAN OF BRATISLAVA

1 Central Station A3
2 Slovak National Council...B/C 2
3 Lenin Museum C3
4 Government Building B2
5 Technical College C2
6 Klement Gottwald Pioneers'
   Palace C2/3
7 New Stage D2
8 Offices of the Slovak National
   Council D3
9 Michalská Gate D3
10 Primae's Palace and Municipal
   Museum E2
11 Manderla Palace orientation
   point E2

12 Saint Martin Cathedral......E3
13 Fortified Castle.............E4
14 Slovak National Gallery.....F3
15 Redoubt F2
16 National Theatre E2
17 P.O. Hviezdoslav Theatre....E2
18 Slovak Museum,.............F2
19 J. A. Komenský University...F1
20 Marionette Theatre..........E1
21 Regional Institute of Public
   Health C1
22 Slovak Syndical Council.....C1
23 Čedok Travel Bureau,
   Štúrova ul. 9b E3
24 Slavín Cemetery ....,..B4

Most of the private houses were built in Renaissance or Baroque style. Among the most valuable Renaissance buildings is the **Segner House** in the Michalská at No 7 (1648); the **Mirbach House** in the Diebrov námestie square (No 8) is an outstanding example of Baroque architecture.

The Gothic **Saint Martin's cathedral (Dom Sv. Martina)** is the most beautiful and most valuable example of church architecture. The building was started in the 14th century and finished in the 15th. The 280 foot tower forms part of the town's fortifications. In the cathedral is the sculptor R. Donner's magnificent work, the lead statue group of Saint Martin. From 1563 onwards the cathedral was the coronation church of the Kings of Hungary; this fact is commemorated by a cushion with a gilded crown on the top of the tower.

Among the other churches the following are specially worthy of notice: the early Gothic sanctuary of the **Franciscan church** and the Gothic **Saint John's chapel** in the same church (1315–18); the Gothic **church of Saint Clare** and its tower (1360); the Renaissance **Jesuit** and **Ursuline church**; the Baroque **church of the Holy Trinity**.

Mention must be made of No 7 Jirásek street. In it there used to be the municipal mint and from 1465 the **Academia Istropolitana** college.

In the museums we find more records of the history of the town and the life of its inhabitants: in the municipal museum in the Old Town Hall and in the Slovak museum at No 12 Vjanský Kai.

Bratislava, which became the seat of the Slovak government departments after the liberation in 1945, is steadily growing and developing. Some new enterprises have sprung up which are able to compete with the most modern factories in the world. The best equipped technically are the chemical works, e.g., the **G. Dimitrov** and **Slovnaft** works.

Bratislava is the centre of the cultural and economic life of Slovakia: the Komenský University, the Technical High School, the High School for Economics and Pedagogy, scientific research institutes and laboratories of the Academy of Sciences (Czech and Slovak); government departments, the Slovak sections of the Czechoslovak Writers' Union and the unions of artists, composers, journalists and architects. A number of newspapers and periodicals are published here; they are the central organs of Slovakia; Bratislava has its own broadcasting station and television studio; also modern film studios.

Theatres: the National Theatre (opera, ballet), the P.O. Hviezdoslav Theatre (drama), the New Stage, the Theatre of the Music College, the Theatre of Music, and the Tatra-Revue Theatre.

Concerts of the Slovak Philharmonic are held in the concert hall.

Exhibitions in the National Gallery and the exhibition rooms of the Slovak section of creative artists.

Among the cultural sights are the Lenin Museum, the Janka Jesenský Museum and the Humel Museum. On Slavían Hill, affording a beautiful view of Bratislava, is the central cemetery where Soviet soldiers who fell in the war lie buried (memorial).

Bratislava has a great many places of entertainment, among others also a number of garden and platform halls in the Culture and Recreation Park. There is a large park on the hills on the west of the town, on the right bank of the Danube, in Patržalká, the Janko Král Park. A path leads out of the park into the picturesque valley, known as Nightingale Valley.

Bratislava has also the well-known Slovak Folk-art Group (Slovenský lud. umel. kolektiv) SLUK and the "Lúčnica" ensemble established here.

Accommodation: Hotel Devín, Riečna ul. 4, Tel. 31241, 39730; Carlton Hotel, Hviezdoslavovo námestie 7, tel: 38141, 30247. Čedok offices, 96 Šturova 52142, 52548; Turista Travel bureau, namestie Slov. nár povstánice 14, tel: 53696, 54007, 50526.

B.   EXCURSIONS FROM BRATISLAVA

Through a district of the town where vineyards grow, one enters the "Koliba", the beginning of the woods of the Little Carpathians with **Kamzík** Hill on which there is a restaurant. Trolleybus No 13 runs as far as the woods. One can continue the walk

to the **Červený Kríž** (Red Cross). Another district
for a half-day excursion is the area between **Želatná
studnička** (the Iron Spring), the **Lamač** and the
Kačín house. Motor buses run directly to the "Iron
Spring" restaurant.

It is also worth mentioning the **steamer trips**
upstream on the Danube to Devín, where stands the
old castle of the Great Moravian Empire, and the
downstream service to Hrušov Gabčikovo and
Komárno.

Stupava (18 km north). Important archaeological
excavations of a castrum of the first century A.D. were
made in the neighbourhood. The 18th-century castle
stands in the middle of a park. There is a famous
pottery workshop and a profilic hunting reserve.

Pajštún (23 km north). Above the village the
ruins of the 13th–century Pajštún castle. Not far from
the castle are the ruins of a watchtower called Dračie
hrádok (Dragon's Castle), the foundations of which
recall the times when the Roman legions were stationed
here. Below the castle the romantic valley Medené
Hámry (caves and springs).

Malacky (38 km north). The 17th–century church
and former monastery, built on the foundations of a
medieval flood refuge and a castle with a park (also
17th century) are its most interesting monuments.
Traditional horse races are run in the town. There are
large fir woods roundabout. On the highway before
Malacky is the summer resort **Kamenný mlýn.**

Vajnory, a suburb of Bratislava (10 km). Slovak
folklore, principally costumes, embroideries and
mural paintings. There are artificial lakes in the
surroundings of Vajnory (bathing and camping).

Podunajské Biskupice (10 km south-east). South of the place, on the Danube, is a hunting research reservation where deers run wild. On the sandy islands in the branches of the Danube, the Cormorant Islands, is a sanctuary for cormorants and other aquatic birds. The biggest cormorant colony in Central Europe, 600–700 pairs, nest in the tall black poplars.

Bernolákovo (18 km north-east), a well-preserved Baroque castle, now the administrative building of a nationally-owned estate.

Senec (26 km north-east), summer resort with artificial lakes and a colony of week-end houses. Large camp for motorists.

Jur pri Bratislave (13 km north) was founded in the middle of the 13th century after the Tartar invasion.

It was given town privileges in 1299. It was made a royal town in 1647. In 1666 it was destroyed by the Turks. In the town museum in the Town Hall we find various records of the town's history as well as interesting documents written by local citizens from Turkish captivity.

The plentiful history of the famous little town which partly subsists through wine-growing, is reflected in its many monuments. Well worth seeing are the old houses with attic living quarters and tiny windows and large wine cellars with casks below them. The parish **church of Saint George** is built in Gothic style. The most valuable artistic monument is however the high altar of the church, a splendid work by an unknown master of soft sandstone. The whole altar is decorated with Renaissance ornamentation. The **Gothic gilt statue group** "The Death of the Blessed Virgin" is also remarkable. The **wooden belfry** near the church has bells made in 1400 and 1460. The churchyard is enclosed by a fortification wall. The **remains of the town walls** are well preserved. The famous writer

Peter Jilemnický once lived in Jur. In his house, behind gardens in the midst of vineyards, is a museum commemorating his work and life.

In the surroundings of Jur there are relatively well-preserved old Slav strongholds (6th–7th century) which arouse wonder because of their mighty and clever system of fortification. On a hill near by, hidden behind trees, are the ruins of the castle of Biely Kameň. In the district is the Šúr reservation, peat meadows with unique species of plants and insects. The biggest race course in Slovakia is at Jur.

Pezinok (20 km north-east) was made a free royal town in 1647 and delivered to the royal court in return for its royal privileges a yearly tribute of 250 buckets of wine. Gold mines existed here until the last century. Among the most important monuments of the town are the Gothic **parish church** (1347) with its remarkable pulpit (early Renaissance) with a Baroque baldaquin, some Renaissance tombs and the Baroque altar (1523); the original evangelical church (1608); the remains of the town fortifications; and the Renaissance **castle** with its park. The castle was built in 1608 on the site of a former flood refuge and is fortified by a moat. Today there are huge wine-barrels made of concrete in its cellars. The living rooms of the castle are used as an elegant bodega. A fine bathing establishment adjoins the castle park.

Pezinok is the birthplace of the 18th–century Baroque portraitist Jan Kupecký. In the house where he was born at No 18 in the street named after him is the Kupecký museum. Valuable objects relating to the town's history are to be found in the municipal **museum** and in the archives of the **Old Town Hall.** Pezinok also has a Museum of Vine-growing. Every autumn there is a harvest celebration and wine-tasting.

In the surrounding district, at **Častá,** at **Slovensky Grob** and, more particularly, at **Viničné**, beautifully embroidered costumes are worn; one can visit artistically painted rooms. The small town of Pezinok is much industrialised; specially, a large brick-works.

Accommodation: Hotel Jelen, 10 Stalingradské námestie, Telephone: 2328.

North-west of the town, on the **Pezinská Baba** in the Little Carpathians is the nearest hikers' hostel to Bratislava at a height of 1,728 feet above sea level. There is a regular motorbus service from Pezinok to the hostel.

Modra (29 km north-east). This ancient small town below the wooded peaks of the Little Carpathians has been known since the 12th century. It was given its first town privileges in the 14th century and in 1613 it was made a free royal borough. Parts of the town fortifications of that time and 17th-century houses by Italian artists are still preserved. Those in the best condition are the **Pezinok Gate** (1618) and the round cannon tower on the south-west rampart. Modra is a centre of viticulture, besides which there is a Research Institute for Viticulture and Vintnery as well as an Agricultural Technical School with similar specialisation.

Modra is also known for the Modra **Popular Art Pottery** in which even connoisseurs can detect all the elements and beauty of popular creative art. The mastery and skill of the plastics produced by the local Pottery Society, which models out of a single piece of clay figures with all the perfection of a skilled sculptor, are quite remarkable.

Modra has played an important part in the enlightenment of Slovakia. Here lived and died (in 1856) a key figure in the national revival of the Slovak people in the 19th century, Ludovît Štur. All over the town we find places with plaques commemorating his activity. There is the Market Square and in the cemetery a memorial on his grave, the work of the sculptor J. Kostka.

Accommodation: Hotel Modra, Štúrova ul. 95, Tel: 42,124.

A place of excursion, as also from Bratislava, is the near-by **Harmonia**, where amid beautiful woodland scenery are many villas, week-end houses and a bathing establishment. Motorbus connection with Modra (4 km). Motorbuses also run further up into the Little Carpathian Mountains to the Zoch Tourist Hostel (1,584 feet above sea level) 9 km. The town is 5 km from the railway station Modra—Čanikovice on the Bratislava—Žilina line.

Červený Kameň castle (40 km north-east), originally a fortress, was already standing in the first half of the 13th century. It was entirely rebuilt in the 16th century as a neo-Renaissance fortress with an almost square ground plan and with four solid round bastions at the corners. The final reconstruction by Count Pálffy towards the end of the 16th century gave the building its present form of a regular castle with four residential wings grouped round the inner courtyard. The interior of the castle has preserved the character of the early Baroque reconstruction done in 17th century. The stone portal, two wells in the courtyard and the remarkable "Salla Terrena" with its magnificent stucco vaulting and the frescoes with fountains and the spring flowing out of an artifical grotto in the background belong to the same period. In 1945 the castle was transformed into a **museum,** in which several wonderful pieces of furniture are contained. Especially fine are two Renaissance rooms with 16th-century Italian furniture, with an interesting collection of Italian Renaissance and early Baroque majolica as well as pieces of Persian, Chinese and Rhineland origin. The Knights' Hall also makes a great impression with some valuable chests and arm-chairs, the collection of hunting weapons and portraits of the Turkish Sultans.

Motor vehicles can drive direct to the castle through the village of **Častá.**

Budmerice (38 km north-east). On the outskirts of Budmerice, in the middle of a wonderful park with a pond and a pool stands the neo-Renaissance castle, built in the 19th century, which reminds one of the French medieval castles. The period interior furnishing of the castle is especially valuable. Today the castle is the headquarters of the Union of Slovak Writers.

C. TRNAVA

Trnava (47 km north-east of Bratislava) lies almost in the middle of the fertile plateau on the little river Trnava (4,818 feet above sea level). West and north of the town rise the Little Carpathian Mountains. Trnava is an important railway junction and fast train station on the Bratislava—Žilina line. Good roads run in all directions.

Its advantageous position on the road from Hungary into the Bohemian provinces soon made Trnava a centre of trade and handicraft. As early as 1238 the town was awarded its civic rights; thanks to the consistent development of its trade and industry it grew considerably in the following century. The town was forti-fied in the same century and several important buildings were erected. Trnava made great strides between the 16th and 18th century, when after the occupation of Buda by the Turks it was for nearly 300 years the see of the Archbishop of Esztergom and thus became the ecclesiastical centre of all Hungary. The number of churches and particularly of monasteries grew to such an extent that the town is still called the Slovak Rome. A university was founded here in 1635 with a theological and a philosophical faculty, a faculty of law and of medicine being added in 1667 and 1769 respectively.

Trnava's share in the Slovak national Renaissance towards the end of the 18th century is also remarkable. The Society of Scholars (Učené tovarišstvo), the foremost scientific and literary association of the Slovaks in the 18th century, was founded here, In the 19th century, after the university transferred to Buda and the archbishop removed to Esztergom, the importance of the town, especially as a cultural centre, declined. But its economic development continued. Industrial undertakings sprang up, chiefly concerned with the manufacture of agricultural products. The town has also continued its development in this direction in the present century, especially since the creation of Czechoslovakia.

Trnava has become an industrial town in the middle of a fertile agricultural region. There are in the town and round about many sugar factories, malt factories, mills, distilleries and brickworks. Today several scientific and research institutes are being erected, principally in connection with agriculture and agricultural production.

The sights of the town

The monumental **Saint Nicholas Church** was built in Gothic style in the 14th century. It was reconstructed at the time when it was used as the cathedral of the Archbishop of Esztergom. Additions were also made to the interior, so that today we find Baroque elements alongside Gothic. The tombs are very precious. It is possible to follow the style of each period from the 14th century on.

The little **Saint Elizabeth church** was built, together with the hospital, in the middle of the 14th century and is the oldest ecclesiastical building in Trnava.

The **Jesuit University Church** was at the beginning of the 17th century the first great Baroque church building in Slovakia. It was built on the model of the "Il Gesù" church in Rome and is one of the biggest churches in Slovakia, with a central nave, 77 yards long, 18 yards wide and 66 feet high. The architecture of the main altar is remarkable.

Old burgher houses. From No 4 Radlinskeho street we can reconstruct the original Gothic ground-plan of the 15th century houses. In the town square we find many typical elements of Renaissance buildings.

Other sights: the regional museum, the former archiepiscopal palace, the University building, the former orphanage, the Pioneer House, the Town Hall and Empire-Style Municipal Theatre.—On the west and east sides of the town nearly all the bastions with their embrasures and the fortification moat, dating from the 14th century, are still preserved.

Accommodation: Hotel Dukla, 30 Town Square, tel: 2499, 2693; Hotel Tatra, 2 Vajanského ulica, tel: 2485. Turista Travel Office, Town Tower, tel: 2079.

Walks and excursions around Trnava

Smolenice Castle (35 km north-west). The original medieval castle dates from the 12th century. The present castle at the foot of the Little Carpathians has a unique situation and offers an unforgettable distant view. It was built at the beginning of this century by Josef Pálffy. The Slovak Academy of Sciences completed and modernized the building in the years 1954–56. Important international conferences and meetings of scientists from all over Europe are held here. Round about there is good shooting with deer, wild boar and moufflon (wild sheep).

Dolná Krupá (15 km north). A Classical castle stands in a beautiful natural park. In a little house still standing near the castle lived Ludwig van Beethoven during his frequent visits to Dolná Krupá.

Dobrá Voda (31 km north) is beautifully situated in an enclosed hollow of the Little Carpathians, below the ruins of a medieval castle (the climb up takes half an hour). The Slovak Academy of Sciences has an estate in the village where the experimental breeding of animals is carried on.

Smrdáky (43 km north-west), a prettily situated health resort at the foot of the Little Carpathians. It has 14 very prolific mineral springs with salt, sulphur and iodine content and the highest active sulphur content of any European spa. Smrdáky specialises in the treatment of rheumatic and skin diseases. The "Musical Summer" is held there (concerts and folk festivals).

Dubník (20 km south-east) near **Šintava** in the district of Galanta is a sanctuary for owls of a rare species (pisorhinascops horned owl).

D. PIEŠŤANY

Piešťany (80 km north-east of Bratislava), the most important Slovak spa, lies on the lower **Považí**, on the bank of the river **Váh** (Waag), 534 feet above sea level. Directly above the town the spurs of the **Považsky-Inovec** rise eastwards to a height of nearly 2,000 feet.

Piešťany is a fast train stop on the Bratislava—Žilina line and the main highway in the same direction runs through the town.

The Romans already knew of Piešťany's natural medicinal springs and by the Middle Ages it can be called a health resort. We know poems of the 17th century which extol the healing properties of the spring. The spa however first won a world-wide reputation for the cure of rheumatic ailments in the last century.

The healing properties of the spa are found in several prolific springs and in the hot mud taken from the peat layers on the banks of a dead arm of the river Váh. The spring waters have a gypsum and sulphur content (56–67° C). The treatment is given in three large baths (the Irma Bath, the Napoleon Bath and the Pro Patria Bath), in which, on the one hand, pools with a mud bottom are immediately next to the springs; on the other hand, there are pools with pure thermal water. The supplementary treatment with gymnastic exercises in the water and in the open air, as well as rehabilitation work, has also reached a high level. Piešťany now specialises in the cure of arthritis, arteriosclerosis, post-accident care and organic nervous ailments.

The prettiest part of the town is the large island formed by the Baths. Here are all the springs with the appropriate baths and clinics. The great park must also be mentioned with its old, bushy lime, chestnut and poplar trees, flowerbeds and a big rock garden with a lake. There grow all kinds of acclimatised flowers and shrubs. The rarest among these is the South American **Victoria Regia** water lily which blooms in the autumn. On the edge of the park is the Eva Thermal Baths with a covered swimming pool, a sports ground and a boat-house.

The **Musical Summer** of Piešťany also enjoys great favour, at which outstanding orchestras and both foreign and native soloists appear.

The town has an interesting **Municipal Museum**. Worth seeing is the collection of crutches presented by patients who have been healed at Piešťany, and the collection of traditional costumes.

The Piešťany **popular costume** is known as being the most elaborately hand-embroidered of all the Slovak costumes. It is worn in the neighbourhood of the spa, at **Moravany**, **Krakovany**, **Trebatice** and **Rakovice**.

At Piešťany itself is the 7-km long **reservoir-lake of Slňava** at the foot of the mountain range of Pavážský Inovec. Accommodation and camping site on the banks of the lake.

Accommodation: for all clinics apply to the Czechoslovak Travel Bureau Čedok or to the Spa Administration, 33 Pavlovova ulica, tel. 2241, 2242, 2783.—Hotel Eden, Thermia Palace, etc.

Excursions and walks from Piešťany

Tourist hostel below the Bezovec (1,837 feet above sea level; 26 km east), a delightful place of excursion in the Považský-Inovec Mountains; good skiing terrain with a ski-lift.

Moravany nad Váhom (7 km north-east), known for the discoveries made there of primitive man. A well-preserved castle with lutherns. The very richly embroidered Piešťany popular costume is worn in the village.

Beckov (4 km north). The ruins of a medieval castle mentioned in records as far back as 1226 stands on a steep crag. The ramparts with part of the watchtowers and the chapel are still preserved. Below the castle stands a small Gothic church and the former Franciscan monastery (1691); also a second church with a Baroque interior.

Čachtice (31 km north-west). The ruins of this legendary, medieval Váh valley castle are above the village of **Višňové**. The castle was notorious for the deeds of the Countess Alžbeta Báthoryčka, who had 68 maidens put to death in order to bathe in their blood. One part of the castle wall with a watch-tower is well-preserved. Below the castle ruins is an interesting labyrinth of caves. Between Piešťany and Trenčín the railway and the road run past the **power stations** of Horná Streda, Nové Mesto on the Váh and Kostolny, which form one of the Váh cascades (dams on the river Váh).

E. TRENČÍN

Trenčín (125 km north-west of Bratislava) lies in the Váh valley, shut in by the **Považsky-Inovec** and the **White Carpathian** mountains. The romantic upper Váh valley begins north of Trenčín; it is characteristic because of the many ruined castles which rise above the river with its numerous dams and power stations.

Trenčín is a fast train stop on the main Bratislava— Zilina line and the main highways from north to south and from east to west also run through the town.

The whole past of the town is closely connected with the many-sided history of Trenčín castle. The area occupied by the present town was already settled in prehistoric times. There is an inscription carved on the Trenčín castle rock dated 179 commemorating the victory of the Roman legions stationed in the Germanic town of Laugaricio (Trenčín) over the German Quadi tribe. After the Slavs had settled here the settlement got the name Trenčín, which was first mentioned in the Vienna chronicles of 1069. In the 11th century the castle had already become the pivotal point of the military frontier region and even the Turks failed to subdue it in 1241. It won its greatest fame at the end of the 13th and the beginning of the 14th centuries, at the time of the oligarchy of Matúš Čáks who ruled the whole of Slovakia from Trenčín castle. In 1405 Trenčín was given the privilege of a royal borough.

Sights and places of interest

Trenčín castle in its present form dates from the 15th century, but the general design of each separate stage of building and reconstruction is still perceptible. The castle has been deserted since the great fire of 1790.

The former **parish church** stood within the plan of the castle in the middle of a high breast-wall terrace. Built originally in Gothic style in the 14th century, it has been several times rebuilt. In the Illésházy chapel connected with the church is a very beautiful **alabaster altar**, ascribed to the sculptor R. Donner; also an epitaph carved on black marble to Kaspar Illésházy (early Baroque, 1649).

The Baroque **Piarist Church of Saint Francis**; the valuable frescoes are ascribed to the Italian master A. Pozza.

The **District Museum** in the namestie (square) No 46, contains valuable exhibits connected with the history of the castle and the town.

The ancient fame of Trenčín castle has today been overshadowed by the very successful industrialisation of Slovakia. Several big concerns of the food and textile industries work in the town itself. In the Trenčín suburb of **Kubra** a chain of **constructional engineering factories** is springing up, extending beyond **Dubnica** as far as **Považská Bystrica**. At the foot of the hill opposite Trenčín castle, below the ancient **Skalka** (Crag) with the towers of the Baroque Benedictine monastery, is one of the Váh power stations, built in only three years.

Trenčín, the Váh valley centre for aquatic sports, has a modern well-equipped boat-house and a swimming bath with a 55 yard long pool.

Accommodation: Hotel Tatra, 5 Pri Lesíku, tel. 2844, 2248, Hotel Trenčín, tel. 2113.

Walks and excursions from Trenčín

The **hostel** below the **Ostrý Vrch** (mountain summit, 1,900 feet) is 1 hour's walk from the motorbus and railway terminus **Soblahov** (9 km).

The **hostel** in **Krásna dolina** is 15 minutes from the railway station **Mnichova Lehota** (16 km).

The **hostel** on the **Inovec** (2,755 feet) is 1½ hours walk from the railway station **Mnichova Lehota** or from **Trenčianske Jastrabie** (2½ hours).

Drietomská dolina (19 km)—camping site.

In many places in the Trenčín district there are historical monuments of secular and ecclesiastical architecture which are well worth seeing. The most important are to be found at: Zamarovce (4 km); a Classical chateau and a well-preserved Baroque church, both 18th century. At Záblatie (4 km), Renaissance castle, at **Adamovce** (14 km) a well-preserved Baroque chateau with a large English park (early 18th century). At **Melčice** (12 km) a 17th-century Renaissance mansion. At **Trenčianske Bohuslavice** (17 km) a late 18th-century Rococo chapel with a very valuable Rococo interior, chiefly wood carvings, metal smithery, stucco work and superb frescoes by the painter A. F. Maulpertsch. At **Haluzice** (19 km) above a deep abyss the tower of a little 13th-century Romanesque church.

Dolná and Horná Súča (13 or 19 km north-west), a picturesque village with lively folklore.

On the **Jankov vršok** (hill, 48 km south-east), above the village of **Uhrovec**, at an altitude of 1,749 feet, is an imposing monument on the scene of the heroic fighting by the "Jan Žižka" Slovak partisan brigade during the Slovak National Uprising in 1944–45; camping site.

At **Uhrovec** the house in which was born a leader of the Slovak national Renaissance in the last century, **Ludovít Štúr**, is used to house the Štúr Museum. The well-preserved **Uhrovec castle** dates in its earliest parts from the 16th century.

Trenčianske Teplice (17 km east). This well-known spa lies in the narrow valley of the Strážovské Mountain 897 feet above sea level.

It has been deduced from archaeological discoveries that the healing properties of the local springs were already known to the Romans, who kept a permanent garrison in Trenčín. As early as 1580 Dr Thomas Jordan wrote a scientific description of the curative effects of the sulphureous mineral water. Only in the 19th and 20th century did the spa become world famous.

The four prolific springs of suitable temperature and with a hydrogen sulphide content are the natural remedies of the spa. The cure is taken in four different baths, built directly over the springs. The finest is the bath in the Sina pump-room. Trenčianske Teplice now specialises in the treatment of rheumatic aliments, neuritis and bronchial catarrh.

Trenčianske Teplice is ideal for convalescence. The whole valley basin right up to the actual centre of the town is one natural park, surrounded by wooded mountains and hills. At the end of the park, near the village of **Baračka** is an **artificial lake** and on the side of a mountain rising above it, a fine **thermal swimming pool,** called the Zelená žaba (green frog).

The annual music festival held at Trenčianske Teplice has a good tradition. The so-called **Musical Summer of Trenčianske Teplice** lasts from June till September.

Accommodation: in the clinics of the Czechoslovak State Baths (tel. 2005, 2040, 2014); the best known is the Krym (tel. 2024, 2060).

On holidays, righly hand-embroidered popular costumes are worn in the neighbouring places: **Trenčianska, Teplá, Dobrá** and **Kubra.**

Púchov-Nosice (39 km north-east). Upstream from Nosice is the "Youth Dam". The great reservoir regulates the water-head of the power stations of the cascades lower down. At **Púchov,** on the so-called

"Púchov Rock" important archaeological excavations have been made.

Vršatec castle (25 km north). The most daringly built medieval castle in Central Europe stands above an abyss on a limestone rock (2,656 feet above sea level). Today it is a ruin above the village of **Vršatské Podhradie**.

Lednica castle (39 km north) above the place of the same name; in the Middle Ages it was the impregnable castle of an unscrupulous baron, accessible through a tunnel hewn through the rock.

F. NITRA

Nitra (100 km east of Bratislava) lies on the left bank of the Nitra river in a fertile plain at the foot of the southern spurs of the Tríbeč Mountains (627 feet above sea level).

Communications: the railway line Nové Zámky—Prievidza and the dense network of roads with direct motorbus connections from Bratislava, Trnava, Banská Štiavnica and Zlaté Moravce.

As archaeological discoveries show, the area occupied by the present town was already settled in prehistoric times. Nitra castle already existed in the third decade of the 9th century as the seat of the Pribina princes. The first Christian church on the soil of Slovakia was also in the castle precincts. In 1025 Nitra became the seat of the crown prince of Hungary. In the following century, thanks to its active international trade, the town below the castle became an important commercial centre and in 1248 was given the privileges of a town. In the 16th and 17th centuries it suffered severely from constant attacks by the Turks who once even captured it and destroyed many historical monuments. The ramparts, which are still standing, were built as defences against the Turks in the second half of the 17th century. The present aspect of the town is the result of its gradual development since the 18th century, during which time it has spread outwards, mainly after 1945.

Sights and places of interest

The Castle. Several centuries of building activity have given it its present appearance. The cathedral and the episcopal palace merit most attention.

The **Cathedral** is composed of three clearly distinguishable divisions: the Saint Emeramus chapel, the oldest part of the castle (13th century); the 14th-century Gothic upper church and the 17th-century lower church. The remarkable Baroque interior of the upper church has a marked artistic merit. The Baroque altar of the lower church (1662) is the work of the Austrian master Johann Pernegger.

The **Episcopal Palace** with its Gothic foundations shows the intrusion of Renaissance from its last reconstruction at the beginning of the 18th century, when it was endeavoured to give the palace a Baroque appearance. The ground floor rooms stand on a floor hewn out of the castle rock.—The **fortifications of the Castle** are well preserved. The oldest parts are still Gothic (walls and Vazul tower), others date from the 16th and 17th centuries.—The **Plague Column** in front of the entrance to the castle was done by the Austrian sculptor Martin Bogerle in 1750.

In the suburb of **Párovce** is the little 12th-century **Saint Stephen's church.** We can see a very valuable Baroque interior furnishing in the Baroque **Piarist church** in the centre of the block of 18th-century Piarist monastery buildings. There are some preserved late Baroque buildings in the Hradná Street. The best is the former **Seminary** (1770).

Nitra is the centre of the political, economic and cultural life of the region. Its industry—mainly food and building materials—is constantly growing and changing the look of the town. High schools, a permanent theatre and the Archaeological Institute of the Slovak Academy of Sciences contribute to the cultural progress of the town.

Accommodation: Hotel Zobor; tel. 2382.

Excursions from Nitra

On the **Zobor Hill** (1,973 feet above sea level; 1–1½ hours walk) there was a Benedictine monastery in the Middle Ages. From here there is a fine view of the town and also in the direction of the Danube. Excellent wine is grown on the slopes of the Zobor and directly below the summit is a picturesque wine tavern with very good local wine.

Of the cultural-historical monuments round Nitra the following should be mentioned:

Drážovce (9 km north). The costly 12th-century Saint Michael's church stands on a projecting hill above the town in the middle of an ancient castle site. In the district is the botanical reservation "Lupka" with rare heath flora.

Horné Lefantovce (22 km north). The present sanatorium in the large English park was originally a monastery, founded in 1369. The castle was rebuilt in Baroque style in the 18th century. The frescoes in the former church have retained a marvellous freshness of colour and are among the most treasured Baroque paintings of Slovakia.

5 km north, **Oponice**. Noteworthy architecture. The Renaissance castle has an old library with some 10,000 volumes. The English-style park surrounding the castle is renowned for its rare species of trees. The second castle of Oponice was built in Baroque style. Three kilometres from the commune, at the foot of the Tríbeč Mountains, are the ruins of Oponice stronghold which was built in the gothic period.

Topolčany (38 km north) was the first 13th-century town built in Slovakia with a regular chequer-board ground plan. The medieval Topolčany castle (18 km from the town) near the village of **Podhradie**, at the foot of the mountain near **Povážsky Inovec**. All that remains of the castle is a watch-tower. Topolčany is an important industrial centre.

East of Topolčany, through the valley of the Vičom stream in the Tríbeč Mountains, an important trading route used to pass in antiquity and in the Middle Ages, between the communes of **Klátová Nová Ves** and Kližské Hradište; there are many mementos, such as fortresses, citadels, strongholds and romanesque churches.

Partizánske (53 km north). In the town is the biggest shoe factory in Slovakia, equipped with modern machinery.

Bojnice (78 km north-east) lies in the Nitra valley in the south-eastern foothills of the **Nitrianská Magura**, the **Strážov Hills**, 976 feet above sea level. There is a regular motorbus service to the spa from the railway junction **Prievidza**.

Bojnice castle was built at the end of the 13th century. Of the original interior of the old castle all that remains are the costly stucco vaulting and the frescoes in the chapel and on the first floor, in the so-called Hunyady tower. The owner, Count Pálffy, had the castle restored in 1899, thereby showing to advantage the styles of all the famous buildings of Central France. By using part of the old walls in the old foundations a completely new castle was built, the effect of which in its lovely surroundings is like some dream-vision out of the Middle Ages owing to the picturesque grouping of the main building. The interior of the castle is furnished with oak furniture. The whole castle is now used as a district museum and the Nitra picture gallery. The collections illustrate by means of valuable exhibits, mostly of the time of the Turkish wars, the history and development of the people of Slovakia. The surroundings of the castle have been converted into a zoological garden. In the adjacent botanical garden there are many exotic trees.

About 500 yards below the castle lies **Bojnice Spa** (Bojnické kúpele). This watering place specialises in the treatment of rheumatic complaints and rehabilitation after accidents. In the limestone rocks, below the Bojnice Saint Martin's church is an interesting **cave**, which according to archaeological research was already inhabited by man before the last Ice Age, approximately 100,000 B.C.

Bojnice has beautiful surroundings. Green woods, rising to the highest summit of the **Magura** and full of woodland fruits and game, undulate above the natural park.

Jelenec (17 km north-east). In the woods above Jelenec the ruins of **Gýmeš** castle. The square tower on the south side and the horse-shoe shaped tower on the north side belong to the oldest parts of the castle. Below the castle is the **Natural Reservation of real chestnut primeval forest**, 300–500 years old. In the environs is a forest preserve with various kinds of game.

Arboretum Mlyňany (34 km east), a well-known acclimatisation park for exotic evergreens (**National Trust park**). A research institute of the Slovak Academy of Sciences works here. Alongside the native oaks, hornbeams and yews which surround and form the reservation, we find here 450 varieties of evergreen deciduous and coniferous trees. There are species indigenous to Asia Minor, the Mediterranean lands, Crimea, the Caucasus, China, Japan, the Himalayas and the American continent.

Those who work at the Arboretum study problems connected with the cultivation of exotic woods in Czechoslovak conditions, their acclimatization, the embellishment of urban communities and of communes, and notably the question of re-afforestation with evergreens. At the census taken in 1962, the park was found to contain 1,079 varieties and species of rare exotic trees.

In the neighbouring **Velké Vozokany** in a field stands the **Lion of Vozokany Memorial**, commemorating the famous victory of Adam Forgachs over the Turks in 1652 during a raid into this district.

Pata (38 km east). A bird sanctuary. Village of Velký Dúr, district of Levice.

Topolčianky (39 km north-east). In the middle of a magnificent English park with rare exotic, acclimatised evergreen trees stands one of the finest Slovakian Classic castles. It is furnished with antique furniture of different periods. One can find accommodation at the castle. In the park there is a hunting lodge, for the park adjoins the largest **hunting grounds** in all Czechoslovakia (1,200 hectares), with abundant deer and wild boar and a bear family. Sportsmen from all over Europe come here. There is also a national stud-farm at Topolčianky.

North of Topolčianky the ruins of the medieval castle **Hrušov** (6 km) and 4 km further north the picturesque mountain village of **Skýcov** which was razed to the ground by German troops in 1945.

G. KOMÁRNO

Komárno (95 km south-east of Bratislava) lies in the middle of the great plain at the confluence of the Váh and the Danube (400 feet above sea level).

The railway line Bratislava—Budapest runs through Komárno. The history of the town goes back to Roman times. Here, on the left bank of the Danube between Komárno and Iža the Romans had a huge, stone-built camp. After the Romans the Avars and finally the Slovaks settled in the region, Komárno became a trade centre and a strategically important fortress under the Hungarian monarchy. It was given its civic rights in 1265. After the Turkish invasion of Hungary vast subterranean military fortifications were laid out in the town, which were for centuries an impregnable obstacle to further encroachments by the Turks to the north and west. In 1767 and again in 1783 the town was visited by an earthquake which caused considerable damage to ancient buildings. After 1818 Komárno became an important Danube port and since 1945 the Gábor Steiner ship-building yards, where freight and passenger steamers are built for inland traffic, have been constantly enlarged. The Komárno ship-building yards and the new settlement give the town its present characteristic silhouette.

Komárno is the birth-place of the famous composer Franz Lehár and of the writer Móric Jókai.

Sights and places of interest

The **fortifications**. These underground fortifications were laid out several hundred years ago and were at the time the most modern in Europe. In their present form they date from after the earthquake in the second half of the 18th century. The system of fortifications consists of some independent units but these are interconnected by wide passages deep below the ground. They have weathered centuries without any serious damage to the walls. The fortress of Komárno was impregnable, witness the inscription under the statue of the "Komárno Madonna" on one of the bastions: "Nec Arte, nec Marte" (neither by ruse nor by force of arms).

The **Saint Andrew's church** was built in 1773 on the site of an old church destroyed by an earthquake. During its erection, bricks and stones from Roman ruins were used. The **church of Saint Rosalia** is built in Empire style. The house in which the **composer Franz Lehár** was born is at the corner of the Stejnerová and the Mostná Streets.

In the **Danube Museum** in the House of Culture are rare archaeological finds, discovered in the environs of the town and belonging to the late Stone Age and the early and middle Bronze Age. In the courtyard is the statue of the writer **Móric Jókai** who was born in the town. Komárno with its renowned theatre tradition is now the seat of the Hungarian National Theatre.

Accommodation: Hotel Centrál, 14 ulica Červenej armády; tel. 2326, Hotel Europe.

At the confluence of the Váh and the Danube, on the left bank of the Váh, stretches a wonderful river beach. Another notable place of excursion is the **Apáli Island** at the confluence of the Váh and the Nítra, where there is an ornithological reservation in wooded meadow.

Excursions and walks from Komárno

Iža (6 km east). From the 1st to the 4th century, the largest Roman camp on Czechoslovak territory stood on the banks of the Danube; its remains have been preserved to this day. The fortified camp shows a square ground plan, each side being 190 yards long; the walls with four gates and 20 towers are 66 feet high. The walls were surrounded by a triple ring of earthworks. The whole castrum had central heating and drainage.

Žitavská Toň (25 km east) is an excavation site of great importance with an Avar-Slovak burial ground (8th century).

Patince (14 km east); a small recreation centre with numerous chalets has been built near the commune, directly on the Danube, round a hot sulphurous spring.

Kovačovské Kopce (Kovačova Hill, 55 km east), a perfect reservation of European importance, with rare flora and fauna, in the municipalities of **Kamenica** on the Horn and **Chabla** and **Bajtava** in the district of Nové Zámky. This is the northern-most point where many heat-loving species of animals and plants appear.

Here, too, is one of the finest sandy beaches on the Danube (camping site).

Chotín (15 km north-east), a site of rich archaeological discoveries of the Hallstatt period. A typical steppe surrounds the town. Part of this region, known as the **Svinský pasienok** (swine meadow) is a botanical reservation park for the protection of sand-loving flora. The people of the village do fine embroidery in their homes.

Bíňa (90 km north-east) is a small village in the district of Nové Zámky and is one of the earliest settlements on Slovakian soil. There is still standing round the village an almost unbroken ring of mighty ramparts that belonged to the medieval fortress of Slav-Avar times. Near the former Premonstratensian monastery a two-steepled church was built in the middle of the 13th century, which is considered one of the most important monuments in the whole of Czechoslovakia. In it Lombard and Saxon influences are combined. Admirable are the richly decorated portal and single figured and foliage designs on the capitals of the pillars.

Hurbanovo (15 km north), with a once known observatory. The observatory building now houses the geophysical institute of the Slovak Academy of Sciences and the seismographical observatory of this region, several times visited by earthquakes. At **Sesíleš** near-by is an experimental nursery of the Czechoslovak Academy of Agriculture for the arable use of sandy soil.

Bajč (29 km north) and **Číčov** (24 km west). In the surrounding country are rich wild duck and pheasant preserves much frequented by foreign sportsmen.

Nové Zámky (29 km north). The town originated as a huge hexagonal fortress against the Turks in the 16th century (1545–60). It was first captured by General Köprülü at the head of 200,000 mercenaries in 1663. In the 18th century the fortifications were demolished and removed. Only traces of the foundations, the remains of bastions, etc. are still left. The present district town is an important railway junction with a considerable constructional engineering industry.

Kolárovo (24 km north-west), the largest village in Slovakia (pop. 14,000) at the confluence of the Váh and the Little Danube. A river fortress against the Turks once stood here.

Kameničná (9 km north-west). Within the parish boundaries in a bird sanctuary, the "Little Island" (Malý Ostrov), a wooded meadow with a protected nesting colony of moorhens (ardea nycyieorax).

Zlatná na Ostrove (12 km north-west), known for gold-buddling of the Danube sand. Today gold is only extracted further upstream, at **Kližská Nemá**. In the "Zlatná" bird sanctuary the Great bustard *(ortia tarda)* is protected.

Near this commune is a bird sanctuary which, in 1962, sheltered some 700 to 800 bustards, the largest European birds. Sportsmen take a special delight in shooting bustards, because it requires extreme skill and mastery.

Čičov (26 km west). Near the commune is Lake Lyon, which is an arm of the Danube. It is planned to transform this region into a nature sanctuary. The locality is renowned for its aquatic and marsh-bird sanctuary, and for its reservation of rare aquatic plants. The waters of the Danube arm near Čičov are very rich in fish. Recreation on the shores of the lake is very pleasant.

Medveďov (39 km west). On the Danube near the commune is the so-called "stag ford" where herds of stags and deer cross from Hungary into Czechoslovakia. On "Cholera" island in the middle of the river, people with contagious diseases (e.g. cholera or plague) used to live in quarantine as late as the first half of last century.

Palkovičovo (40 km west). Has the largest pisciculture cooperative on the Danube. Fishing is the main occupation of the population. This stretch of the Danube abounds in a special variety of sturgeon called "vyza".

Gabčíkovo (46 km west). Autumn shooting of wild ducks and geese, which is organized every year in the surroundings of Gabčíkovo, Baka and Šamorín, is very popular both with Czechoslovak and foreign sportsmen. The commune also has a research station for the study of fast-growing trees (poplars, willows).

Baka (50 km west). Bird sanctuary "Osprey Island" for the protection of the unique haliaetus albicilla (a kind of sea-eagle). There are also a rare cervine species, the grassland stag.

13.   SOUTH-EAST SLOVAKIA

The landscape of the Juhoslovenský Kras (the South Slova-kian karst), which forms the core of this region, characterises the whole; further the Košice basin in the river plain of the Hornad and the Bodva and finally also the Spišské rudohorie (the Spiš Ore Mountains). The centre of the area is mountainous while fer-tile plains extend in the south and east.

South-East Slovakia can be divided into three approximately equally large regions: the Košice basin, the mountains and forests of the Spiš Ore Mountains and the arid South Slovakian plain. The economic distribution of these regions is also different. The Košice plain yields a surplus of agricultural products; in the frontier region between the South Slovakian karst and the Spiš Ore Mountains there are valuable mineral deposits where iron ores are chiefly extracted; in the Spiš Ore Mountains besides ore the timber resources are also exploited for manufacture. The whole engineering industry is concentrated at Košice; Rožňava is the centre of the Gemer iron-ore works. The Hnilec valley area which is equally rich in iron ore belongs to the Spiš iron works sphere.

From a tourist point of view, South Slovakia is remarkable for its wealth of historical monuments, especially in the region of the South Slovakian karst from Moldava and Jasov to beyond Plešivec. This area has very many well preserved castles and chateaux, a number of which are now cultural institutions; specially worth seeing is the unique original beauty of the karst phenomena in the Juhoslovenský kras—the karst plains with pot-holes, ravines, caves and gorges; the Dobšinská ice-cave Ladová jaskyňa; the hunting grounds abounding with game and the beautiful holiday resorts.

Communications: In two directions railways and motor high-ways connect South Slovakia with the rest of Czechoslovakia. The main railway line Žilina–Košice–Čierna nad Tisou runs through Košice, the starting point for trips into South-east Slovakia; here four lines meet: from Prešov in the north, from Michalovice in the east, from Miškolz in the south and from Rožňava in the west. The aerodrome at Košice guarantees a regular air service between South-East Slovakia and Prague and Bratislava. Another starting point is Plešivec, the terminus of the main line Vrùtky–Plešivec (with direct connections from Prague) which joins the line to Bratislava at Zvolen. The national high-

way from the west runs through the Hron valley through Rožňava or from the south through Lučenec and Plešivec.

The most important cultural, economic and political-adminis-
trative centres of South Slovakia are: Košice, the seat of the
East Slovakian district administration, then Plešivec, Rožňava
and the Plešivec and Dobšiná caves in the South Slovakian
Karst.

Sights and places of interest

Natural reservations: "Zrúcania hradu Slanec" (ruins of
Slanec castle), Zádielska dolina, Herlany—Malé Brdo.

Regions of interest to tourists: Zádielska dolina, Spišské rudohorie (the Špiš Ore Mountains), Juhoslovenský kras (the South
Slovakian Karst) Slovenský raj (the Slovakian paradise).

Castles and chateaux: Slanec, Barca, Turňa and Krásna Hôrka.

Hunting grounds: Betliar.

Climatic and holiday resorts: Lake Izra, Štos, Uhorňan lake,
the baths of Thurza.

Other important sights: the Herlany geyser, the Jasov caves,
the Domica cave, the ice-cave at Silice, the caves of Gombasek,
the ice-cave ravine at Barazdaláš, Dobšinská Ladová jaskyňa
(ice-cave), the Hnilec dam at Dedinky.

Circular tour through South-east Slovakia: Košice—Jasov
(28 km)—Turna nad Bodvou (47 km)—Zádielska dolina (52 km)
—Turňa nad Bodvou (57 km)—Krásna Hôrka (84 km)—
Domica (117 km)—Rožňava (145 km)—Betliar (152 km)—
Ladová jaskyňa (191 km)—Hnilec Dam at Dedinky (209 km)—
Gelnice (273 km)—Košice (316 km).

KOŠICE

Košice, (pop. 95,000) the metropolis of South-east
Slovakia, spreads along the eastern spurs of the Spiš
Ore Mountains in the broad basin of the Hornád river
(676 feet above sea level). Košice is an important
railway and road junction and has also an airport
with regular air services to all parts of Czechoslovakia.

The origins of the town go back to the 9th century: it developed into a town after the annihilation of the Tartar hordes at
the end of the 13th century. Its advantageous geographical

position gave it importance as the centre of trade with the eastern provinces. In the 15th century Košice was already one of the most important towns of Hungary. In 1657 a university with two faculties was founded here. As the seat of the administration of the district of Abauj and of the later larger district of Košice the town made rapid progress and continuously spread. Košice recorded a significant development after 1918 and especially since the liberation in 1945.

The Declaration of the **Košice Government Programme** of the National Front of the Czechs and Slovaks was made here on the 5th April 1945; at that time the town—in the recently liberated territory of Czechoslovakia—was the seat of the government and of the Slovak National Council. Today it is the seat of the East Slovakian District National Committee, the political, economic and cultural centre of South-east Slovakia and the second most important Slovak town.

In Košice are numerous industrial undertakings, especially engineering factories, some high schools and scientific research institutes.

Sights

The Gothic **Saint Elizabeth's Cathedral** is the town's outstanding monument; the building was started in 1378 and only completed in the following century. The edifice is superb Gothic and the highest achievement of Gothic art in Slovakia; the interior decoration is also especially fine. The **main altar,** 37 feet high and 9 yards wide, is a notable piece of wood carving (1474–77). The master who executed the three best central plastics is still unknown. Especially valuable too are the stone sculptures and reliefs. The Gothic **Saint Michael's chapel** next to the cathedral dates from the first half of the 14th century.

21

The **Dominican Church** with the early 14th-century monastery building with a sextuple Gothic vaulting was rebuilt in Baroque style in 1700.

There is a remarkable concentration of historical and artistic sights in Leninova Street. The **Levoča House** at No 60 Leninova Street was built in the 15th century and later several times adapted. The **Technical Museum** at No 94 Leninova St. was originally built in the 17th century as the Commandant's residence.

The **former District Administration building** of the district of Abauj at No 76 Leninova St. dates from the 17th century, the new Košice District Administration building (No 31 Leninova St.) was built in 1779. The exquisite style of the late Baroque Classic façade is remarkable. The **Town Hall** (No 63 Leninova St.) was built in neo-Renaissance style in 1870. The **Dessewffy Palace,** which today houses the East Slovakian district **picture gallery** (No 78 Leninova St.), was built at the beginning of the 19th century in Classic style, as was the **Forgách Palace**, now the National Scientific Library (No 12 Leninova St.). Both palaces have characteristic courtyards with loggias and arcades in Renaissance and Classic styles. The **National Theatre** (1898) is an imitation of Renaissance style. The **Jacob's Palace** is a replica of the Rákoczi castle at Siebenbürgen.

Of the town's fortifications the so-called **Katova bašta** (executioner's bastion) has survived from the 13th century and has been converted into a museum (No 13 Hrnčiarska St.); also the **Miklušova vaznica** (prison) with the original medieval torture chamber. Old fortification walls and ramparts are still visible at different places.

Accommodation: Hotel Slovan, 5 Leninova ulica; Telephone 22 33 16.

Walks and excursions in the surroundings of Košice

Herlany (30 km north-east). The Herlany geyser is a European phenomenon. It erupts at intervals of 32 hours; the geyser spurts for 30 minutes at a time to a height of 82–132 feet. The quantity of water erupted is approximately 8,800 gallons. The geyser is in an enchantingly beautiful spot in the Slanec mountain country, surrounded by the oak and pine woods of a magnificent park. The geyser is notable as being the only one in the world to erupt cold water.

Lake Izra (36 km south-east). Below **Mount Milíč** in the Tokaj mountains, in a picturesquely situated valley on the shore of the lake, at an altitude of 1,610 feet above sea level, is a beautiful convalescent home. On the road to Lake Izra above the village of **Slanec** (25 km from Košice) on a conical hill are the ruins of the 13th-century Slanec **castle** with a well preserved tower. The woods on the castle hill are under National Trust protection. Specially effective is the old beach and oak avenue leading up to the castle; the trees have a circumference of 11 ½ to 14 ½ feet.

Barca (6 km south). In this village archaeologists have excavated dwelling-caves of the Old Aurignac Age (i.e. 70,000–100,000 years ago). They are the oldest dwelling caves in Europe. The oldest of the three local castles dates from between the 14th and 15th centuries. The last reconstruction was made in Classical style.

Seňa (22 km south). Here is the site of the oldest archaeological discoveries in Czechoslovakia: the stone tools of Diluvian man about 400,000 years old. The **castle** dates from the beginning of the 19th century.

Zádielska dolina (the Zádiel valley; 45 km south-west). The entrance to the valley, one of the loveliest parts of the South Slovakian Karst, is from the railway station of **Dvorníky-Zádiel**. From **Zádiel** a 3 km long **canyon** has been eroded by the **Blatnica torrent** with magnificently coloured cliffs and towering rocks on either bank. Also typical are the numerous waterfalls; the 330 feet high needle-shaped rock, called **Cukrová homola** (sugar-loaf) is remarkable. There is a tourist hostel at the end of the valley; in the canyon itself there are many small caves. The Zádielská dolina is under National Trust protection as a natural park for the sake of the fauna and the flora of the canyon.

Jasov (28 km west). The little town arose around the 13th-century Premonstratensian monastery. The quadrangular monastery building now standing dates from the 18th century; there is a voluminous library in the monastery. The superb **Baroque church** has valuable murals and altarpieces, the work of the important Baroque period painter J. L. Kracker; they were painted between 1762 and 1765. Near the town in a conspicuous limestone cliff are the **Jasov caves** with magnificently coloured stalactite filigree and little greenish-blue lakes. The cave has eight terraces; in one of the upper terraces is an inscription dated the 25th February 1452. Near the original entrance valuable finds were made from the time when the caves were used as dwellings by primitive man.

Štós (47 km west). A climatic health resort and convalescent establishment on the southern spurs of the Spiš Ore Mountains in the middle of dense pine woods. 19 km further west is another fine convalescent establishment on the shores of **Lake Uhorňan**.

Juhoslovenský kras (South Slovakian Karst)

The karst region, known as the "Juhoslovenský kras", spreads over a wide area of 800 square km on the Czechoslovak-Hungarian frontier in the middle of South Slovakia. Characteristic of this country are the vast high plateaux abounding in superficial karst phenomena. The most typical are the various caves, gorges, crevasses and sudden cul-de-sac valleys. One plateau is separated from another by canyon-like valleys with a drop of 1,300 feet. Besides numerous beauties typical of karst scenery we also find in this region lovely, peaceful valleys and well preserved castles in ancient little towns and market towns. The best places to start from to see these sights are Plešivec and Rožnava.

Plešivec is on the south-west edge of the Slovakian Karst. The town is shut in on three sides by the steep slopes of the Karst. Plešivec is an important railway junction on the Zvolen–Košice line and a starting point especially for the **Silická planina,** the **Domica** cave, the **Gombasek** cave, the **Barazdaláš** gorges and the **Silická ladnica** (ice-cave).

Jaskyňa Domica (Domica cave, 11 km south-east). The motor-bus service from Plešivec runs to the cave. Its stalactite formations are notable for the beauty of their colour and imposing size. The underground river **Styx**, which has been formed by the cave and runs through it, can be navigated **by boat**; the trip permits a good inspection of the cave. In the Neolithic Age cave-dwellers lived in Domica cave. It has its continuation beyond the Hungarian frontier and its total length is 21 km. In front of the entrance to the cave is a modern **tourist hostel** with inn accommodation. The tourist hostel houses a minor museum with exhibits of the Neolithic Age and some interesting karst formations. The **Gombasecká jaskyňa** (the Gombasek cave, 6 km north-east). The best way to get to the cave is from the village of **Gombasek**; it is a relatively new cave with slender stalactites 10 feet high. There is a new **tourist hostel** near the cave.

The **Barazdaláš gorge** (11 km north-east) is north of the road from Gombasek to Silica; the nethermost cave-terrace is 600 feet deep.

Silická ladnica (the Silica ice-cave, 15 km north-east). This unique karst phenomenon, a sloping, gorge-like cave, 280 feet deep, is 2 km south of Silica. In the middle part of the cave a thick layer of ice and an icing of the rock is maintained all the year round; so is the frozen waterfall 43 feet high.

Rožňava

is an old mining town where iron ore was produced and gold mines prospected for as early as the 12th century; it was at the time a free and royal mountain town. Today Rožňava is a district capital on the main line from Zvolen to Košice.

Sights

The 14th–16th century Gothic **Cathedral** stands on the site of an earlier old castle and has a rich interior decoration. Particularly noteworthy is a signed pastoforium (1509) and an altar-piece (1513) with scenes of mining life. There are some houses in the **main square** of artistic and historical merit, particularly Nos 17 and 19, the 18th-century **Town Hall**, the former **Mint** (17th century) and the 18th-century **Episcopal Palace**. We find some Baroque houses in the Brzotínská ulice. The **District Museum** contains valuable collections relating to mining life.

Accommodation: Hotel Gemer, 2 námestie Baníkov; Telephone 307.

Excursions in the outskirts of Rožňava

Krásna Hórka (7 km east). A well preserved medieval **castle** stands above **Krasnohorské Podhradie** on a steep, conical hill. In the 17th century the castle was rebuilt in Renaissance style as a residence and it now houses a **museum** with the original interior. In 1903–04 the owner of Krásna Hôrka castle had a **mausoleum** built for his wife about 1 km from Krásnohorské Podhradie. It is an ornate vault-chapel surrounded by a park, a typical Slovak Secession style building. Costly kinds of marble were used in the building of the mausoleum; the execution of the bas relief is especially remarkable. A very interesting work is the altarpiece, a mosaic composed of 4,000 stones of different kinds.

Štítnik (15 km west). This little old town, whose origins go back to the 12th century, is in one of the loveliest valleys of the Gemer. The 13th-century Gothic **church** with beautiful pointed arches has an unusually valuable original interior furnishing, notably pews, frescoes, tomb inscriptions and a more recent Renaissance altar.

Betliar (7 km north-west). In a well-treed park, covering more than 185 acres, with pavilions, grottoes, little lakes and exotic shrubs, stands the former **hunting lodge**. It dates from the 18th century and was built on the foundations of an old 16th-century Renaissance castle. Towards the end of the 18th century the castle was renovated in the usual Gemer Glassic style. The last reconstruction was done at the turn of the last century. The contemporary interior, valuable pictures of the Realistic School and different collections, especially one of exotic hunting trophies, have been kept in the lodge. Close by is a hunting reserve abounding in deer.

The **ice-cave of Dobšiná** (46 km north-west) is world-famous for the richness of its ice formations and is one of the most beautiful and largest ice-caves in the world. The entrance to the cave is at an altitude of

3,197 feet, the climb up from the road takes half an hour. The cave is about 440 yards long, over 45 yards wide and the maximum height from top to bottom is nearly 300 feet. The so-called **Great Hall** (Velká sieň) is the roomiest cave, 132 yards long, 38–66 yards wide and 36–39 feet high. In the **Pillar Corridor** the single pillars reach an imposing height of 16–40 feet and measure 6½–13 feet across. They are partly hollow with an exterior "decoration" of various ice "ornaments". The lower part of the cave consists of a compact **mass of ice,** 70 foot thick, which forms the floor of the Great and Little Hall. Steps and passages have had to be hewn out of the ice here. The **Ruffiny Corridor** is 220 yards long and 50–66 feet high. Here too the ice masses are as enormous as can only be seen elsewhere in the Polar regions. It takes 1 hour to visit the cave.

Accommodation: Hostel "U Dobšinskej ladovej jaskyni", tel. Ladová jaskyňa 2; a tourist chalet. The ice-cave is recommended as a starting point for a whole number of other **walking tours** in the Slovakian Ore Mountains with its pre-eminent natural beauties.

The Slovakian Paradise can be reached via Havrania skala and Kláštorisko via Glac in 4–5 hours.

To the Hnilec Dam at Dedinky in 1½ hours by the Hnilec valley and to the top of the Stolica (4,884 feet above sea level), the highest peak of the Ore Mountains, 4 hours from Gemer.

Volovec (4,133 feet above sea level), a favourite place of excursion near Rožňava in the Ore Mountains. Below the Volovec is a tourist hostel (3,748 feet); the climb from Rožňava through Čučma takes 1½ hours.

14. CENTRAL SLOVAKIA

Geographically Central Slovakia is completely shut in; its delimitations from the neighbouring regions are clearly defined. Mountains and hollows everywhere form its boundaries. Politically and administratively almost the whole region belongs to one district; the district of Central Slovakia with its capital at **Banská Bystrica**. The Pohronská tabula and the mountain ridges of the Hronský Inovec and the Vtáčnik divide it from South-west Slovakia, the Žiar, the Great Fatra and the Lower Tatra from North Slovakia, the Gemerské rudohorie (Gemer Ore Mountains) and the mountain basin of Rimava from South-east Slovakia. The basin of Ipel and Rimava with the two rivers of the same names form the frontier with Hungary. Mountains, river valleys and mountain hollows are typical of the landscape. Chiefly in the north mighty, continuous mountain chains constitute the frontier and also command the central part of the region. The Hron valley runs through the whole region from the east to the south-west border, constantly widening and ending only in the Pohronská tabula. On the southern frontier the mountains gradually give way to the plain.

Central Slovakia is 50% covered with woods, chiefly beech. Arboriculture, the manufacture of wood, lumbering and the transport of wood are the main occupations of the people of the upper Hron valley. Alongside many small factories, the biggest industrial concerns, "Smrečina" at Banská Bystrica and "Bučina" at Zvolen, manufacture wood. Numerous mineral deposits are another source of wealth. Mining has long been implanted here and the Roman Emperor Marcus Aurelius mentions the mines in the 2nd century A.D. and the high state of development of mining in the Hron valley. The plenitude of raw materials has helped not only the development of mining, but also its industrial manufacture. It is only the southern part of the country that is covered with fertile fields; there are extensive hollows along the whole length of the Czechoslovak-Hungarian frontier. Where the mountains drop down into the valley livestock, particularly sheep, are raised. An Alpine economy thrives in many mountain villages; the whole region is rich in mineral springs, which favour the growth of watering places. Owing to the richness of the country in natural beauties and in cultural-historical places another economic factor has developed, namely tourism.

From a touristic standpoint the region is remarkable for its natural beauties, valuable cultural-historical buildings, a traditionally and constantly developing industrial art and its plentiful game preserves. In the mountains of Kremnica, of the Lower Tatra and of the Slovakian Ore Mountains there is a whole number of summer holiday and winter sports resorts. At Banská Štiavnica, Banská Bystrica and Kremnica well-preserved historical gems of medieval art (under National Trust protection) invite a thorough inspection; old feudal castles and chateaux are to be found everywhere besides. Characteristic features of the native folklore are the gay popular costumes, with original lacework, melodic popular songs, rhythmical dances and beautifully carved ornaments and utensils made of wood.

In the many hunting grounds of Central Slovakia, countless roe and fallow deer, wild boars, hares and pheasants tempt the sportsman; there are also wild geese and wild duck in the Hron and Ipel river areas. Capercailzie pair in the neighbourhood of the Králova Hôla, on the Prašivá and at Dobroč. Botanists can enjoy the many natural parks. The bitterest fighting during the Slovak National Uprising in August 1944 took place in Central Slovakia. After the rebels had been driven back into the mountains there was heavy fighting with partisan groups. All over the region many memorials honour the heroism of this numerically small nation in the struggle against the superior might of Hitler's army.

Communications: Railways, roads and air lines connect Central Slovakia with the rest of the Republic. The main railway lines and motor highways run through the most important junction of Zvolen. The most important railway lines are from Bratislava to Košice, from Prague via Žiúlina (Vrútky) to Plešivec and on to Košice, the national highways from Bratislava through Nítra lead partly through the upper Hron valley into the High Tatra and East Slovakia and partly via Lučenec into the region of South-west Slovakia. The national highway from Žilina in North Slovakia runs through Kremnica. All the above-mentioned lines of communication have good connections with abroad. All the most important towns of Central Slovakia lie on these main roads and railways. The chief cultural, economic and administrative centres are Brezno, the district town of Banská Bystrica, Kremnica, Zvolen, Banská Štiavnica and Lučenec.

Sights and places of interest

Towns under National Trust protection: Banská Bystrica, Kremnica, Banská Štiavnica.

Natural park reservations: the primitive forest of Dobroč, the primitive forest of Badín, Polana, "Sitno-Križná", the "Arboretum" at Banská Štiavnica. The valley of Harmanec (the largest yew-tree forest in Europe).

Regions of interest to tourists: the Lower Tatra, the Slovakian Ore Mountains, the Great Fatra, the mountains of Kremnica.

Castles and chateaux: Muráň, Zvolen, Kremnica, Svätý Antol, Filakovo, Modrý Kameň.

Hunting grounds: Dobroč, Švermovo, Drastavica, Polana, the Hron and Ipel river areas.

Spas: Sliač, Číž, Dudince, Brusne, Sklené Teplice.

Folklore: Čierny Balog, Polomka, Helpa, Švermovo, Dobrá Niva, Detva, Abelová.

Other special sights: The Slovak National Uprising Museum at Banská Bystrica, the Izbica cave at Harmanec, the mint at Kremnica, the Dionýz Šúr Mining-life Museum at Banská Štiavnica, the Horné Strhary geyser.

Circuit through Central Slovakia

Banská Bystrica—Sliač (20 km)—Zvolen (30 km)—Kremnica (65 km)—Sušov (82 km)—Banská Štiavnica (112 km)—Svätý Antol (120 km)—Krupina (135 km)—Bzovík (146 km)—Zvolen (185 km)—Víglašský hrad (199 km)—Detva (217 km)—Lučenec (252 km)—Ožďany (271 km)—Rim. Sobota (282 km)—Brezno (332 km)—Čierny Balog (354 km)—Brezno (354 km)—Srdiečko (379 km)—Brezno (404 km)—Slov. Lupča (437 km)—Banská Bystrica (449 km).

A. BREZNO

Brezno (1,643 feet above sea level) lies in the Hron valley. The main railway line and motor highway of Central Slovakia run through the town from west to east. Since the Middle Ages Brezno has been the mining region of the upper Hron valley and looks back upon a glorious tradition as a mining town; in 1655 Brezno became a free and royal town. Today there is a large constructional engineering factory at Brezno, which has specialised in building bridges.

Excursions in the neighbourhood of Brezno

Čierný Balog (11 km south) is a typical lumberjack town and consists of a number of small settlements of shepherds and wood-workers. Many of its inhabitants were burnt alive in their dwellings by Hitler's army because of their support of the Slovak National Uprising. In the near-by municipality of **Dobroč** in the Vepor Ore Mountains is a large natural park (under National Trust protection) with 300-year-old woods covering 125 acres: the primitive forest of Dobroč. Here, there is also a **hunting preserve** with plenty of wild boar and capercailzie.

Tále-Srdiečko (25 km north). Tále is reached from **Bystra** (with a remarkable cave) across the lovely Bystra depression immediately below the southern slope of the main ridge of the Lower Tatra. It is an important tourist centre of the Hron valley.

Here we find the large modern "Partizán" Hotel, tourist chalets and a ski lift. A road, which is kept in a perfect state of repair, goes from Tále to the central range of the Lower Tatras where the "Srdiečko" mountain hotel has been built on the south side of the Chopok, at an altitude of 4,075 feet. Near the hotel is a new ski lift. The hotel also is the starting point of a chair lift from the valley to the Chopik (6,578 feet), through the intermediary station of "Kosodrevina". By means of the station at the top of the Chopok, the Srdiečko Hotel is connected with the Demanová valley and with the Jasna on the north side of the main chain of the Lower Tatra mountains. The tourist region of the Bystra valley, with Tále and Srdiečko, is the starting point for the ridges and peaks of the Lower Tatras. Communication is by chair lift. From the station at the top, a path along the ridge, leads in two hours to the highest peak of the Lower Tatra Mountains, the Ďumbier (6,708 feet). If we go west, we come to the Chabenec peak (6,414 feet) in about 3½ hours.

Polomka (21 km north-east) is a place which still keeps up its old traditional folklore, particularly the wearing of beautiful **popular costumes**. Polomka is the starting point for mountain tours in the Lower Tatra (4–5 hours to the top of the **Velký Bok**) and up the **Fabova Hola** in the Gemer Ore Mountains (3–4 hours).

Helpa (33 km north-east) is another place on the upper course of the Hron where **old popular customs** have been preserved; there are architecturally interesting buildings and costumes to be seen.

Švermovo (53 km north-east) is a village typical of the region below the Králova Hôl, in which bloody battles were fought during the Slovak National Uprising. It was razed to the ground by the Germans. There is a hunting preserve with plenty of deer in its area. Starting point for the climb up the **Králova Hola** (3-hour walk, 6,390 feet).

Muráň (64 km east). Above Muráň rise the battlements of a medieval **castle**. It is accessible for motor vehicles. On the road from Červená Skala to Muráň, not far from Muráňská Huta is the former **hunting lodge** of Ferdinand of Coburg and the sanatorium **Predná hora**.

B. BANSKÁ BYSTRICA

Banská Bystrica (1,194 feet above sea level) is the metropolis of Central Slovakia and is magnificently situated at the mouth of the Bystrica brook. The town is surrounded by mountains, the spurs of the Kremnica range, the Great Fatra, the Lower Tatra and the Slovakian Ore Mountains. Banská Býstrica has good fast train services in all directions and is the junction of national highways running north, east and south.

Rich silver mines and copper ore deposits in the whole surrounding district attracted German miners here at the beginning of the 13th century. Banská Bystrica was given its civic rights in 1255. At the beginning of the 16th century it gained a monopoly in the European silver and copper market. With the decline of the mines in the following centuries the town lost its importance to a considerable extent. The national liberation in 1918 again brought prosperity to the town both economically and culturally.

The historic occasion when on the 19th August 1944 the liberated Slovak broadcasting station of Banská Bystrica announced to the world that the Slovak people had taken up the battle against Hitler's army and called for a national rising is written in letters of gold in the history of the town. Banská Bystrica became the seat of the Slovak national organizations, of the staffs of the military and partisan groups who led the uprising.

Banská Bystrica is today the seat of the National Committee of Central Slovakia, the political, economic and cultural centre of Central Slovakia and one of the most beautiful towns in all Slovakia; there is a proverbial saying about the beauty of the town: "Live in Bystrica and go to heaven when you die." The very lively building activity is characteristic of the town and its environs. Here, in the framework of the industrialisation of Slovakia, new important undertakings and whole new quarters of the town, many official buildings, palaces, hospitals and schools have come into being. The town has a broadcasting station, a district newspaper, an opera house, an art gallery, a lovely natural amphitheatre and a remarkable sports stadium (with a winter stadium). The place is situated in the middle of a **winter sports region** (ski lift up the Urpín, ski jump at Srnkava) and all the surrounding country is excellent skiing terrain extending down to the very streets of the town.

Sights and places of interest

Banská Bystrica is under the National Trust protection for Ancient Monuments; the most treasured are two cultural-historical blocks of buildings: the burgher houses round the main square and castle.

The **burgher houses** date from the town's efflorescence in the 15th and 16th centuries; outwardly and inwardly they can compare with the buildings of any opulent Central German town. Among the most costly exterior decoration of the houses are: the sgraffito decoration of the façades which are frequently surmounted by attics, the rich stucco ornamentation of the vaulting, magnificent wings in the inner courtyards and arcaded balconies. Among the best preserved are the houses in the square námestie Slovenského národného povstania: No 1, a burgher house, No 4, the Thurz House which has been turned into a museum and No 16.

Of the old **castle buildings**, the historic heart of the town, which stand on a hill, the present námestie Červenej armády, there still remain the mighty castle gate with embrasures and entrance buildings, the royal residence in Gothic style, the guard house (pretorium) with arcades in the upper storey and two Gothic churches. Both churches have unusually valuable interior furnishings of the Baroque period and partly also of the Gothic period. The most precious is the Gothic altar, also early 16th century, attributed to the master Paul of Levoča. The towers of the castle buildings form the characteristic silhouette of the town.

The **Slovak National Uprising Museum** is installed in the Old Town Hall (1510). It contains numerous documents and records of the Slovak insurrection in 1944. The **District Museum** is in a Gothic house dating from 1479 and known as the House of King Matthias. Here there are valuable collections of native applied art, colour printing, stained glass, carvings, besides other exhibits illustrating the history of Banská Bystrica.

No 8 in the Street maršála Malinovského has an interesting chamber-like arched vault, loopholes and an inscription dated 1610. In 1620 in this house Gábor Bethlen was elected King of Hungary by the Hungarian Diet. The little Saint Elizabeth's church at the end of this street dates from 1303.

Accommodation: Hotel Národný dom, 7–9 ulica Februárového vitasztva; tel. 237 37; Hotel Hradec, namestie Slovenského národného povstania 12, tel. 2202.

Excursions in the environs of Banská Bystrica

The **hut on the Hrb** (3,047 feet above sea level, 22 km east) is a starting point for the Slovakian Ore Mountains. By automobile or motorbus to the Podlipa-Lubietova stop (cross roads) and from there on foot, following the blue signs, 1½ hours walk.

Sporthotel Donovaly (3,333 feet above sea level, 29 km north), grandly situated above the village of **Donovaly**, a favourite starting point for trips into the mountains. In winter the whole surroundings of the hotel are excellent skiing terrain. In 1944 the Slovak National Council met in the hotel and decided to call the people to arms. The road to Donovaly runs through the interesting valley of the Starohorský potok through typical mountain villages.

1½ km from the **Harmanec-Jaskyňa** railway station is a remarkable stalactite cave, with its entrance high up in the hills, and approached by a well-marked footpath. There is a small hostel at the entrance. In the opposite direction from the railway-station the green-marked path leads into the High Fatra mountains. The climb to the mountain hotel below the Kralova studnia (4,191 feet), via the Krasny Kopec, takes 2½ hours. The valley of Harmanec is a **National**

Trust park for the protection of the richest natural habitat of the Carpathian yew in Europe; here there are trees from 500 to 600 years old.

The **Kremnica Mountains** (west). On the slope of the Kremnica Mountains towards Bystrica are some mountain huts available to summer tourists and winter sportsmen. The tourist hostel on the **Suchý vrch** (2,508 feet above sea level) can be reached from Tajov by the blue-marked path in one hour and a half; to the mountain hut on the **Králiky** (3,013 feet, with ski lift above the hut) a green-marked path leads from the village of Králiky (10 km) in one hour and a yellow-marked path from Tajov, also in one hour, up to the tourist hostel on the **Tajov** (2,867 feet).

Radvaň n/Hronom (4 km south) with a fine 15th-century Gothic church and the **three Radvaň castles**; the lowest built like a fort and situated in the middle of a park is the best. Ever since the 14th century the Radvaň **Annual Market** has been held here.

Kremnička (7 km south). A memorial honours the 747 victims of Fascism who were killed in the Slovak National Uprising and whose mortal remains lie buried here in a mass grave.

Badínsky prales (the primitive forest of Badín; 12 km south). Above Badín itself (4–5 km) stretches a **primitive forest** covering 44 acres; the trees are mostly beeches and pines. There is a **stud farm** where platinum and silver foxes are bred; also mink.

C. KREMNICA

The town of Kremnica (2,112 feet above sea level) is built on terraces in the picturesque hollow of the Kremnica Mountains; it is entirely surrounded by high mountains, dominated by the seven Kremnica peaks.

The town lies on the main line Zvolen—Vrútky and the national highway, which also runs from north to south.

Kremnica was given its civic rights as a free and royal town in 1328 by reason of the extraordinarily rich discoveries of gold there. It soon became the administrative seat of King Charles Robert's mint. The 14th and 15th centuries were the golden age of the Kremnitz gold mines and thus of the town itself; famous Kremnitz gold ducats were known all over Europe.

Stubborn fighting raged in Kremnica and especially in the neighbouring mountains during the Slovak National Uprising. The town is under National Trust protection as an Ancient Monument and offers the visitor many things worth seeing.

Sights and places of interest

The 15th and early 16th-century **patrician houses** are of great artistic merit and are the best preserved Gothic houses in Slovakia. The most important in the Inner Town are: No 1 (now the seat of the Municipal National Committee), No 3, No 7 (now the Museum of Native Lore), No 8 with a specially precious coffered ceiling and Nos 12 and 14 (the former town hall). Outside the main square houses Nos 22, 23, 28, 36 (with a sort of diamond vaulting) and No 101. The little **Miners' Houses** with a wooden balcony on the upper storey. The tiny houses are scattered about in the valley around the town.

The **castle**, from where the visitor enjoys a beautiful view of the town, is the best preserved medieval castle in Slovakia. The present **castle church** was originally the main tower of the defence system, converted in the years 1468–85 into a Gothic style church. The church has a remarkable quadrangular ground plan and is divided into two naves by a row of pillars; the interior furnishing is mostly Gothic. The Romanesque **Rotunda,** the original castle church (now Saint Andrew's chapel) dates from the 14th century. Near it are some battlements which can be reached by a draw-bridge and the interesting "Banická bašta" (miner's bastion), a tower which was part of the defences. A covered passage under the well of the staircase of the castle bastion still leads into the castle square above the main square of the town. The old **castle town hall**, the oldest house in Kremnica, near the bastion, has recently been renovated. From the castle an underground passage branching off into many houses, leads into the town. The double defence wall of the castle is well preserved and is in places nearly 40 feet high; there is a moat between the two walls.

The **town walls** begin and end at the walls of the castle complex. They were built in the 15th century and parts are still standing, among them the Dolná brána (the lower gate) and four defence towers, of which the **Červená veža** (the Red Tower) was also later used as a prison and the town executioner's lodging and is the most remarkable. The **Dolná brána** is really a double gate with a richly decorated façade; it is adorned by bas-reliefs of Ferdinand I of Hapsburg and his wife. In front of the Dolná brána stands a memorial to the Slovak National Uprising by the sculptor Fraňo Štefunka. The Plague Column, a tripartite monumental statuary group, is the work of the Vienna sculptors Vogerle and Stanetti (1765–77). The stone fountain is also by Stanetti. The former **hospital church**, once dedicated to Saint Elizabeth, is a late Gothic work from the turn of the 14th century.

The **Municipal Archives** possess the most valuable original documents on various scientific subjects in Slovakia. The most thoroughly represented are mining, smelting and coining.

In the District **Museum of Native Lore**—besides valuable and unique specimens of native applied art—

the monumental decorations of the former assembly hall are remarkable, not to mention pictures by the academic painter Gejza Angyal, who was born at Kremnica. The original 14th-century **Kremnica Mint** still stands in the Horná Street. The Mint was removed to its present site in the middle of the 15th century; today it is a modernly equipped concern where coins and badges of all kinds are struck. It can be visited by sightseers.

Accommodation: Hotel Central, tel. 262.

Excursions in the environs of Kremnica

The neighbouring **Kremnica Mountains** rise all round the town. Among the favourite excursions are the climb up the **Kremnický štít** (3,323 feet above sea level) with a **geological natural park** for the protection of its andesite formations, up the **Jarabica** (3,095 feet), the **Krahulský štít** (3,164 feet), the **Trnovník** (3,267 feet) and to the heights of Mount Calvary, the **Sibeničný vrch** (Gallows Hill) and the **Revolta.**

Skalka (10 km north-east), a pleasant excursion and starting point, close to the ridge of the Kremnica Mountains, with a tourist hostel (3,899 feet above sea level) and a good, comfortable hotel (3,797 feet). A road suitable for motor vehicles runs to the hotel. Yellow signs indicate the footpath up through the Bystrica valley; the climb takes 2½ hours. The Skalka is chiefly visited in winter because of its excellent skiing terrain. Winter tours, starting from the tourist hostel, take one far out into the region of Zadné and Predné Pléne, onto the slopes below the tunnel, along the main ridge and to the mountain huts on the slopes of the Kremnica Mountains in the direction of Banská Bystrica (Tajov, Králiky, Suchý vrch). The shortest ascent of Skalka takes only half an hour, from the Krahule bus station.

Žiar n/Hronom (20 km south). In the little town is a 16th-century castle, rebuilt in the 18th century.

Handlová (22 km west). Here is the most important brown coal mining district in Slovakia. Handlová is the starting point for tours in the Kremnica Mountains to the Sokolská chata on the Remät (2,079 feet above sea level, 6 km) and up the **Vtáčnik**.

D. ZVOLEN

Zvolen (967 feet above sea level). The town lies in the heart of Central Slovakia in the Hron river basin and is surrounded by the spurs of the mountains. Zvolen is an important railway junction where the main lines to Bratislava, Vrútky, Margecany and Plěsivec cross; the town has a similar importance for road traffic. The **air-port** Sliač-Tri Duby provides a regular service.

A notable building is **Zvolen Castle**; it has peculiar differences from the usual old feudal buildings of its time. It was built in the years 1370–80 as a royal residence for King Ludovít Velký (Louis the Great) in the then prevalent Italian and French taste. The castle has the form of a regular rectangle, consisting of four wings round the central courtyard. Although it has been several times reconstructed, the castle has preserved its original character. The restored castle also contains a forest museum.

Excursions in the environs of Zvolen

Dobrá Niva (14 km south) is an erstwhile miners' settlement, founded in the 13th century. The little **Romanesque church**, later rebuilt in Baroque style, remains from that time. The local people wear an interesting popular costume.

Detva (32 km east) and the district for a very considerable distance round it form one of the most interesting ethnographical regions of Slovakia. The district itself is in fact the prototype of settlement known as a **"lazy"**.

The "lazy"—small isolated settlements—with houses peculiar to Detva are scattered in larger or smaller groups from the centre of Detva far out into the wooded country of **Polana.** Characteristic to these little Detva houses are their carved wooden roof-plates and yard-gates. The local dress is particularly interesting. The wood-carvers of Detva carve with perfect skill not only objects of daily use, such as whisks, ladles and other kitchen utensils, but also yokes for domestic animals. Specially remarkable are the carved wooden crosses in the Detva cemetery. They used also to carve popular musical instruments, especially the three-mounted shepherd's horn (typical of Detva), and others too, such as the "drumble". The studded shepherd's staff with an axe-head is also unrivalled in its originality. Old popular customs are still kept up locally.

The songs and dances of the Detva are equally interesting; they are remarkable for their fiery spirit, poetic feeling, rebellious love of freedom, a natural gaiety and playfulness. It is a genuine experience to witness a Detva marriage with its extremely complicated ceremonial. Today however the living conditions there have greatly changed. Industry has penetrated the Detva "lazy" and at Hrinová near by the modern constructional engineering factories of Podpolana are already at work.

A foot-path leads from Detva up the Hostelry on the Predna Polana (4,309 feet above sea level) in the Polna mountains. The climb takes three hours.

Polana (34 km east) is a hunting preserve covering 27,500 acres stretching from Detva and Hrinova as far as Čierny Balog. Stags, wild boar and bears as well as smaller game are under protection. The highland white fir of primitive forest character is typical of Polana. The highest peak of the chain, the **Detvianska Polana** (3,810 feet) is of volcanic origin.

Sliač Spa (10 km north) lies in magnificent surroundings. The Sliač springs were already known in the 13th century and are curative especially for diseases of the heart muscles and the blood system; the efficacy of cure lies in the water from the carbon dioxide isothermal springs. There are altogether five mineral springs at Sliač, of which the **Prameň kúpelny** is used for baths, the other four—the Adam, Bystrica, Lankey and Štefámik springs—for drinking. Every year in July and August a Spa Festival called the "Cultural Summer in Sliač" is held in the town. Accommodation can be obtained through the Spa Administration (tel. 2241).

E.   BANSKÁ ŠTIAVNICA

Banská Štiavnica. The town is picturesque and situated in quasi-terraces on the slopes of the steep **Štiavnica Mountains**. Whereas the lower part of the town is 1,815 feet above sea level the upper town rises to a height of 2,640 feet. Banská Štiavnica is connected with the main railway line Bratislava–Zvolen by the Trať mládeže (a section of line built entirely by the Youth Organisation); it runs through Hronská Dúbrava. A dense network of roads extends from the town in every direction. Banská Štiavnica is also under National Trust protection as an Ancient Monument. The area occupied by the present town and its environs was already settled in the Stone and Bronze Ages. The first glorious epoch in the history of this mining town falls in the first half of the 13th century when it was given its civic privileges. The second begins at the turn of the 15th–16th centuries and its prosperity then was mainly due to the successful production of silver.

Sights and places of interest

The **old castle** dates from the 13th century and was originally a Gothic church. During the Turkish wars in the 16th century the castle was rebuilt in Renaissance style as a fortress. The early 13th century charnel-house is particularly well preserved. Today it houses the Historical Archives and Municipal Museum of Banská Štiavnica and Banská Belá.

The **Saint Nicholas Cathedral** was originally Romanesque and so was the late Romanesque basilica; Baroque adaptations were made of both buildings; these still remain and show splendid frescoes, costly paintings and altars.

The **Town Hall** dates from the 15th century. The original Gothic building was later reconstructed in Renaissance style.—The so-called little Slovak **Saint Catherine's church** was built in the 15th century in Gothic style and its interior furnishing is especially fine. The Gothic fonts of the same date as the erection of the church are remarkable.

The Frauenberg church is a typical late Gothic edifice with diamantine sacristy vaulting and flame-like vaulting above the holy of holies.

The **New Mansion** (nový Panský zámok) was built in the years 1554–71 as a fortress-like observation post against the Turks; it is specially well preserved.

In the main square in the centre of the town the striking **houses** are the 15th–17th century style houses with notably decorated doorways, bays, balconies and staircases, partly still in Gothic style. In the middle of the square stands a **Plague Column**, a tripartite Baroque monument (1756–64).

In the Dionýz Štúr Museum, devoted to mining life, are numerous documents and exhibits relating to the history of mining and its technique. In 1627 gunpowder was used for the first time in the world for blasting in this mining area. In the first half of the 18th century pit water was pumped up with machines invented by Matej Kornel and Josef Karol Hell, both natives of Štiavnica. In order to set these pumping machines in action 25 reservoirs and some culverts were built to conduct the whole volume of water from the Banská Štiavnica mines into the river Hron, a distance of over ten miles. It took nearly a hundred years to build the plant. Until the opening of the Simplon tunnel in 1906 this drainage channel was the longest tunnel in the world.

Accommodation: Grand Hotel, 2 námestie Náradného povstania; tel. 370.

Excursions in the environs of Banská Štiavnica

"Sitno-Krížna-Pokhaus" is a partially protected hunting preserve for the local roe-deer.

"Arboretum v Kysihýbli" is also State protected territory within the municipality of Banská Štiavnica and is used for research in the acclimatisation and possible uses of exotic trees.

Svätý Antol (19 km south-east) is a late Baroque 18th-century castle with valuable interior furnishing; it is now State property. The castle is built in the form of a regular square.

Jazero Klinger (Lake Klinger, 5 km south) is the bathing beach of **Banská Štiavnica**, lying in lovely wooded surroundings. A footpath leads to the beach from the "Pod Klingerom" motorbus stop.

Jazero Počúvadlo (13 km south) is a municipal recreation resort in a beautiful park and is specially suitable for aquatic sports. Not far from the lake is a **tourist hostel**. Some 500 yards above the lake rises the legendary and much celebrated peak of the **Sitno** (3,363 feet above sea level). The whole mountain is under protection as a **natural park** and has an abundant flora, specially rose bushes. From the shore of the lake a footpath with blue signs takes one to the mountain hut at the top of the Sitno in one hour. There is a remarkable **Romanesque church** in **Ilija** at the foot of the mountain.

Drastavica (south-west). A **hunting preserve** for the protection of herds of roe-deer and moufflons covers an area comprising some of the villages in the districts of Banská Štiavnica and Nové Bane (Beďan, Dekýš, Jablonovec, Počúvadlo, Štiavnické Bane, Unliská and Vysoká).

Dudince (32 km south); spa with mineral springs with a high content of active sulphur, salts and carbonic gas. The temperature of the water attains 28 degrees Centigrade.

Sklené Teplice (15 km north); bathing resort specializing in the treatment of rheumatism, and starting point for excursions into the Štiavnica Mountains.

Krupina (23 km south-east). A medieval town with a Romanesque **basilica**, later rebuilt in Baroque style. Well-preserved remains of **ramparts**. "Vartovka" watch tower against Turkish assaults in the Middle Ages. Nearby, a perfectly preserved fortified castle (Bzovík, and ruins of the Čabraď stronghold).

F. LUČENEC

Lučenec. The town lies in the middle of the wide Lučenec basin on the main railway line Zvolen–Plešivec and on the road from Zvolen to Rožňava. It has also an air service.

Lučenec was founded in the 13th century and was the scene of violent fighting during the Turkish raids into Slovakia in the 16th–17th centuries. No historical monuments remain in the town itself. Lučenec is however the **starting point** for worth-while excursions roundabout.

Accommodation: Hotel Slovan, 14 Železničná; tel. 456.

Excursions in the surroundings of Lučenec

Filakovo (16 km south-east). **Filakovo Castle** stands on an isolated hill overlooking the town; it is a medieval castle and its possession was often contested in bygone times. Today one of its towers is used as a residence. A museum is installed in the former Franciscan church building. The Baroque church is 18th century, the Baroque castle 19th.

Rimavská Sobota (30 km east). In the area of the town is a partly protected ornithological natural park for the protection of the native bird life and the nesting-trees "Kurínec".

Číž (53 km east) is a rather small **spa** with the most efficacious iodine springs in Europe.

Modrý Kameň (44 km west). On a tongue of rock above the town stands a medieval **castle**. Modrý Kameň is the centre of the new **brown-coal mining district** of Velký Krtíš-Pôtor with notable residential settlements. In the neighbouring **Horné Strháre** a new **geyser** is active (the water rises to a height of 40 feet; capacity 33–35 gallons per minute).

Abelová (32 km north-west) is a mountain settlement in the hills of Abelová, well worth seeing and noted for its sheep-rearing. The colourful women's popular costumes of Abelová and the neighbouring **Polichna** are among the most beautiful in Slovakia.

Divín (25 km north-west). Ruins of a **medieval fortified castle** in gothic style, dating from the 13th century, and of a 17th-century castle which is architecturally very interesting. Starting point for excursions into the Jarovie mountains.

Halič (9 km north-west). A commune with a well-preserved 18th-century **castle** which shows a successful synthesis of three styles, medieval, Renaissance and baroque.

Hajnačka (29 km south-east). On a conic-shaped hill of volcanic origin a powerful feudal castle was built on the site of a prehistoric stronghold. Behind the commune opens the vista of the Filakovo plateau (Mount Ragač, 1,762 feet; 1 hour excursion). South of Hajnačka, near the commune of Stará Bašta, on a table-shaped basalt mountain, stands the "pagan fortified castle" (a prehistoric stronghold). Farther west, ruins of Šomoška castle.

Hodejov (36 km east); ruins of a fortified castle which was destroyed by the Turks in the 16th century. Cold curative springs with a high carbonic gas content.

Oždány (19 km east); interesting reconstruction of a fortified castle.

15. EAST SLOVAKIA

The region of East Slovakia covers an extensive area consisting of several geographical divisions. Its frontiers with the countries north of it are preponderantly mountains, plains and rivers. The East Beskids form the boundary with Poland, the mountains in the region of the rivers Uh and Vihorlat the boundary with the USSR, the Theiss plain with Hungary, the Slovak Ore Mounts and the Slanec Mountains with South-West Slovakia, the Lower Tatra with North Slovakia.

Typical of the whole region are first the highlands, e.g. Šariš, Lubovňa, Ondava wedged into the foothills of Levoča, Čerchov and the Vihorlat. There are depressions only on the edge of this region.

We can divide the whole of East Slovakia into fairly isolated and naturally and economically differentiated districts. The boundaries between these districts were the result of natural conditions and were already fixed in the early Middle Ages when they once formed district administrational "gaus". On the west there is the Spiš (Zips), shut in by mountains, with medieval towns which developed from the settlements of German colonists after the ranges of the Turks; in the centre the Šariš which, with its numerous mining areas constitues the transition from the mountainous Spiš to the third region of Zemplin, right in the east, characterized by wide river valleys and the Theiss (Tisza) plain.

In the west of East Slovakia there are principally mountains, pasture land and well developed industry whereas in the eastern half wheat, corn, sugar-beet, tobacco and rice are cultivated on fertile soil and at a lower altitude. The northern and eastern parts were formerly bare of industries; it is only recently within the framework of the industrialisation of Slovakia that many factories have been built, especially in the surroundings of Prešov or are under construction, so that this hitherto retarded part of Czechoslovakia is gradually reaching the economic level of the rest of the country. In connection with the general industrialisation and accelerated building of houses in East Slovakia the building materials industry is making great strides.

From a touristic standpoint, East Slovakia is remarkably rich in historical monuments, chiefly in the Spiš and Šariš areas. The historic centres of many towns have been placed under National Trust protection. In the Spiš area they are the former trade centres Levoča (Leutschau) and Kežmarok

(Käsmark), the small guild town Spišská Sobota and the former centre of the ecclesiastical administration of East Slovakia, Spišská Kapitula. In Šariš the towns Prešov and the venerable royal town Bardejov. The culture of the Renaissance period has left in the Spiš—as the result of the reciprocal penetration of elements from the Danube area and of northern influences—characteristic attic house signs and graffito façades on private houses as well as on castles and church buildings, as at Betlanovce, Strážky and Kežmarok, but also in the Šariš area at Fričovce. There are valuable cultural-historical monuments in almost every place in the former confederacy of the towns of the Spiš.

The natural beauty of East Slovakia is in no way surpassed by this wealth of cultural monuments. The **Slovenský raj** (the Slovakian Paradise), the **Pieniny**, the **Morské oko** below the Sninský kameň are gems in the truest sense of the word. The whole region is rich in mineral springs, near which many watering places have arisen. There are extensive hunting grounds in the eastern forests, where in addition to the usual game, bears and wolf packs are not lacking.

Communications: East Slovakia has railway, road and air connections with the rest of Czechoslovakia. The most important town of East Slovakia, **Prešov**, has direct air services to Prague and Bratislava. The Poprad-Tatra airfield lies quite close to the Spiš; travellers in the Zemplin area use the airfield at **Košice**. The main line Žilina–Košice which crosses the Spiš ensures railway connection with Prague and Bratislava. Via Košice and Kysak the whole region is connected with the international lines to the U.S.S.R. and Hungary. The most important stretches of railway line are Žilina–Košice–Čierna (on the Theiss), Michalany–Medzila-borce, Košice–Prešov–Čirč and Prešov–Strážske–Humenné. The most important road junction is Prešov where the cross-country highways from the west from Prague and Bratislava through Poprad,

from the south from Košice and from the east from
Michalovce (Užhorod) converge.

The chief cultural, economic, political and administrative
centres are Kežmarok, Levoča, Prešov, Bardejov and Michalovce. The most notable tourist centres are the Pieniny and the
Slovakian Paradise.

Sights and places of interest

Towns under National Trust protection: Kežmarok, Spišská
Sobota, Levoča, Spišská Kapitula, Prešov, Bardejov.
Natural parks: Pieniny, Dreveník, Šimonka, Senné.
Tourist areas: the Pieniny, the Slovakian Paradise, the
Vihorlat, the Morské oko, the Čerhov Mountains and the Ondava
valley.
Castles and chateaux: Kežmarok, Lobovnia, Červený
Kláštor, Betlanovce, Spišský Štiavník, Markušovce, Spišský hrad
(Zips castle), Šarišský hrad (Šariš castle), Fričovce, Kapušany,
Zborov, Čičava.
Hunting grounds: Poprad, Dunajec, Zlatá Baňá-Šimonka,
Ondava highlands, Velké Zálužice, Remetské Hamry, Eastern
Beskids.
Spas: Vyšné Ružbachy, Sivá Brada, Bardejov Spa, Cigelka.
Folklore centres: Svídník, Nižné Ružbachy, Jakubany,
Zamagurie, Matiašovský Potok-Bijacovce, Hervartov, Richvald,
Zlaté, Velké Zalužice, Pozdišovce.
Other noteworthy sights: Svit, the Tatra Museum at Poprad,
the Svidník-Dukla Pass Memorials and the little wooden church
of Tokajík.
Circular tour of East Slovakia: Prešov—Spišské Podhradie
(44 km)—Levoča (60 km)—Červený Kláštor (Pieniny (123 km)—
Stará Lubovňa (168 km)—Bardejov (224 km)—Svidník (260 km)
—Dukla (281 km)—Svidník (302 km)—Kapušany (352 km)—
Prešov (360 km).

A. KEŽMAROK

Kežmarok (Käsmark) lies in the valley of the Poprad
river, on the northern edge of the Spiš basin (2,066 feet
above sea level); the town lies off the railway and main
highway with which it is connected through Poprad
(15 km).

The town was founded in the 12th century during the Saxon colonisation of the Spiš. It was no sooner given the privileges of a free royal town than it began a rivalry with Levoča for primacy within the confederacy of the free towns of the Spiš. Today it is a tourist centre for excursions into the High Tatra, into the Spišská Magura and, first and foremost, into the Pieniny.

Sights

The fork-shaped ground plan is typical of towns founded at important road junctions. The buildings are predominantly the work of native Spiš architects. The dwelling houses of Kežmarok with their typical shingle roofs and arched doorways represent a more developed form of country house, influenced by Renaissance architecture.

The 15th-century Gothic **parish church of the Holy Cross** has a remarkable side altar, a Renaissance steeple and a belfry close to the church; both towers are topped by buckler-shaped attics typical of East Slovakian Renaissance.

The five-towered 15th-century **castle** resembles a fortress and bounds the main square; it was rebuilt in the 17th century and is embellished by a Renaissance attic. During the Slovak National Uprising the Gestapo tortured and murdered local patriots in the rooms of the castle. There is now a **Municipal Museum** in the castle.

The **chapel of Thököly Castle** has a costly Renaissance interior.—The 17th-century Evangelical **wooden church**—now converted into a museum—is one of the roomiest wooden churches in Europe. The wooden pulpit is especially noteworthy.

Accommodation: Hotel Sport, 36 nám. Sovietskej armády; tel. 158.

Excursions in the environs of Kežmarok

Poprad (15 km south-west) is the best starting point for excursions into the High Tatra and the Spiš and an important railway and road junction. The **Tatra Museum** at Poprad has unusual exhibits from the National Trust natural park. In the neighbouring **Svit** (7 km) are modern chemical and textile factories amidst beautiful surroundings.

Spišská Sobota (14 km south-west). This small town is the best preserved unit of Spiš Renaissance architecture and is under protection as an ancient monument. Plain Renaissance and Baroque buildings with their steep roofs and graduated shingle roofs have been well preserved; also the interior of the houses in their original form. The little 13th-century **Gothic church** in the main square with its Renaissance belfry is specially worthy of note; the belfry was later rebuilt in Baroque. Inside the church there is among other things a late Gothic side-altar which certainly came from the workshop of the master Paul of Levoča. Spišská Sobota is now a suburb of Poprad.

Nižné Ružbachy (22 km north-east). The architecture of the peasant houses here is specially interesting, as is the furnishing of the rooms. The inhabitants have remained true to their popular costumes.

Výšné Ružbachy (25 km north-east). This watering place is situated in enchantingly beautiful surroundings among the pine woods of the north-east slope of the **Spišská Magura** (2,036 feet above sea level). The mineral springs are alkaline and aerated with a natural average temperature of 19–24° C. The baths are particularly suited for the treatment of different kinds of psycho-neuroses and states of exhaustion. A special attraction of the spa is the modern **bathing beach** with a little island, which—immediately below the Dukla clinic—is supplied directly with water from the mineral springs. Camping possibilities.

Accommodation: Hotels Magura and Dunajec.

Lubovňa Castle (36 km north-east) stands above the ancient town of Stará Lubovňa on a hill in the romantic valley of the Poprad river. The castle was rebuilt in Renaissance style and is well preserved. Until 1772 it was the residence of the Polish starost who governed the 13 towns of the Spiš, surrendered to Poland as a pledge by King Sigmund in 1412.

The Pieniny

The Pieniny region is one of the most remarkable geological phenomena in the world and is under National Trust protection as an agricultural and natural science park.

One enters the Pieniny by the road from Poprad through Kežmarok and Spišská Stará Ves (59 km by regular motorbus service, or from Prešov (90 km).

The Pieniny owes its overwhelming natural beauties to the Dunajec river and its endemic flora. The Dunajek gorge through the limestone cliffs which rise to a height of 1,000–1,650 ft above the river level gives the Pieniny an alpine character. Navigation on the river begins at **Červený Kláštor**, in the so-called "harbour" opposite the monastery ruins. A **trip on rafts** leaves an unforgettable impression. On the opposite bank of the Dunajec proudly rises the summit of the loveliest crest of the Pieniny, the picturesque Tri Koruny. The trip is made on peculiar rafts, consisting of 4 or 5 narrow, long boats constructed out of hollowed poplar and pine tree-trunks bound together. Two raftsmen—local mountain folk—steer them with long poles during the exciting trip which takes three quarters of an hour. At Červený Kláštor there are interesting remains of the former **monastery**, founded by Carthusian monks in 1319. The Gothic monastery church (1360) and the whole lay-out of fortifications with adjoining dwellings and domestic buildings have been well preserved. Exceptionally interesting is the monastery courtyard, in which there were ten independent hermitages for the monks. The monastery is State cultural property and has been renovated and reconstructed as the Pieniny museum.

In Červený Kláštor on a narrow, flat stretch of land at the foot of the wooded Venglisiek ridge are some buildings of the former spa known as **Smerdžonka.** The springs give out cold, sulphureous water with Glauber salt and mineral content. Every year in the neighbourhood of Červený Kláštor a **water slalom regatta** is held on the Dunajec with international competition. The lovely region is visited by many tourists and fishermen (salmon in the Dunajec).

The **folklore** throughout the so-called **Zamagurie** region of the **Spišská Magura** is worthy of note. Popular costumes are still worn in the villages Osturňa, Velký Lipník and Matiašovský Potok. The wooden houses merit attention.

B. LEVOČA

The town of Levoča (Leutschau) spreads over a massively rising slope of the southern spurs of the Levoča Mountains (1,890 feet above sea level). A branch line to the terminus Levoča runs off from the main railway line at Spišská Nová Ves. Roads to Levoča run through Poprad, Spišská Nová Ves, Prešov and Kežmarok.

The town was founded in 1245 by the inhabitants of the earlier, original Levoča, who had fled to Kláštorisko na Skale in the Slovakian Paradise during the Tartar invasion. The advantageous position of the town at the crossing of the trade routes to Hungary, Poland and Silesia favoured its rapid prosperity and development into an international commercial centre. The town quickly flourished owing to the industriousness of its handicraftsmen, especially the linen and cloth weavers and later the guild of metal founders and goldsmiths, whose products found their way to the Orient. In 1271 Levoča was the capital of the federation of the 24 towns of the Spiš. As a free and royal town Levoča occupied a leading political and economic position in the whole region of the Spiš, the provincia Saxorum, until the 18th century. In the following century the further development of the town stagnated because of the changed economic conditions, so that its original medieval character has been preserved to the present day.

Sights

The consistenly developed ground plan of the town with its regular rectangular main square, dating in its present form from the 14th century, the chequerboard arrangement of the blocks of houses, the systems of little streets along the ramparts, the specially carefully constructed fortifications with the still-standing town gates, the Town Hall and the church in the main square and finally the monastery building near the ramparts. Many artistic monuments still bear witness to the former wealth of the town. In the main square a whole number of houses in Gothic and Renaissance styles have been preserved; artistically even more valuable are the well preserved interior furnishings of the ecclesiastical and some secular buildings. The Gothic

parish church of Saint James is a unique artistic 14th–century complex. Most precious is the interior furnishing of the church, notably the unique Gothic altars. A pearl among these treasures is the main altar of the church, the life's work of the architect Paul. The altar is 60 feet high and 6½ yards wide and is one of the largest in Central Europe. It is one of the finest examples of Gothic carving in Slovakia and can stand comparison with the best works of that period in all Europe. Among the other Gothic monuments in the church are the side-altars, the wooden priedieu of the Senators and the bronze fonts; the chief Renaissance works are the wooden, stone and marble tombs and the wooden pulpit; recently, valuable frescoes have been uncovered.

The **Minorite** church and monastery near the former Polish Gate are other magnificent Gothic buildings.

The remains of secular Gothic architecture are preserved in individual buildings only in the burgher houses in the main square. Chiefly deserving of notice are the **Gothic portals** of Nos 7, 10, 45, 49 and 60. **Arcades, balconies** and **loggias** in the courtyards of Nos 27, 45, 49 and 57 in the main square.

The **Thurzo House** (No 6 in the main square) is the best-known Renaissance building, even though it shows exterior features of a renovation in Classic style (1824) and a graffito façade. The interior furnishing of the house in Renaissance style has remained untouched.

The **Town Hall,** completed in 1615, is also a remarkable building. The original Gothic part was given additional arcades on ground level and also on the upper floors.

The **Museum of the Spiš**, in a part of the Town Hall building, may be regarded as another historical monument.

Accommodation: Hotel Družba, 18 Cesta Slobody; tel. 381 and 335.

Excursions in the environs of Levoča

Betlanovce (20 km south-west). A Renaissance period castle (1564) with attic gables and graffito decoration, one of the finest Renaissance buildings in the Spiš. In the neighbouring **Spišský Štiavnik** is another Renaissance castle surrounded by a park.

Spišský Čtvrtok (12 km east). The **chapel annex** to the original Romanesque church is one of the best works of Gothic architecture in the whole of Czechoslovakia. The chapel, still preserved in Gothic style, was built in 1473 as a family vault for the Zápolskys.

In the neighbouring village of **Dravce** is a little 14th–century church with remarkable frescoes done at the time of its foundation.

Spišská Nová Ves (12 km south) was from 1772 onwards the seat of the administration of the 24 towns of the Spiš. When in session the "ambassadors" of these towns lived in a private residence on the right bank of the Hrenad river, known as the "Šestnáska" (sixteen) where the little houses of these ambassadors are still preserved.

Today Spišská Nová Ves is an important mining and industrial centre. It is the starting point for **excursions into the Slovakian Paradise** and the Slovakian Ore Mountains. There is a permanent **theatre** in the town.

Markušovce (23 km south). 15th-century castle ruins stand above the place and below the castle a 16th-century Renaissance stronghold with semi-round corner towers. Inside is a museum of objets d'art.

Sivá Brada (14 km east). There are mineral calcium saline springs in the hills on the way to Spišské Podhradie. The old spa Sivá Brada lies on the south side at the foot of the hills.

Spišské Podhradie (16 km east) is a classic example of the culture of the social life of old Hungary. Nearly 600 feet above the town are the ruins of **Spiš castle** (Zips castle). On a broad, low hill stands the **Spišská Kapitula**, the seat of the abbot and the later bishop. And between them, lower down the valley, lies the small town Spišské Podhradie.

Spišské Podhradie developed in the 12th–13th centuries from a settlement below the castle into an important town with a flourishing handicraft. It was one of those Spiš towns which were pledged to the Polish kings for 360 years. In the main square are the Town Hall (1546), built by the Polish starosts of the Spiš towns. In the parish church a copper font and a 13th–century side-altar piece have remained, both from the original Gothic church.

The **Spišská Kapitula** was erected on the Saint Martin's Mount at an altitude of 1,627 feet above sea level. The former ecclesiastical quarter, surrounded by ramparts, is now under National Trust protection. One still enters the town through the old gates. Despite later alterations in Gothic style the **cathedral** is still an important example of Renaissance architecture. During its reconstruction in the 15th century a **chapel** was built onto the cathedral as the Zápolský family vault; it is one of the most impressive Gothic buildings in Slovakia. Inside the cathedral we find frescoes depicting the coronation of King Charles Robert, painted in 1317; many well preserved works of 15th–century Gothic panel painting on the originally Gothic altars, plastics and artistically carved pews. Noteworthy also is the episcopal **residence** and the lane with the **canon's dwellings**.

Spišský hrad (Zips Castle) was built in the 13th century. Until the 18th century it was the political and economic centre of the whole district. It is the most extensive ruined castle in Czechoslovakia, spreading terrace-wise to the top of the steep limestone crag (2,092 feet).

Dreveník (18 km east) is a remarkable tufaceous limestone mountain (2,023 feet above sea level), about 45 minutes from Spišské Podrhadie. It is cleft by deep ravines and has many sheer precipices, subterranean passages, caves and labyrinths; the mountain is covered with rare flora and is besides an outstanding archaeological excavation site. It is partly under National Trust protection as a geological and botanical natural park for the preservation of its vegetation and travertine formation.

Žehra (22 km east). In the ancient 13th–century little **church of the Holy Ghost** are specially valuable 13th–15th–century frescoes. The outer walls of the church date from 1275. The Baroque castle is also worth seeing.

Bijacovce (21 km east). On the mountain above the village are a picturesque cemetery, a Romanesque chapel and an early Gothic little church with Romanesque elements. The peasant houses on either side of the brook are worth attention. The Baroque-style fort is 18th century. Bijacovce was the focus of the peasant uprising in 1831. Some typical popular costumes and customs are still in use today.

Slovenský raj (the Slovakian Paradise)

The Slovakian Paradise is the name given by tourists to a part of the Slovakian Ore Mountains (Rudohorí) in East Slovakia between Poprad and Spišská Nová Ves. In the relatively small area of this chalk highland there are a number of peculiar sights which have earned for it the name "Slovakian Paradise". Specially attractive are the many **tiesňavy** (little, narrow canyons), each one of which is a world unto itself. The deep, narrow gorges often measure no more than a yard across the bottom and above them rise sheer, overhanging cliffs up to 1,000 feet into the sky. Abysses with gigantic waterfalls and cascades, underground streams with numerous springs, deep-dug erosion pits, pot-holes and caves succeed one another. The three loveliest and most visited canyons—**Kyssel, Suchá Belá** and **Velký Sokol**—are provided with iron ladders and small bridges which facilitate the ascent.

Other sights are: the view from Tomašova, the Hernad river gorge, the artificial water basin on the Biely-Potok called the Klausa, the Glacská lúka, the great waterfall in the central Piecky (100 feet), the three-tiered waterfall in the Sokolia dolina, Medvedia jaskyňa (the Bears' Cave) and rare alpine flora, amongst them gentian and specially edelweiss. The finest view is from the Havranie skala (the Ravens' Rock).

Kláštorisko (2,445 feet above sea level) is the tourist centre of the Slovakian Paradise. Hither, in the years 1241–42, into this natural fortress the inhabitants of the Spiš escaped from the Tartars and in memory of their salvation the mountain was named **Skala útočišťa**—Lapis Refugii (the Rock of Salvation). Later a Carthusian monastery was built here, but it was destroyed in 1543 when robber barons seized the monastery. From Kláštorisko there is a unique view of the range of the High Tatra Mountains.

The quickest way up to the top is from Letanovce following a red-marked path, the so-called Kartuziánsky chodník (Carthusian path) in 1½ hours.

From **Hrabušice** Kláštorisko can also be reached by automobile. From **Spišská Nová Ves** via Čingov the climb takes 3½ hours. From **Spišské Tomašovice** by way of the view-point above the Hornád valley 2½ hours. All paths to Kláštorisko are very carefully marked, as is the case everywhere throughout the Slovakian Paradise.

C. PREŠOV

Prešov, the second largest town in East Slovakia, sprawls in the valley of the Torys river at the foot of the Čerhov, the Slaníc Mountains and the Šariš highland (907 feet above sea level). The town is an important railway and road junction from where rail and motor-bus lines run in four directions all over the region. Connection with the main line Žilina–Košice is via Kysak and there is a regular air service to and from Prague and Bratislava. In the 15th century Prešov was a free and royal town.

Sights

Prešov with its remarkable fusiform main square and its old fortification ruins is under National Trust protection. The Renaissance-style **burgher houses** have richly decorated façades and particularly, plastic arcades and attics embellished by graffito painting. The most important are the **Rákoczi House**, the **Caraffa House** and the **Werther House**. The churches—the 14th-century Gothic Catholic church, the 16th–century Baroque Evangelical church and the 17th–century Rococo Orthodox church—represent three different architectural styles with specially valuable interior decoration. Prešov is an important cultural centre for the Slovak and Ukrainian population of the district. The town has a broadcasting station, the Jonás Záborsky Theatre, the **Ukrainian National Theatre**, the Šariš Museum in the Rákóczi House, the **pedagogical faculty** of the Slovak University, a higher Slovak and Ukrainian **Teachers' Academy**, a popular observatory and various scientific institutes. Prešov also possesses the most modern artificial **swimming baths** in Czechoslovakia and a magnificent Dubrara open-air swimming pool.

Accommodation: Hotel Dukla, 2 Slovenskej republiky rad; tel. 3015.

Excursion from Prešov

Fričovce (24 km west). A well preserved early 17th-century **castle** with attics, graffito and figural ornamentation. 4 km north rises the excellent aerated mineral spring **Salvator.**

Cemjata (9 km south-west) is a place of excursion for the people of Prešov in lovely mountain scenery and with abundant aerated mineral springs.

Solivar (3 km south). In this suburb of Prešov there are flooded rock salt deposits from which salt is simply extracted. Noteworthy are the salt deposits in the shape of fine spires.

Zlatá Baňa (18 km south-east). Starting point for the ascent of the **Šimonka** (3,603 feet above sea level), the highest peak of the Slánské Mountains with abundant hunting grounds. The Šimonka is under National Trust protection as a **forest park** for the preservation of endemic plants.

Kapušany (8 km north-east). On the hill above Kapušany are the ruins of a medieval **castle**. The ascent takes three quarters of an hour; there is a grand view from the ruins.

Velký Šariš (5 km north-west). On a hill (1,887 feet) above the place, in the middle of a copse stand the ruins of a medieval **castle** as old as the 11th century and once the seat of the district administration of Šariš. The climb up to the castle takes roughly one hour.

Sabinov (17 km north-west). The fortifications round the town and its gates have been preserved. The originally Gothic **cathedral** bears traces of reconstruction in 1503; the valuable interior furnishing also dates from then. Next to the church rises a **belfry** (1657). The Sabinov region is remarkable for its orchards.

Lipany (28 km north-west). The **Saint Martin's church** (1513), originally Gothic, but rebuilt in Renaissance style has a particularly valuable interior furnishing, notably side-altars, fonts and an arcaded gallery.

D. BARDEJOV

The town lies on a terrace (900 feet above sea level) where the Lukavice brook runs into the Topla river. It is the terminus of the railway line to Prešov, to which it is also connected by national highway. The foundation of Bardejov goes back to the 9th century; after the Tartar invasion the town was rebuilt by foreign colonists and became a free royal town in 1376.

Sights

Bardejov is one of the best preserved old towns in Slovakia and represents an almost unspoilt architectural whole with relatively only few interferences to the original buildings; the town makes a decidedly medieval impression.

The regular rectangular **main square**, surrounded by buildings in Gothic and Renaissance styles, is still paved with cobblestones, as was customary in earlier times in the squares and streets of Slovak towns.

The **burgher houses,** dating from the end of the 15th and beginning of the 16th centuries, with their façades showing high wall signs above their main fronts overlook the main square. Original stucco decoration, frescoes and mural paintings still remain.

The **Town Hall** in the middle of the main square was built in the transition period from Gothic to Renaissance. In front of the building, a small cannon has been placed; it came from the ruins of the near-by Zborov Castle.

The huge Gothic **parish church of Saint Aegidius**, which shuts off the south side of the main square is—in so far as well preserved decoration and interior furnishing is concerned—a real museum with costly 15th and 16th–century collections; it is actually the prototype of a late medieval church. The building was started in the 14th century and completed in the 15th. Amongst the most precious features inside are the Gothic aisle altars, the Gothic pews against the walls round the Holy of Holies, the tower-like stone pastoforium, the bronze baptismal font, the statue of Saint Aegidius, a rich collection of chalices, exquisite panel paintings and splendidly coloured rosettes.

The **battlements of the town fortifications** date from the year 1352, when the whole town was fortified. Many bastions, gates with embrasures, partly with the original plastering, still remain.

In the old Town Hall building is the Šariš **Fatherland**

Museum with very valuable exhibits relating to the history of Bardejov. Rich collections of the national economic section are in two new museums at Nos 1 and 2 Rhodyho ulica.

Accommodation: Hotel Dukla, tel. 209.

Excursions in the environs of Bardejov

Hertník (11 km south). The Renaissance-style castle with well preserved remains of fortifications dates from the 17th century. A path with green signs leads from Hertník up to the hut on the **Čerhov** (3,234 feet above sea level). The ascent takes 2½ hours.

Hervartov (9 km south-west). Here there is a little 15th-century gothic wooden church; also remarkable small **log houses** with shingle and thatched roofs and gaily painted outer walls.

Richvald (11 km west). A typical little village of the upper Šariš region with beautiful popular costumes.— **Zlaté** (11 km north-west) is another typical village where the inhabitants still wear popular dress.

Bardejov Spa (**Bardejovské kúpele**, 6 km north). This watering place is magnificently situated; its origins go back to 1247 and the first baths were built as early as 1505. Digestive ailments are treated there. Cultural performances are given here in the summer season under the slogan "Summer at Bardejov Spa".

Zborov (10 km north). There was bitter fighting here during the First World War. Two km south are the ruins of a 13th–century **castle**, originally built in Gothic style.

Svidník (36 km east). This small town has been rebuilt on the ruins and ashes of its predecessor. On a hill above the town stands an obelisk 100 feet high to the memory of the Soviet army; here lie buried more than 9,000 Soviet soldiers who fell in the winter of 1944–45 during operations in the Dukla-Prešov area. In the rectory not far from the memorial is an exhibition with souvenirs of the Dukla Pass battle. The Russian general Kutuzov stayed in this building in 1805 on his way home after the Battle of Austerlitz.

A visit to Svidník is especially recommended during the annual national costume festival; on that occasion performances by dance and song groups are given in a out-door amphitheatre.

In the villages roundabout Svidník there are a whole number of small **wooden churches**, built in Byzantine style and embellished with old artistic icons and paintings. They date from the 17th to the 18th century. The finest are in the villages along the road from Bardejov to Svidník; in Nižný, Vyšný Mirošov and Vyšný Orlík; on the road from Svidník to Dukla: in Lodomírova, Hunkovce, Krajná Polana and Nižný Komárnik. At **Kružlova**, whither the road from Svidník branches through Kapušov, is the oldest wooden church in Slovakia.

Dukla (57 km north-east). The cenotaph to the Heroes of Dukla stands on the spot where on the 6th October 1944 the soldiers of the 1st Czechoslovak Brigade emerged from the frontier forest after months of heavy fighting for the Dukla Pass to behold the first Slovak village on their native soil, Vyšný Komárnik. The monument—a tall pylon with a hall of honour—shuts off the south side of thr cemetery to which the remains of over 1,000 Czechoslovak soldiers were transferred.

E. MICHALOVCE

Michalovce lies on the river Laborec in the middle of the fertile Zemplin; railway connection via Michalany (main line Košice—Čop) by the branch line Michalany–Medzilaborce. The national highways from Košice and Prešov run through the town and continue to Užhorod and into the U.S.S.R. The town was founded in 1046.

Sights

Parish church, originally gothic, rebuilt in Baroque style in the 18th century (valuable interior). Former **Sztáray castle**, built in the 17th century on the site of an old stronghold and now converted into a folk museum of the Zemplín region. The **Štift Palace** where the district assembly used to hold its sessions.

Accommodation: Hotel Park, tel. 353, 249.

Excursions in the neighbourhood of Michalovce

Velké Zálužie (4 km east), a place with rich folklore. The colourful Zemplin costume is worn and popular songs are sung. A pheasantry in the neighbourhood offers promise of an excellent bag.

Morské Oko (33 km north-east). In the volcanic **Vihorlat** highland at an altitude of 2,072 feet above sea level lies a magnificent mountain lake (35 acres) in lovely surroundings—the Morské Oko (hunting and fishing). On the shore of the lake is a mountain hut. Above the lake stretches the rocky massif of the **Sninský kameň** (4,821 feet) with a unique panorama of the whole surroundings (the ascent takes 1 hour). The Morské Oko can be approached by motorbus via **Remetské Hámre** (33 km), from where it is a 2 hours walk by a path with blue signs, or else by mountain railway. **Remetské Hámre** is one of the most plentifully stocked hunting grounds in Slovakia with a little old hunting lodge.

Tokajík (78 km north-east). A small village in the Ondava highland near Stropkov. The place was razed to the ground in the war, but has since been rebuilt. A large memorial to the victims of the Nazis has been put up.

Pozdišovce (6 km south-west) is a pottery community with a tradition of more than 500 years. Here **crockery ware** with beautiful old Slovak designs, based on the gaily coloured patterns of native folklore, is produced.

16.   NORTH SLOVAKIA

North Slovakia forms a geographical unit, separated from the neighbouring regions almost entirely by mountains. The Javorníky Mts. and the Moravian-Silesian Beskids form the boundary with Moravia, the Slovakian Beskids and the Western Tatra the frontier with Poland, the Lower Tatra and Kremnica Mts. divide it from Central Slovakia and, finally, the Žiar Mts. and the Strážov highland from South-west and West Slovakia.

The Váh (Waag), the main river of North Slovakia, with many tributaries on either side, flows through the whole region.

In the west lies the upper Považie (Váh valley) with its centre at Žilina, then the Turiec valley basin with its centre at Martin, Orava (a region on the river of the same name) and the valley basin of Liptov, stretching from Ružomberok to Liptovský Hrádok. From the tourist standpoint the most interesting parts are the region of the Roháče in the Western Tatra and the Vrátná area in the Malá Fatra (Little Fatra).

The greater part of this region consists of mountains, often wooded and often bare, and pasture-land, while in the river valleys we find few cultivated fields. Potatoes and oats do best. On the other hand, the woodworking industry is extraordinarily developed; wood pulp factories at Žilina, Martin and Ružom berok, the wood industry at Bytča, at Krásno on the Kysuca, at Turany, Martin and Ružomberok. There are besides important constructional engineering factories at Považská Bystrica, Kysúcke Nové Mesto, Martin and on the Orava; textile factories at Žilina, Ružomberok and Lipt. Mikuláš. The region derives its energy from the power station built on the cascades of the Váh and the dams of the Liptov valley basin as far as the "Youth Dam" at Puchov, which are yearly increasing in number by further new building.

From the point of view of the tourist the region of North Slovakia is remarkable for the beauty of the Western Tatra Mts. (round the Roháče), of the Lower Tatra (chiefly in the area of Jasná and the near-by, world-famous stalactite caves of Demänová) and the Little Fatra in the Vratna area. We find valuable cultural-historical monuments concentrated in some medieval towns. Several 13th–century castles along the Váh survived the Tartar invasion. Many villages and settlements are known for the wealth of their folklore. The river abounds in fish, amongst others also the rare Danube salmon-trout; there are trout in its tributaries, in the mountain brooks and streams as well as in the Čierny Váh (the Black Waag) and in the Belá. Besides deer and wild boar, the game includes bears and lynxes. Many mineral springs with spas at Rajecké Teplice, Turčianské Teplice, Lubochňa, Lúčky and Korytnica complete the natural resources of North Slovakia.

Communications: Connection with the whole of Czechoslovakia is assured by railways and motor-roads. The most important town of the region, Žilina, is the chief junction of Slovakia, connecting Prague (via Bohumín and Púchov) and Bratislava with Central, South-west and East Slovakia, and also with the High Tatra. International railway connection is assured by direct fast trains and carriages from Prague, Bratislava and Košice. The direct Budapest—Warsaw line also runs through Žilina. The chief towns of the region are on the main railway and highway network from Prague and Bratislava to Žilina and from there on through the Váh valley in the High Tatra and East Slovakia. Martin and Dolný Kubín are the only exceptions. The most important railway services between this region and all Czechoslovakia and the rest of Slovakia are: Prague—Bohumín—Žilina—Košice, Prague—Púchov—Žilina—Košice, Bratislava—Košice, Košice and Plešivec—Vrútky. The main highways run into North Slovakia from Bratislava, Ostrava, Prešov (through Poprad) and Kremnica.

The most important cultural, economic and administrative centres of North Slovakia are: Žilina, Martin, Ružomberok, Liptovský Mikuláš and Liptovský Hrádok.

Tourist centres in the region: Vrátna, Orava, Roháče and the valley basins of Demänová and Jasná.

Sights and places of interest

National Trust parks: Súlovské skály (Súlov Rocks), Liptovský Ján, the Bešeňová region, the valley basin of Demänová.

Hiking areas: Súlovské skály, the Little Fatra (Vrátna), Martinské hole (the bald Mt. Martin), Oravice, Roháče, the Western Tatra, the Lower Tatra (Jasná, Čertovica).

Castles: Budatín, Hričov, Lietava, Strečno, Orava, Bytča Kunerád, Diviaky, Liptovský Hradok, Považská Bystrica.

Fishing and hunting: Orava, Belá, the Čierny Váh Valley.

Spas: Rajecké Teplice, Turčianske Teplice, Kortnica, Lúčky.
Folklore: Čičmany, Sliače, Liptovská Osada, Lipt. Lužná, Východná, Važec, Vyšná Boca, Ždiar.
Other sights: the memorial on Zvonica Hill, the Orava dam, the Slovakian Karst Museum at Lipt. Mikuláš, the Demänová valley basin—stalactite caves.

Žilina–Vrátna (35 km)—Zázrivá (52 km)—Oravský Podzámok (82 km)—Orava Dam (113 km)—Oravice (140 km)—Tvrdošin (161 km)—Dolný Kubín (196 km)—Ružomberok (214 km)—Korytnica (241 km)—Ružomberok (268 km)—Královany (287 km)—Martin (311 km) —Strečno (329 km)—Žilina (341 km).

A. ŽILINA

Žilina is situated in North-west Slovakia in the Váh valley (1,135 feet above sea level) at the confluence of the Kysuca and the Rajčianka.

Žilina is the most important junction in Slovakia (190 km to Bratislava, 214 km to Brno, 430 km to Prague). It has also connections by air.

The town originated at the beginning of the 13th century at the crossing of five important trade routes and immediately after its foundation was given the rights of a free royal town. The original measurements of the market place, surrounded entirely by one-storey houses and a regular network of streets, still remain. There are open arcades on all sides of the market place.

It lost its privileges as a free, royal town, by rebelling against the emperor. A considerable part of its people joined the Slovak National Uprising and we can find in nearly every street of of Žilina memorial tablets to those who fell during the insurrection.

Sights

The 13th-century Romanesque little **church of Saint Stephen,** surrounded by ramparts with loop-holes, stands where once the old Žilina stood. It is one of the earliest Romanesque buildings in Slovakia. There are valuable frescoes inside the church.

The originally Romanesque **parish church** (1300) has the features of its frequent reconstructions. The most evident are the early Gothic elements of the building. The isolated Renaissance tower is 16th century. The **Žilina Book** is a collection of laws and orders once obeyed by this free royal town. It is the oldest juristic document written in the Slovak tongue.

Žilina is today the political, economic and cultural centre of North Slovakia. Industrial production is steadily developing.

The town has a permanent **theatre** (Peter Jilemnický's Workers' District Theatre) and exhibition rooms with works by artists living in the Žilina district. In the **Municipal Museum** are valuable exhibits of wire-binding and carving. In the Sports Centre of Žilina, besides summer sports grounds, there is also a winter stadium with an artifical ice track. On the Bôrik, from where there is a fine view of the town and its surroundings with the circle of mountains, there is also a beautiful **natural park.**

Accommodation: Hotel Polom, 77 ul. Slov. nár. povstania; Telephone 2 39 04; **Hotel Metropol,** Hviezdoslavova Nr. 4, Telephone 2 39 00; **Information,** Ul. Slov. nár. povstania Nr. 11.

Excursions from Žilina

Budatín Castle (2 km north) lies at the confluence of the Kysúca and the Váh. The origin of this later reconstructed castle goes back to the 13th century. The castle is now furnished as a museum and picture gallery.

Hričov Castle (15 km west), one of the most beautifully situated Slovakian castles, stands on a high rock above **Hričovské Podhradie.** It was first mentioned in the 13th century. It has been deserted since the 18th century.

Bytča (17 km west). This fortified water-castle (1571–1604) is the finest Renaissance monument in North Slovakia. The most remarkable feature is the so-called wedding palace in the castle courtyard, the walls of which are richly decorated with graffiti. This much industrialised little district town is the starting point for excursions to the Súlov Rocks.

Sulovské skaly (the Súlov Rocks, 22 km south-west). A rock city caused by the erosion of the Strážov highland. The rock city is broken by the so-called **Súlov Gate** which forms the entrance to the Súlov valley. The mass of rocks and fantastically shaped towers reaches to **Roháč** (2,669 feet), the most striking point of the Súlov Rocks. On a limestone crag in the middle of the rock city stand the ruins of **Súlov Castle** (12th century). The Súlov Rocks, in which there are a rock amphitheatre and a canyon are under National Trust protection.

The castle of **Povážska Bystrica** (27 km south-west). The medieval castle ruins, of which the walls and the stone window-frames still remain, stands directly above the Váh and the village of **Povážske Podhradie.** Wonderful view over the Váh valley (the Považie). In the village is a Renaissance castle (1631) and another (1775) in Rococo style. A ferry takes one across the river to the village.

Lietava Castle (9 km south). This picturesque ruin of one of the largest Slovakian castle is southeast of **Lietava** on the eastern edge of the vertiginous mountain range. The first written mention of the castle was made in 1318.

Rajecké Teplice (15 km south-east). A magnificently situated spa in the wide Rajčianka valley at the foot of mountains wooded with beech and partly with spruce. The thermal water is used for the treatment of rheumatic complaints, chronic bronchial catarrh and sinus trouble.

Kunerád (20 km south). The luxurious **hunting lodge,** built in 1916, below Mount Martin was used during the Slovak National Uprising as partisan headquarters. The lodge was set on fire in the course of the fighting. After being restored it is intended to use it as a sanatorium.

Rajec (21 km south). An ancient little town with much handicraft production. The Romanesque 13th–century little **Saint Ladislaus church** has lost its original appearance owing to later re-building. In the middle of the market square stands the rectangular, ancient Town Hall. In the neighbouring villages, particularly in **Rajecká Lesná, Fačkov, Čičmany** and **Domaniža** the people still wear popular costumes.

Čičmany (38 km south-west). A village renowned for its unique folklore. The peculiar popular costume is elaborately and artistically embroidered. The architecture of Čičmany with its ornamentally painted house-walls is original. A typical house—the one-storey wooden house that belonged to the Jokl family—is in the Prague National Museum.

Teplička (5 km east). On the south-east edge of the place is the **three-towered castle** that belonged to General Johannes Löwenburg. Nearby a door and a section of a wall can be seen; they are the remains of the city's fortifications. Valuable frescoes in the 16th-century **church**. A chapel is built onto the north side of the church (1729), an exact copy of the Italian

Loretto chapel. The Hungarian nobles formed an anti-Habsburg conspiracy at Teplička in 1664.

Strečno (12 km south-east). The river Váh flows from Turiec into the Žilina basin through a romantic valley to which many legends and stories are attached; for example, the legends of Margita and Besná from the days when raftsmen still navigated the Váh. In the Middle Ages two castles guarded the entrance of the narrow valley, one on the left and the other on the right bank. Both stand on impregnable rocks.—**Starý Hrad** (old castle) on the right bank of the river dates from the 11th–12th century. It was still inhabited in the 18th century, but today only the bare walls remain. A tourist path (½ hour) leads from Strečno railway station up to the castle.—**Strečno** Castle is on the left bank, above Strečno itself. It was built in the 13th century. The road passes directly beneath the sheer cliff on which the ruin, of this important castle stand. The possession of it was more than once contested down the centuries by the imperial troops and the rebels in the Austro-Hungarian monarchy. The castle fell into ruins at the end of the 17th century and was abandoned. The ascent can be made from Strečno.—On **Zvonica** Hill the 28 foot pylon, erected in memory of the French partisans who died here in the Second World War. A road practicable for motor vehicles branches off the highway and leads up to the memorial.

Trnové (5 km south-west) has an ancient wooden church dedicated to Saint George which is well worth seeing.

The Vrátna valley constitutes another attractive excursion from Žilina.

Žilina offers a magnificent view of the Little Fatra Mts., north-east of the town. The most frequented part of these mountains is one of the loveliest valleys in Slovakia, the Vrátna valley, a tourist centre with every modern convenience. The valley is easily accessible from the Žilina highway (38 km). It forms a symmetrically enclosed whole, dominated by the narrow main ridge like a defence wall and those of the neighbouring ridges covered with meadows—known as "greens". Here pastureland alternates in charming contrast with woods, bare slopes, dwarf pines and naked rocks. In the Vrátna valley there are shelters for hikers, several sleighs and chair-lifts. Starting point is the original village of Terchová, the birthplace of the robber chieftain Juro Jánošík, who in the 18th century championed the rights of the serf Slovak people and became a legendary revolutionary hero. The wooden houses and women's costumes of Terchová are worth seeing. The highway runs through a natural gate along the Tiesňavy (narrows). The serpentine highway winds steeply up past the waterfalls of the foaming torrent. The whole length of the Tiesňavy is surrounded by strangely shaped limestone formations.

Behind the Tiesňavy the valley widens considerably and we presently stand enraptured before the extraordinarily beautiful Vrátna panorama with the dominating main ridge of the Křiváň in the Great Fatra to Stoh. The view towards the tourist hostel, beautifully situated on the lovely sunny south-east slope of the Sokolie rocks is also fascinating. About 1 km behind the Tiesňavy, at the so-called "Rázcestie" (fork) the broad Grúň mountain ridge divides the Vrátna valley in two. One branch of the valley, the left, runs south-east below the Great Rozsutec, the finest peak of this range, to Štefanová; the other runs right in a south-westerly direction below the Great Fatra-Kriváň to the lift up the Vrátna. At the foot of the Grúň, at the so-call Paseky (wood-cutting) a ski-lift is in operation in winter. There is another tourist hostel above the station on the Grúň. From the Rázcestie to the actual heart of the Vrátna, to the hostel and the lift in the same building, the distance is 3 km.

The Vrátna hostel (2,442 ft) is equipped with 90 beds. From here a chair cable railway takes one in 12 minutes up to the Snilovske saddle (4,107 ft above sea level) on the main ridge of the Little Fatra. The lift is able to carry 220 persons per hour in one direction. The lift is most used in winter when it carries vast numbers of skiers up to this skiing paradise on the main ridge, in the huge depression below the Chleb and the Great Fatra-Kriváň (5,646 ft).

The terrain below the Chleb has a decidedly alpine character and is the best descent terrain in the whole of Czechoslovakia, for which reason international championships in descent tactics are regularly held here. The international course runs from the Chleb ridge (5,425 ft) to the lower chair cable rail station. There is a large hostel on the other side of the Chleb (4,719 ft).

The hostel on the Chleb is the starting point for summer and winter tours to all parts of the mountains. From it one enjoys a wonderful view of all the most important Slovakian mountain chains.

The hiker's hostel on the Rozsutec (3,937 ft above sea level) is picturesquely situated in the romantic corner of the Vrátna below the cleft summit of the Great Rozsutec (5,299 ft). The limestone and dolomite peaks, forked above deep abysses, rise imposingly. The Rozsutec is often climbed also from the frontal side, from the quaint little village of Zázrivá where there is a nice hostel for tourists.

Amongst the sights of the Vrátna one must also include the Diery (potholes), deep and narrow canyons with many waterfalls which the torrents of the streams flowing down from the Little and Great Rozsutec have worn out of the rocks. The Diery can best be reached from Štefanová, from the second branch of the valley where there is also a rather small tourist hostel.

B. MARTIN

The town of **Martin** lies in the fertile basin of **Turiec** (986 feet above sea level). The main railway line from north to south runs through Martin and it is connected via Vrútky with the Košice—Žilina line. Same connections by road.

Martin was given its civic rights in the 14th century, and in the middle of the 18th century it became the capital of a district. The town's industry only began with the creation of the Czechoslovak Republic and has developed mainly in recent years. Since the last century Martin has been a centre of Slovak national life and was when Slovakia was being forcibly Magyarised the chief town of Slovakia. Also after the Slovak Rebellion in 1848–1849 Slovak national institutions were concentrated here, such as the "Matica Slovenská" (Slovak capital fund), which spread culture and enlightenment in Slovak among the population; the Slovak grammar-school, the "Živena" Union of Slovak Women, the Slovak Museum Society. The news-papers "Národnie noviny" (National News) and the "Slovenské pohľady" (Slovak Review) were published here in Slovak. In 1861 the political demands of the Slovaks for national liberation were also drawn up at Martin in the "Memorandum of the Slovak nation to the Austro-Hungarian Emperor".

The Slovak National Uprising in August 1944 started in Martin, which had been captured by partisan units on the 26th August 1944, three days before the official proclamation of the rebellion.

Sights

The Gothic **church,** in which valuable medieval frescoes have been discovered and restored. Near the church archaeologists found old tribal burial grounds. Today too Martin plays an important part in the cultral life of Slovakia. Here are the headquarters of the Matica Slovenská, the Slovak **National Museum,** the Slovak **Museum Society** and the permanent **Army Theatre.** Visitors to the town will find many memorial tablets commemorating eminent Slovak creative artists and politicians. Many of these are buried in the town cemetery.

In the years of Slovakia's industrialisation a large constructional engineering factory was built at Martin, which with the wood-working and food industries has given it the stamp of a modern industrial town.

Accommodation: Hotel Slovan, Telephone 42.

Excursions from Martin

Hostel on the **Martinské hole** (Martin Mounts, 4,290 feet above sea level, 12 km east). To the hos-tel on foot takes 2½ to 3 hours. The hostel can also be reached by powerful cars and in winter by sleigh.—**Priekopa** (6 km north). A huge cenotaph to those who fought in the National Uprising.—**Vrútky** (9 km north). A small town with a remarkable tradition and a museum of the Workers' Press.—Further, **Sklabinský Podzámok** with Sklabina **Castle.**

Necpaly (12 km south-east). In the place two well preserved 17th- and 18th-century **castles.** In the late 13th-century **church** are valuable murals. Necpaly is the starting point for walking tours in the Great Fatra, to the hostel below the Borišov, 4,290 feet (4 hours walk).—**Kláštor pod Znievom** (13 km north). The ruins of the 13th century **Zniev Castle** rise above the little town. The Gothic church also dates from the same time. In the monastery church is a remarkable picture, painted on wood (1229).

Mošovce (19 km south). In the market square an 18th-century Renaissance style castle; near the town is a fine bathing beach. Mošovce is the birthplace of Ján Kollár, poet and theorist of the pan-Slav idea.

Turčianske Teplice (24 km south). Abundant springs with gypsum content, 40–42° C. Rheumatic ailments and injuries after accidents are treated here in bath-tubs and pools. The spa is beautifully situated in the middle of a park and was already known in the 14th century. The little town is the starting point for **walking tours** in the **Great Fatra,** to the hotel on the **Králova studňa** (4,191 feet above sea level), 6 hours walk.

C. THE ORAVA

The Orava is an extensive territory, surrounded on every side by mountains, in the region of the river of the same name. The Orava and its tributaries abound in fish. The waters of the upper course of the river are retained by the huge Orava Dam; its reservoir, covering an area of 17½ square miles, regulates the water level of many power stations in the Považie (Váh valley). The Orava leaves a powerful impression on every visitor. Industrialisation is chiefly noticeable at Istebné, Dolný Kubín, Mokrad, Nižná and Trstená. If we travel through the Orava valley by train or by car, we come across many reminders of old popular culture. The peculiar wooden houses with their shingle roofs and gables turned towards the streets are interesting. The houses have front gardens and behind the village are wooden granaries. Noteworthy are the little wooden churches (15th–17th century) with well preserved Renaissance paintings. The most interesting are to be found at Zábrežie, Tvrdošin, Istebné and Leštiny.

The people of the Orava have also kept up their peculiarity in dress, that worn by the men being more remarkable than that worn by the women.

The river Orava made the gateway to the Orava at Královany where it flows into the Váh. By the railway crossing at Královany both rail and highway run through the beautiful Královany valley into the Orava country. One could believe that one was travelling upstream through a paradise. Tourist paths lead up to the hostels in the Little Fatra and the Oravská Magura. From Bystrička below the Rozsutec one can get to the hostel on the Rozsutec (4,125 ft) in 2½ hours. Flocks of sheep graze on the mountain slopes.

Via Istebné and Veličné we come to **Dolný Kubín,** the chief town of the Orava, with the imposing **Choč** (5,323 feet) towering above it. Here the greatest Slovak poet, Pavel Orságh Hviezdoslav, lived for many years and died.

From Dolný Kubin the path leads to the **hostel on the Kubinská hola** (4,092 feet). The climb takes 2½ hours. On our further ramble through the Orava our way is blocked at **Oravský Podzámok** by the best preserved and most visited Slovakian castle, the medieval **Orava Castle** (Oravský zámok). The limestone rock forms a natural protection for the castle and, as has appeared from the most recent archaeological discoveries, the spot was already settled in primitive times. The oldest written mention of the castle dates from the 12th–century. It has now been turned over to a museum. Under the rough-casting of the walls original paintings in colour have been discovered and the reconstructed painting on the highest part of the castle gives the impression of a wall composed entirely of large squares. From the highest point of the castle, a look-out tower 370 feet above the Orava, one can enjoy an unforgettable view of the surroundings.

Tvrdošín, a small town with a unique little wooden church (15th century) in the cemetery above the town. Here the railway and a highway branch off to Poland and to **Oravice** via **Trstená** and **Suchá Hora**; a second road leads to the Orava Dam and to **Námestovo.**

Oravice, a hollow picturesquely situated amidst meadows and woods with a fine, new tourist hotel. An ideal holiday resort—Starting point for summer and winter tours in the West Tatra, the Roháče, up the Magura and the Skorušina.

There are several recreation centres and camping sites (tents) on the banks of the Orava reservoir. Boat excursions on the lake. To enthusiastic tourists we would warmly recommend the ascent of Mount **Babia Gora**, starting from the commune of Oravská Podhora. During that excursion you go through an interesting forest of 200-years-old spruce-firs. The climb takes about three and a half hours. The most important tourist centres in the surroundings of Lake Orava are the communes of **Ústie nad priehradou, Prístavište, Slanická Osada, Námestovo,** and **Slaná Voda**; the last-named used to be a spa with healing springs containing iodine and bromine. Capacity of accommodation: 100 beds. To the "Priehrada" Hotel at Ústie nad priehradou and the "Magura" at Námestovo, modern hotels have been added, namely the "Goral" hotel above Prístavište, and the "Slanica" hotel at Slanická Osada. Above the "Goral" Hotel are numerous tourists chalets.

At the end of the lake a little island with a tiny Baroque church projects from the water, the last reminder of the flooded village of Slanica, the birthplace of Anton Bernolák who first stirred the Slovaks to national consciousness. The view of the mighty, generally snow-capped, peaks of the Babia Gora (5,692 ft), which tower above the lake on the northern side, leaves an unforgettable memory of the majestic beauty of "Lake Orava".

The **Roháče** may be called from a touristic standpoint the western part of the West Tatra, sloping towards the Orava. The main ridge of the West Tatra from Volovec to Salatín and the lateral slopes which run off from Volovec as far as Rákon, form the heart of the Roháče, a vast basin which begins at the Zverovka and the Tatliak hostel. In this relatively small area so much beauty is however combined that for the last 20 or 30 years the Roháče has been the "craze" for Czechoslovak tourists.

In summer hikers can enjoy the wildness of the main ridge whose peaks are without exception over 6,600 ft high, the beautiful ridges and banks and the wooded slopes dropping down into deep valleys. In the valleys we find unspoilt virgin forest and in the hollows many large and small lakes. The beauty of the Roháče is chiefly revealed in the glorious valley bottoms. The torrential streams of the Roháče mountains froth and foam through these narrow valleys, where meadows, clearings and woods lie close together.

Still more impressive is the enchanting beauty of the snow-capped Roháče, especially in spring. At that time we can see whole pilgrimages of skiers trekking through the valleys of the Roháče. Tourists and skiers tend to concentrate round the hotels on the Zverovka and the Tatliak Hostel below the Roháče.

The hostel on the Zverovka (3,389 ft above sea level) is splendidly situated and can comfortably accommodate 100 persons. The Zverovka is an important starting point for whole day tours in the Roháče along marked tourists paths: to Osobitá, Salatín, Pachola and in the Spálená valley. The ascent from here is shorter than from the higher Tatliak Hostel. One great advantage of the hostel is that a road practicable for motor vehicles leads up to it through Kralovany-Podbiel and Zuberec. There is a regular motorbus service from Podbiel railway station to Zuberec, from where the hostel can be reached in 2 hours walk.

The Tatliak Hostel on the Roháče is a simple, but comfortably equipped tourist hostel (4,950 ft above sea level) with

118 beds. The hostel is in the lower part of the huge Roháče hollow, where the Roháče ends in the forest and the terrace-like Smutná valley begins. From here there is a unique view over the Roháče hollow proper with the dominating peak of the Ostrý Roháče. The hostel is the best starting point for shorter or longer tours into the Roháče or up to the saddles and summits. Amongst the favourite excursions are the ascents to the Roháče lakes on to the Roháče and Volovec, to the Smutné saddle, Plačlivô, and up to the Ostrý Roháč, the Tri kopy and the Baníkov. The road to the hostel as far as the fork by the bridge in the Studená valley is the same as to the hostel on the Zverovka. From here the climb to the foot through the Roháče valley takes 1½ to 2 hours.

D. RUŽOMBEROK

Ružomberok lies in the Liptova valley basin at the confluence of the Revuca and the Váh at the foot of the Great Fatra Mountains (1,636 feet above sea level) and is a fast train station on the main Žilina–Košice line. Highways also run through the town from west to east and from north to south.

Ružomberok was founded at the beginning of the 14th century by German immigrants as a miners' settlement and was given its privileges as a mining town in 1339. The extraction of ore and the advantageous position of the town on the road from Pohronie to the Orava helped its development. Archaeological discoveries and a well-preserved fortress mound prove that the near-by Mt. Mních was already inhabited in prehistoric times.

Ružomberok is today an important town with a well developed (preponderantly technical) wood-working industry. The town is known as a tourist centre and the starting point for mountain parties in holiday resorts, spas and quaint little villages, remarkable for the multiplicity of their folklore.

Sights: The Liptova Museum with valuable exhibits documenting the mining of the past and the Montane colonisation of Liptova in the 13th century.

Accommodation: Hotel Kultúrny dom, 32 ul. čsl. armády; tel. 2129 and 2149.

Excursions from Ružomberok

Lubochňa (12 km east). The former climatic health resort has been made into a sanatorium. A narrow gauge railroad runs through the beautiful Lubochňa valley, nearly 20 km long, almost into the heart of the High Fatra Mountains, as far as the hostel on the Borišov (4,290 feet). The Lubochnianka valley is an excellent hunting ground (stag, deer, wild boar, bears).

Likavka Castle (12 km north). Above Likavka in less than an hour we can reach a ruined castle standing on a mighty limestone rock, 4,290 feet up. The castle was destroyed in 1707. Fine view of Ružomberok and the surrounding country.

Choč (5,323 feet, 18 km north) is the highest peak of the Choč Mountains, dominating Liptov and Orava. The ascent on foot takes 2½ hours from Valašská Dubová which can be reached by motorbus.—**Lúčky** (17 km north-east) is a spa below the Choč in magnificent pine-woods. The spring water has a gypsum and argil content and a temperature of 27° C. The spa specialises in the treatment of gynaecological diseases. —**Sliače** (11 km east). A characteristic village known for its popular songs, dances, costumes and embroideries.—**Lipt. Osada—Lipt. Lužná** (17–25 km south). Typical mountain villages at the foot of the Lower Tatra, where the people still wear the Liptov popular costume.

Korytnica (2,805 feet, 22 km south). A grandly situated spa below the Prašivá massif in the Lower Tatra. The spa specialises in the treatment of intestinal and gastric ailments. The modern, comfortable and uniquely situated Sport Hotel at Donovaly (3,333 feet) can be reached from here on foot in 1½ hours. The **Hotel Malina** (5 km south-west), the chief skiing centre

of Ružomberok with excellent terrain and a ski lift.—
Smrkovica (10 km south-west). A beautiful hiking and
skiing centre in the Great Tatra, reached by a cable
railway.

E. LIPTOVSKÝ MIKULÁŠ

The town of **Liptovský Mikuláš** lies in the heart of
the Liptov-Váh valley basin. The ideal position of the
town, surrounded on the north by the West Tatra,
on the south by the Lower Tatra and the famous
Demänová valley grottos, has made Liptovský
Mikuláš the most important tourist centre in Slovakia.
The town lies on the main railway and road network
linking East and West Slovakia.

Liptovský Mikuláš has played an important part in Slovak
history. The town was known as the place where the legendary
bandit Juro Jánošík of Terchová was condemned and executed.

Sights:

The Saint Nicholas (Mikuláš) parish church, one of
the oldest Gothic churches in Slovakia, was built in the
first half of the 13th century. The most precious treasures it contains are three late Gothic altars. One of
them, consecrated to the altar sacrament, is a unique
example in the history of art. In the altar shrine there
are none of the usual figures, but a plastic Gothic
monstrance with the altar sacrament serving as the
main decoration. There is only one such altar besides
this one in Europe.

The Janko Král Museum of Literature. A museum of
the literary past of the whole Liptov region with material relating to over 50 writers who were born here or
worked in Liptov for a long time. The museum is

housed in the so-called Selig House, which has been preserved in its historical form. The Slovakian Karst Museum, at No 2 Hviezdoslavova ulice, gives a general picture of the wealth of the Slovakian stalactite caves and the karst. The Peter Michal Bohúň Picture Gallery in the Tranovská exhibits the works of creative artists.

Accommodation: Hotel Europa, 2 Gottwaldova ul.; tel. 352, 355; Hotel Kriváň, 12 Štefánikova ul.; tel. 354.

Excursions from Liptovský Mikuláš

Palúdzka adjoins Liptovský Mikuláš. A structurally remarkable **wooden church** (1674), the biggest wooden church in Slovakia.—**Parížovce** (7 km west). A Gothic castle. Excursions into the Prosiecka and Kovačianska valleys with their concretions, grottoes and geysers. —**Bešeňová.** Within the boundaries of Bešeňová is the geological reservation known as the "Travertine Field" for the protection of typical travertine or tufaceous limestone formations.—**Okoličné** (5 km east). The 15th-century **Franciscan church** is the finest Gothic building in the Liptov.

Demänovská dolina (the Demänová valley)—Jasná

The Demänová valley stretches southwards from Liptovský Mikuláš well into the heart of the Lower Tatra in the direction of the Chopok and Ďumbier peaks. Its grottoes have made it the most frequently visited valley in the Slovakian mountains. Its picturesque beauty is enhanced by the white trias limestone cliffs which stand out against the dark green of the pines. By the **Jasná** we mean several interconnected valleys and slopes, surrounded by the mountain chain of the Krupova hola along the Dereše and Polana as far as the Sina; tourist hostels, a chair cable railway up the Chopok and a ski lift from Záhradky to the top of the Priehyba. The whole area of the Demänova

valley and the Jasná with its unusual abundance of flora and
fauna is a protected natural park. In the subterranean karst of
the Demänová valley there are a large number of pot-holes,
passages and spacious grottoes. The best-known are the **Dráčia**
(Dragon ice grotto) and the **Slobody** (Liberty) grotto. Near the
caves, in the forest near the road, is a caravan site.

The Dračia cave is one of the first known Central European
caves. It was mentioned as early as 1299 and was scientifically
explored in 1719. The entrance to the grotto is at the last stop
but one on the motorbus route Liptovský Mikuláš—Demänovské
jaskyne (Demänová grottos), 11 km from Lipt. Mikuláš.

The Slobody grotto was discovered in 1921 and made accessible to the public in 1924. Later new vast caves—named the
Peace grottoes (Mieru)—were discovered and also a connection
between the most important grottoes in the whole has been
found. It is now only a question of time before the whole 12 km
long conglomery can be made accessible to the public in its
entirety. Below the entrance into the Peace grotto is the terminus
of the motorbus route from Liptovský Mikulás. The climb up
to the grotto entrance takes 10 minutes.

Mention must also be made of the Okno (window) grotto
with paleolontological finds and the Pustá Cave with an underground chasm 250 ft deep.

The subterranean space of the grottos and their dazzling
beauty were created by the little Demänovka river and its
tributary the Lučianka. Flowing over a limestone bed, they
often disappear underground, meet in the Liberty Grotto,
flow through the nethermost caves and finally the Demänovka
emerges in the form of a geyser. The Liberty Grotto is remarkable
for the splendid colouring of its stalactites. The most beautiful
places in the caves are the many domes, waterfalls, galleries,
lakes, halls and other interesting formations. Peculiar to the
Demänová grottoes, besides the colossal quantity of stalactite
formations, are the completely crystallized calcareous stones,
chiefly the so-called grotto pearls, water roses, little onions,
vases and the like.

The visit of the caves takes 1½ hours.

From the motorbus terminus below the Liberty
Grotto a footpath marked by red signs goes up to
Jasná; the climb up takes 1 to 1½ hours. The highway
is practicable for automobiles as far as the Mikulášská

hostel, for coaches up to the Biela púť saddle. 15
minutes from the saddle there is a symbolic cemetery
on the Ostredok.

Jasná offers ideal conditions for summer and winter
tours and for skiing. The chair cable railway runs up to
the main ridge, to the summit of the Chopok (6,616
feet) and from there on the south side to Srdiečko.

At the entrance of the Liberty Caves at Demänová is a large
tourist hotel. A road which is practicable for cars, crosses the
Demänová valley, via Lúčky and Zahrádky, and leads over the
Biela Puť pass to Jasna where there is a chair-lift station for
Chopok and the Mikulášska chata chalet near Lake Vrbické
pleso which has several hotels and tourist chalets; of the latter,
the loveliest is the Mikulášská chata chalet at an altitude of
3,651 feet. The chair-lift, with a run of 7,218 feet, leaves from
the valley which lies at an altitude of 4,051 feet, and goes up
to the main ridge of the Lower Tatras (the Chopok, 6,578
feet); it then descends by the south side into the Bystra valley
where we come to the "Srdiečko" Hotel. Tourist paths lead
from the Demänová valley to the main ridge (Ďumbier, Polana,
Chopok). The runs down below the Chopok are very popular
with the skiers from November to May.

F. LIPTOVSKÝ HRÁDOK

Liptovský Hrádok (2,102 feet above sea level), a
small town in the Upper Liptov at the confluence of the
little river Belá and the Váh, shut in on all sides by
mountains. Liptovský Hrádok is a fast train station on
the main line Žilina–Košice; also the main highway
runs through the town from west to east.

A partly preserved old **castle** is evidence of the medieval settlement. Until the 19th century ore, extracted in
the surrounding district, in many high-lying valleys of
the Lower Tatra and often on the main ridge at an
altitude of 4,950 feet, was manufactured. Today
Liptovský Hrádok is a forestry and industrial wood-

working centre and a training ground for the young generation of foresters.

Because of its unique situation Liptovský Hrádok is a much frequented and favourite holiday resort and at the same time a starting point for excursions roundabout. In the spring and the summer those who come here are mostly water sportsmen. There is a nice, comfortably equipped boathouse where the Belá flows into the Váh, which is also used as a hikers' shelter. This is the usual place to start the romantic boattrip down the Váh and here are also the best conditions for an ideal water slalom course on the Váh and on the Belá. Many anglers visit these waters. Hikers rove beyond Liptovský Hrádok; into the West Tatra, into the Jamnická, Ráčková, Bystrá and Kamenistá valleys; in the western part of the High Tatra up the Podbanské with the Tichá and Koprová valleys and a possible ascent of the Kriváň; in the eastern part of the Lower Tatra up the mountains Králova hola, Velký Bok, Velká Vápenica and the Čertovica; and also through the Svätojanská valley up the Ďumbier. In winter excellent skiing terrain can be found still nearer the town.

Accommodation: "Loděnice" Hostelry, tel. 68; Hotel Smrek; tel. 20.

Excursions from Liptovský Hrádok

Smrekovica (4,247 feet, south). View-point of the little town Liptovský Hrádok. Red signs mark the way up through Bukovica and Brtkovica; the climb takes 2½ hours. Behind Smrekovica, near Mounts Ohnište and Slemä, beautiful stalactite formations; edelweiss (leontopodium alpinum) even grows here.

The **Ďumbier** (6,748 feet, south) is the highest peak of the Lower Tatra and can be reached through the

Svätojanské valley. The path starts from the Workers' Convalescent Home "Ďumbier" at Liptovský Ján (9 km by motorbus to here); blue signs, 5–6 hours.

In the **West Tatra** (north) through the Kamnická, Ráčková and Bystrá valleys. Motorbuses run from Liptovský Hrádok to Pribylina (10 km). From there marked paths lead into these valleys.

Kriváň (8,236 feet, north-east). By motorbus to Podbanské (22 km). From there the climb to the summit of this majestic peak of the High Tatra takes 4–5 hours.

Východná (17 km east). A village at the foot of the Tatra, in which is united the most natural beauty and active popular creative art.

The wooden and stone little houses are show-pieces of peasant architecture. The domestic utensils used every day are made by local carvers. The older inhabitants still wear popular costume. Above the village an open air amphitheatre, in which every year at the end of July or the beginning of August the biggest Slovak national festival is held. For two days in succession one can see the costumes and dances and hear the songs and music of every region.

Važec (21 km east). Another village at the foot of the Tatra where folkdress is still preserved. On the outskirts of the village an interesting stalactite cave. A new hostelry has been built.

The **valley of the Black Váh** (6 km east). Parallel to the main ridge of the Lower Tatra a beautiful valley stretches for 35 km from Králova Lehota; through it runs a narrow gauge railway from Liptovský Hrádok. The valley is an excellent place for shooting and fishing in the wonderful surroundings of vast woods and is much frequented by foreign visitors.

Králova hola (6,412 feet, east). A unique view-point in the Lower Tatra. One can get there by forest railway

from Liptovský Hrádok as far as Liptovská Teplička;
from there the climb, following the green-marked path,
takes 4 hours.

Čertovica, the pass over the Lower Tatras range,
(4,085 feet, 25 km south). A much frequented and favourite starting point for walks. Excursions and tours
into the lovely surroundings of the east and west parts
of the main ridge of the Lower Tatra. Coming from
the north through the picturesquely situated, ancient
village of **Boca** (gold was extracted here as early as the
11th century), which straggles on either side of a stream
in a relatively narrow valley below the slopes of the
Rovná holá and the Fišiarka, up to the Čertovica.
Here and at **Vyšná Boca** are several tourist hostels.
The best equipped are the Sport Hotel below the
Čertovica (3,676 feet) and the hostel above the Čertovica (4,125 feet), both directly on the highway which
crosses the main chain of the Lower Tatra to the
Čertovica pass.

In summer, there are interesting tourist excursions to the
ridge of the range. Going west, we come to the **Ďumbier** and the
Chopok (red markings, 3½ hours and 5 hours respectively);
going east, we come to Homolka and Velký Bok (5,669 feet,
red markings, 5 to 6 hours' walking). In winter, there are excellent skiing grounds below the Čertovica pass. There is a ski-lift
below the pass, and another near the "Sport Hotel".

17. THE HIGH TATRA MOUNTAINS

The main chain of the Tatra broken by numerous ridges rises steeply to a hight of 8,580 feet. Granite walls which have undergone glacial erosion frame the massif. Slopes and summits have literally been carved by erosion. In the deep valleys, terraces (often with lakes), alternate with ravines. Glacial and post-glacial periods account for the various geological phases. The irregular valleys are connected by powerful cascades.

On fine days, the range offers a stupendous view from the Kriván, Solisko, Slavkov or Baranie peaks. Tourists will be enchanted by the wide, poetic Mengušovská Valley and the Batizovská's charm. The Velká Studena Dolina (Great Cold Valley) is also very much visited. Its lakes are a pleasant aim for excursions.

This sector is under National Trust protection and is known as the Tatra National Park (TANAP). Purposeful interest is taken to preserve the character and aspect of this whole region and its plant and animal life. We find in the Tatra 600 chamois, roughly 600 marmots, bears, lynxes, etc.

Accommodation can be found in the many recreation homes run by the Czechoslovak Trades Unions, in hotels, tourist hostels, inns and also in camping sites reserved for this special purpose. The number of climatic health resorts and clinics is also growing steadily.

A caravan site also constitutes an excellent starting point for excursions in the High Tatra range.

The history of the country as a summer holiday and climatic health resort is comparatively recent. Soon after the Middle Ages mining and smelting flourished here, in the 16th and 17th centuries came hunters and shepherds, in the 18th tourists and scientific explorers arrived and in the second half of the 19th the greater part of the settlements were established. Now the most important places in the Tatra are linked by a fine highway, the "Freedom Road", running for 56 km from the Štrba mountain lake to the Lysá Polona. The western and central part between the Lake Štrba (Štrbské pleso) and Tatranská Lomnica is also connected by an electric railway 24 km long.

Communications. The main Košice—Žilina railway line has connections with the High Tatra. Liptovský Hrádok is the station for the Podbanské and the Kriváň; Štrba for Lake Štrba (12 km by motor bus); Poprad in the Tatra for Starý Smokovec (12 km) and Lake Štrba (30 km); and one can travel by electric train as far as Tatranská Lomnica (17 km). The distance from Prague to Poprad is 607 km, from Bratislava 339 km. Fast trains with through coaches and sleepers run from both cities to Poprad. There are also direct air services from Prague and Bratislava to the Poprad-Tatry air-field. The main highways from north, central and east Slovakia also run through Poprad.

The chief tourist centres are: Štrbské Pleso, Starý Smokovec, Tatranská Lomnica, Tatranská Kotlina, Ždiar and Javorina.

Štrbské Pleso

Štrbské Pleso (4,455 feet) lies on the lake of the same name (41 acres). From the lake one enjoys a fascinating view of the peaks of the north-west of the range. In the glorious scenery the most impressive is the **Vysoká** massif. There are well equipped hotels on the lake, the **Hviezdoloslav** and the **Kriváň** (now a sanatorium); also a trades union convalescent home and tourist hostels.

The tour up the Podbanské (the west gate to the High Tatra) by the main path via the "Tri Studnicky" (Three Springs) game-keeper's house in 3 hours; to the most celebrated peak in the Tatra—the **Kriváň** (8,236 feet), the goal of national pilgrimages, in 4–5 hours; to the view-point **Patria** (7,276 feet) in 2–2½ hours. To **Lake Poprad** (4,993 feet, tourist hostel) on the main path in 1½ hours; up the **Rysy** (8,260 feet) with one of the grandest panoramas of the High Tatra in 4–5 hours (below the Rysy, at an altitude of 7,543 feet, a tourist hostel); and up the Ostrva (6,547 feet) by way of Lake Poprad in 2½ hours. Most popular of all are the walk round **Lake Štrba**; the excursion to **Lake Poprad** in 1 to 1½ hours and the visit to the **Symbolic Cemetery** on the Ostrava.

Lake Štrba is also much frequented in winter. A ski lift (sleigh) runs up the **Solisko** to a height of 6,570 feet. There is a large ski-jump at the beginning of the Mlynica valley.

At **Vyšné Hágy**, east of Štrbské Pleso, is a sanatorium for consumptives. There are also sanatoria at **Tatranská Polianka**.

Starý Smokovec

Starý Smokovec (3,276 feet) below the Slavkov peak is the political, economic and cultural centre of the region. It is the oldest settlement in this part of Slovakia, now forming a whole with the neighbouring Nový, Horný and Dolný Smokovec. In all parts of Smokovec are hotels, inns, sanatoria and T.U. convalescent homes. The Grand Hotel (tel. Starý Smokovec 301–303) is a luxury hotel with restaurant.

Up the **Hrebienok** (4,224 feet) by the cog-wheel railway (2 km) in 11 minutes or on foot in ½ hour. Tourist paths lead in all directions from Hrebienok.

To the **Sliezsky dom** hostel (5,834 feet) in the Velická valley below the Gerlach massif 2 hours; the Slavkov peak can be climbed in 3 to 3½ hours; to the Studeno-vodské waterfalls "Dlhý", "Velký" and "Obrovský" (the "Long", the "Great" and the "Giant") in 15 to 30 minutes: to the **Zbojnická hostel** ("Brigands' Hut", 6,461 feet) in the Velká Studená Dolina, 3 hours: to the **Téry Hostel** (652 feet) on the upper terrace of the Malá Studená Dolina 3 hours and up to the **Skalnaté**

Pleso (Stone Lake, 4,681 feet) 2 hours. There are also T.U. convalescent homes in the surroundings, the Bílik hostel (4,174 feet, 3 mins.), the Kamzik hostel (4,299 feet, 15–20 mins.) and the Kapitan Nálepka hostel (5,148 feet, 1 hour).

From Hrebienok one can also undertake more difficult tours from the south to the north side of the mountains, from the southern valleys to the northern over high passes. From the Velicka valley we can cross the Polish ridge and from the Velká Studená Dolina the Prielom to the Bielovodská and Javorina valleys; and from the Malá Studená Dolina over the Sedielko into the Javorová and Javorina depression. These tours take 8 to 12 hours.

The Zbojnická and Téry hostels offer further opportunities for mountain climbing, rambles over the saddles and ridges in which there are no paths.

Starý Smokovec is also well equipped for winter sports. A ski-lift operates from Hrebienok via Horná lúka up to the Maximilanka. At Smokovec there is a toboggan run illuminated at night, a ski descent and two small sleighs in the practice fields; the championship ski-jump at Tatranská Polianka.

Tatranská Lomnica

Tatranská Lomnica (2,970 feet) is uniquely situated. Hotels, notably the Grand Hotel, convalescent homes and villas in the middle of an enormous natural park, above which rise the Skalnaté Pleso (5,740 feet) and the Lomnica peak. Lomnica is the starting point for tours in the eastern part of the High Tatra and in the neighbouring Belá Belanské Tatra.

Accommodation: Grand Hotel Praha, tel. 9 63 01. From the Grand Hotel Praha (3,065 feet) an aerial cableway takes one in 12 minutes to the Skalnaté Pleso (4 km) and from there in another 11 minutes to the top of the Lomnica peak (2 km); altitude 8,615 feet.

To the **Skalnaté Pleso** (5,256 feet), an interesting mountain lake. In the place of the same name are an observatory in the building of the Enzian Hotel cableway and two minutes from the station the Skalnatá chata (Stone Hut).—The climb over the Lomnica saddle up the **Lomnický peak**, the second highest mountain in the High Tatra, where there is an observatory, takes 3 hours (11 minutes by the cableway); to the view-point **Velká Svišťovka** (6,732 feet) to 1½ hours to the **Brnčalova chata** near the Zelené Pleso (Green Lake, 5,118 feet) 2½ hours and into the valley of the Biela voda (White Water) to the **Kežmarska hostel,** 3 hours.

To Studenovodské vodopády (waterfall) from Tatranská Lomnica through a dense wood in 2 hours; through Matliare or Biela Voda into the Biela Voda Kežmarská valley or straight to the Brnčal hostel near the Brnčal hostel near the Zelené Pleso 3 hours, or to the Kežmarská hostel 3½ hours.

Both hostels are starting points for further tours. From the Brnčalova chata one can wander into the Great and Little Zmrzlá dolina (frozen valley) where skiing is possible even in summer, to the Jastrabia veža (tower) and to the Baranie rohy (Ram's horns); from the Kežmarská hostel, on the other hand, to the Kopské sedlo (saddle), into the Belanské Tatra and to Ždiar and Javorina beyond the saddle.

The best skiing terrain for downhill tactics is on the Skalnaté Pleso. A chair lift goes up to the Lomnica saddle (7,237 ft). The international downhill championships are run from the Skalnaté Pleso to the half-way station of the cableway "Start" and on again down to Tatranská Lomnica. There is also a bobsleigh run and a ski-jump.

Belanské Tatry

The "Freedom Road" runs from Tatranská Lomnica to Tatranská Kotlina, Ždiar, Javorina and on to the Lysá Polana on the Czechoslovak–Polish frontier (see Nagel's POLAND). There is a motorbus service between these places and the chief settlements.

Tatranská Kotlina (2,481 feet) is the starting point for excursions and tours in the Belanské Tatry. To walk along the ridge as far as the Kopské saddle takes 6 hours. Twenty minutes from the motorbus stop are Belá stalactite caves (2,749 feet). There is a TB sanatorium.

Ždiar (2,600 to 2,900 feet) is in contrast to other places, which are holiday and health resorts, a peasant village where cattle are bred. It straggles in bigger and smaller groups of houses for 7 km along the Freedom Road on the slopes of the Spišská Magura. Ždiar is known for its folk costumes, which can be seen on Sundays and holidays, at various festivities and family celebrations. The houses of Ždiar are also remarkable: forts with enclosed yards, round which the farm buildings are built. There is only one entrance to the whole. A small exhibition of the local costumes, embroideries and other applied art products can be seen at Ždiar.

There are two chalet-hotels, **Ždiaranka** and **Protežka,** and a rest home. A mule-track leads to the ridge of the Belanské Tatra and the Široké pass (6,010 feet).

Javorina (3,359 feet), the northernmost place in the Tatra, lies in the lovely region of the north-east spurs of the Belanské Tatry. Javorina is a starting point for rambles in the valleys, the Bielovodská, Javorová and Svišťová, from where one can cross the mountains into the southern valleys.

The most important marked tourist passes

Through the Javorová valley over the Kopské saddle to Tatranská Lomnica: 6–7 hours.

Through the Javorová valley over the Sedielko (7,854 ft) to the Téry hostel in the Malá Studená Dolina (the little Cold Valley) and to Starý Smokovec: 8–10 hours.

Through the Bielovodská over the Prielom (7,557 ft) to the Zbojnická hostel in the Velká Studená Dolina (the Great Cold Valley) and to Starý Smokovec: 10–12 hours.

Through the Bielovodská valley over the Polish ridge (7,656 ft) to the Sliezky dom in the Veliká Dolina to Starý Smokovec: 10–12 hours. 1 km beyond Javorina on the way to the Lysá Polana and the Bielovodská valley is a period hunting lodge.

Practical
Information

CZECHOSLOVAKIA

TOURIST INFORMATION

All tourist information on Czechoslovakia is supplied by the Čedok agency which is both a Tourist Association and a travel agency.

In Czechoslovakia

Čedok–Praha: Na Příkopě 18, Praha 1, tel. 22 42 51.
Čedok–Brno: Divadelní 3, tel. 347 00.
Čedok–Bratislava: Štúrova 9/b, tel. 521 42.

Accommodation:
Čedok Accommodation office: Panská 5, Praha 1, tel. 22 70 04.

Tours of Prague:
Čedok, Na Příkopě 18, Prague 1, tel. 22 42 55.
Information from the hotel reception office.

Information:
Visas, air tickets, local and international rail tickets, sleepers, tickets for cultural events, sports and fashionable events, round trips, hotel accommodation, exchange, interpreters and guides, chauffeur-driven or self-drive car hire, cures in spas, hunting and fishing, stays in the mountains and in Czechoslovak beauty spots.

Abroad

Čedok–London (W1): 45 Oxford Street, tel. REGent 00 41.
Čedok–Paris (1er): 32, avenue de l'Opéra, tel. RIC 38-45.
Čedok–Bruxelles: 60, boul. de l'Impératrice, tel. 11 34 12.
Čedok–Wien (I): Parkring 12.
Čedok–Bern: Muristrasse 53, tel. 43 64 57.
Čedok–Kopenhagen: Vester Farimagsgade 6, tel. BYN 121.

I. TOURIST CENTRES

There are several ways in which you can visit Czechoslovakia: you can join an organized tour, or come in your own car, by air or by train and stay in a centre from which you tour the region.

Prague is an excellent tourist centre, with comfortable hotels, and is easily accessible from all parts of Europe. There is also Brno in Moravia and Bratislava in Slovakia. Tourists who come for a rest will find a whole range of summer resorts and high-altitude health resorts; while skiers will find an abundance of well-equipped winter sports resorts.

Watering Places

Countless medicinal springs are scattered all over Czechoslovakia. Round many of them world-famous spas have grown up. The best-known spa is Karlovy Vary (Karlsbad) which celebrated its sixth centenary in 1958. The other spas have also an old tradition and many illustrious names can be found in the list of those who have taken the cure here. Most spas are open all the year round. Visitors are advised to take advantage of the reduced cure tax during the off season. All formalities in connection with a stay at a spa are dealt with by the Czechoslovak Travel Agency Čedok, 18 Na příkopě, Praha I, or by **Balnea**, Staré Město, Pařížka 11, tel. 646 77. Information on Czechoslovak spas, Václavské nám. 55, Praha I, tel. 23 41 64.

The chief Czechoslovak spas and their particulars:

Karlovy Vary (Karlsbad)—District Karlsbad. The spa lies in the valley of the river Teplá, on the northern edge of the so-called "Imperial Forest" in West Bohemia. Connections: by rail: Praha—Chomutov—Karlovy Vary (187 km)—Cheb. Highway: Praha—Karlovy Vary (125 km). By air: Praha—Karlovy Vary (summer flight plan). Accommodation: Grand Hotel Čedok, Moskva (formerly Pupp), the largest spa hotel in Czechoslovakia and the Čedok Hotels Central, Horník, Atlantic, Sevastopol.

Treatment for: chronic liver and bilious complaints, disorders of the urinary ducts, metabolic and gastric ailments, gastric ulcers, internal and allergic skin diseases.

Mariánské Lázně (Marienbad)—District Karlovy Vary. In West Bohemia, 2,072 ft above sea level. Connections: by rail: Praha—Plzeň—Cheb (189 km from Praha). By road: Praha–Plzeň–Cheb (166 km). Accommodation: Hotel Čedok Palace, Parkhotel Čedok Esplanade and pensions belonging to the Spa Administration.

Treatments for: Ailments of the urinary ducts, metabolism, digestive organs, gout, gall-stones, nervous disorders, ailments of the respiratory organs, skin diseases.

Piešťany—District Bratislava. This spa is situated in South Slovakia on the bank of the river Váh, 534 ft above sea level. Connections: fast trains Bratislava—Žilina (through sleeping-car from Praha). By road: Bratislava—Žilina. Accommodation:

Thermia Palace and other pensions belonging to the Spa Administration.

Treatment for: rheumatic and gouty arthritis, recovery after accidents, neuralgia, myalgia, rehabilitation.

Františkovy Lázně (Franzensbad)—District Karlovy Vary. Franzensbad lies in West Bohemia and is sheltered to the north by mountains, 1,485 ft above sea level. Connections: fast trains Praha—Plzeň—Cheb (227 km). By road: Praha—Karlovy Vary—Františkovy Lázně. Accommodation: Hotel Slovan, Hotel Pavlík and other pensions belonging to the Spa Administration.

Treatment for: Gynaecological illnesses, rheumatic arthritis, gouty arthritis, care after accidents.

Luhačovice—District Gottwaldov. This spa is in South Moravia, on the river Ostrava, 1,037 ft above sea level. Connections: by rail: terminus of the local line Újezdec u Luhačovice. Újezdec is a fast-train stop on the line Praha—Brno—Vlára (387 km). By road: Uherské Hradiště—Luhačovice. Accommodation: Hotel Čedok Alexandria and pensions belonging to the Spa Administration.

Treatment for: catarrh of the upper respiratory passages, bronchial asthma, bronchitis, care after operations of the respiratory organs.

Teplice Lázně v Čechách (Bad Teplice in Bohemia)—District Ústí nad Labem. The spa is in North Bohemia in the valley of the Bělá river at the foot of the Krušné Hory (Ore Mts.), 752 ft above sea level. Connections: Fast trains Praha—Ústí n.L.—Chomutov (126 km). By road: Praha—Louny—Teplice Lázně (92 km). Accommodation: Hotels Thermia and De Saxe.

Treatment for: rheumatic arthritis, gouty arthritis, care after accidents, arteriosclerosis, morbus Buerger.

Poděbrady—District Praha. Poděbrady lies in the Elbe depression, 53 km east of Praha, 617 ft. above sea level. Connections: Fast trains Praha—Hradec Králové (55 km). By road: Praha—Hradec Králové. Accommodation: Hotel Tlapák and pensions belonging to the Spa Administration.

Treatment for: heart and arterial ailments.

Jeseník (Gräfenberg)—District Olomouc. The spa lies above the small town of Jeseník. The founder of the spa was the famous nature cure practitioner V. Priessnitz. Connections: fast trains Praha—Hanušovice—Hlucholazy—Opava—Bohumín (262 km). By road: Praha—Svitavy—Jeseník—Ostrava.

Treatment for: nervous disorders, allergic illnesses, chronic bronchitis.

Sliač—District Banská Bystrica. Sliač is in Slovakia, on the bank of the river Hron, 1,211 ft above sea level. Connections: Fast trains Banská Bystrica—Zvolen (motorbus connection to Sliač), twice daily through fast trains Praha— Sliač (579 km) with sleeping-car to Banská Bystrica. By road: Branch road off the highway Banská Bystrica—Bratislava. By air: Praha—Bratislava—Sliač. Accommodation: Spa Administration pensions.

Treatment for: heart complaints and care after heart operations.

Štrbské Pleso—District Vysoké Tatry. The spa is in the west part of the High Tatra, on the south slope of the Tatra Mts., on the shore of the lake of the same name, 4,458 ft above sea level. Connections: fast trains Praha—Košice. Motorbus connection from Štrba or by narrow gauge railway from Poprad. By road: Štrba—Tatranská Lomnica (589 km from Praha). Accommodation: Grand Hotel Hviezdoslav, Hotel Kriváň.

Treatment for: bronchial asthma, radium or X-ray poisoning symptoms, chronic poisoning from industrial poisons.

Trenčianske Teplice—District Žilina. The spa lies in the valley of the Teplička river in Slovakia. The valley is sheltered by high, wooded hills, rising from 2,000 to 3,000 ft. Connections: Fast trains to Trenčianske Teplice on the Bratislava-Èilina line, from there by motor-train to the spa. By road: Branch road off the Bratislava-Žilina highway. Accommodation: Spa Administration pensions.

Treatment for: chronic rheumatic fever, care after accidents, ailments of the upper respiratory system, metal poisoning.

II. SUGGESTED ITINERARIES

The choice of an itinerary depends, above all, on the amount of time available. You cannot hope to get to know Czechoslovakia in less than two weeks. The ideal way to see the country is to divide your journey into several parts by returning several years running and seeing each region: one year, Prague and Bohemia, then Moravia and West Slovakia, and finally the Tatras and Central and East Slovakia.

The best solution is to have your own car. Czechoslovak roads need not worry drivers: they are mostly excellent, and the road network is constantly being improved.

A. Trips into Bohemia: 7 days

From the German Federal Republic or Austria (or through both countries), you can make a short trip to Czechoslovakia, getting to know Prague (or perhaps Brno) and the main regions in the west of the country. Below is a suggestion for an itinerary:

Enter Czechoslovakia by Pomezi-Cheb; visit Karlovy Vary, Mariánské Lázně, Plzeň, Prague (three days in Prague), the northern and north-eastern outskirts of Prague (one day), České Budějovice, Lipno, Domažlice; leave by Rozvadov.

Alternative from České Budějovice: leave by Dolní Dvořiště, to Linz (Austria).

B. Bohemia-Moravia and West Slovakia: 12 days

As under A as far as Prague. Then, Liberec, Janské Lázné, Hradec Králové, Brno (two days, with the surroundings), Gottwaldov, Luhačovice, Trenčín, Piešťany, Nitra, Bratislava (two days). Leave in the direction of Vienna.

C. Tour of Czechoslovakia: 21 days

As under B as far as Gottwaldov. Then Ostrava, Žilina, Poprad, Prešov, Košice, Brezno, Banská-Bystrica, Trenčín, Piešťany, Nitra, Komárno, Bratislava (it is possible to go on to Vienna). Then Břeclav, Znojmo, Telč, České Budějovice, Lipno (from here it is possible to go on to Linz), Domažlice, leave by Rozvadov.

Travellers who have no car will find a whole range of organized luxury-coach tours arranged by Čedok. Below is a list of the principal tours:

1. One-day excursion through the surroundings of Prague

Prague – Karlštejn Castle – Jíloviště (lunch at the Hubertus Hotel) – Štěchovice dam – Konopiště hunting lodge.

Departure: every Tuesday, Thursday and Saturday at 9 a.m. from the Čedok Office in Prague.

2. One-day excursion through the surroundings of Prague

Prague – Lidice – Křivoklát Castle – ruins of the castles of Točnik and Žebrák – Beroun.

Departure: Every Wednesday, Friday and Sunday at 9 a.m. from the Čedok Office in Prague.

3. Three-day excursion to the north of Prague

Visit to buildings and monuments of cultural value, to the national cemetery at Terezín, the Železný Brod school of glassware, Poděbrady Spa, short stay at the Pec pod Sněžkou sports centre in the country of the Giant Mountains, and visit to other places of interest.

Departure: every Tuesday at 9 a.m. from the Čedok Office in Prague.

4. To the Spas and on the trail of folk traditions

Visit to the Domažlice region, the most interesting region of Bohemia for folk traditions, and visit to the three world renowned spas in West Bohemia (Mariánské Lázně, Františkovy Lázně and Karlovy Vary).

5. Bohemia and Moravia: 7 days

Visit to cultural and industrial centres, to the most popular tourist regions of Bohemia and Moravia (The Bohemian Paradise, historic places under National Trust in South Bohemia, Brno, Olomouc, Telč, Ostrava, Gottwaldov, etc).

Departure: every Thursday at 9 a.m. from the Čedok Office in Prague.

6. Through Czechoslovakia: 12 days

Visit to the most interesting tourist regions of Czechoslovakia, with coach trips round the cultural and industrial centres (Karlštejn, Lidice, Karlovy Vary, Mariánské Lázně, Plzeň, Český Krumlov, Hluboká, Telč, Brno, Gottwaldov, High Tatra, Piešťany, Bratislava, etc).

Departure: every Monday at 9 a.m. from the Čedok Office in Prague.

Even if you come to Czechoslovakia by air or rail, you can get to know the beauties of the country: the Čedok Travel Agency offers a whole range of modern **self-drive cars** which you can rent at the following charges (subject to change):

Make of car	Daily rates 1—7 days	Weekly rates (from 8 days)	Charge per km
Škoda "Octavia" ..... (4 places)	4,5 dollars	30 dollars	0,05 dollar
Škoda "Felicia" ...... (2/4 places)	3,5 dollars	23 ,,	0.06 ,,
Volga "Pobieda" ..... (5 places)	5 dollars	31.5 ,,	0.065 ,,
Moskvitch .... (5 places)	4 dollars	30 ,,	0.065 ,,

A deposit of 100 dollars must be made on taking possession of the car; this will be fully reimbursed when the rented car is returned.

For all cars, of whatever make, a basic charge of 3 dollars is payable in addition to the rates given above.

Czechoslovak Automobile Club: Prague I, Opletalova Street, tel. 22 35 44.

III. PASSPORTS AND CUSTOMS REGULATIONS

Visas

Every tourist must have a valid passport.

Czechoslovak visas can be obtained from Čedok-accredited travel agents; a list of the latter is supplied by Čedok on demand.

It takes 2 days for the visa to come through (2 photos required). Price: 20 shillings.

The issuing of the visa is no longer subject to the purchase of hotel vouchers payable to the travel agency before departure, with full board and lodging.

On arrival in Czechoslovakia these vouchers are exchanged for Czechoslovak crowns with which the tourist settles the charges for his stay. The rate of exchange is about twice as favourable to the tourist as the official rate. Purchase of hotel vouchers is not compulsory.

The Czechoslovak crowns received in exchange for hotel vouchers must be spent in Czechoslovakia. They cannot be changed into any other currency.

If a foreign visitor wishes to prolong his stay in Czechoslovakia after his arrival there, he may purchase hotel vouchers for the number of days he wishes to stay on in Czechoslovakia at a Čedok hotel or agency. Transit visas are valid for only a very short stay.

If a traveller wishes to stay in Czechoslovakia for a while, he must ask the Czechoslovak consular authorities abroad expressly for a transit visa with validity for a stay in the country. This visa may be granted if the tourist purchases at least two days' hotel vouchers. The country must be entered by the frontier post indicated on the visa, and on leaving the country tourists must again leave by the frontier post stated on their visa. If a visitor decides to leave by a different frontier post, he must obtain permission to that effect during his stay in Czechoslovakia.

Prolongation of your stay: Bartolomějská 14, Prague.

Customs Regulations

There is a customs check on entering and on leaving Czechoslovak territory. It is done quickly and courteously.

The following may be imported duty-free: personal effects, a camera and reasonable amount of film, a pair of binoculars, a portable typewriter, a portable radio, a musical instrument. Tourists must, however, declare these objects on a form which they are given on entering and which they must keep carefully and return on leaving. 250 cigarettes, 2 litres of wine, 1 litre of liquor, and some food for the journey may also be imported duty-free.

On leaving, foreign travellers may export freely: souvenirs and objects bought in Czechoslovakia, to a total value not exceeding 200 crowns. But they must be careful to keep all bills of their purchases and all certificates of currency exchange. See p. 422.

Motor vehicles may be imported freely. For further details, see under the heading "Motoring".

IV. CURRENCY AND EXCHANGE

In Czechoslovakia there are metal coins of 1, 3, 5, 10, 25, and 50 hellers and of 1 crown, and bank notes to the value of 3, 5, 10, 25, 50 and 100 crowns. (kčs)

Unlimited amounts of any foreign currency may be imported into Czechoslovakia. Visitors must declare the amount of foreign currency carried, and this will be entered on the customs declaration form. Import and export of Czechoslovak currency are forbidden. Foreign currency may be change without any limitation as to amount, in all branches of the Czechoslovak State Bank **(Státni Banka Československá)**, at the Čedok exchange offices and at some hotels and some customs offices. When changing foreign currency visitors receive a special bonus in addition to the official rate of exchange of the State Bank. This means, in practice, that foreign visitors receive a tourist rate about double that of the official rate of exchange; foreign letters of credit or cheques are changed so that tourists receive double their nominal value.

Travellers Cheques of the Czechoslovak State Bank may be exchanged against cash as soon as the frontier is crossed. As it is forbidden to import Czechoslovak currency, Travellers Cheques are a very convenient means of payment. They are established for sums of 25, 100, 200 and 500 crowns. When crossing the Czechoslovak frontier, travellers have these cheques certified by a "Certificate for persons resident abroad concerning the import of foreign currency into Czechoslovakia". Travellers cheques can be exchanged at the **Státní banka Československá** and its branches, in **Čedok** exchange bureaux and at some big hotels.

The rates of exchange are subject to fluctuation, and it is advisable to enquire before leaving at a bank or travel agency. To give an idea, the "tourist" rate of exchange is as follows: 100 crowns = about 6.15 U.S. dollars; £2.4; 27.0 Swiss francs; 34.50 French francs; 311 Belgian francs; 3,900 Italian lire.

V. MOTORING

Customs posts

Cars may cross the frontier at only a few post listed below.

German Federal Republic: Schirnding—Pomezí (Cheb); Waid-haus—Rozvadov.

Austria: Berg—Bratislava; Gmünd—České Velenice; Wullo-witz—Dolnî Dvořiště; Klein Haugsdorf—Hautě u Znojma; Drasenhofen—Mikulov; Horni Dvořiště—Wullowitz.

U.S.S.R.: Užgorod—Vyšné Nemecké.

German Democratic Republic: Schmilka—Hřensko (Děčín); Radiumbad Brambach—Vojtanov; Altenberg—Cínovec.

Poland: Chaloupky—Bohumín; Cieszyn—Český Těšín; Lysa Polana—Javorina; Kudowa—Běloves—Náchod.

Hungary: Rajka—Bratislava—Rusovce; Komárom—Komárno; Hidas Németi—Milhošt; Balassagyarmat—Slovenské Dar-moty; Sátoraljaujhely—Slovenské Nové Mesto.

Customs documents

The Czechoslovak authorities allow the temporary import of a vehicle withou1 a **carnet** or a triptych.

Car insurance is compulsory, even for foreign cars. The "green card" is recognized as long as it expressly lists the Czechoslovak Republic. If you do not possess the necessary insurance, you must contract one at the frontier for 14 or 45 days respectively.

This covers third party risks on Czechoslovak territory. The owner of the vehicle must report any accident in which a third party is injured or where another's property is damaged, to the State Insurance Company in the nearest chief town or directly to the Insurance Company (Praha 2, Spálená 14, tel. 22 48 83) which will take the matter in hand.

Highway Code

Although the Czechoslovak highway code is much the same as that of all major European countries, it might be useful to indicate some of its special features and principles. It is also useful to get to know the road signs.

In the open country, there is practically no speed limit for motorbicycles and cars. But the speed must be adjusted to traffic conditions, the state of the vehicle and of the road so that the driver at all times has full control of his vehicle. Other vehicles may go up to a speed of 60 km/h in the open country. In localities, motorbicycles and passenger cars may not exceed 50 km/h, other vehicles, 40 km/h. Exceptions to this rule are shown on road signs.

Keep to your right! In Czechoslovakia, overtaking is allowed only on the left.

At crossings of roads of the same class, vehicles on rails (trams) have priority over motor vehicles, and motor vehicles over others. If two vehicles of the same category arrive simultaneously at a crossroads, the one coming from the right has priority. At a crossing where there is not enough room in the middle for vehicles, drivers turning left must first veer as much as possible to the left half of his side of the road, i.e. towards the middle. He may only turn directly left if he does not obstruct vehicles coming from the opposite side. Generally, a car making a turn should stop in the middle of the crossing so as not to obstruct the flow of traffic and then wait till the road is clear. In the middle of a crossing, drivers must stop at a distance of not less than 1 m (3 feet) from the rails of the line on his side of the road. Generally, a left-hand turn should be executed by driving round the centre of the crossing on the right. Of course, there is no right-hand priority where a policeman or traffic light is directing the traffic.

Overtaking trams (or vehicles on rails) requires special care. It is generally forbidden to overtake them at stops where there is no pedestrian refuge. Where there is one, vehicles may pass at a moderate speed. If there is no tram at the stop, refuges may be passed on the left or the right. But it is forbidden to pass when another vehicle is passing them at the other side. Overtaking trams on the left is also forbidden. Generally speaking, all overtaking is forbidden at blind corners, at the approach of a hill top, on a level crossing, in a tunnel, or near such places, at a crossing or when another vehicle is overtaking. Where a road sign forbids overtaking, this applies also to three-wheeled vehicles.

Priority goes to vehicles on a main road; the driver coming from a secondary road must wait. If a crossing is preceded by the sign: "Yield Priority" (equivalent of "Major Road Ahead") or "Stop. Yield Priority" (equivalent of "Halt"), the driver must wait for all categories of vehicles approaching from the major road. Where the "Stop" sign is placed along a road, drivers must halt before the crossing, at a spot from which they have a clear view of the other road. Priority of passage goes to vehicles of the fire brigade, ambulances, mines and armed forces. When a driver hears their alarm signal, he must facilitate their passing by drawing to the side of the road and stopping.

If trams or other vehicles on rails directly cut across other vehicles at a right-hand turn, they have priority if they signal the right-hand turn in advance. They have no such priority at left-hand turns.

There are also rules for stopping at a **filling station**. A car may stop at a distance of no less than 3 m (9 feet) from a car at a petrol pump, and other cars behind that one must keep a distance of 1 m (3 feet). The engine must be switched off during filling. No smoking, engine repair, or holding an open flame within 20 yards of a petrol pump.

Road signs in Czechoslovakia are either placed on posts or directly on the road. Of those directly on the road, an unbroken line along the road indicates that drivers must not cross that line; a broken line may be crossed in accordance with the general rules of the highway code; an unbroken line at the side of the road indicates that stopping is forbidden. A horizontal line across the road shows where cars must stop at a halt road, traffic signs, etc. Horizontal broken lines across the road indicate pedestrian crossings. Arrows show the obligatory direction and the position cars should take up at a crossroads.

Vertical road signs fall into three distinct groups, each with its special shape. The first group comprises danger signs, placed on a white triangle with a red border. The best known are: "Left (right) bend", "Crossroads", "Guarded level-crossing" with a small barrier, "Unguarded level-crossing" with a train engine, "Dangerous hill" giving the gradient, "Road narrows" with two lines drawing closer, "Road works", "Danger of skidding", "Pedestrian crossing", "Children crossing", "Other dangers" indicated by a thick black vertical line in a red triangle, and finally a blank triangle with red borders, placed on its point, which means "Major Road Ahead". The second group comprises absolute prescriptions or interdictions. They are shown on a disc with a red circle round them. A white disc means "All traffic forbidden". A white line through a red disc means "No entry—one-way street". "Overtaking forbidden" is shown by two vehicles side by side, a black figure in a red circle shows the speed limit, a red triangle on its point with the letters STP, the whole in a red circle, means "Halt"; "Clo-Zoll" in a red circle means, "Stop for the customs post ahead". A blue sign crossed with a red stroke means "No horn". A disc crossed with a thick black stroke means "End of interdiction". The third group comprises simple indications. These signs are shown on blue rectangles. A white P means "parking", and H, "hospital", etc.

Traffic lights are red, amber and green, as elsewhere. An intermittent amber light indicates a spot where specially careful driving is necessary. Traffic policemen bend their raised arm to indicate "Accelerate", move their forearm up and down to say "Slow". A raised arm means the same as the amber light. Pedestrians, too, must respect the signals of the traffic police. When turning right, drivers must watch for pedestrians crossing on that side.

Beware of drinking! This warning applies to drivers of motor vehicles, for the drinking of any spirits whatever before driving is forbidden in Czechoslovakia. Disregard of this law may lead to imprisonment in case of an accident. "Spirits" in this context, means all spirits, wine, and beer. Drivers must give way to faster vehicles, and must make as little noise as possible when passing through localities.

Motor Fuels. As in other European countries, three kinds of motor fuel can be bought in Czechoslovakia. "Normal" petrol (80 octanes) at 2.10 Kčs. the litre (1 litre = 0.2 gallons), or Special petrol (90 octanes) at 2.40 Kčs. a litre and "super" at 3 Kčs. Special petrol is obtainable in all fair-sized towns. All brands of high quality oils are available at petrol stations and garages. At every service station you can have an oil change, as also at most pumping stations.

Foreign visitors can obtain petrol at reduced rates by means of "Tuzex vouchers". Foreigners can buy petrol with Tuzex vouchers at all pumping stations with "Special" petrol. These will be found in all chief towns, in spas and several very small towns. Tuzex vouchers can be bought in departmental branches of the State Bank, at all frontier posts, in some hotels and at all Tuzex stores which are listed on p. 423.

Foreign visitors can also procure Tuzex vouchers at branches of the Czechoslovak State Bank at Prague, Brno, Bratislava, Mariánské Lázné, Ústí nad Labem, Liberec, Hradec Křalové, České Budějovice, Gottwaldov, Ostrava and Banská Bystrica.

You can also buy these vouchers in your own country. Below we are listing agencies and Automobile Clubs which sell Tuzex vouchers:

Austria: E. Bezenek, Gluckgasse 1, Wien I; Südland Transporte Peregringasse 2, Wien IX; Oesterreichischer Automobil Motorrad und Touring Club, Schubert Ring 7, Wien I.

Belgium: Voyage Galilée, 15, avenue Galilée, Bruxelles.

Canada: Omnitrade Ltd., 1247 Guy Street, Montréal, P.Q.

Denmark: De Ferende Dansko Motorejere, Frederiksborggade 18, Kobenhavn.

U.S.A.: Utsch & Associates, Inc., Broadway 39, New York 6, N.Y.

France: Banque Commerciale pour l'Europe du Nord, 21, rue de l'Arcade, Paris 8e.

Great Britain: Automobile Association, Leicester Square, London W.C.2; The Royal Automobile Club, Pall Mall, London S.W.1; Gondrand Frères. 31 Greechurch Lane, London, E.C.3.

Greece: Kosmos Travel Agency, Constitution Square, Athens.

Italy: Automobile-Club d'Italie, via Marsala 8, Roma.

Norway: Norges Automobil-Forbund, Kongensgatan 5, Oslo.

Netherlands: H. Van Assem Import, Laan van Meerdervoort 203 B, Den Haag.

German Federal Republic: Alimex, Handels GmbH, Neuhauser Str. 34, München.

Sweden: Sver Persson, Packhusplatsen 2, Göteborg.

Switzerland: Palatinus GmbH, Schweizergasse 10, Zürich.

Self-drive car hire

see page 409.

Useful addresses in Prague

Parking

There is a whole series of supervised and paying parking lots in the centre of the town.

Praha 1, Nové Město, V Jámě
Praha 1, Staré Město, Havelská
Praha 1, Staré Město, Námestí Republiky
Praha 1, Staré Město, Ovocný trh
Praha 1, Nové Město, Námestí M. Gorkého
Praha 1, Nové Město, Opletalova

Day-and-Night Petrol Pumps

(open also on Sundays and holidays)
Praha 1, Nové Město, Opletalova and in the large garages.

Garages and car-cleaning service

Praha Nové Město, Opletalova 9, tel. 22 11 76
Praha-Žižkov, Sudomeřická 1644, tel. 27 36 80
Praha-Dejvice, Čkalova 26, tel. 32 71 06

Repair Workshops

Breakdown assistance

Praha 3, Žižkov, 1644, Sudomevičká, tel. 27 27 27.
   crowns. Tel. 24 24 41.
Prague 2, Vinohrady, Španělská 3, tel. 24 71 31 (Škoda).
Prague 3, Žižkov, Koněvova 143, tel. 83 92 50 (Moskvitch).
Prague 3, Žižkov, Sudomeřská 32, tel. 27 43 09 (Volkswagen).
Prague 4, Záběhlice, Zábělická 26, tel. 92 26 49 (Austin, Ford Cortina).
Prague 5, Motol, Pleňská, tel. 52 26 21 (Renault).
Prague 6, Břevnov, Břevnovská 29, tel. 35 29 64 (Wartburg, Ford Taunus, Ford Cortina).
Prague 6, Bubeneč, tř. Čs. armády 13, tel. 32 20 88 (Hillman).
Prague 8, Karlín, Vítkova 7, tel. 24 17 44, 24 34 57 (Volga, Poběda).
Prague 8, Libeň, Pelc-Tyrolka 474, tel. 84 07 25.
Prague 9, Vysočany, Spojovací 41, tel. 83 86 84 (Citroen).
Prague 10, Vršovice, tř. SNB 60, tel. 92 96 85 (Fiat).
Prague 10, Vršovice, Ruská 194, tel. 92 23 40 (Simca).

Taxis

Rates in town: 4 crowns basic rate, plus 1.80 crowns per kilometre (waiting, 20 crowns an hour).

Between 9 p.m. and 6 a.m. the basic rate is increased by 2 crowns.

Distances

Athens	2162	Lisbon	2923
Belgrade	994	London	1202
Berlin	338	Madrid	2262
Bern	813	Moscow	1857
Brussels	878	Oslo	1309
Bucarest	1430	Paris	1063
Budapest	581	Rome	1371
Copenhagen	1039	Sofia	1398
Dublin	1554	Stockholm	1324
Helsinki	2335	Tirana	1740
The Hague	974	Warsaw	602

VI. COMMUNICATIONS

Railways

Czechoslovakia is often called the heart of Europe. Not unjustly, for its central position makes possible rapid and smooth communications with every other part of Europe. The Baltic-Orient express crosses the Czechoslovak frontier at Děčín and leaves the country, after travelling 688 km (Ústi nad Labem, Praha, Brno, Břeclav, Štúrovo), to continue its journey to Budapest and Belgrade (connection with the Simplon-Orient express). Through trains from Moscow to Vienna via Warsaw join this line and through trains run from Berlin and Prague to Vienna with further connections to Venice and Rome. The service between Berlin and Vienna via Prague is maintained by the "Vindobona" motor-express.

Another important international railway connection from east to west is the Orient Express (Warsaw, Ostrava, Olomouc, Praha, Plzeň, Mariánské Lázně, Cheb), 601 km in Czechoslovak territory, and on via Nuremberg (connection with Brussels and London) to Stuttgart, Kehl and Paris. Other international trains run on the line Praha (or Karlovy Vary)–Cheb, Vojtanov, Brambach (radium spa), Leipzig, Berlin.

A cursory glance at the communications map of Czechoslovakia is sufficient to show that the country itself has a dense railway system.

The return trip Paris–Prague (direct coaches and sleepers) takes about 20 hours each way.

Distances between the main European rail centres and Prague:

		km
Amsterdam	Cologne–Frankfurt–Nuremberg	1143
Ankara	Sofia–Belgrade–Budapest	2627
Athens	Niš–Belgrade–Budapest	2188
Belgrade	Subotica–Budapest–Szob	988
Berlin	Dresden	375
Bern	Zurich–Vienna	1338
Brussels	Cologne–Frankfort–Nuremberg	1063
Bucarest	Szob–Siharkereztes	1522
Budapest	Szob	613
Budapest	Komarno	629
Copenhagen	Warnemünde–Berlin	913
Frankfurt	Nuremberg	610
Helsinki	Stockholm–Berlin	1865
Istanbul	Sofia–Belgrade–Budapest	2071
The Hague	Cologne–Frankfurt–Nuremberg	1199
Lisbon	Irun–Paris–Nuremberg	3375
London	Ostende–Cologne–Nuremberg	1424
London	Calais–Paris–Nuremberg	1728
Luxembourg	Coblentz–Frankfurt–Nuremberg	904
Madrid	Irun–Paris–Nuremberg	2710
Milan	Venice–Vienne–České Velenice (Gmünd)	1256
Moscow	Kiev–Čop	2556
Moscow	Warsaw–Lichkov	2070
Munich	Markttredwitz–Cheb	523
Oslo	Malmö	1438
Paris	Strasbourg–Nuremberg–Cheb	1261
Paris	Belfort–Bâle–Buchs–Vienna	1878
Rome	Florence–Venice–Vienna–Gmünd	1557
Sofia	Niš–Belgrade–Szob	1390
Stockholm	Malmö–Berlin	1382

km

Warsaw	Petrovice–Malovice	778
Warsaw	Lichkov	745
Vienna	České Velenice (Gmünd)	352
Vienna	Břeclav	406

Distances between Prague and the principal Czechoslovak towns (in km):

Banská Bystrica	565	Mariánské Lázně	189
Blansko	233	Olomouc	253
Brno	255	Ostrava	358
Bratislava	396	Piešťany	477
Břeclav	314	Plzeň	113
České Budejovice	167	Poděbrady	55
České Velenice	183	Poprad (High Tatras)	607
Cheb	220	Poprad (via Púchov)	574
Domažlice	173	Prešov	719
Františkovy Lázně	227	Přerov	275
Gottwaldov	314	Sliač	579
Horní Dvořište	223	Štrba	589
Jánské Lázně	197	Tábor	101
Jeseník-Lázně	262	Teplice v Čechách	126
Jihlava	173	Trenčianské Teplice	439
Karlovy Vary	187	Ústí ned Labem	109
Košice	718	Vrchlabí	164
Kutná Hora	6	Železný Brod	114
Liberec	137	Žilina	469
Luhačovice	387		

Air lines

Czechoslovakia can be reached directly or with very easy connections from all the air ports of the world. There are direct air services to Moscow (jet liner TU 104), Helsinki, Warsaw, Stockholm, Copenhagen, Berlin, London, Brussels, Amsterdam, Frankfurt, Paris, Vienna, Rome, Zurich, Belgrade, Tirana, Sofia, Bucharest and Budapest. The inland air lines are also highly developed. Some 70 smaller towns, not connected with the regular flight network, can if wished be reached by aero-taxi. There are new connections with New York, Montreal and Singapore (ČSA). Bratislava is linked with Amsterdam and New York.

CZECHOSLOVAK AIRLINES OFFICES

Československé aeroline (ČSA), Revoluční 3, Prague I; Telephone
6 57 41. Trams Nos 2, 3, 5, 11 and 19 stop in the náměstí Republiky. Information about flights inland and abroad, sale of
tickets, circular flights, departure of motorbuses for the airport.

General representation of foreign airlines

Aeroflot, Praha-Ruzyně air-field, Telephone 32 15 41.
Air France, 10, Václavske Namesti, Nove Město, Praha I,
Telephone 23 75 15.
Air India International, 20 Na příkopě, Nové Město, Praha III,
Telephone 23 48 44.
BEA: Štěpanská 63, Tel. 24 08 47.
Alitalia: 5 Revoluční, Prague I, Telephone 63 258.
KLM (Royal Dutch Airlines), 19 Václavské náměstí, Nové
Město, Praha XIX, Telephone 23 19 56.
Pan Am: Pařizska 11, tel. 6 97 41.
Sabena, Belgian World Airlines, Na Přikopě, 6, Nové Město,
Praha I, Telephone 22 59 77.
Swissair, 34 Vodičkova, Nové Město, Praha II, Telephone
23 76 24.

Prague airport in Ruzyně, Telephone 32 15 41. Transport by
motorbus provided by the ČSA (Czechoslovak Airline) to the
aerodrome, starting 105, 95 or 30 minutes before the departure
time of the aeroplane according to destination (enquire)
from the ČSA office, or by No 11 tram to the stop Divoká
Šárka with connection with No 108 motorbus to the aerodrome. ČSA bus fare: 6 crowns.

    BEA has a London–Prague flight (by jet; flying time, 1 hour 50).
    Air France has several flights a week to Prague, from Orly
(by Caravelle). Flying time: 1 hour 35. Return fare, tourist class:
542 FF.
    Sabena has a Brussels-Prague flight (1 hour 40 by jet). Return
fare, tourist class: 5040 BF.
    Swissair has a flight from Zurich to Prague (by jet, flying time,
1 hour 10). Return fare, tourist class: SF 428.
    SAS has a flight to Prague from Copenhagen (1 hour 40, by
DC–8).
    KLM has an Amsterdam–Prague flight (flying time 3 hours 25)
with stop-over at Frankfort.

Alitalia has a Rome–Milan–Prague flight.
JAT has a Belgrade–Prague flight (2 hours, by IL-62).
Austrian Airlines has a Vienna–Prague flight.
Pan Am has a flight from New York (London)–Prague.

The **Czechoslovak National Airline, ČSA,** covers a wide domestic and international network. It has modern Tupolev-104 and Ilyushin-62 planes. The principal international lines include the following:

Prague–Caire–Bombay–Rangoon–Djakarta;
Prague–Sofia–Ankara–Damascus–Bagdad;
Prague–Zurich–Rabat–Dakkar–Konakry–Bamako;
Prague–Shannon–Gander–Havana;
Prague–Moscow; Prague–Warsaw;
Prague–Paris;
Prague–Budapest–Sofia (or Bucarest);
Prague–Berlin; Prague–Stockholm–Helsinki;
Prague–Brussels and Prague–Amsterdam;
Prague–Zurich; Prague–Rome;
Prague–London;
Prague–Vienna; Prague–Belgrade–Tirana.
Prague–Montreal–New York
Bratislava–Prague–Amsterdam–New York.

Domestic lines include: Prague–Karlovy Vary; Prague–Brno; Prague–Ostrava; Prague–Bratislava; Prague–Košice, etc.

VII. SHOPPING

Tourists find much to tempt them in Czechoslovakia, and Prague stores will fascinate them particularly. We shall list some of these later. But the most interesting are the **Tuzex** stores which offer very advantageous rates.

In Tuzex stores you can buy both Czechoslovak and foreign goods, at favourable prices. There is a wide choice, including foodstuffs, drinks, cigarettes and textiles, glassware, porcelain, jewellery (garnet), traditional crafts, costume jewellery, etc.

In Tuzex stores, whose addresses we are listing below, you will find especially attentive service. A qualified staff, speaking the principal languages, is at your service.

When arriving in Czechoslovakia you need only ask for Tuzex vouchers when changing your foreign currency in a bank (**Státní banka Československá**, Prague (Na Příkopě 12, Praha 1, Tel. 23 51 18) or its main branch offices, or at the **Živnostenská banka**, Prague); with these vouchers you can make your purchases at all Tuzex stores. Your foreign currency will be exchanged at the current rate of the State Bank against Tuzex vouchers. Tuzex price lists are available at the bank itself, at Čedok Travel Agencies, in Czechoslovak Airline offices, in the chief hotels and customs offices.

The Státní banka československá and the Živnostenská banka will exchange your unused Tuzex vouchers—without special formality—against the currency in which you originally bought them or against Czech crowns at the current rate at a small additional charge.

All goods purchased at Tuzex can be exported freely, or dispatched to an address abroad by the shop. The bill established by Tuzex fully replaces the export permit and all further customs formalities are dispensed with.

LIST OF **TUZEX** AGENCIES:

Praha 1, Ovocný trh 2; Praha 2, Tylovo nám. 3; Praha 1, Palackého 13; Praha 1, hotel **Alcron**; Praha 7, Veletržní palác; Praha-Ruzyň, letiště; Karlovy Vary, hotel **Moskva**; Brno, Rooseveltova 18; Bratislava, Gorkého 13; Žilina, Hodžova 9; Poprad, Gottwaldovo nábřeží 1045; Košice, Leninova 11; Prešov, Stalinova 39; Michalovce, Pasáž 738.

Large Stores in Prague:

Bilá Labuť (White Swan), Praha 1, Nové Město, Na poříči 23. Perla, Praha 1, Staré Město, ul. 28, října 1.

Dum módy (Fashion House), Praha 1, Nové Město, Václavské nám.

Darex (Women's fashions and trousseaux), Praha 1, Nóve Město, Václavské náměstí 11.

Děský dům (Maison de l'Enfant), Praha 1, Staré Město, Na příkopě 15.

Materials:

Obchod textilem, Praha 1, Nové Město, Národní 40.
Praha 1, Staré Město, Rytířská 20.
Dum vlny a hebvábí (wool and silk), Praha 1, Staré Město,
Na příkopě 1.

Hats:

Women's: Praha 1, Nové Město, Václavské nám. 4.
Men's: Praha 1, Nové Město, Václavské nam. 12.

Clothes for women:

Praha 1, Nové Město, Václavské nám. 44.
Praha 1, Nové Město, Vodičkova 30.

For men:

Praha 1, Nové Město, Václavské nám. 18.
Dům oděvů, Praha 1, Nové Město, Na poříčí 14.

Linen:

Prim (for men), Praha 1, Nové Město, Na příkopě 8.
Silon (in synthetic materials), Praha 1, Nové Město, Na příkopě
16.
Modeta (Lingerie for women), Praha 1, Nové Město, Na příkopě
16.

Shoes:

Dům obuvi (shoes, leather goods, pedicure), Praha 1, Nové
Město, Václavské náměsti 6.
Ton mody (luxury shoes), Praha 1, Nové Město, Na příkopě.

Jewellery:

Praha 1, Staré Město, Národní 25.
Praha 1, Nové Město, Na Příkopě.

Perfume, beauty products:

Rosana, Praha 1, Nové Město, Na příkopě 16.
Praha 1, Staré Město, Národní 35

Gems:

Praha 1, Národni 26.

Antiques:

Praha 1, Národni 24, tel. 23 65 75.
Praha 1, Václavské námestí 60.

Cameras:

Praha 1, Vodičkova 33.
Praha 1, Václavské námestí 57.

Foodstuffs:

Dum potravin, Praha 1, Nové Městro, Václavské náměstí 59.
Gastronomy Store, Praha 1, Staré Město, Na příkopě 9.

Books:

Praha 1, Nové Město, Václavské nám.
Praha, Nové Město. Na příkopě 22.

Records:

Divadlo hudby (Theatre of music), Praha 1, Nové Město,
   Opletalova 5.
Praha 1, Staré Město, Národni 31.

Toys:

Dětský dum, Praha 1, Staré Město, Na přikopě 15.
Praha 1, Nové Město, Václavské nám. 48.
Praha 1, Nové Město, Národní 32.
Praha 1, Staré Město, Mŭstek 4.

Glass and porcelain:

České sklo a keramika (Bohemian glass and pottery), Praha 1,
   Staré Město, Národní 43.
Výběrové sklo a porcelán (Luxury glass and china), Praha 1,
   Nové Město, Na přikopě 16.
Krystal (crystal), Praha 1, Nové Město, Vodičkova 41.
Praha 1, Staré Město, ul. 28. října 9.

Souvenirs and presents:

Praha 1, Staré Město, ul. 28 října 3.
Praha 1, Nové Město, Václavské náměstí 52.
ULUV (traditional craftsmen's works), Praha 1, Nové Město,
Národní 37.

Foreign export concerns

Artia, import and export of cultural goods, 30 Ve smečkách,
   Nové Město Praha II, Telephone 24 60 41.
Centrotex, import and export of textile and leather goods,
   47 Dukelskych hrdinů třida, Holešovice, Praha VII, Telephone
   38 01.

Cechofracht, sea travel agency, 11 Na Příkopě 8, Praha I, Telephone 21 29.

Chemapol, import and export of chemical products and raw materials, 9 Panská, Nové Město, Praha III, Telephone 24 49 41.

Forromet, export and import of foundry products, 27 Opletalova, Nové Město, Praha I, Telephone 22 08 41 to 45.

Glass export, export of glassware, 1 Václavské náměstí, Nové Město, Praha III, Telephone 24 73 51.

Koospol, import and export of foodstuffs and agricultural products, 47 Dukelskych hrdinů třída, Holešovice, Praha VII, Telephone 38 20.

Kovo, import and export of precision machinery, 47 Dukelskych hrdinů třída, Holešovice, Praha VII, Telephone 38 20.

Ligna, export and import of wood and wood and paper industrial products, 41 Vodičkova, Nové Město, Praha I, Telephone 22 64 51.

Metalimex, import and export of ores, metals and solid fuels, 34 Štěpánská, Nové Město, Praha II, Telephone 24 04 61.

Motokov, import and export of automobiles and light industry products, 47 Dukelskych hrdinů třída, Holešovice, Praha VII, Telephone 38 01.

Pragoexport, import and export of articles of attire, fancy goods, etc, 34 Jungmannová, Nové Město, Praha II, Telephone 22 03 54.

Strojexport, export of machinery and machine plant, 56 Václavské námestíí, Nové Město, Praha II, Telephone 24 50 41.

Strojimport, import of machinery and machine plant, 5 Konviktská Staré Město, Praha I, Telephone 23 05 91.

Technoexport, export of complete industrial plant, 56 Václavské náměstí, Nové Město, Praha II, Telephone 21 31.

Czechoslovak Ceramics, import and export of china-ware, 1 V jámě, Nové Město, Praha II, Telephone 24 77 41.

Tuzex, retail sale of goods in exchange for foreign currency, 13 Rytírská, Staré Město, Praha I, Telephone 22 73 55.

Czechoslovak Chamber of Commerce, information office for foreign trade, 28 října, Staré Město, Praha I, Telephone 21 39. Nos 3, 5, 7, 11, 19, 22 and 23 trams stop Václavské náměstí-Mustek.

Turista (Travel Bureau), 32 Václavské náměstí, Nové Město, Praha II, Telephone 23 47 41 to 43. Trams Nos 3, 7, 11, 14, 15, 18, 19, 21, 22 and 23 and omnibuses Nos 52, 53, 55, 61 stop Václavské náměstí. Information centre and travel service for Czechoslovakia.

Central Information Office, 20 Na příkopě, Praha I, Telephone 54 44 44. Nos. 2, 5, 7, 9, 17, 20, 22 and 23 stop Narodní divadlo (National Theatre). General information.

VIII. EMBASSIES AND CONSULATES

Foreign Representations in Prague

Albania, Praha 6, Bubeneč, Pod kaštany 22, Telephone 7 53 29.
Allied Permit Office for Germany, Praha 6, Nové Město, Štepánská 18, Telephone 23 86 54.
Argentina, Praha 3, Nové Město, Washingtonova 25, Telephone, 22 38 03.
Austria, Praha 16, Smíchov, Viktora Huga 10, Telephone 4 00 47.
Belgium, Praha 1, Malá Strana, Valdštejnská 6, Telephone 53 66 27.
Brazil, Praha 6, Bubeneč, Na Zátorce 19, Telephone 6 29 02.
Bulgaria, Praha 2, Nové Město, Krakovská 6, Telephone 22 13 19.
Canada, Praha Hradčany, Mickiewiczova 6, Telephone 32 71 24.
China, Praha Majakovského 22, Telephone 32 61 41.
Denmark, Praha 2, Královské Vinohrady, Koperníkova 10, Telephone 25 47 15.
Egypt, Praha 12, Královské Vinohrady, Italská 39, Telephone 24 78 94.
Finland, Praha 5, Střešovice, Sibeliova 6, Telephone 6 96 43.
France, Praha 1, Malá Strana, Velkopřevorské náměstí 2, Telephone 53 30 42.
German Democratic Republic, Praha 2, Nové Město, Gottwaldovo nábřeží 32, Telephone 22 92 63.
Greece, Praha 2, Královské Vinohrady, Helénská 2, Telephone 24 75 97.
Great Britain, Praha 1, Malá Strana, Thunovská 14, Telephone 53 33 47.
Guatemala, Praha 3, Nové Město, Na příkopě 12, Telephone 22 18 51.

Haiti, Praha 12, Královské Vinohrady, Polská 3, Telephone 5 75 53.

Hungary, Praha 1, Malá Strana, Šeříková 1, Telephone 4 04 77.

India, Praha 1, Malá Strana, Valdštejnská 6, tel. 53 62 43.

Indonesia, Praha Bubeneč, Pod Kaštaný 24, Telephone 71647.

Iran, Praha 6, Bubeneč, Na Zátorce 18, Telephone 7 43 73.

Italy, Praha 1, Malá Strana, Nerudova 20, Telephone 53 26 46.

Korea, Praha 6, Bubeneč, V bubenečskych vilách 9, Telephone 7 47 19.

Mexico, Praha 1, Malá Strana, Maltézské náměstí 6, Telephone 1 9 7 59.

Netherlands, Praha 1, Malá Strana, Maltézské námestí 1, Telephone 53 13 78.

Norway, Praha 1, Malá Strana, Karmelitská 14, Telephone 6 08 56.

Papal Nuncio, Praha 2, Nové Město, Voršilská 12, Telephone 4 36 03.

Poland, Praha 1, Malá Strana, Valdštejnská 8, Telephone 6 32 75.

Rumania, Praha 1, Malá Strana, Nerudová, Telephone 6 65 32.

Salvador, Praha 2, Nové Mesto, Jungmannovo náměstí 7, Telephone 24 01 12.

Sweden, Praha 1, Hradčany, Úvoz 13, Telephone 53 33 44.

Switzerland, Praha 1, Hradčany, Hradčanské námestí 1, Telephone 53 73 03.

Syria, Praha 1, Malá Strana, Valdštejnská 6, Telephone 6 17 91.

Turkey, Praha 5, Střešovice, Pevnostni 3, Telephone 32 55 01.

U.S.S.R., Praha 6, Bubeneč, Pod kaštany 1, Telephone 37 82 52.

U.S.A., Praha 1, Malá Strana, Tržiště 15, Telephone 53 14 56.

Vietnam, Praha 16, Smíchov, Holečkova 6, Telephone 4 14 16.

Yugoslavia, Praha 1, Malá Strana, Mostecká 15, Telephone 6 63 26.

Czechoslovak Diplomatic Representation

Abyssinia, Addis Abeba, B.P. 1372.

Afghanistan, Kabul, Shar-i-now.

Albania, Tirana, Rruga Donika Kastrioti.

Argentina, Buenos-Aires, Calle Calleo 1175.

Australia, Sydney, 23, Kambala Rd., Bellevue Hill, Melbourne, S.C.2, "Stanhill" 34, Queens Rd.

Austria, Vienna XIV., Penzingerstrasse 11–13.

Belgium, Brussels, 152, Av. A. Buyl.
Bolivia, La Paz, Plaza Izabel la Catolica 1007.
Brazil, Rio de Janeiro–Ipanema. Rue Prudente de Morais 403.
Bulgaria, Sofia, Rue Mar. Tolbuchin 16.
Burma, Rangoon, 326, Prone Road.
Canada, Montreal, 1305 Pine Ave. W.
China, Peking, 55, Nan-Chang-Chieh.
Columbia, Bogotá, Carrero 9, Nr. 75–70.
Congo, Leopoldville, Av. de la VIII Armée, P.B. 3154.
Denmark, Copenhagen, Svanemollevej 48.
Ecuador, Quito, Calle Juan Leon Mera 650.
Egypt, Cairo, 18, rue Aicha, el Teymorieh Garden City.
Finland, Helsinki, Armfeltintir 14.
France, Paris VII, 15, Avenue Charles Floquet.
German Democratic Republic, Berlin N 54, Schönhauser Allee 10.
German Federal Republic, Berlin-Dahlem, Podbielski-Allee 54.
Great Britain, London W8, 6–7 Kensington Palace Gardens.
Greece, Athens, 1, Sékéri.
Holland, The Hague, Stadhouderslaan 1.
Hungary, Budapest, Vorosilov ut 22.
India, New Delhi 2, 22/39, Kantilya Marg Diplomatic Enclave.
Indonesia, Djakarta, Djalan Madura 29.
Iran, Teheran, 4, Avenue Rarzane Fischer Abad-Damghan.
Iceland, Reykjavik, Smaragata 16.
Italy, Rome, Via Luisa di Savoia 16.
Lebanon, Beirut, Rue Verdoun, B.P. 1529.
Mexico, Mexico D.F., Avenida Horicio 213, Zona 5.
Mongolia, Ulan Bator.
New Zealand, Wellington C. 2, 49 Thompson Street.
Norway, Oslo, Thomas Heftyes Gate 32.
Pakistan, Karachi, 99, Clifton, off Partab Singh Sethi Road.
Peru, Lima, Avenida Arica 268, San Miguel.
Poland, Warsaw 10, Koszykowa 18.
Rumania, Bukarest, Strada Vasile Lascar 43–45.
Sweden, Stockholm, Tysta-Gatan 10, Stockholm.
Switzerland, Berne, Muristrasse 53; Zürich, Retelbergstrasse 49.
South Africa, Cape Town, 49 Belmont Avenue, Oranjezicht.
Sudan, Khartum, POB 1047.
Syria, Damascus, Abou Roummaneh, Rue El-Jilas, Haus Zoulnoun El Monayed Azem.
Turkey, Ankara, Cankaya caddesi 375–377.
Uruguay, Montevideo, Calle Louis B Cavis 2996.
U.S.A., 3900 Linnean Ave., Tel. 363 63 16.
Yugoslavia, Belgrade, Bulevar Revolucije 22.

IX. SPORTS, SHOOTING AND FISHING

Czechoslovakia enjoys a good reputation in the sporting world. The most popular sports are football, ice hockey, athletics, basket ball, parachute jumping, boxing, table tennis, water sports, handball, etc. Czechoslovak sportsmen have won considerable successes in all these sports both at home and abroad. The summer season in Czechoslovakia has plenty of sports tournaments of every kind.

Without doubt the mass gymnastic displays are something unusual. Every five years the so-called Spartakiade is held. The whole country is represented. This sporting occasion carries on the tradition of the famous Sokol festivals. Tens of thousands of athletes appear at the same time in the Prague stadium with accommodation for 140,000 people.

All Czechoslovak towns, spas and tourist centres offer visitors ample opportunities for sporting activity. The Czechoslovak mountains have ideal skiing terrain, every scenically beautiful region is criss-crossed with well marked footpaths and roads. Favourite mountain country, especially attractive to tourists is: the High Tatra (Vysoké Tatra), the Giant Mts. (Krkonose), the Beskids (Beskydy) and the Fatra. Mountain-climbers particularly favour the "Bohemian Paradise" (Český ráj) with its strange sandstone formations. There are opportunities for aquatic sports of every kind on rivers, ponds and lakes. Riding can best be enjoyed in the health resorts. One of the loveliest golf courses on the Continent is near Mariánské Lázně (Marienbad).

There are facilities for shooting and fishing all the year round. The Czechoslovak Travel Agency Čedok arranges individual and party shoots for foreign visitors. The commonest kinds of game and fish are: stag, fallow deer, moufflon, roe deer, wild boar, bear (only in East Slovakia), chamois, hare; bustard, capercailzie, red grouse, wild goose, wild duck, partridge, pheasant; trout, salmon-trout, silurus and species of carp.

X. USEFUL INFORMATION (PRAGUE)
Post and Telegraph offices

General Post Office, 14 Jindřišská ulice, Nové Město, Praha III, Telephone 23 17 51 to 57. Continuous day and night service, despatch of letters and parcels, telegrams and telephone.

Despatch and customs formalities for parcels for foreign countries, acceptance and payment of duty on parcels from abroad: Post Office 1, Hybernská, Nové Město, Praha III (in the courtyard), Telephone 24 18 07.

Important telephone numbers:

Calls for places outside Czechoslovakia: 048.
Enquiries (for inland calls): 27 51 51
Enquiries (for calls for abroad): 27 83 56.
To dictate telegrams: 07.
Local directory enquiries: 030.

ACCOMMODATION

There are many international hotels offering every comfort. The staff speak several languages. There are also exchange offices in these hotels.

Luxury hotels

Alcron, Praha 1, Nové Město, Štěpánská 40, tel. 24 57 41 to 9.

Esplanade, Praha 1, Nové Město, Washingtonova 19, tel. 22 25 52.

International, Praha 6, Dejvice, náměstí Družby, tel. 32 10 51.

Jalta, Praha 1, Nové Město, Václavské nám. 45, tel. 23 63 90.

Class I

Europa, Praha 1, Nové Město, Václavské nám. 29, tel. 23 05 95.

Flora, Praha 3, Vinohrady, Vinohradská 121, tel. 27 42 42.

Palace, Praha 1, Nové Město, Panská 12, tel. 23 71 51.

Paříž, Praha 1, Staré Město, U Obecního domu 1, tel. 6 27 51 to 54.

Slovan, Praha 1, Vinohrady, tř. Vítězného února 12, tel. 22 32 16.

Tatran, Praha 1, Nové Město, Václavské nám. 22, tel. 24 05 41.

Class II

Axa, Praha 1, Nové Město, Na poříčí 40, tel. 22 54 11.

Central, Praha 1, Staré Město, Rybná 8, tel. 6 67 21.

Hybernia, Praha 1, Nové Město, Hybernská 24, tel. 22 04 31.

Merkur, Praha 1, Nové Město, Těšnov 9, tel. 6 96 56.

Meteor, Praha 1, Nové Město, Hybernská 6, tel. 22 92 41.

Morava, Praha 2, Vinohrady, Bělehradská 110, tel. 25 45 44.

Opera, Praha 1, Nové Město, Těšnov 13, tel. 6 29 44.

Zlata Husa, Praha 1, Nové Město, Václavské nám. 7, tel. 23 69 51.

Motel STOP, Praha 5, Plzeňská, tel. 52 32 55.

Restaurants

Good food is one of the pleasures of travelling. The Czechoslovak cuisine—its meals washed down with the famous Czech beer or local wines—has an excellent reputation. There are so many inns and restaurants that a choice is difficult.

Restaurants with an international cuisine

Alcron, Praha 1, Nové Město, Štěpánská 40.

Esplanade, Praha 1, Nové Město, Washingtonova 19.

Flora, Praha 3, Vinohrady, Stalinova 121.

International, Praha 6, Dejvice, nám. Družby.

Jalta, Praha 1, Nové Město, Václavské nám. 45.

Praha, Praha 7, Letná, Letenske sady.

Some picturesque restaurants and taverns

Barrandov, Praha 5, Hlubočepy (terraces with splendid views of Prague—open in summer).

U Fleků, Praha 1, Nové Město, Křemencova 11, (picturesque former brewery).

U Kalicha, Praha 1, Nové Město, Na bojišti 12, (famous inn of the good soldier Švejk).

U Lorety, Praha 1, Hradčany, Loretánské nám. 18, (tavern in a romantic setting).

U tří pštrosů, Praha 1, Malá Strana, Dražického náměstí 12, (typical of the old Malá Strana quarter).

U Markýze, Praha 1, Nové Město, Nekázanka 8, (with French cuisine).

U sv. Tomáše, Praha 1, Malá Strana, Letenská 12, (old Prague brewery).

U Šuterů, Praha 1, Nové Město, Palackého 4, (typical Prague tavern with wide choice of South-Moravian wines).

Valdštejnská hospoda (Waldstein Inn), Praha 1, Malá Strana (picturesque old inn).

Vikárka, Praha 1, Hradčany, Vikárská 4, (in a romantic setting in the outskirts of Prague Castle).

Zlatá Studně (Golden Well), Praha 1, Malá Strana, Pod Hradem 166, (terraces with splendid view of Prague).

Museums

National Museum, Praha 1, Nové Město, Václavské náměsti 68 tel. 23 35 41. Closed on Tuesdays.

Náprstek Museum, Praha 1, Staré Město, Betlémské námestí 1, tel. 22 76 91.

Ethnographical section of the National Museum, Praha 5, Smíchov, Petřínské sady 98, tel. 53 13 07.

Music section of the National Museum, Praha 1, Malá Strana, Velkopřevorské náměstí 4, tel. 53 06 10.

V. I. Lenin Museum, Praha 1, Nové Město, Hybernská 7, tel. 24 61 73.

Kl. Gottwald Museum, Praha 1, Staré Město, Rytířská ulice 29, tel. 24 84 51.

City of Prague Museum, Praha 3, Nové Město, ul. Jana Švermy 1554, tel. 22 04 06.

Alois Jirásek Museum, Praha 6, Břevnov, Obora Hvězda, tel. 35 26 14.

Museum of Czech Literature, Praha 1, Hradčany, Strahovské nádvoří 132, tel. 53 14 51.

Bedřich Smetana Museum, Praha 1, Staré Město, Novotného lávka, tel. 23 56 70

Antonín Dvořák Museum, Praha 2, U Karlova 20, tel. 22 82 14.

National Technical Museum, Praha 7, Holešovice, Kostelní 42, tel. 77 11 50.

Museum of the Czechoslovak Army, Praha 3, Žižkov, U památníku 2.

Military History Museum, Praha 1, Hradčany, Hradčanské náměstí 2, tel. 53 64 88.

Crafts and Trades Museum, Praha 1, Staré Město, ul. 17. listopadu 2, tel. 6 33 74.

State Jewish Museum, Praha 1, Staré Město, Jáchynova 3, tel. 6 33 74.

Czechoslovak Physical Education and Sports Museum, Praha 1, Malá Strana Újezd, 450, tel. 53 21 16.

Post Museum, Praha 5, Smíchov, Holečkova, tel. 54 11 25. The museums are usually closed on Mondays.

Exhibitions and art galleries

A large number of exhibition halls and art galleries show the art of past centuries as well as that of modern times. Czech artists at all periods liked to reproduce the art of their day, and the collections in the galleries contain gothic and baroque works of art as well as masterpieces of Czech painting and sculpture of the 19th and 20th centuries. The following are the most interesting exhibitions and galleries:

Collection of antique art, Praha 1, Hradčany, Hradčanské náměstí 15. tel. 53 68 67.

19th-century Czech painting, Praha 1, Malá Strana, Valdštejnská ulice, tel. 53 68 44.

Graphic collection, Praha 1, Staré Město, Staroměstské náměstí 12, tel. 6 61 01.

Modern Art, Praha 1, Staré Město, Náměstí primátora Vacka, tel. 6 59 53.

Collection of Czech sculpture, Castle Zbraslav, tel. 59 11 93.

Gallery of the Riding School of Prague Castle, Praha 1, Hradčany, U Prašného mostu, tel. 09 41.

Mánes Gallery, Praha 2, Nové Město, Gottwaldovo nábřeží 250, tel. 29 90 12.

Aleš Exhibition Hall, Praha 1, Malá Strana, Besední 3, tel. 53 28 30.

New Exhibition Hall, Praha 1, Nové Město, Voršilská 3, tel. 4 73 13.

Hollar, Praha 1, Staré Město, Smetanovo nábřeží 6, tel. 23 37 26.

Youth Gallery, Praha 1, Nové Město, Vodičkova 10, tel. 22 59 02.

V. Špála Gallery, Praha 1, Nové Město, Národní 30, tel. 23 98 95.

Fronta, Praha 1, Nové Město, Spálená 53, tel. 23 65 38.

Gallery of the National Central Committee, Praha 1, Staré Město, Staroměstské náměstí 1.

Purkyně, Praha 1, Nové Město, Na příkopě 16, tel. 22 38 60.

Obecní dum Exhibition Hall, Praha 1, Staré Město, námešti Republiky 5, tel. 6 30 01.

U Hybernů, Praha 1, Nové Město, námesti Republiky, tel. 22 55 38.

Panorama of the Battle of Lipany, Praha 7, Holešovice, Julius Fučik park of culture and recreation, tel. 37 73 41.

The Liebscher diarama of the "Struggle of the People of Prague against the Swedes", with an adjoining hall of mirrors. Praha 1, Malá Strana Petřin (accessible by cable car).

Galleries and exhibition halls are generally closed on Mondays. Varnishing of new exhibitions is announced on posters.

Theatres

The 22 permanent theatres in Prague are attended by an average of three and a quarter million spectators a year. There are also 2 opera companies attached to the National Theatre.

National Theatre, Praha 1, Nové Město, Národní třida, tél. 23 12 51.

Tyl Theatre, Praha 1, Staré Město, Železná 11, tel. 23 05 16.

Smetana Theatre, Praha 3, Vinohrady, tř. Vítězného února, tel. 22 60 00.

Lanterna magica, Praha 1, Nové Město, Národní třída 40, tel. 23 85 12.

Central Theatre of the Czechoslovak Army, Praha 3, Vinohrady, náměstí Míru. 25 70 91.

D 34, Praha 3, Nové Město, Na poříčí 26, tel. 24 12 19.

Realist Theatre Z. Nejedlý, Praha 5, Smíchov, Kirova 557, tel. 54 50 27.

S.K. Neumann Theatre, Praha 8, Libeň, tř. Rudé armády 34, tel. 82 24 92.

Municipal Theatre, Praha 1, Nové Město, Hybernská 10, tel. 22 28 19.

Municipal Theatre (Divadlo komedie), Praha 1, Nové Město, Jungmannova 1, tel. 23 10 26.

DISK, Praha 1, Staré Město, Karlova 8, tel. 23 39 15.

ABC Theatre, Praha 1, Nové Město, Vodičkova 28, tel. 24 77 31.

Rokoko Theatre, Praha 1, Nové Město, Václavské náměstí 38, tel. 24 12 39.

Na Zábradlí Theatre, Praha 1, Staré Město, Anenské náměsti 5, tel. 24 81 31.

Semafor Theatre, Praha 1, Nové Město, Ve smečkách 26, tel. 24 93 49.

Karlin State Theatre, Praha 3, Karlín, Křižíkova 10, tel. 22 08 01.

Municipal Theatre "Na Fidlovačce", Praha 4, Nusle, tel. 93 24 97.

Jiří Wolker Theatre, Praha 1, Staré Město, Dlouhá třída 29, tel. 6 71 21.

Spejbl and Hurvínek Theatre, Praha 2, Vinohrady, Rímská 45, tel. 2 10 58.

Central Marionette Theatre, Praha 1, Nové Město, nám. M. Gorkého 28, tel. 22 36 37.

Music

The musical life of Prague centres round the three operatic stages and several concert halls, the largest of which are the **Smetana Hall** and the **Hall of the Artists' House**.

The concerts held in the gardens of the old palace of Prague are very popular. Record lovers should visit the Theatre of Music which has especially the masterpieces by dead composers and musicians from all over the world. Masterpieces of classical music are occasionally performed in Prague churches. Besides, the Prague Spring Festival, organized every May, brings eminent musicians and music lovers from all parts of the globe.

The following places are most popular with music lovers:

House of Artists, Praha 1, Staré Město, nám. Krasnoarmějcu, tel. 6 93 93.

Smetana Hall, Praha 1, Staré Město, náměsti Republiky, Obecni dum.

Theatre of Music, Praha 3, Opletalova 5, tel. 22 45 37.

Libraries

The most important libraries are the **National Library** and the **University Library** (with some two million volumes) housed in the Klementinum, and the famous **Strahov** Library close to the Archives of national literature which give a detailed survey of the development of Czech literature from its beginnings to the present.

Other things of interest

People's Observatory of the City of Prague, Praha 1, Petřín, tel. 4 63 05.

Planetarium, Praha 7, Holešovice, Julius Fučik Park of Culture and Recreation.

Zoo, Praha 8, Troja, tel. 7 32 96.

Botanic Gardens, Praha 1, Nové Město, Na Slupi 1, tel. 23 39 97

Cafés and miscellaneous attractions

Julius Fučík Park of Culture and Recreation, Praha 7, Holešovice, tel. 37 73 41 (open daily, except Monday; amusement centre).

Prague Music Hall, Praha 1, Nové Město, Vodičkova 30, tel. 24 37 20 (with various programmes by Czechoslovak and foreign performers).

Lucerna, Praha 1, Nové Město, Vodičkova 36, tel. 24 61 51 (international programme at the Night Club).

Alhambra, Praha 1, Nové Město, Václavské náměstí 5, tel. 22 33 55 (singing, dancing and diverse attractions).

Cafés with music

Alcron, Praha 1, Nové Město, Štěpánská 40, tel. 24 57 41 (music daily from 8 p.m. to 2 a.m.).

Alfa, Praha 1, Nové Město, Václavské náměstí 28, tel. 23 32 20.

Barrandov, Praha 5, Hlubočepy, tel. 54 54 09 (open only in summer, terminus tram No 5).

Mánes, Praha 1, Nové Město, Gottwaldovo nábřeží 250, tel. 23 22 54.

Pasáž, Praha 1, Nové Město, Václavské náměstí 5, tel. 22 00 72.

Savarin, Praha 1, Nové Město, Na příkopě 10, tel. 22 47 78.

Vltava, Praha 1, Staré Město, Revoluční 25, tel. 6 43 94.

Night clubs

Embassy Bar, Praha 1, Nové Město. Václavské nám. 5, tel. 22 06 44 (open 9 p.m. to 3 a.m.).

Est Bar, Hotel Čedok Esplanade, Praha 1, Nové Město, Washingtonova 19, tel. 22 25 52 (open 9 p.m. to 3 a.m.).

Olympia Grill, Praha 1, Malá Strana, Vítězna 7, tel. 53 06 88 (open 8 p.m. to 3 a.m.).

Opera Grill, Praha 1, Staré Město, Divadelní 24, tel. 23 75 88 (open 7 p.m. to 2 a.m.)

Trilobit Bar, Barrandov, Praha 5, Hlubočepy, tel. 54 53 09 (open in summer only, 9 a.m. to 4 a.m.).

Cinemas

First runs:

Sevastopol, Praha 1, Staré Město, Na příkopě 31, tel. 23 89 01.

Other cinemas in the town centre:

Alfa, Praha 1, Nové Město, Václavské náměstí 28,.tel. 22 07 24.

Blaník, Praha 1, Nové Město, Václavské náměstí 56, tel. 23 80 85.

Čas, Praha 1, Nové Město, Václavské náměstí 41, tel. 22 66 90.

Hvězda, Praha 1, Nové Město, Václavské náměstí 38, tel. 22 91 87 (continuous programme).

Jalta, Praha 1, Nové Město, Václavské náměstí 43, tel. 23 93 23.

Lucerna, Praha 1, Nové Město, Vodičkova 36, tel. 24 60 82.

Praha, Praha 1, Nové Město, Václavské náměstí 17, tel. 23 74 65.

Světozor, Praha 1, Nové Město, Vodičkova 39, tel. 23 65 10.

Metro, Praha 1, Staré Město, Národní 25, tel. 23 19 53.

Paříž, Praha 1, Nové Město, Václavské nám. 22, tel. 24 05 10.

Kino Mladých, Praha 1, Klimentská 4, tel. 645 04 (films for children and young people).

Information on programmes:

Central Information Bureau, Praha 1, Nové Město, Národní 10, tel. 54 44 44, and SLUNA, Praha 1, Nové Město, Václavské náměsti 5 (Lucerna Passage), tel. 23 71 27.

Health Services

All information from telephone No 333.

Polyclinics:

Praha 1, Revoluční 19, tel. 6 13 41 to 44.
Praha 1, Palackého 5, tel. 23 74 53 to 55.
Praha 2 (Foreign visitors), Karlovo nám 32, tel. 24 00 51.

Emergencies:

(only from 7 p.m. to 7 a.m. continuous on Sundays and holidays).
Praha 1, Staré Město, Dlouhá 11, tel. 6 17 18.
Praha 1, Nové Město, Jungmannova 14, tel. 24 77 71.
Praha 1, Nové Město, Kimentská 9, tel. 6 70 64.

Emergency Dental Service

(only from 7 p.m. to 7 a.m.).
Praha 1, Nové Město, Vladislavova 22.

Ambulances:

In case of accidents or serious illness call 37 37 37.
Transport of sick people by ambulance: tel. 333.
Prague City Ambulance Service: Praha 7, Holešovice, Třída Dukelskýck hrdinú 21, tel. 333.

Chemists:

(continuous day and night service).
Praha 1, Staré Město, Na Příkopě 7, tel. 22 08 81.
Praha 1, Nové Město, Hyberáská ul., tel. 22 31 73.
Day-time service in the centre of town:
Praha 1, Nové Město, Jindřísská 11, tel. 23 74 37.
Praha 1, Nové Město, Václavské nám. 8, tel. 23 88 24.
Praha 1, Nové Město, Václavské nám. 27, tel. 23 03 33.

Ophthalmic cases:

Praha 1, Nové Město, Václavské nám. 17, tel. 23 92 87.
Praha 1, Nové Město, Václavské nám. 51, tel. 23 07 12.

XI. LIST OF PLACES OF ETHNOGRAPHICAL INTEREST

Bohemia and Moravia

Prague: Ethnographical sections of the National Museum in the Kinský Gardens, Petřín Park, Smíchov—Collections of

Czechoslovak popular art, costumes and folklore of other Slav peoples. Near the Museum an original wooden church from the village of Medvědvovce (Carpathian-Ukraine) has been erected.

Náprstek Museum in the Old Town (Betlémské náměstí)—Oriental collections and exhibits.

Agricultural Museum in the Old Town (Husova 7)—Collections of implements and models of buildings.

Turnov: In the surrounding villages there are a whole number of wooden peasant houses with richly decorated gables and verandas (e.g. Přepeře, Dolánky, Přísovice, among others).

Domažlice: Chode costumes in the Old Chode Castle Museum.

Plzeň: the collections in the Museum.

Soběslav: ancient peasant houses with richly decorated walls and painted gables (e.g. in the villages Komarov, Klečaby, Zálší, Mažice). Popular art collections in the Museum.

Veselí nad Lužnicí: popular art collections in the Museum.

Brno: Ethnographical Section of the Museum with collections of ceramics, popular costumes, folklore, Mendel's Museum, etc.

Rožnov: the Wallachian Open Air Museum, in an extensive park, contains models of typical popular buildings to their original scale. In the middle stands a little church. Many objects of popular art are exhibited inside the buildings.

Moravské Slovásko (Moravian Slovakia): Gottwaldov.

Slovakia

Piešťany: in the villages round about the people wear richly embroidered costumes to church on Sundays (e.g. in Pobedin, Častkovice, Trabatice, Rakovice, Moravany, Krakovany).

Trenčianske Teplice: ditto, in the villages Omšení, Velká Kubra and Malá Kubra, Trenčianska Teplá.

Čičmany: picturesque villages with unique rustic popular buildings; ancient customs, dress. About 22 km south of Žilina, via Rájec.

Ždiar: a picturesquely situated village on the eastern edge of the High Tatra. Typical peasant houses, which form an organic whole; beautiful popular costumes are worn to church on Sundays.

Detva: a region east of Zvolen where, in the villages Detva, Očová, Hriňová and others, both men and women wear popular costume sometimes on working days but mainly on Sundays. This region is also known for its popular art products.

Martin: Museum with unique ethnographical collections.

There are some whole villages in the rest of Slovakia where the ancient style of building is preserved. Picturesquely painted houses and cottages make a striking contrast with modern schools and other public buildings and often with the factories which have been erected in Slovakia since 1945.

XII. CAMPING

Even when you are only passing through Czechoslovakia to another country you can get to know the beauties of Czechoslovakia. Čedok has prepared itineraries leading from one frontier post to another:

1. Schirnding (FGR) – Pomezí – Praha – Hradec Králové – Náchod – Běloves – Kudowa (Poland).

2. Waidhaus (FGR) – Rozvadov – Praha – České Budějovice– Dolní Dvořiště – Wullowits (Austria).

3. Waidhaus (FGR) – Rozvadov – Praha – Brno – Žilina – Vysoké Tatry – Prešov – Vyšné Německé – Užhorod (USSR).

4. Waidhaus (FGR) – Rozvadov – Praha – Brno – Český Těšín – Cieszyn (Poland).

5. Waidhaus (FGR) – Rozvadov – Praha – Brno – Bratislava – Petržalka – Berg (Austria).

6. Wullowitz (Austria) – Dolní Dvořiště – České Budějovice – Praha – Hradec Králové – Náchod – Běloves – Kudowa (Poland).

7. Wullowitz (Austria) – Dolní Dvořiště – České Budějovice – Telč – Brno – Český Těšín – Cieszyn (Poland).

8. Wullowitz (Austria) – Dolní Dvořiště – České Budějovice – Telč – Brno – Žilina – Vysoké Tatra – Vyšné Německé – Užhorod (USSR).

9. Wullowitz (Austria) – Dolní Dvořiště – Praha – Hřensko – Schmilka (GDR).

10. Klein Haugsdorf (Austria) – Hatě or Drassenhofen (Autriche) – Mikulov – Brno – Český Těšín – Cieszyn (Poland).

11. Klein Haugsdorf (Austria) – Hatě Mikulov – Brno – Nové Mesto nad Váhom – Žilina – Vyšné Německé – Úžhorod (USSR).

12. Berg (Austria) – Petržalka – Bratislava – Nové Mesto nad Váhom – Žilina – Vyšné Německé – Užhorod (USSR).

13. Waidhaus (GFR) – Rozvadov – Praha– Brno – Bratislava – Rusovce – Rajka (Hungary).

Caravan Camping Sites:

Kokořín: Caravan site near the town of Mělník (16 km) in the midst of lovely country; nearby is the stronghold of Kokorin.

Přihrazy: Caravan site in a very picturesque part.

Knižecí rybník
near Tábor: 4 km from Tábor in a charming nook of the forest. Very pleasant.

Cerna v Posumavi: Caravan site near the Lipno dam, about 22 km from Český Krumlov; very popular, especially with motorists interested in angling.

Habr u Volduch: set in the midst of dense forests on the banks of a lake near the Rozvadov – Pilsen – Prague main highway. Very popular both with Czechoslovak and foreign tourists.

Anín: This camping site (tents and chalets) is splendidly equipped and very popular, especially with foreign motorists. It lies on the banks of the river Otava, in the midst of the Šumava forests, some 7 km from the town of Sušice.

Stará Oleška: A newly laid out camping site, set in attractive country, not far from the frontier (8 km from Děčín).

Plzeň
(Pilsen): Well-equipped with tents and chalets, this camping site lies on the periphery of the town of Plzeň, on the shore of Lake Bolevec.

Seč: Newly laid out, near the Seč dam, on the edge of the wood. Very popular, especially with fishing and water sports enthusiasts.

Sedmihorky: One of the best Czechoslovak caravan sites, in the midst of the "Bohemian Paradise", where tourists can enjoy every comfort. Starting point for excursions in the beautiful surroundings.

Brno-Obora: Chalets (near the Kníničky dam) where motorists can stay.

**Rožnov pod
Radhoštěm:** The camping site at Rožnov pod Radhoštěm near the Valašské Meziříčí-Žilina road, is a good centre for those who want to explore the beauty spots of the Beskids range.

Senec: Large, urban-style camping site.

Banská Bystrica: Camping site for motorists 7 km from the town of Banská Bystrica, near the commune of Tájov.

Vyšné Ružbachy: Camping site for motorists.

Demánová: Caravan site near the highway, not far from the famous stalactite and stalagmite caves.

Štrba: Excellent centre for excursions into the High Tatra range.

Motorists' camping sites (Prague):
Prague 4, Branik, Uledáren 55.
Prague 5, Motol (No. 5 highway, 6 km).

HOTELS

Hotel vouchers may be obtained from any foreign travel agency which has signed a regular contract with Čedok for the issuing and sale of these vouchers. They are no longer compulsory. In return for the vouchers, visitors will obtain the exchange value of the amount marked on the voucher, at the tourist rate. This applies to vouchers delivered to individual travellers.

The price naturally depends on the category of the hotel (service charge included). Local tax amounts to 4 Kčs per person, per day, in season, and 2 Kčs off season. Half-board is compulsory in Prague, at mountain resorts and in spas. The following rates, in U.S. dollars, are indicative:

De luxe category: Single room with bath: 11.70; double room: 19.80.

Category I: Single room with bath: 9.40, without bath: 8.10; double room with bath: 15.05, without bath: 13.00.

Category II: Single room with bath: 5.55, without bath: 4.45; double room with bath: 9.45, without bath 7.55.

The following is a list of hotels recommended by Čedok. Category A on our list corresponds to Čedok's de luxe and Category I rates; Category B to I and II, and Category C to II and III.

Hotels and addresses	Tel.	Class	Beds
Banská Bystrica			
Narodný Dům	2 37 37	B	30
Benecko (Jilemnice)			
Hančova Bouda	15	B	34
Krakonoš..........................	12	C	26
Martinova Bouda	8	C	23

Hotels and addresses	Tel.	Class	Beds
Panorama	20	C	22
Richtrova Bouda		C	23
Benešov nad Ploučnicí			
Hotel Jelen	90	C	—
Bilina			
Hotel Praha	20 20	C	—
Bratislava			
Carlton	3 81 41	A	179
Devín	3 12 41	A	390
Břeclav			
Grand Hôtel, Leninova 10	5 53	B	31
Brno			
Grand Hôtel Brno, Tr. 1. maje 18/20 ...	2 13 63	AB	180
International, Husova 16	2 04 11	A	—
Continental, Leninova 20	5 86 16	B	—
Slavia, Solnicni 15/17	3 11 84/5	B	134
Slovan, Lidicka 23	3 54 90	B	195
Černý Důl (Vrchlabí)			
Lesni Bouda	07	C	50
Náchodska Bouda	06	C	18
České Budějovice			
Slunce, Žižkovo nám. 36	29 22	B	70
Zvon, Žižkovo nám. 262	26 61	B	103
Hotel Malše	25 22	B	—
Grandhotel Vlata	20 82	B	—
Český Krumlov			
Hôtel Krumlov	3 57	B	97
Cheb			
Hvězda, Krále Jiřího	25 49	B	—

Hotels and addresses	Tel.	Class	Beds
Děčín			
Grand, Rybalkovo nám.	24 16	C	63
Pošta, Stalinovo nám.	28 31	C	38
Spori	5 26	B	—
Domažlice			
Chodsky Hôtel, U nadraži 178	3 05	C	50
Krym, Náměstí 49/50	4 53	C	36
Dvůr Králové			
Kvéten, Revolučni 20	6 90	B	30
Františkovy Lázně			
Bajkal	5 01	B	—
Slovan, Leninova 5	3 05	B	37
Frenštát pod Radhostem			
Tanečnica		B	140
Vlčina	53 51	A	71
Gottwaldov			
Moskva	25 41	A	492
Harrachov			
Duha	4	C	32
Hubertus	22 92 48	B	64
Praha	63	C	15
Hradec Králové			
Avion, Obrancu Miru 806	64 09	B	52
Bystrica, Čsl. armady 295	42 01	B	118
Paříž, Šmeralovo nam. 552	35 34	B	—
Jablonec n. Nisou			
Corso	23 23	B	54
Zlaty Lev, Kostelní vrch 1	53 41	B	—

Hotels and addresses	Tel.	Class	Beds
Jeseník			
Jeseník, Revoluřni 141	6 26	B	41
U Nadrazi, Puškinova 288	6 29	B	38
Jevany			
Jevany	58	C	67
Jičín			
Slavie, Riegrova	91	B	30
Astra	30	B	20
Jihlava			
Grand Hôtel, Husova	39 81	C	38
Jilemnice			
Grand	67	B	13
Jiloviště u Prahy			
Hubertus	4 48 81	A	70
Jindřichův Hradec			
Grand Hôtel	4 10	B	35
Karlovy Vary			
Atlantic	47 15	B	69
Central	51 01	B	100
Elefant, Tr. Duk. hrdinu 343	34 06	B	35
Hornik		B	66
Moskva (Pupp)	21 21	A	512
Sevastopol		B	77
Karlštejn			
U Karla IV	21	C	41
Kladno			
Sport, Ul. Cs. Armady	22 21	C	43
Kolín			
Savoy, Rubešova 61	24 85	B	51

Hotels and addresses	Tel.	Class	Beds
Košice			
Slovan	22 33 16	A	112
Kutná Hora			
Cerny Kun, Kollarova 314	2 51	C	48
Lázně Libverda (Frýlant)			
Parkhotel	63	C	23
Liberec			
Impérial, Ul. 1 máje	40 62	A	261
Zlatý Lev, Guttenbergova 3	31 51/3	A	126
Litoměřice			
Labuť, Zítkova 5	24 51	C	62
Luhačovice			
Alexandria	3 10	A	55
Malá Skála (Turnov)			
Jizera	2	C	58
Malá Skála-Vranove			
Mala Skála	7	C	39
Malá Upa (Trutnov)			
Devětsil............................		C	30
Mariánské Lázně			
Cristal, Ul. Odborářů 61	20 74	B	96
Esplanade	21 64	A	103
Golf, Zabud 55	27 12	A	48
Palace	22 22	A	60
Mělnik			
Modrá Hvězda, Nám. Rudé Armady 97	2 28	C	12
Zámecká Pivnice	8 15	C	16
Mladá Boleslav			
Domov, *Staroměstské* n. 97	20 50	C	11
Věněc, Staroměstské n. 87	24 93	C	142

Hotels and addresses	Tel.	Class	Beds
Náchod			
Beránek, Náměstí	4 02	B	61
Nitra			
Stalingrad		B	64
Nové Město nad Metují			
*Metuj*e	37	C	59
Olomouc			
Družba	23 67	B	47
Narodni Dům, 8. kvetna 21	48 06, 49 66	B	119
Palace, 1. máje 27	32 84, 40 96	B	91
Ostrava			
Ostrava, 1. Tyršova 6	2 27 33	AB	260
Palace, 1. Gottwaldova 63	2 34 26	A	148
Otrokovice-Gottwaldov			
Společenský Dům	92 25 51	A	101
Pardubice			
Grand Hotel, tř. Míru	2 03 31	B	—
Zlata Štika		B	60
Pec pod Sněžkou (arr. de Trutnov)			
Devin	2 30	C	55
Horec	2 04	B	38
Hvezda	2 42	C	27
Kolinska Bouda	03	C	65
Piešťany			
Eden	22 45	B	70
Plzeň			
Continental, Zbrojnicka 8	2 52 55/57	A	117
Slovan, Smetanovy sady 1	37 90	B	180
Písek			
Bila Ruze, Halkova ul. 169	26 26	B	40
Otava		B	

Hotels and addresses	Tel.	Class	Beds
Poděbrady			
Praha, II, Riegrovo n.	7 88	C	33
Zalozna, I, Jirikovo nám. 10	6 94	C	11
Poprad			
Tokajik	4 12	B	90
Gerlach	—	—	—
Prachovské Skály			
Skalni Mesto	6	B	60
Praha			
Alcron, Nové Město, Stepanska 40	24 57 41/9	A	200
Ametyst, Vinohrady, Makarenkova 11.	25 01 16	B	108
Atlantic, Nové Město, Na porici 9	6 55 56	B	91
Axa, Nové Město, Na porici 40	22 54 11	B	182
Belvédère, Letna, Tr. Obrancu miru 19.	37 49 22	B	122
Central, Staré Město, Rybna 8	6 67 21	B	110
Centrum, Nové Město, Na Porici 31 ...	6 40 54/56	B	98
Družba, Nové Město, Vaclavské nám. 16	24 06 07	B	78
Esplanade, Nové Město, Washingtonova 19	22 25 52	A	115
Evropa, Nové Město, Václavské nám. 29	23 65 41 23 05 95	A	174
Flora, Vinohrady, Stalinova 121	27 42 41	A	311
Florida, Vinohrady, Blanicka 10	25 22 55	C	52
Hybernia, Nové Město, Hybernska 24 .	22 04 31/2 22 74 57	B	99
International, Praha-Dejvice	32 01 63	A	584
Jalta, Václavské nám. 45	23 79 51	A	125
Krivaň, Nové Město, Nám. I.P. Pavlova 4	22 58 15	B	110
Merkur, Nové Město, Tesnov 9	6 05 64	B	90
Meteor, Nové Město, Hybernska 6	22 92 41	B	138

29

Hotels and addresses	Tel.	Class	Beds
Moraň, Nové Město, Na Morani 15 ...	24 42 67	B	99
Opéra, Nové Město, Tesnov 13	6 29 44/45	B	85
Palace, Nové Město, Panska 12	23 71 51	A	182
Pariž, Staré Město, U Obecniho domu 1	6 27 51	A	150
Regina, Staré Město, Dlouha tr. 41	6 33 08	B	95
Skrivan, Vinohrady, Londynska 50	5 27 01	C	24
Slovan, Vinohrady, tr. Vitezneho unora 12	23 52 02	A	138
Tatran, Nové Město, Václavské nám. 22	24 05 41/44	A	98
Zlata Husa, Nové Město, Václavské nám. 7..................................	23 69 51	B	118
Solidarita, Praha 10, Soudružská 2081	77 46 15	A	—
Motel Stop, Praha 5, Plzeňská 103 ...	53 32 56	B	—

Prešov
| *Dukla* .... | 30 15 | B | 155 |

Prichovice (Jablonec)
| *Hvezda* .... | 14 | C | 37 |

Prostějov
| *Grand*, Palackého 3/5 .... | 52 57/8 | A | 73 |

Rabyne (Benešov)
| *Nova Rabyne* .... | 2 | C | 64 |

Rožnov pod Radhoštem
| *Koruna* .... | 2 57 | B | 20 |

Rumburk
| *Savoy* .... | 3 02 | C | 14 |

Ružomberok
| *Kulturny Dom* .... | 24 19 | B | 60 |

Smrzovka (Jablonec)
| *Slavie* .... | Jablonec 9 33 49 | C | 17 |

Hotels and addresses	Tel.	Class	Beds
Špindlerův Mlýn			
Alpsky Hotel	9 32 42	B	35
Davidova Bouda..................	2 23	B	70
Hradec	2 56	C	19
Klinova Bouda	2 58	C	75
Krakonos........................	3 34	C	50
Labska Bouda....................	2 21	C	74
Lucni Bouda	2 59	B	280
Martinovka......................	3 35	C	47
Medvedi Bouda...................	4 33	C	67
Moravska Bouda	2 69	C	54
Savoy	9 35 21	B	98
Slavoj	3 08	B	53
Snezka	3 26	C	127
Spolecensky Dum	3 10	C	66
Start	3 05	C	49
Svaty Petr......................	3 38	C	18
Starý Smokovec			
Grand Hôtel	3 01	A	155
Šumperk			
Grand, Gottwaldova 1	5 51	B	52
Tábor			
Jordan, Zapoteckeko nám. 505	34 02	B	140
Slovan, Stalinova 678	34 35	B	45
Lužnice, Libušina 54	9 61 19	B	—
Tatranská Lomnica			
Grand Hôtel Praha	9 63 01	A	166
Telč			
Cerny Orel, Stalinovo nám. 7	29	C	26
Teplice			
Thermia............................		B	96

Hotels and addresses	Tel.	Class	Beds
Radnice, K. Marx	20 19	B	—
Hotel de Saxe, Leninova 35	20 32	B	—
Trenčín			
Tatra	28 44	B	85
Turnov			
Slavie, Palackého 46	11	B	—
Trutnov			
Moskva, Spojencu 44	21 62	C	36
Uherské Hradiště			
Grand		B	36
Ustí nad Labem			
Palace, Mala Hradebni 87	29 14	B	130
Varnsdorf			
Sport, Gottwaldova 886 ,...........	3 26	B	—
Žilina			
Metropol........................	2 39 00	B	—
Polom	2 39 04	B	—

VOCABULARY

Note on pronunciation: To any one whose native tongue is English and who does not know any Slav language the pronunciation of words composed mainly of consonants appears at first glance to be very difficult. An attentive ear and a few general principles however will help. It is not necessary to make them too complicated. Briefly, all Czech words without exception are stressed on the first syllable. Vowels are pronounced more or less as in English when unaccented. v is long (ah), í and ý are pronounced as ie (as in piece), ú and ů=oo (as in moon). ě=ye (e.g. květen, pronounced kvyeten), ď and ť=dy and ty. c is ts and č is ch (as in church). s and z are both pronounced much the same as the English s, the s being more sibilant than the z; š and ž both like sh; (if you wish a distinction the ž is more like the French j (as je). The most difficult is ř which is pronounced rsh. Finally, j is pronounced as y (in yes).

Tell me, please	řekněte mi, prosím
Have you?	máte?
Where is?	kde je?
Bring	Přineste
Thank you	děkuji
Do you speak English?	mluvite anglicky?
French?	francousky
German?	německy
Do you understand?	rozumíte?
I do not understand	nerozumím
Speak slowly, please	mluvite pomalu, prosím
I am asking for information	prosim o informaci
I am sorry	lituji
I am glad	jsem rád
Give me something to eat	dejt mi něco k jídlu
Give me something to drink	dejte mi něco k pití
I do not feel well	není mi dobře
Good day	dobrý den
Good evening	dobrý večer
Good bye	na shledanou
Pleasant journey	štastnou cestu

Months and days of the week

January	leden
February	únor

March	březen
April	duben
May	květen
June	červen
July	červenek
August	srpen
September	září
October	říjen
November	listopad
December	prosinec
Week	týden
Monday	pondeli
Tuesday	úterý
Wednesday	středa
Thursday	čtvrtek
Friday	pátek
Saturday	sobota
Sunday	neděle
next (prox.)	příští
last (ult.)	minulý

Time

Morning	ráno
Noon	poledne
Afternoon	odpoledne
Evening	večer
Hour	hodina
Three quarters of an hour	tři čtvrti hodiny
An hour and a quarter	hodinu a čtvrt
An hour and a half	hodiny a půl

Customs

I have nothing to declare	nemám nic k proclení
No tobacco	žádny tabák
A suitcase	jedna brašna
A trunk	jeden kufr
Clothes	šaty
Linen	prádlo
Baggage	zavazadlo
Used articles	použité předměty
See for yourself	podívejte se
Triptyque	triptyk

| Passport | pas |
| Identity papers | osobní doklady |

Motoring

Car	vůz, auto
Motor cycle	motocykl
Bicycle	jízdní kolo
Petrol, gas	benzin
Oil	olej
The tank is full	nádrž je plná
Wheel	kolo
Tyre, inner tube	pneumatika, duše
Mudguard	blatník
Steering wheel	volant
Brake	brzda
Headlight	reflektor
Gear changing	řazení rychlostí
Clutch	spojka
Driving licence	povolení k jízdě
Car registration	doklady k vozu
Number plate	poznávací číslo
Garage	garáž
Service station	service
Greasing	promazat

Hotel and Restaurant

A two-bedded room	dvoulůžkový pokoj
on the street (side)	do ulice
on the courtyard	do dvora
How much?	kolik?
Are tips included?	včetně spropitného?
I wish to eat here	chci jíst zde
Breakfast	snídaně
Black coffee	černá káva
Milk: cold, hot	mléko: studené, teplé
White coffee	bílá káva
Chocolate	čokoláda
Butter	máslo
Jam	jam, džem
Bread	chléb
Cheese	sýr
Egg	vejce

Tea	čaj
Lunch	oběd
Dinner	večeře

Post

Where is the main post office?	kde je hlavní pošta?
Where is the nearest post office?	kde je neibližší pošta?
I want a stamp	chci známku
Postcard	dopisnice
Money order	peněžní poukázka
Telegraphic money order	telegrafická poukázka
I want to send a telegram	chci podat telegram
How much does each word cost?	kolik stojí každé slovo?
Reply paid	odpoveď placena
Urgent	pilný
What is the postage?	jaké je poštovné?

Other common words

Bridge	most
Castle	zámek
Stronghold	hrad
Church	kostel
Bank, shore	břeh
Crossing	křižovatka
Quarter, district	obec, okres
Plain	rovina
Wood	les
Town	město
Spring, fountain	studna
Garden, park	zahrada, park
Avenue	třída
Hotel	hotel
Inn	noclehárna
Island	ostrov
Lake	jezero
Mountain	hora
Pass	průsmyk
Harbour	přístav
Gorge	roklina
Rock	skála

Street	ulice
Watch-tower	strážní věž
Square	náměstí
Town Hall	radnice
Valley	údolí

Numbers

1	jeden
2	dva
3	tři
4	čtyři
5	pět
6	šest
7	sedm
8	osm
9	devět
10	deset
11	jedenáct
12	dvanáct
13	třináct
14	čtrnáct
15	patnáct
16	šestnáct
17	sedmnáct
18	osmnáct
19	devatenáct
20	dvacet
100	sto
200	dvěstě
300	třista
400	čtyřista
500	pětset
1,000	tisíc
10,000	deset tisíc

INDEX

Printed in Switzerland

This guide has been printed by
Nagel Publishers and Printers in Geneva (Switzerland)
Legal Deposit No 387
Printed in Switzerland

ČESKOSLOVENSKO
TCHÉCOSLOVAQUIE
CZECHOSLOVAKIA
TSCHECHOSLOWAKEI

Hlavni smery silnicni dopravy – Route principale – Main Road – Hauptstrasse.

Zeleznice – Chemin de fer – Railway – Eisenbahn

Mista se 1.000.000 obyv. avice – Villes de plus de 1.000.000 hab. –
Town population over 1.000.000 inhab. – Stadt mit mehr als 1.000.000 Einw.

Mista se 100.000 obyv. avice – Villes de plus de 100.000 hab. –
Town population over 100.000 inhab. – Stadt mit mehr als 100.000 Einw.

Mista se 50.000 obyv. avice – Villes de plus de 40.000 hab. –
Town population over 50.000 inhab. – Stadt mit mehr als 50.000 Einw.

Mista se 20.000 obyv. avice – Villes de plus de 20.000 hab. –
Town population over 20.000 inhab. – Stadt mit mehr als 20.000 Einw.

Mista mensi – Autres localités – Other localities – Soonstige ortschaften

```
0                    50                   100 km.
```

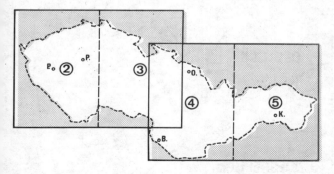

2

DEUTSCHE DEMOKRATISCHE REPUBLIK

GERA

Mittweda Freiberg Pirna DRESDEN Varnsdorf Zittau

Glauchau

Greiz KARL-MARX-STADT Elbe Luzické h.

ZWICKAU Děčín

Reichenbach Aue Annaberg Teplice Usti N. Bor Mimoň
Nád Labem Česká Lípa

Plauen Litvínov Duchcov Bílina Litoměřice Doksy

KRUŠNÉ HORY Chomutov Most Mnich Hradiš

Jáchymov KLINOVEC Roudnice n.L. ML. Boleslav
1244 Ohře

Nejdek Kyselka Žatec Louny Mšené Mělník

Frant.- Kralupy- St. Boleslav
Lázné n.Vlt.

Karl. Vary Podbořany Kladno Slaný Brandýs

Cheb Kynžvart Kožlany Rakovník PRAHA Kouřim

Mariánské Beroun Říčany
Lázně Beroun Kartštejn Střechovice Sázava

Tachov Konstant. Lázně Tocník Zdice Benešov Šternt

Stříbro Mže PLZEŇ Vltava Vlašim

Přimda Rokycany Votice BLANÍ

Dobřany Brdy Příbram

Nepomuk Orlík Sedlčany

CERCHOV Domažlice Klatovy Zvíkov Tábor
1042 Vltava

Všeruby Horažďovice Písek Bechyně

Cham. Pabi Strakonice Č

Sušice Veselí n.L. Jin dř. Hra

Zel. Ruda POLEDNIK Prachatice Hluboká Třeboň
1314

DEUTSCHE ŠUMAVA ČERNÁ H. 1362 Č. Budějovice
Zwiesel 1314 BOUBIN

Straubing Volary C. Krumlov N. Hrady Č. Velk

Deggendorf Vltava Černá v PoŠum Rožmberk Gmünd

Isar VITKŮVKÁMEN Novohradské h.
1053 Vyšší Brod KAMENEC
1069

Donau Passau Freistad

BUNDESREPUBLIK ÖSTER

Inn

3

© EDITIONS NAGEL

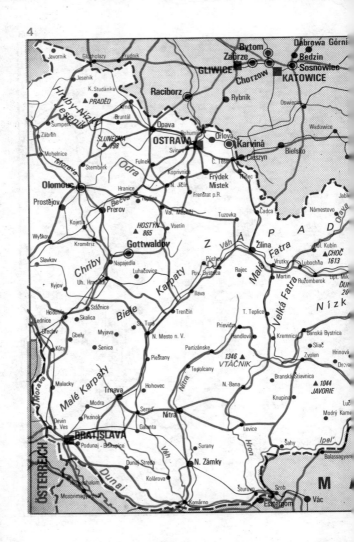

5

Imprimé en Suisse   Printed in Switzerland

ENG

Algeria	China	Greenla◌
Andorra	Costa Rica	Guatema◌
Angkor (Cambodia)	Cyprus	Holland
Arab Emirates	Czechoslovakia	Hondura◌
Austria	Denmark and Greenland	Hungary
Bahrain	Düsseldorf	Iceland
Balearic Islands	Düsseldorf and Duisburg	India an◌
Belgium and Luxembourg	Egypt	Indonesi◌
Belize	El Salvador	Iran
Bolivia	Europe	Ireland
Brazil	Finland	Israel
Bulgaria	Florence and its environs	Italy
Burma*	France	Ivory C◌
Cambodia (Angkor)	French and Italian Riviera	Japan
Canada	Germany (Federal Republic)	Kuwait
Central America	Germany (Democratic Republic)	Leningra◌
Ceylon (Sri Lanka)	Great Britain	Liechten◌
Châteaux of the Loire	Greece	Luxemb◌

FRE

Algérie	Chine	Grèce
Allemagne (République Fédérale)	Chypre	Groenla◌
Allemagne (République Démocr.)*	Costa Rica	Guatema◌
Amérique Centrale	Côte d'Azur et Riviera Italienne	Hollande◌
Angkor (Cambodge)	Côte d'Ivoire	Hondura◌
Autriche	Danemark et Groenland	Hongrie
Bahrein	Düsseldorf	Iles Balé◌
Belgique et Luxembourg	Düsseldorf et Duisbourg	Inde et ◌
Belize	Egypte	Indonési◌
Birmanie*	Emirats du Golfe	Iran
Bolivie	Espagne	Irlande
Brésil	Etats-Unis	Islande
Bulgarie	Fédération des Emirats Unis	Israël
Cambodge (Angkor)	Finlande	Italie
Canada	Florence et ses environs	Japon
Ceylan (Sri Lanka)	France	Koweit
Châteaux de la Loire	Grande-Bretagne	Leningra◌

GER

Ägypten	Finnland	Island
Algerien	Florenz und Umgebung	Israel
Balearen	Frankreich	Italien
Belgien und Luxemburg	Französische und Italienische	Japan
Brasilien	Riviera	Jugoslaw◌
Bulgarien	Griechenland	Leningra◌
Dänemark und Grönland	Grönland	Marokko
Deutschland (Bundesrepublik)	Großbritannien*	Der Mon◌
Deutschland (Demokr. Republik)	Holland	Moskau
Düsseldorf	Indien und Nepal	Nepal
Düsseldorf und Duisburg	Irland	Norwege◌

5-7, rue de l'Orangerie, 1211 GENEVA 7
Tel. (022) 34 17 30 - Telegrammes: NAGELEDIT-GENÈVE   **NAGEL**